MINI
JAPANESE
DICTIONARY
JAPANESE-ENGLISH
ENGLISH-JAPANESE

JN219956

Tokyo | Rutland, Vermont | Singapore

"Books to Span the East and West"

Tuttle Publishing was founded in 1832 in the small New England town of Rutland, Vermont [USA]. Our core values remain as strong today as they were then—to publish best-in-class books which bring people together one page at a time. In 1948, we established a publishing outpost in Japan—and Tuttle is now a leader in publishing English-language books about the arts, languages and cultures of Asia. The world has become a much smaller place today and Asia's economic and cultural influence has grown. Yet the need for meaningful dialogue and information about this diverse region has never been greater. Over the past seven decades, Tuttle has published thousands of books on subjects ranging from martial arts and paper crafts to language learning and literature—and our talented authors, illustrators, designers and photographers have won many prestigious awards. We welcome you to explore the wealth of information available on Asia at **www.tuttlepublishing.com.**

Published by Tuttle Publishing, an imprint of Periplus Editions (HK) Ltd.

www.tuttlepublishing.com

© 2019 by Periplus Editions (HK) Ltd

All rights reserved.

ISBN 978-4-8053-1470-8

Distributed by:

North America, Latin America and Europe
Tuttle Publishing
364 Innovation Drive, North Clarendon,
VT 05759-9436 USA.
Tel: 1(802) 773-8930
Fax: 1(802) 773-6993
info@tuttlepublishing.com
www.tuttlepublishing.com

Asia Pacific
Berkeley Books Pte. Ltd.
3 Kallang Sector #04-01,
Singapore 349278
Tel: (65) 6741-2178
Fax: (65) 6741-2179
inquiries@periplus.com.sg
www.tuttlepublishing.com

Japan
Tuttle Publishing
Yaekari Building, 3rd Floor,
5-4-12 Osaki, Shinagawa-ku,
Tokyo 141 0032
Tel: (81) 3 5437-0171
Fax: (81) 3 5437-0755
sales@tuttle.co.jp
www.tuttle.co.jp

28 27 26 25   11 10 9 8 7
Printed in China   2502CM

CONTENTS

Introduction

This Mini Dictionary is an indispensable companion for visitors to Japan and for anyone in the early stages of learning Japanese. It contains all the 13,000 or so Japanese words that are most commonly encountered in colloquial, everyday speech.

For the sake of clarity, only the common Japanese equivalents for each English word have been given. When an English word has more than one possible meaning, with different Japanese equivalents, each meaning is listed separately, with a clear explanatory gloss. The layout is clear and accessible, with none of the abbreviations and dense nests of entries typical of many small dictionaries.

The language of this dictionary is that spoken universally throughout the islands of Japan, by some 120 million people. Japanese is not clearly related to any other languages of the world. There was no written form of Japanese until the early centuries CE, when the system that had long been in use in China was borrowed and adapted.

Written Chinese does not relate directly to the sounds of the language; instead it makes use of a very large number of characters representing different syllables, to each of which is linked both a meaning and a sound. The characters derived initially from the stylized representation of concrete objects, to which the abstract meanings needed for the expression of the complete language were added by processes of combination and metaphor.

The pronunciation of each of these characters is not obvious from the written form but must be learnt separately in each case. To make matters more complex, in Japanese each character (kanji) is usually associated with several possible pronunciations. One or more (the **on** readings) are derived from the Chinese syllable originally represented by the character, and others (the **kun** readings) from native Japanese elements of equivalent or associated meaning. Each reading is used in different contexts (for example when used alone or in compound words, as part of the general vocabulary or in proper names) and the choice is only partly predictable.

The Chinese language does not make use of inflections (changes to the form of a word to indicate grammatical information such as tense or number), so it can be effectively written in characters representing unvarying syllables. By contrast Japanese has many inflections, and the variable word endings and particles need to be represented in writing to prevent ambiguity. To this end a set of syllabic symbols (kana "borrowed names"), derived from Chinese characters but with only sound values and no meaning component, are used in conjunction with kanji.

Thus in written Japanese the roots of words are represented by kanji, with the inflections and particles being in hiragana ("rounded kana"), derived from simplified cursive forms of certain kanji. Small versions of hiragana, known as furigana ("applied kana"), are also sometimes written above kanji to show their readings, for example in material for children or foreigners, or in case of ambiguity or some obscure characters used in personal names.

A second version of the same set of syllables, with more angular forms and known as katakana ("side kana," being derived from a part only of certain kanji) is also used for purposes such as transcribing foreign words and names, for representations of natural sounds, and sometimes for emphasis.

In this dictionary every Japanese word and phrase is also clearly spelled out in the Roman alphabet (romaji).

In contrast with the complexity of the writing system, the pronunciation of Japanese is quite straightforward for English speakers: it is not a tonal language and syllables are evenly stressed. Distinguishing clearly between long and short vowels is important, as in several cases a completely different meaning can result. Long vowels are pronounced with twice the length of short vowels, effectively creating an extra syllable. In this dictionary they are indicated by a bar over the vowel concerned; elsewhere you may find them written with a double vowel, or with long **e** represented as **ei** and long **o** as **ou**, but these practices can be misleading to English speakers.

The Japanese-English section of the dictionary is alphabetized according to the romanized forms, with short vowels preceding the equivalent long vowels.

Pronunciation

Japanese is made up of strings of syllables (*a*, *ka*, *ta*, etc.) which join together following simple rules of pronunciation (e.g. *anata* is *a-na-ta*). Unlike English, each syllable has mostly even stress and combinations of vowels (*e-i*, *a-i*, etc.) do not represent completely new sounds.

Vowels

Japanese has five vowels, pronounced either long or short. Distinguishing the length is very important as sometimes the meaning depends on the difference (e.g. *oji-san/ojii-san*, terms of address to a middle-aged man and an old man respectively). Note that a final *e* is always pronounced.

a	like *a* in *America*	**a**sa
	like *ah* in *ah!*	mā
e	like *e* in *pet*	d**e**su, sak**e**
	like *ere* in *there*	on**ē**-san
i	like *i* in *pit*	n**i**ch**i**
	like *ee* in *keep*	ch**ī**sai
o	like *o* in *top*	y**o**ru
	like *aw* in *law*	ky**ō**
u	like *u* in *put*	har**u**
	like *oo* in *coop*	ch**ū**

Vowel combinations

Basically, each vowel should be pronounced separately. The most common combinations are:

ai	like *igh* in *high*	**h**ai

ao	like *ao* in the British pronunciation of *Laos*	**nao**
ei	like *ay* in *play*	**rei**
ue	like *ue* in *pueblo*	**ue**

Consonants

Most consonants are pronounced in a similar manner to English. Some that are a bit different are:

f	in native words, *fu* is like *foo* in *food*, but without pressing the teeth against the lips;	**fuyu**
	in loanwords, like *f* in *finger*	**firumu**
n	at the end of a word, may be more like *ng* in *thing*	**yen**
r	like *tt* in the American pronunciation of *butter*	**are**

(You can use *l* for *r* at the beginning of a word and after *n*.)

Note: when *i* and *u* follow *k, s, t, p, h* or come between two of them, they become very shortened and are often not heard at all (e.g. **desu** becomes **des** and **mimashita** becomes **mimashta**).

Japanese–English

A

abareru v 暴れる to rage, to storm, to rampage

abiru v 浴びる to bathe oneself in; to douse, to shower

abuku N あぶく bubble

abunai ADJ 危ない dangerous

abunai! EXCL 危ない! Watch out!

abura N 脂 fat

abura N 油 oil, grease

aburakkoi ADJ 油っこい・脂っこい oily, greasy, fatty

aburu v あぶる to roast, to grill

achikochi, achira kochira PRON あちこち, あちらこちら here and there

achira PRON あちら that one (*of two*) over there, the other one (*over there*); over there, that way, yonder

achiragawa ADV あちら側 over there, the other side

āchisuto N アーチスト artist

adana N あだ名 nickname

adobaisu N アドバイス advice

adokenai ADJ あどけない innocent, childlike

adoresuchō N アドレス帳 address book

afureru v 溢れる to overflow

afutā-sābisu N アフターサービス (*maintenance and repair*) service, servicing

agaru v 上がる to rise; to feel self-conscious/nervous

ageru v 上げる to raise up, to lift; to give

ageru v 揚げる to fry; (*a flag*) to raise; to fly a kite

ageru v 挙げる (*a wedding ceremony*) to hold

ago N あご chin, jaw

ahiru N アヒル duck

ai N 愛 love

aibō N 相棒 partner

aida N 間 interval, space, between; while

aidagara N 間柄 relationship

aidea N アイデア idea

aidoku suru v 愛読する to like reading

aijin N 愛人 mistress

aijō N 愛情 affection

aikawarazu ADV 相変わらず as usual/ever/always

aikokushin N 愛国心 patriotic spirit, nationalism

aikon N アイコン (*computer*) icon

aikyō N 愛きょう charm, attractiveness: *aikyō ga aru* 愛きょうがある nice, attractive, charming

aimai na ADJ あいまいな (*word*) vague, muddled, unclear

ainiku ADV あいにく unfortunately

airashi'i ADJ 愛らしい lovely, sweet

airon N アイロン iron(ing)

Airurando N アイルランド Ireland

Airurando(-jin) no ADJ アイルランド(人)の Irish

aisatsu N 挨拶 greetings

aishō ga ii ADJ 相性がいい to be compatible with, to fit together well

aiso/aisō ga ii ADJ 愛想がいい amiable, sociable, agreeable

aisukōhī N アイスコーヒー iced coffee

aisukurīmu N アイスクリーム ice cream

aisuru V 愛する to love

aisutī N アイスティー iced tea

aite N 相手 the other fellow; companion; adversary

aitī (IT) N IT (アイティー) information technology

aitsu N あいつ that person

aizu N 合図 signal, sign

aji N 味 taste; flavor

ajia N アジア Asia

ajike no nai, ajikenai ADJ 味気のない、味気ない dreary, insipid, flavorless, flat

ajimi o suru V 味見をする (*salty, spicy*) to taste

aji o shimeru V 味をしめる to get a taste of success

ajiwau V 味わう to taste it

aka N 赤 (*color*) red

akachan N 赤ちゃん baby

akai ADJ 赤い red

akaku naru 赤くなる to turn red; to blush, to flush

akari N 明かり light, lamp

akarui ADJ 明るい bright, light; clear; cheerful, colorful

akashingo N 赤信号 (*signal*) red light

akemashite omedetō 明けま

しておめでとう Happy New Year!

akeru v 開ける to open

akeru v 空ける to leave empty, to vacate

akeru v 明ける to open up, (*the day/year*) begins

aki N 秋 autumn, (*season*) fall

akichi N 空き地 field, empty space

akiraka ni suru v 明らかにする (*make known*) to reveal

akirameru v 諦める to give up (*on*)

akiru v 飽きる (*get tired*) to weary of; to get enough of

akogareru v 憧れる to adore, to admire; to long for

akubi suru v あくびする to yawn

akuhyō N 悪評 (*unfavorable*) criticism

akui N 悪意 ill will, malice

akujōken N 悪条件 bad/un-favorable/adverse condition

akuma N 悪魔 devil, Satan

akusento N アクセント accent

akusesarī N アクセサリー an accessory

akusesu suru v アクセスする (*Internet*) to access

akushitsu na ADJ 悪質な malignant, pernicious, vicious

akushon N アクション action

akushū o hanatsu v 悪臭を放つ to stink

akushu N 握手 handshake

akushumi N 悪趣味 bad/poor taste

amachua N アマチュア an amateur

amaeru v 甘える to presume on someone's goodwill, to act like a baby

amai ADJ 甘い sweet; permissive, lenient

amari N 余り remainder, surplus, over, more than; leftover

amari ADV あまり [+ NEGATIVE verb] not very, not much, not many

amari nai あまりない There are not so many. I/We have not much.

amari ni ... sugiru あまりに～過ぎる too, excessively

amaru v 余る to be left over, to remain, to be in excess

amayadori suru v 雨宿りする to take shelter from the rain

amayakasu v 甘やかす to pamper, to coddle

ame N 飴 candy, sweets

ame N 雨 rain

Amerika N アメリカ America

Amerika gasshūkoku N アメリカ合衆国 United States

Amerika(-jin) no ADJ アメリカ (人)の American

ami N 網 net

amu v 編む to knit, to braid

an N 案 proposal, suggestion, idea; plan

ana N 穴 hole; slot

anata PRON あなた you

anchi uirusu sofuto N アンチウイルスソフト (*computer*) antivirus software

ane N 姉 older sister

ani N 兄 older brother

anka na ADJ 安価な inexpensive

ankēto N アンケート questionnaire

anki N 暗記 memorizing

anmari ADV あんまり too much, overly; [+ NEGATIVE] not (*very*) much

an'nai N 案内 information, guidance

an'nainin N 案内人 guide, lead

ano PRON, ADJ あの that (*over there*)

anohito PRON あの人 he/him, she/her

anohitotachi PRON あの人達 they/them

anshin N 安心 peace of mind; relief; security; confidence

anzen na ADJ 安全な safe, secure

anzenberuto N 安全ベルト safety belt

anzu N アンズ apricot

aogu v 扇ぐ to fan (*oneself*)

aoi ADJ 青い blue; pale

aojashin N 青写真 blueprint

aoshingō N 青信号 (*signal*) green light

apāto N アパート flat, apartment

appaku suru v 圧迫する to put pressure on; to oppress, to suppress

appudē´to N アップデート update

apuri(kēshon) N アプリ(ケーション) (*computer*) application

ara'arashi'i ADJ 荒々しい fierce

Arabia, Arabu N アラビア, アラブ an Arab

Arabia(-jin) no ADJ アラビア (人)の Arabian

arai ADJ 荒い・粗い (*not smooth*) rough

araiotosu V 洗い落とす to scrub

arakajime ADV あらかじめ beforehand, earlier, in advance

aramā INTERJ あらまあ goodness!

arappoi ADJ 荒っぽい rough

arashi N 嵐 storm

arasoi N 争い contention, struggle; disturbance, war

arasou V 争う to contend for; to argue, to quarrel

arasu V 荒らす to devastate, to damage, to ruin

arau V 洗う to wash

arawareru V 現れる to appear, to become visible; to show up

arawasu V 表す to show, to express

arawasu V 現す・表す (*make visible*) to reveal

arayuru ADJ あらゆる all, every

are PRON あれ that

arera PRON あれら those

areru V 荒れる to go to ruin/waste, to get dilapidated; to get rough/wild; to rage

arerugī N アレルギー allergy

arifureta ADJ ありふれた very common, commonplace

arigachi na ADJ ありがちな common, typical [IN NEGATIVE SENSE]

arigatō (gozaimasu) ありがとう（ございます）thank you

arigatō to iu V ありがとうと言う to say thank you

arikitari no ADJ ありきたりの commonplace, so typical [IN NEGATIVE SENSE]

arimasen V ありません is not

aru V ある there is, we've got; (*located*) it is

arubaito N アルバイト side job, part-time job

arukōru N アルコール alcohol

aruku V 歩く to walk

asa N 朝 morning

asagohan N 朝ご飯 breakfast

asai ADJ 浅い shallow

asase N 浅瀬 shallows

asatte N 明後日 day after tomorrow

ase N 汗 sweat

aseru V 褪せる to fade, (*color*) to bleach

aseru V 焦る to feel rushed/pressed

ashi N 足 foot

ashi N 脚 leg

ashiato N 足跡 footprint

ashidori N 足取り step

ashikubi N 足首 ankle

ashisutanto N アシスタント assistant

ashita, asu N 明日 tomorrow

asobi N 遊び fun, amusement; a game, play; a visit

asobu V 遊ぶ to have fun, to play; to visit

asoko PRON あそこ (*that place*) over there

assari (to) shita ADJ あっさり (と)した simple, plain, light, easy; frank

asshuku fairu N 圧縮ファイル (*computer*) compressed file

ataeru V 与える to give, to provide, to grant

atama N 頭 head; *atama ni kuru* 頭にくる to get mad at

atamakin N 頭金 downpayment, up-front money; deposit

atarashi'i ADJ 新しい new; fresh

atari N 当たり a hit; good luck, lucky

atari hazure ADJ 当たり外れ unpredictable, risky

atari ni ADV 辺りに (*area*) around; thereabouts; such as

atarimae no ADJ 当たり前の natural, ordinary, proper; suitable, sensible

ataru V 当たる to hit, to face; to apply; be correct

atatakai ADJ あたたかい warm

atatamaru V あたたまる to warm up

atatameru V 温める to heat

ateru V 当てる to guess; to hit; to appropriate; to touch

ato N 跡 mark, track, trace

ato de PREP, ADV 後で after(wards), later

ato ni mawasu V 後に回す to postpone, to leave something until later

atokatazuke N 後片付け cleanup

atorie N アトリエ studio, workshop, atelier

atoshimatsu o suru V 後始末をする to deal with the aftermath, to pick up the pieces

atotsugi N 跡継ぎ successor

atsui ADJ 厚い (*things*) thick

atsui ADJ 暑い・熱い (*temperature*) hot

B

atsukamashi'i ADJ 厚かましい impudent

atsukau V 扱う to treat, to deal with

atsumeru V 集める to assemble; to collect, to accumulate

atsuryoku N 圧力 pressure

au V 会う to meet, to see

au V 合う to match with

awa N 泡 bubble; foam

awaseru V 合わせる to join, to go along; to combine

awateru V あわてる to get flustered/confused

ayafuya na ADJ あやふやな indecisive

ayamari N 誤り error, mistake

ayamaru V 謝る to apologize, to say sorry

ayashi'i ADJ 怪しい questionable, suspicious; uncertain; weird; unreliable

ayatsuru V 操る to manipulate, to bribe, to manage

aza N あざ bruise, macula

azukaru V 預かる to take in trust, to keep, to hold

azukeru V 預ける (*leave behind with someone*) to deposit

bā N バー (*serving drinks*) bar

ba'ai N 場合 situation, occasion, case, circumstance

bābekyū N バーベキュー barbecue

baffarō N バッファロー buffalo

bāgen N バーゲン (*reduced prices*) sale

bai N 倍 (*multiplying*) times; double

Baiburu N バイブル Bible

baikin N ばい菌 germ

baiku N バイク motorbike

baindā N バインダー binder

baio tekunorojī N バイオテクノロジー biotechnology

baiorin N バイオリン violin

baipasu N バイパス bypass

bairingaru N バイリンガル bilingual

bairitsu N 倍率 magnification, magnifying power

baishunfu N 売春婦 prostitute

baiten N 売店 (*of vendor*) stall, booth, kiosk

bajji N バッジ badge

baka N 馬鹿 fool, idiot

17

bakabakashi'i, bakarashi'i ADJ 馬鹿馬鹿しい, 馬鹿らしい absurd, foolish

bakemono N 化け物 monster, ghost

baketsu N バケツ bucket

bakkin N 罰金 fine, (*punishment*) penalty

bakku, baggu N バック, バッグ bag

bakkuappu N バックアップ backup, support

bakuchi N 博打 gambling

bakudai na ADJ 莫大な immense, vast, enormous

bakudan N 爆弾 bomb

bakuhatsu suru V 爆発する to blow, to burst, to explode

bakuzen to ADV 漠然と vaguely, obscurely

bamen N 場面 scene

ban N 晩 evening, night

ban N 番 (*one's*) turn; lookout

-ban 〜番 (*counts numbers or orders*)

banana N バナナ banana

banchi N 番地 (*house number*) address

bando N バンド strap, (*watch*) band, belt; (*music*) band

bangō N 番号 (*assigned*) number

bangohan N 晩ご飯 (*dinner/supper*) evening meal

bangumi N 番組 (*broadcast*) show, program

banken N 番犬 watchdog

bankoku-hakurankai, banpaku N 万国博覧会, 万博 international exposition

banira N バニラ vanilla

-banme 番目 [NUMERAL] +th

ban'nin N 番人 watchman

ban'nō N 万能 versatility, ability to do anything

bansō N 伴奏 musical accompaniment

bara N バラ (*flower*) rose

barabara ni naru V ばらばらになる to scatter; in pieces

baransu N バランス balance:

basho N 場所 place

bassuru V 罰する to punish

basu N バス bus

basugaido N バスガイド bus tour guide

basuketto N バスケット basket

basukettobōru N バスケットボール basketball

basurōbu N バスローブ bathrobe

basurūmu N バスルーム bath, bathroom

basutei N バス停 bus stop

batā N バター butter

baton tatchi N バトンタッチ passing the torch, having someone take over

batsu, batten N ばつ, ばってん cross (= X [means "wrong"]), a black mark

batsu, bachi N 罰 retribution, punishment

batsu no warui ADJ ばつの悪い embarrassed, embarrassing

batta N バッタ grasshopper

battā N バッター (*baseball*) batter

battari ADV ばったり unexpectedly

batto N バット (*baseball*) bat

bebīshittā N ベビー・シッター babysitter

beddo N ベッド bed

bekkan N 別館 (*building*) annex

ben N 便 feces

bengoshi N 弁護士 lawyer

benjo N 便所 toilet, lavatory

benki N 便器 bedpan, toilet bowl, lavatory pan

benkyō N 勉強 study

benkyōzukue N 勉強机 desk

benpi N 便秘 constipation

benri na ADJ 便利な handy, convenient

benshō N 弁償 compensation

bentō N 弁当 box lunch

beruto N ベルト belt

bessō N 別荘 villa, vacation house

bēsu N ベース base, basis; (*baseball*) base

bēsubōru N ベースボール baseball

besuto N ベスト(服) vest

besuto o tsukusu V ベストを尽くす to do one's best

besutoserā N ベストセラー bestseller

Betonamu N ベトナム Vietnam

Betonamu(-jin) no ADJ ベトナム(人)の Vietnamese

betsu no PRON, ADJ 別の (*different*) another; other; extra

betsubetsu (na/no) ADJ 別々 (な/の) separate, individual

betsuryōkin N 別料金 (*charge*) extra

bīchi N ビーチ beach

bideo dekki N ビデオデッキ VCR, video recorder

19

bijin N 美人 beautiful woman, a beauty

bijinesu N ビジネス business

bijinesu hoteru N ビジネスホテル economy hotel

bijinesuman N ビジネスマン businessperson

bijutsu N 美術 art

bijutsukan N 美術館 art museum, art gallery

bikkuri suru V びっくりする to get startled, to get a surprise

bimyō na ADJ 微妙な delicate, subtle, fine, nice

bin N 瓶 bottle

binbō na ADJ 貧乏な poor (needy)

binīru-bukuro N ビニール袋 plastic bag

binkan na ADJ 敏感な sensitive

bira N ビラ leaflet, handbill

biri no ADJ びりの the last, the tail end, the rear

binsen N 便箋 (letter-)writing paper

binsoku ni ADV 敏速に quickly

bīru N ビール beer

biru(dingu) N ビル(ディング) building

Biruma N ビルマ (Myanmar ミャンマーの旧称) Burma

Biruma(-jin) no ADJ ビルマ(人)の Burmese

bisshori ADV びっしょり completely soaked

bisuketto N ビスケット biscuit

bitaminzai N ビタミン剤 vitamin pills

biyōin N 美容院 beauty parlor

biza N ビザ visa

bochi N 墓地 cemetery, graveyard

bōeki N 貿易 trade, exchange

bōeki-shōsha/-gaisha N 貿易商社/会社 trader, trading company

bōenkyō N 望遠鏡 telescope

bōgai N 妨害 disturbance

bōgyo suru V 防御する to defend

bōhanberu N 防犯ベル burglar alarm

bōi N ボーイ waiter

bōifurendo N ボーイフレンド boyfriend

boin N 母音 vowel (sound)

bōken N 冒険 adventure

boki N 簿記 bookkeeping

bokoku N 母国 mother country, homeland

bokujō N 牧場 ranch

bokushi N 牧師 (*Christian*) minister, preacher, priest

bokushingu N ボクシング boxing

bon N 盆 tray

bōnasu N ボーナス (*wage*) bonus

bōnenkai N 忘年会 year-end party

bonsai N 盆栽 bonsai, dwarf trees (*in pots*)

borantia N ボランティア volunteer

bōringu N ボーリング bowling

bōru N ボール ball

bōrugami N ボール紙 cardboard

bōrupen N ボールペン ballpoint pen

bōryoku N 暴力 (*brute force*) violence

boryūmu N ボリューム volume

bōshi N 帽子 (つばの広い) hat

boshū suru V 募集する to recruit, to collect

botan N ボタン button

bōto N ボート boat

bu N 部 department, part, division, section

-bu SUFFIX 部 (*counts books or bound things*) copy

bubun N 部分 part, portion

buchō N 部長 department/division/section head, manager

budō N ブドウ grapes

budō N 武道 martial arts

buhin N 部品 (*machine*) part

bujoku N 侮辱 insult

buka N 部下 a subordinate

buki N 武器 arm, weapon

bukimi na ADJ 不気味な ghastly, eerie

bukiyō na ADJ 不器用な clumsy

bukka N 物価 commodity prices

bukkirabō na ADJ ぶっきらぼうな blunt, brusque, curt

Bukkyō N 仏教 Buddhism

Bukkyōto N 仏教徒 Buddhist

bumon N 部門 sector, branch, department, section

bun N 分 part, portion, share; state, status

bun, bunshō N 文, 文章 sentence, text

bunbōgu N 文房具 stationery

bungaku N 文学 literature

bunka N 文化 culture

bunkatsu N 分割 division, split-up

bunken N 文献 literary document

bunko(-bon) N 文庫(本) pocketbook

bunmei N 文明 civilization

bunpō N 文法 grammar

bunrui N 分類 classification

bunseki suru V 分析する to analyze

buntsū suru V 文通する (*write letters*) to correspond

burajā N ブラジャー bra

burandē N ブランデー brandy

burando N ブランド brand

burasagaru V ぶら下がる to hang (down)

burasageru V ぶら下げる to hang (down), to suspend

burashi N ブラシ brush

burausu N ブラウス blouse

burauza N ブラウザ browser

burei na ADJ 無礼な impolite, rude

burēkā N ブレーカー circuit breaker (box)

burēki N ブレーキ brake

burīfu N ブリーフ (下着) briefs

burīfukēsu N ブリーフケース briefcase

burōdobando N ブロードバンド broadband

burogu N ブログ blog, weblog

busahō na ADJ 不作法な rude, blunt

bushi N 武士 Japanese warrior, samurai

busho N 部署 (*in the office*) department

busshitsu N 物質 matter, substance

buta N 豚 pig

butai N 舞台 stage

butai N 部隊 detachment of troops, unit, outfit

butaniku N 豚肉 pork

butsukaru V ぶつかる to collide with, to run into

butsukeru V ぶつける to hit

butsuri(gaku) N 物理(学) physics

buttai N 物体 object, thing

buzoku N 部族 tribe

byō N 秒 (*of time*) second

-byō SUFFIX 秒 (*counts seconds*)

byōdō na ADJ 平等な equal

byōin N 病院 hospital

byōki N 病気 disease, illness

byōki no ADJ 病気の ill, sick

byōnin N 病人 an invalid, a patient

byōsha suru V 描写する to describe

C

cha N 茶 tea

chairoi ADJ 茶色い brown

chakujitsu na ADJ 着実な steady, constant

chakumero N 着メロ music ringtone, ringing tone (*cellular phone*)

chakuriku N 着陸 landing, touching ground

chakuseki suru V 着席する to take a seat

chāmingu na ADJ チャーミングな charming, attractive

chan'neru N チャンネル (*TV*) channel

chanpion N チャンピオン champion

chansu N チャンス chance

chanto ADV ちゃんと (*without incident*) safe(ly), securely

charenji N チャレンジ challenge

charitī N チャリティー charity

chawan N 茶わん cup, (*tea ceremony*) tea cup; rice bowl

chawanmushi N 茶碗むし (*made from broth and egg*) steamed egg in a cup

chekku N チェック (*bank*) check; look-over

chekkuauto N チェックアウト check-out

chekku'in N チェックイン check-in

chero N チェロ cello

chesu N チェス chess

chi N 血 blood

chichi N 父 father

chichūkai N 地中海 the Mediterranean

chideji N 地デジ terrestrial digital broadcasting

chie N 知恵 wisdom

chigai N 違い difference, discrepancy

chiheisen N 地平線 horizon

chihō N 地方 area, district, region, province

chihō no ADJ 地方の local

chi'i N 地位 rank, position, status

chi'iki N 地域 area, region

chijimu N 縮む to shrink

chijō N 地上 above ground, on the ground

chijoku N 恥辱 shame, disgrace

chika N 地下 underground

chikagoro N, ADV 近頃 lately, recently

chikai N 誓い vow, pledge, oath

chikai N 近い near, close by

23

chikai uchi ni ADJ 近いうちに in the near future

chikaku ADJ, ADV 近く close, nearby

chikaku de ADV 近くで around, nearby

chikamichi N 近道 short cut

chikan N 痴漢 (*sexual*) molester, groper

chikara N 力 force, power, strength

chikashitsu N 地下室 basement

chikatetsu N 地下鉄 subway

chikau V 誓う to swear, to vow, to pledge

chikayoru V 近寄る to approach, to draw/come near

chikazuku V 近づく (空間、時間) to approach (*in space and time*); to draw/come near

chikoku N 遅刻 late

chiku N 地区 section, (*area*) sector

chikyū N 地球 Earth

chimei N 地名 the name of a place/land

chimitsu na ADJ 緻密な close, minute, elaborate

chingashi suru V 賃貸しする to rent out

chingin N 賃金 wages

chinmoku N 沈黙 silence

chinō N 知能 intelligence

chinō-shisū N 知能指数 intelligence quotient

chippu N チップ (*gratuity*) tip

chira(ka)su V 散ら(か)す to scatter, to strew

chiri N 地理 geography

chiri N ちり dust

chiritori N ちり取り dustpan

chiryō N 治療 (医療) cure, (*medical*) treatment

chīsai, chīsa na N 小さい, 小さな little, small

chisei N 知性 intellect, mind, intelligence, mentality

chisetsu ADJ 稚拙 childish

chishiki N 知識 knowledge

chitchai ADJ ちっちゃい little, small

chitsu N 膣 vagina

chizu N 地図 map

chīzu N チーズ cheese

chō, chōcho N 蝶, 蝶々 butterfly

chōbo N 帳簿 account book

chōchin N ちょうちん lantern

chōchō N 町長 town mayor

chōdo ADV ちょうど exactly, just

chōhōkei N 長方形 rectangle

chōjo N 長女 eldest sister

chōjō N 頂上 top, summit, peak

chōkaku shōgai no ADJ 聴覚障害の deaf

chōkan N 朝刊 morning paper

chokin N 貯金 deposit, savings

chokin suru V 貯金する (*money*) to deposit, to save

chokki N チョッキ vest

chōkoku N 彫刻 carving, sculpture

chokorēto, choko N チョコレート, チョコ chocolate

chokumen suru V 直面する to face

chokusetsu N 直接 direct

chōmiryō N 調味料 spice, seasonings

chōnan N 長男 eldest son

chōnekutai N 蝶ネクタイ bowtie

chōsa suru V 調査する to examine

chōsei suru V 調整する to organize, to arrange; to adjust

chōsen N 挑戦 challenge

chosha N 著者 writer, author

chōshi N 調子 tune; condition; trend

chōshi ga ii/warui ADJ 調子がいい/悪い be in good/bad condition

chōsho N 長所 strong point, merit, advantage

chōshoku N 朝食 breakfast, morning meal

chōten N 頂点 climax, peak, high-point

chotto ADV ちょっと just a little; just a minute; somewhat

chū N 中 middle; medium

chūdoku N 中毒 addiction, poisoning

chūgakkō N 中学校 middle school, junior high school

Chūgoku N 中国 China

Chūgoku(-jin) no ADJ 中国(人)の Chinese

chūi N 注意 note, notice; attention

chūibukai ADJ 注意深い cautious, careful, mindful

chūingamu N チューインガム chewing gum

chūkan N 中間 middle; ··· *(no) chūkan* ··· (の)中間 between...

chūkohin N 中古品 secondhand goods

chūkurai no ADJ 中くらいの average; *(size)* medium

chūmoku N 注目 notice; attention

C

chūmon N 注文 (*placed for food, goods*) order

chūnen N 中年 middle age

chūō N 中央 middle, center

chūō no ADJ 中央の central

chūsen N 抽選 lottery, drawing

chūsha N 注射 injection

chūsha suru V 駐車する (*car*) to park

chūshajō N 駐車場 parking lot/ garage

chūshakinshi 駐車禁止 No Parking

chūshi N 中止 (*abeyance*) suspension

chūshi suru V 中止する to suspend, (*in the midst*) stops

chūshin N 中心 center, middle

chūshin no ADJ 中心の central

chūshōkigyō N 中小企業 medium-sized and small companies

chūshoku N 昼食 lunch, midday meal

Chūtō N 中東 the Middle East

chūto (de) ADV 中途(で) on the way, halfway

chūto hanpa na ADJ 中途半端 な half-done, incomplete

D

dabokushō N 打撲傷 bruise

dabudabu no ADJ だぶだ ぶの baggy, loose, full, voluminous

daburu N ダブル a double (*room*); double(-*size*) drink; double-breasted suit

daeki N 唾液 saliva

daen N 楕円 ellipse, oval

daenkei no ADJ 楕円形の (*shape*) oval

daga CONJ だが but

dageki N 打撃 hit, strike; blow, shock

dai N 題 title; topic, theme

dai N 台 stand, (*low*) table

dai- PREFIX 第 [+ NUMBER] number ...; [NUMERAL]-th; (*separate word except when attached to a single-unit numeral*)

-dai N 代 charge (*fee*), bill; age, generation

-dai SUFFIX 台 (*counts vehicles or machines*)

daiben N 大便 feces, defecation

daibiki (de) N 代引き(で) C.O.D., collect on delivery

daibingu N ダイビング dive

daibu ADV 大分 quite, very, much

daibubun N 大部分 most part, the majority

daidai ADJ, ADV 代々 generation after generation, for generations

daidokoro N 台所 kitchen

daietto N ダイエット diet

daigaku N 大学 college, university

daigakuin N 大学院 graduate school

daigishi N 代議士 Diet member

daihon N 台本 script

daihyō N 代表 representative

daihyō-teki na ADJ 代表的な representative, typical, model

daiji na ADJ 大事な important, precious

daijin N 大臣 (*cabinet*) minister

daijōbu ADJ 大丈夫 OK, all right; safe (and sound); no need to worry, no problem

daikibo na ADJ 大規模な large scale

daikin N 代金 the price/charge, the bill

daikirai na ADJ 大嫌いな loathing, aversion

daikon N 大根 Japanese radish

daimei N 題名 (本、映画) (*of book, film*) title

dainashi N 台無し ruin, spoil

dairi N 代理 commission, agent, agency

dairi-nin N 代理人 agent

dairiten N 代理店 agency

daisan no ADJ 第三の third

daishi N 台紙 mount, (*art*) board

daisuki na ADJ 大好きな favorite

daitai N, ADV だいたい more or less, in general, on the whole, approximately

daitan na ADJ 大胆な bold

daitōryō N 大統領 (*of a nation*) president

daiyaku N 代役 substitute, alternate

daiyamondo, daiya N ダイヤモンド、ダイヤ diamond

daiyaru N ダイヤル dial

daiyō N 代用 substitution

daizu N 大豆 soy beans

dakara CONJ だから so, because of that, and so; therefore; that's why

... dake de naku... mo mata ～だけでなく～もまた not only ... but also

daku v 抱く to hold in the arms

damaru v 黙る be/become silent; to shut up

damasu v だます to cheat, to deceive

dame だめ don't!, no good

dame na ADJ 駄目な no good, no use, won't; bad, broken, malfunctioning

danbō N 暖房 (*room, house*) heating

danbō setsubi N 暖房設備 (*equipment*) heating

danbōru (bako) N 段ボール箱 (*box*) cardboard

danchi N 団地 housing development

dango N 団子 dumpling

danjiki suru v 断食する to fast

dankotoshita ADJ 断固とした determined, stubborn, (*definite*) firm

dan'na N 旦那 my husband; (*shop, etc.*) master; **dan'na-san/-sama** 旦那さん/様 (*your/someone else's*) husband

dansei N 男性 male

danshi N 男子 boy

danshi seito N 男子生徒 schoolboy

dansu N ダンス dance

dantai N 団体 organization, group

dare PRON だれ who, anyone, anybody: *dare de mo* だれでも anybody, anyone, everybody; *dare ka* だれか somebody, someone

dashi N だし soup stock, broth

dasu v 出す to put out; (*food/ drink*) to serve; to produce; to pay, to spend; (*mail*) to send; to begin

dāsu N ダース dozen

datō na ADJ 妥当な adequate

... de PREP 〜で in, at

... de kenka suru v 〜で喧嘩する to fight over

... de mo ADV 〜でも even/also (*being*) ..., even if it be; ...or something

... de mo nai ADV 〜でもない nor, neither

... de nai kagiri CONJ 〜でない 限り unless

... de nakereba 〜でなければ if not

de wa CONJ では well then; in that case; and so; and now

... de wa nai ADV 〜ではない no, not

28

... de warareta ADJ 〜で割られた divided by

deau V 出会う: **(... ni) deau** (〜に) 出会う to encounter, to meet, to run/bump into

deguchi N 出口 exit, way out

deiriguchi N 出入り口 gate(way), doorway

dejitarukamera N デジタルカメラ digital camera

dekakeru V 出掛ける to start off/out, to go out, to depart

dekigoto N 出来事 event, happening, incident

dekimono, o-deki N できもの、おでき swelling, sore, boil, pimple

... dekiru VERBAL AUXILIARY 〜できる can, be able to; be possible; be produced; be done, finished, ready

dekirudake できるだけ as much as possible

dekoboko no ADJ でこぼこの bump(y), (*road, etc.*) rough; uneven

demo CONJ でも but, however, even so, though

demo N デモ demonstration

demukaeru V 出迎える to meet, to greet, to welcome

denchi N 電池 battery

dengon N 伝言 message

denki N 電気 electricity, light

denki kiki N 電気機器 electrical appliance

denki sōjiki N 電気掃除機 vacuum cleaner

denki sutando N 電気スタンド desk/floor lamp

denki sutōbu N 電気ストーブ electric heater

denkyū N 電球 light bulb

denpa N 電波 electric wave, radio wave

denpō N 電報 telegram

denpun N でんぷん (*for cooking*) starch

denpyō N 伝票 (*restaurant bill*) check

denryoku N 電力 electric power

denryū N 電流 electric current

densenbyō N 伝染病 contagious/communicable disease, epidemic

densetsu no ADJ 伝説の (*legend*) traditional

densha N 電車 train, streetcar

denshi jisho N 電子辞書 electronic dictionary

29

denshi keijiban N 電子掲示板 bulletin board (system), BBS

denshi manē N 電子マネー (*Internet*) e-cash, e-money

denshi mēru N 電子メール (*system, message*) email

denshi mēru adoresu N 電子メールアドレス email address

denshi renji N 電子レンジ microwave oven

denshi shoseki N 電子書籍 digital book, e-book

denshi shuppan N 電子出版 electronic publishing

dentō N 伝統 tradition

denwa N 電話 telephone

denwa ni deru V 電話にでる to answer the phone

denwa no koki N 電話の子機 (*telephone*) extension

denwa o kakeru V 電話をかける (*telephone*) to dial

denwa (o) suru V 電話(を)する to call on the telephone, (*on the telephone*) to ring

denwabangō N 電話番号 telephone number

depātto N デパート department store

depparu V 出っ張る to stick out

deru V 出る to go/come out, to

exit; to emerge, to appear; be served; to leave, to start

... deshō ～でしょう probably, probably (it) is; I think; don't you think so?

desuku N デスク desk

dēta N データ data

dētabēsu N データベース (*computer*) database

detarame N でたらめ nonsense

detarame na ADJ でたらめな irresponsible, unreliable

dēto N デート date (*time; engagement*)

dezain N デザイン design

dezāto N デザート sweets, dessert

dī-bui-dī N ディーブイディー DVD

disupurē N ディスプレー (*computer*) display

dō N 銅 bronze, copper

dō ADJ どう how, why; (*in*) what (*way*)

-do SUFFIX 度 (*counts times, occasions or degrees*)

doa N ドア door

dōbutsu N 動物 animal

dōbutsuen N 動物園 zoo

dochira PRON どちら which one (*of the two*); where, who

dochira de mo どちらでも either one of the two

dochira ka どちらか one of the two

dochira ka (ippō) no どちらか (一方) の either

dochira mo どちらも (*not*) either one; neither one; both

dochiragawa どちら側 which one

dochira-sama どちら様 who (*are you*)

dodai N 土台 basis

dōfū suru V 同封する (*in envelope*) to enclose

dōga N 動画 animation, moving image

dōgu N 道具 tool, utensil, instrument

dōhan suru V 同伴する to accompany

dōi N 同意 agreement

dōitashimashite どういたしまして don't mention it! you're welcome!

Doitsu N ドイツ Germany

Doitsu(-jin) no N ドイツ(人)の German

dōitsu no ADJ 同一の identical

dōji ni ADV 同時に at the same time

dojō N 土壌 earth, soil

dōjō suru V 同情する to sympathize (with)

doko PRON どこ where, what part/place

doko de mo ADV どこでも anywhere

doko e どこへ where to

doko ka N どこか somewhere

doko made どこまで where to; how far

doko ni mo... nai ADV どこに も〜ない nowhere

doku N 毒 poison

dokuritsushita ADJ 独立した free, independent

dokusha N 読者 (*person*) reader

dokushin no ADJ 独身の (*not married*) single

dokusho N 読書 reading books

dokutoku no/na ADJ 独特の characteristic, peculiar, unique

dōkyūsei N 同級生 classmate

domein mei/nēmu N ドメイン 名/ネーム (*Internet*) domain-name

donaru V 怒鳴る to shout, to yell

donata PRON どなた who, anyone, anybody

donburi N どんぶり (*large*) bowl

don'na どんな what kind of

dono ... ADJ どの... which ... (*of more than two*)

dono-gurai/kurai ADV どの位 how many/much/far/long

donokurai desu ka どのくらいですか how many/much/far/long?

dono yō ni ADV どのように how

don'yorishita ADJ どんよりした (天気) (*weather*) dull

doraggu sutoa N ドラッグストア drugstore

doraibu N ドライブ drive

dorai kurīningu N ドライクリーニング dry cleaning

doraiyā N ドライヤー dryer, drier

dore PRON どれ which (*one*)

dore de mo PRON どれでも whichever/any of them

dore ka どれか some/any one of them

dore mo PRON, ADJ どれも any

doro N 泥 mud; (*filth, dirt*) muck

dōro N 道路 road

dorobō N 泥棒 thief, robber, burglar

dōryō N 同僚 co-worker, colleague

doryoku N 努力 effort

dōseiai no ADJ 同性愛の homosexual

dōshite ADV どうして why; how

dōshite mo ADV どうしても anyway, possibly, one way or another, somehow or other

dotchi, dochira PRON どっち, どちら which one (*of the two*)

dote N 土手 (*of river*) bank

dōwa N 童話 fairy tale

dōyara ... rashi'i ADV どうやら ～らしい apparently

dōyō N 童謡 (*traditional*) children's song

dōyō ni ADV 同様に alike

do-yōbi N 土曜日 Saturday

dōzo INTERJ どうぞ (勧めるとき) please (*go ahead*)

dōzō N 銅像 (*bronze*) statue

E

e N 絵 picture, painting, drawing

... e PREP ～へ (場所) to, toward

... e mukau V ～へ向かう to head for, toward

... e yōkoso INTERJ ～へようこそ welcome to

eakon N エアコン air conditioning/conditioner

eamēru N エアメール airmail

earobikusu N エアロビクス aerobics

echiketto N エチケット etiquette

eda N 枝 branch

edamame N 枝豆 green soy beans

ee INTERJ ええ yes

efu-tī-pī (FTP) N エフ・ティー・ピー FTP (*computer*) File Transfer Protocol, FTP

egaku V 描く (*picture*) to draw

eibun N 英文 English text

eien ni ADV 永遠に for ever, eternally, permanently

eiga N 映画 film, movie

eigakan N 映画館 cinema, movie house

Eigo N 英語 (*language*) English

eigyō N 営業 business

eigyōjikan N 営業時間 business hours, operating hours

Eikaiwa N 英会話 English conversation

Eikoku N 英国 United Kingdom

Eikoku(-jin) no ADJ 英国(人) の British

eikyō N 影響 effect, influence

eikyū no ADJ 永久の permanent

eisei N 衛星 satellite

eisei-teki na ADJ 衛生的な sanitary

Eiwajiten N 英和辞典 English-Japanese dictionary

eiyaku N 英訳 English translation

eiyō N 栄養 nutrition, nourishment

eiyū N 英雄 hero, heroine

eizō N 映像 picture, image

eizu N エイズ AIDS

eki N 駅 train station

ekiben N 駅弁 box lunches sold at train stations

ekisu N エキス extract

ekitai N 液体 liquid

ekkususen N エックス[X]線 X-ray

en N 円 circle

-en SUFFIX 円 (*counts money*) yen (¥)

enchō N 延長 extension

endōmame N エンドウ豆 peas

enerugī N エネルギー energy

engan N 沿岸 the coast

engei N 園芸 gardening

engeki N 演劇 drama, play

engi N 演技 performance; acting

enjin N エンジン motor, engine

enjiru V 演じる to play, to act, to perform

enjo N 援助 assistance, support, backing

enkai N 宴会 banquet, party

enkatsu ni susumu V 円滑にすすむ to go smoothly

enki suru V 延期する to postpone, to put off, to delay

enmoku N 演目 program

enpitsu N 鉛筆 pencil

enryo suru V 遠慮する to hesitate, to hold back

enshutsu N 演出 production, (*play, movie*) staging

ensōkai N 演奏会 concert

ensoku N 遠足 picnic, outing

ensō suru V 演奏する to perform, (*musical instrument*) to play

enzetsu N 演説 (*public*) speech

erabu V 選ぶ to pick, to choose, to select, to elect

erai N 偉い great, grand, (*person*) superior; awful

erebētā N エレベーター lift, elevator

ereganto na ADJ エレガントな elegant

eri N 襟 (*of clothes*) collar

eru V 得る to earn, to get

esa N えさ bait

essē N エッセー essay

esu-enu-esu N エスエヌエス social networking service, SNS

esukarētā N エスカレーター escalator

F

faiawōru N ファイアウォール (*Internet security*) firewall

fairu N ファイル file

fakkusu N ファックス (*machine*) fax

fakkusubun N ファックス文 (*message*) fax

fan N ファン (*admirer*) fan

fantajī N ファンタジー fantasy

fasshon N ファッション fashion

fasunā N ファスナー zipper

fāsutofūdo N ファーストフード fast food

ferī N フェリー ferry

fēsubukku, feisubukku N フェースブック、フェイスブック Facebook

Firipin N フィリピン Philippines

firumu N フィルム (*camera*) film

firutā N フィルター filter

fisshingu N フィッシング (*fraud, Internet*) phishing

fōku N フォーク fork

fuan na ADJ 不安な uneasy, anxious

fuben na ADJ 不便な unhandy, inconvenient

fubo N 父母 father and mother, one's parents

fubuki N 吹雪 snowstorm

fuchūi na ADJ 不注意な careless

fudan ADV 普段 usually, ordinarily

fudōsan N 不動産 real estate

fudōtoku na ADJ 不道徳な immoral

fueru V 増える to enlarge, to increase; to grow in quantity/number, to get bigger, to swell

fūfu N 夫婦 husband and wife, (*married*) couple

fugōkaku N 不合格 failure

fuhei N 不平 complaint, discontent, grumbling

fuhitsuyō na ADJ 不必要な unnecessary

fuhō no ADJ 不法の illegal

fui ni ADV 不意に suddenly

Fuji (-san) N 富士(山) Mount Fuji

fujin N 婦人 lady, woman

fujin N 夫人 wife; *-fujin* –夫人 Mrs. ...

fujiyū na ADJ 不自由(な) inconvenient, restricted; needy; weak

fukai ADJ 深い deep

fukanō na ADJ 不可能な impossible

fūkei N 風景 scenery, landscape

fukeiki N 不景気 depression, recession, hard times

fukisoku na ADJ 不規則な irregular

fukō N 不幸 misfortune

fukō na ADJ 不幸な unhappy, unfortunate, unlucky

fukō ni mo ADV 不幸にも unfortunately

fukōhei na ADJ 不公平な unfair

fuku N 福 happiness

fuku V 拭く to wipe

fuku V 吹く to blow

fuku N 服 clothes, clothing

fuku- PREFIX 副– vice-, assistant-

35

fuku-shachō N 副社長 (*of a company*) vice-president

fukubu N 腹部 abdomen

fukumu V 含む to include; to hold in the mouth; to contain; to imply; to bear/keep in mind

fukuramu V 膨らむ to swell up, to bulge

fukusha N 複写 reproduction, copy

fukushi N 福祉 welfare

fukushū N 復習 (*study*) review

fukushū N 復讐 revenge, vengeance

fukusō N 服装 dress, clothes, costume

fukuzatsu na ADJ 複雑な complicated

fukyō N 不況 business slump, depression

fuman N 不満 discontent

fumei no ADJ 不明の unknown, obscure

fūmi N 風味 flavor

fumō no ADJ 不毛の barren

fumu V 踏む to step on, to tread

fun N 分 minute

-fun (-pun) SUFFIX 分 (*counts minutes*)

funanori N 船乗り sailor

funatabi o suru V 船旅をする to sail

funbetsu no aru ADJ 分別のある (*sensible*) reasonable

fune N 船 ship, boat

funmatsu N 粉末 powder

funshitsubutsu N 紛失物 lost property

funsui N 噴水 fountain

furaipan N フライパン frying pan

Furansu N フランス France

Furansugo N フランス語 (*language*) French

Furansu(-jin) no ADJ フランス (人)の French

fureru V 触れる to touch; to come in contact with; to touch upon, to mention, to refer to

furi na ADJ 不利な unfavorable

furikaeru V 振り返る to turn around; to transfer

furimuku V 振り向く to look back

furin N 不倫 adultery

furo N 風呂 bath: *furo ni hairu* 風呂に入る to take a bath

furoba N 風呂場 bathroom

furoppīdisuku N フロッピーディスク floppy disk

36

furōsha N 浮浪者 homeless person

furu V 振る to shake, to wave

furueru V 震える to shake

furui ADJ 古い old; (*not fresh*) stale; secondhand, used

furumau V 振舞う to act, to behave

furūto N フルート flute

furūtsu N フルーツ fruit

furyō N 不良 rogue (*child*), delinquent juvenile

furyō no ADJ 不良の bad, no good

fusawashi'i ADJ ふさわしい suitable, fitting, worthy; becoming

fusegu V 防ぐ to prevent; to defend, to protect

fuseikaku na ADJ 不正確な inaccurate

fushi N 節 joint; knot, knob; tune; (*in a statement*) point

fushigi na ADJ 不思議 な strange, mysterious; wonderful; suspicious; odd, funny, uncanny, weird

fushin na ADJ 不審な doubtful, suspicious

fushinsetsu na ADJ 不親切な unkind

fushizen na ADJ 不自然な unnatural

fushō N 負傷 injury

fushōji N 不祥事 scandal

fusoku N 不足 shortage, insufficiency

futa N ふた lid, cover

futago N ふたご twins

futegiwa N 不手際 mismanagement

futeiki no ADJ 不定期の irregular

futekisetsu na ADJ 不適切な irrelevance, inappropriate

fūtō N 封筒 envelope

futō na ADJ 不当な unfair, unjustified

futoi ADJ 太い fat, plump, thick

futōitsu N 不統一 disunity

futoji N 太字 boldface

futokui na/no ADJ 不得意な/の poor/weak at

futon N 布団 padded quilt, futon

futoru V 太る to get fat

futsū ADV 普通 normally, commonly, usually, regularly, typically, ordinarily

futsūdensha N 普通電車 (*non-express*) local train

futsuka N 二日 two days; second day (*of a month*)

futsuka-yoi N 二日酔い hangover

futsūyūbin N 普通郵便 surface mail

futtō suru V 沸騰する to boil

fu'un N 不運 bad luck

fuyasu V 増やす to increase

fuyō no ADJ 不要の unneeded, unnecessary

fuyō no ADJ 不用の useless, disused

fuyōkazoku N 扶養家族 dependent family/relatives

fuyu N 冬 winter

fuyukai na ADJ 不愉快な unpleasant, displeasing, displeased

fuyuyasumi N 冬休み winter break/vacation

fuzokuhin N 付属品 attachments, accessories

fuzoroi na ADJ 不揃いな irregular

G

ga N 蛾 moth

... ga aru ～がある there is, there are

... ga hoshi'i V ～が欲しい to want

ga iru ～がいる there is, there are

gacchi suru V 合致する to fit

gachō N ガチョウ goose

gādeningu N ガーデニング gardening

gādoman N ガードマン guard

gai N 害 damage, harm, injury

gaido N ガイド guide

gaiken N 外見 appearance

gaikōkan N 外交官 diplomat(ic officer)

gaikoku-jin, gaijin N 外国人, 外人 foreigner

gaikoku no ADJ 外国の foreign

gaikokukawase N 外国為替 foreign exchange

Gaimushō N 外務省 Ministry of Foreign Affairs

gaisen N 外線 outside line/ extension (*phone*)

gaishoku N 外食 eating out

gaishutsu N 外出 going out

gaishutsu-chū V 外出中 be out

gaitō N 外套 coat, overcoat

gaka N 画家 painter, artist

gake N 崖 cliff

gakka N 学科 (*school*) subject

gakkari suru V がっかりする to be disappointed/discouraged

gakki N 楽器 musical instrument

gakkō N 学校 school

gaku N 額 amount, sum

gakudō N 学童 schoolchild

gakuhi N 学費 academic fees

gakumon N 学問 knowledge, learning, education

gakureki N 学歴 educational background

gakusei N 学生 student

gakusha N 学者 scholar

gakushū suru V 学習する to study, to learn

gaman N 我慢 perseverance, patience: *gaman suru* 我慢する be patient

gamen N 画面 (*computer*) screen

gamu N ガム (*chewing*) gum

gan N がん cancer

ganbaru V 頑張る to stand firm, to bear up, to hang in there; to try hard(er)

ganbō N 願望 desire

Ganjitsu N 元日 New Year's day, first day of the year

ganko na ADJ 頑固な stubborn, determined

ganryō N 顔料 paint

gansho N 願書 application

gappei suru V 合併する to merge, to unite, to combine

gara N 柄 pattern, design

garakuta N がらくた junk

garasu N ガラス (*material*) glass

garēji N ガレージ garage

gasorin N ガソリン gasoline, petrol

gasu N ガス (*natural*) gas

gatsu N 月 month

gāze N ガーゼ gauze

gehin na ADJ 下品な vulgar

geijutsu N 芸術 art

geijutsu-ka N 芸術家 artist

geisha N 芸者 geisha

geka N 外科 surgery

geki N 劇 play, drama

gekijo N 劇場 (*drama*) theater

gekkyū N 月給 monthly salary

gēmu N ゲーム game

gen N 弦 string

gendai no ADJ 現代の modern

gendo N 限度 limit

gengo N 言語 language

gen'in N 原因 cause, origin, root

genjitsu no ADJ 現実の actual, real

genjū na ADJ 厳重な strict

genkan N 玄関 entrance, way in, front door

39

genkei no ADJ 原型の original

genki N 元気 how are you?

genki ga ii ADJ 元気がいい cheerful

genki ga nai ADJ 元気がない cheerless(ly)

genki na ADJ 元気な fine, energetic, healthy, cheerful

genki ni naru V 元気になる to get better

genkin N 現金 cash, money

genkotsu N げんこつ fist

genryō N 原料 (*raw*) materials

gensaku N 原作 (*writing*) the original

genshi no ADJ 原始の primitive

genshiryoku N 原子力 atomic energy

genshō N 減少 reduction, decrease

gensoku N 原則 a basic principle, a rule

gentei N 限定 limitation

genzai N, ADV 現在 presently, nowadays

genzō suru V 現像する (*film*) to develop

geppu N げっぷ belch

geri N 下痢 diarrhea

geshuku N 下宿 lodgings, room (*and board*)

gesui N 下水 sewage

geta N 下駄 (*shoes*) wooden clogs

getsumatsu N 月末 the end of a month

getsu-yōbi N 月曜日 Monday

gia, giya N ギア, ギヤ gearshift

gichō N 議長 chairperson

gifuto N ギフト gift

gi'in N 議員 member of parliament

giji N 議事 transactions

gijutsu N 技術 technique, technology

gijutsusha N 技術者 technician, engineer

gikai N 議会 parliament, assembly, congress; (*the Japanese*) Diet

gimon N 疑問 question, doubt

gimu N 義務 (*responsibility*) duty

gimukyōiku N 義務教育 compulsory education

gin N 銀 silver

ginkō N 銀行 (*finance*) bank

ginkōin N 銀行員 bank clerk

giri no ane/ani N 義理の姉/兄 (*older*) sister/brother-in-law

giri no chichi N 義理の父 father-in-law

giri no haha N 義理の母 mother-in-law

giri no imōto/otōto N 義理の妹/弟 (*younger*) sister/brother-in-law

giri no musuko N 義理の息子 son-in-law

giri no musume N 義理の娘 daughter-in-law

Girisha, Girishia N ギリシャ, ギリシア Greece

Girisha/Girishia(-jin) no ADJ ギリシャ/ギリシア(人)の Greek

giron N 議論 argument, discussion

gisei N 犠牲 sacrifice

giseisha N 犠牲者 victim

gishiki N 儀式 ceremony

gitā N ギター guitar

giwaku N 疑惑 doubt, suspicion

gizō N 偽造 forgery

go NUM 五 five

go N 語 word

go N 碁 the board game Go

... go PREP ... 後 after, later, since

go-busata shite orimasu ご無沙汰しております I have been neglectful (*in keeping in touch with you*).

gochagocha(shita) ADJ ごちゃごちゃ(した) messy, jumble

gochamaze ADJ ごちゃ混ぜ jumble

gochisō N ご馳走 (*something special*) treat, delicious meal

gochisō-sama (deshita) INTERJ ごちそうさま(でした) (*greetings after meal*) thank you for the treat

gōdō no ADJ 合同の combined, united, joint

go-fujin N ご婦人 (女性への敬称) (*term of address*) madam

gogaku N 語学 language learning

go-gatsu N 五月 May

gogo N 午後 afternoon, p.m.

go-han N ご飯 (*cooked*) rice; meal, dinner

gōhō no ADJ 合法の legal

gōi N 合意 agreement

gōin na ADJ 強引な forcible, highhanded

gojū NUM 五十 fifty

gōka na ADJ 豪華な luxurious, deluxe

gokai N 誤解 misunderstanding

gōkai na ADJ 豪快な dynamic

gōkaku N 合格 (*an exam*) passing

41

gōkan N 強姦 rape

gōkei no ADJ 合計の total

gomakasu V ごまかす to cheat, to deceive, to misrepresent

gomen kudasai ごめん下さい Hello—anybody home?

gomen'nasai ごめんなさい sorry!; excuse me!

gomi N ごみ garbage, trash

gomu N ゴム rubber

goraku N 娯楽 pastime

gōri-teki na ADJ 合理的な rational, reasonable, sensible

gōru N ゴール goal

gorufu N ゴルフ golf

go-ryōshin N ご両親 your parents

gōryū N 合流 merger, confluence

gosho N 御所 imperial palace

go-shujin N ご主人 your husband

gotakō o inorimasu ご多幸を祈ります best wishes

gōtō N 強盗 robber; robbery

... goto ni ADJ ～毎に each, every

gozen N 午前 morning, a.m.

guai N 具合 condition, shape, (*of health*) feelings

guchi o kobosuru V 愚痴をこぼ

す to complain, to gripe

gūgūru N グーグル Google

guntai N 軍隊 army, troops

grafu N グラフ graph

... gurai ADV ～ぐらい (*an amount; the same extent as*) about; at least

gurasu N グラス (*for drinking*) glass

guratsuita ADJ ぐらついた (*wobbly*) loose

gura(u)ndo N グラ(ウ)ンド playground

gurē no ADJ グレーの (*color*) gray

gurēpufurūtsu N グレープフルーツ grapefruit

gurīn no ADJ グリーンの (*color*) green

gurōbu N グローブ (*baseball, boxing*) glove

gurume N グルメ gourmet

gurūpu N グループ group

gūzen ni ADV 偶然に accidentally, by chance

gūzō N 偶像 idol

guzuguzu suru V ぐずぐずする to delay, to dawdle

gyakkō suru V 逆行する to go backwards

gyaku no/ni ADJ, ADV 逆

の/に opposite, contrary, backwards
gyanburu N ギャンブル gamble
gyō N 行 (*words*) line
gyōji N 行事, event, ceremony
gyōmu N 業務 business, work
gyōmujikan N 業務時間 business hours
gyōretsu N 行列 (*queue*) line
gyōsei N 行政 (*of government*) administration
gyōseki N 業績 achievements
gyoshō N 魚醤 fish sauce
gyūniku N 牛肉 beef
gyūnyū N 牛乳 milk

H

ha N 歯 teeth, tooth
ha N 刃 (*knife*) edge, (*razor*) blade
ha N 葉 leaf
habahiroi ADJ 幅広い wide
habuku V 省く to cut out, to save, to omit
haburashi N 歯ブラシ toothbrush
hachi NUM 八 eight
hachi N 鉢 pot, bowl
hachi N 蜂 bee
hachi-gatsu N 八月 August

hachijū NUM 八十 eighty
hachimitsu N 蜂蜜 honey
hada N 肌 skin
hadagi N 肌着 underwear
hadaka no ADJ 裸の naked, nude
hadashi N 裸足 barefoot
hādodisuku N ハードディスク hard disk
hādowea N ハードウェア (*computer*) hardware
hae N ハエ (*insect*) fly
haeru V 生える to grow, to come out
hagaki N 葉書 postcard
hagane N はがね steel
hagasu V はがす to peel off, to tear off
hage N はげ bald spot, baldness
hagemu V はげむ to work hard
hageshi'i ADJ 激しい violent, severe, fierce, acute
hageshiku utsu V 激しく打つ (*strike*) to beat
haha N 母 mother
hai N はい yes
hai N 肺 lungs
hai N 灰 ashes
-hai (-bai, -pai) SUFFIX 杯 (*counts cupfuls, bowlfuls*)
haibijon terebi N ハイビジョン テレビ high-definition TV

haibun N 配分 distribution

haichi N 配置 layout, allocation, location, placement, setup

haifu N 配布 distribution, circulation

haigan N 肺がん lung cancer

haigō N 配合 composition

haigūsha N 配偶者 spouse

hai'iro no ADJ 灰色の gray

haikanryō N 拝観料 admission fee

haiki N 廃棄 disposal, abolition, rejection

haikibutsu N 廃棄物 waste(s)

hairu V 入る to enter

hairyo N 配慮 consideration

haisha N 歯医者 dentist

haishi suru V 廃止する to abolish

haitatsu N 配達 delivery

haiyū N 俳優 actor, actress

haizara N 灰皿 ash tray

haji, hashi N 端 edge; (tip) end

haji N 恥 shame, embarrassment

hajikeru V はじける to pop, to snap

hajiku V はじく to snap it; (water) to repel

hajimari N 始まり start, beginning

hajimaru V 始まる (start) to begin

hajime N 初め the beginning; in the beginning

hajimemashite INTERJ 初めまして (on being introduced) How do you do?

hajimeru V 始める to begin, to start

hajimete ADV 初めて for the first time

hajiru V 恥じる to feel shame, to feel embarrassed

haka N 墓 grave

hakadoru V はかどる to make good progress

hakari N はかり scales

hakariwakeru V 量り分ける to weigh out, measure out

hakaru V 計る to scale

hakaru V 測る to measure

hakaru V 量る to weigh

hakase, hakushi N 博士 doctor (Ph.D.)

hakidasu V 吐き出す to vomit, to spit out

hakike ga suru V 吐き気がする to feel sick

hakimono N 履物 footwear

hakka N ハッカ peppermint

hakkā N ハッカー (computer) hacker, hack

hakkan N 発汗 sweat

hakken suru N 発見する to discover

hakkiri to ADV はっきりと plainly, clearly, distinctly

hakkō suru V 発行する to publish, to issue

hakkō suru V 発酵する to ferment

hakkutsu N 発掘 exhumation

hako N 箱 box, case

-hako (-pako) SUFFIX 箱 (*counts boxed or boxful of things*)

hakobu V 運ぶ to carry, to convey

haku V 掃く to sweep

haku V 履く (*on feet or legs*) to wear, (*shoes, socks, pants*) to put/slip on

haku V 吐く to vomit, to spit out

hakubutsukan N 博物館 museum

hakurankai N 博覧会 exhibition, exposition

hakuryoku ga aru ADJ 迫力がある powerful

hakushi N 白紙 blank sheet of paper: *hakushi ni modosu* 白紙に戻す to withdraw, to take back

hakushu N 拍手 clapping

hamabe N 浜辺 beach

hamaki N 葉巻 cigar

hamidasu V はみ出す to protrude, to run off the edge, to stick out, to go over

hamigakiko N 歯磨き粉 toothpaste

hamono N 刃物 cutlery, knives

hamu N ハム ham

hamusando N ハムサンド ham sandwich

hana N 花 flower

hana N 鼻 nose; (*elephant*) trunk

hanabi N 花火 fireworks

hanaji N 鼻血 nosebleed

hanami N 花見 flower viewing

hanamizu N 鼻水 snivel, nasal mucus

hanamuko N 花婿 bridegroom

hanareru V 離れる to separate, to become distant, to leave

hanashi N 話 (*tale*) story, speech

hanashiau V 話し合う to discuss, to confer, to negotiate

hanashi-chū ADJ 話し中 (電話) (*telephone*) busy, engaged

hanasu V 話す to speak, to talk, to tell

hanasu V 放す to release, to let loose/go, to set free

hanasu v 離す to separate (*something*) from; to detach, to disconnect

hana-ya N 花屋 florist, flower shop

hanayaka na ADJ 華やかな colorful, showy, gorgeous, glorious, bright

hanayome N 花嫁 bride

hanbāgā N ハンバーガー a hamburger

hanbāgu N ハンバーグ (*patty*) hamburger

hanbai N 販売 sale

hanbai'in N 販売員 salesperson

hanbaiki N 販売機 vending machine

hanbaiten N 販売店 sales outlet

hanbun N 半分 half

handan suru v 判断する to judge, to give judgment

handobaggu, handobakku N ハンドバッグ, ハンドバック handbag, pocketbook

handoru N ハンドル steering wheel; handle

hane N 羽(根) feather; wing

hanei N 反映 reflection

hanei N 繁栄 prosperity

haneru v 跳ねる to jump, to splash

hanga N 版画 woodblock print

hangā N ハンガー hanger

hangyaku N 反逆 rebellion

hangyakusha N 反逆者 rebel

hanhan N 半々 half-and-half

han'i N 範囲 scope, range, limits: (*… no*) *han'i-nai* (…の)範囲内 within the limits (*of …*)

hanigo N 反意語 antonym

hanikamu v はにかむ to act shy, to be bashful

hanjō N 繁盛 prosperity

hanjō suru v 繁盛する to thrive, to prosper

hankachi N ハンカチ handkerchief

hankagai N 繁華街 downtown, center (*of city*)

hankan o kau v 反感を買う to provoke one's antipathy

hankei N 半径 radius

hanketsu N 判決 judgment

hanko N はんこ a "chop" (= signature seal), name stamp

hankō N 犯行 crime, perpetration

hankō suru v 反抗する to oppose, to resist

hankyō suru v 反響する to reflect

hanmā N ハンマー hammer

han'nichi N 半日 half a day, a half-day

han'nin N 犯人 criminal, culprit

han'nō N 反応 reaction, response

han'nō suru V 反応する to react

hansamu N ハンサム handsome

hansei N 反省 reflection

hansen no ADJ 反戦の antiwar

hansoku N 反則 foul

hantai suru V 反対する to object, to protest, to oppose

hantō N 半島 peninsula

hantoshi N 半年 half a year

hantsuki N 半月 half a month

hanzai N 犯罪 crime

hanzaisha N 犯罪者 criminal

hanzubon N 半ズボン short-pants

happa N 葉っぱ leaf

happyō suru V 発表する to announce, to publish

hara N 腹 stomach, belly: *hara ga heru* 腹が減る to get hungry

harahara suru V はらはらする to get anxious, to be scared

harau V 払う to pay

hareta N 晴れた (*weather*) clear

hari N 針 needle

harigane N 針金 wire

haru N 春 (*season*) spring

harumaki N 春巻 egg rolls, spring rolls

haruyasumi N 春休み spring break/vacation

hasamaru V 挟まる (*in, between*) to get caught, to become sandwiched

hasami N はさみ scissors; (*crab*) claw

hasamu V 挟む to insert, to put between

hasan suru V 破産する to be bankrupt

hashi N 橋 bridge

hashi, haji N 端 edge; (*tip*) end

hashi N 箸 chopsticks

hashigo N 梯子 ladder

hashika N はしか measles

hashira N 柱 post, column, pillar

hashiru V 走る to run

hasu N 蓮 lotus

hata N 旗 flag

hatachi N 二十歳 20 years old

hatake N 畑 field

hataki N はたき duster

hataraku v 働く to work, to labor; (*a crime*) to commit

hatasu v 果たす to fulfill

hatsubai N 発売 sale, release

hatsugen N 発言 utterance

hatsuka N 二十日 20 days; 20th of the month

hatsukoi N 初恋 first love

hatsumei N 発明 invention

hatsunetsu N 発熱 fever

hatsuon suru v 発音する to pronounce

hatten N 発展 development

hau v 這う to crawl

hayai ADJ 速い fast, rapid, quick

hayai ADJ 早い early

hayakunaotte 早く治って get well soon!

hayari no ADJ 流行りの fashionable, popular

hayasa N 速さ speed

hayashi N 林 grove

hayasu v 生やす (*hair, teeth*) to grow it; (*sprout*) to let it grow

hazukashi'i ADJ 恥ずかしい ashamed, embarrassed; embarrassing, disgraceful; shameful; shy

hazumu v 弾む to bounce

hazureru v 外れる to get disconnected, to come off; to miss, to fail

hebi N 蛇 snake

heibon na ADJ 平凡な (*not fancy*) plain

heikin N 平均 average

heisa N 閉鎖 (道) (*road*) closed

heitai N 兵隊 soldier

heitan na ADJ 平坦な flat, smooth

heiten N 閉店 (*shop*) closed

heiwa N 平和 peace

hen na ADJ 変な strange

henji N 返事 answer, (*spoken*) response, reply

henka N 変化 change

henkan N 変換 conversion

henkan suru v 変換する to replace, to transform

henshin N 返信 answer, (*written*) response

henshin suru v 変身する to transform

henshū N 編集 editing

henshūchō N 編集長 editor in chief

henshūsha N 編集者 editor

hentō N 返答 response

herasu v 減らす to reduce

48

herikoputā N ヘリコプター helicopter

heru V 減る to decrease, to dwindle, to go down

herumetto N ヘルメット helmet

heta na ADJ 下手な unskillful, inept, clumsy, poor, inexpert

heya N 部屋 room

hi N 日 sun; day

hi N 火 fire: *hi ga tsuku* 火がつく to be caught on fire

hiatari ga ii ADJ 日当たりがいい sunny

hibana N 火花 spark

hibiku V 響く(音が) *(tune, noise)* to echo, to resound

hidari N 左 left

hidarigawa N 左側 left-hand side

hidarikiki no ADJ 左利きの *(person)* left-handed

hidoi ADJ ひどい severe, terrible, unreasonable, vicious, bitter

hifu N 皮ふ skin

higai N 被害 damage, injury, casualty

higasa N 日傘 parasol

higashi N 東 east

higashiguchi N 東口 the east exit/entrance

hige N ひげ beard; mustache

higeki N 悲劇 tragedy

higure N 日暮れ sunset

hihan N 批判 judgment, criticism

hihan-teki na ADJ 批判的な critical

hihyō N 批評 criticism, review

hi'iki N ひいき illegitimate favor, patronage

hi'ita PREP 引いた less, minus

hiji N ひじ elbow

hijō ni ADV 非常に very, extremely

hijōguchi N 非常口 emergency exit

hijōji, hijōjitai N 非常時, 非常事態 emergency

hijōkaidan N 非常階段 emergency stairs

hikaeru V 控える to refrain, to withhold

hikaeme na ADJ 控えめな modest

hikage N 日陰 shade, *(from sunlight)* shadow

hikaku N 比較 comparison

hikaku-teki ADV 比較的 relatively, comparatively

hikan-teki na ADJ 悲観的な pessimistic

hikari kēburu N 光ケーブル optical cable

hikaru V 光る to shine; to glow

-hiki (-piki) SUFFIX 匹 (*counts small animals, fish or bugs*)

hikiageru V 引き上げる to pull up; to refloat; (*price, wage, fee*) to raise

hikidashi N 引き出し drawer

hikidasu V 引き出す to pull/draw out; (*money*) to withdraw

hikiniku N 挽き肉 chopped/minced/ground meat

hikitoru V 引き取る to take over, to look after, to receive

hikitsugu V 引き継ぐ to take over for

hikiukeru V 引き受ける to take charge of; to guarantee

hikkosu V 引っ越す (*house*) to move

hikō N 飛行 flight

hikōki N 飛行機 airplane

hiku V 引く to pull, to draw; to drag, (*a boat*) to tug; (*a cold*) catches

hiku V 弾く (*a stringed instrument*) to play

hikui ADJ 低い (*not high*) low, short

hikyō na ADJ ひきょうな cowardly

hima N 暇 time; leisure, spare time; leave; (*of servant*) dismissal

himei N 悲鳴 a scream

himitsu N 秘密 secret

himo N 紐 string, cord, tape, strap, ribbon

hin no ii/aru ADJ 品のいい/ある elegant

hinamatsuri N ひな祭り (*3 March*) the Dolls Festival

hinan N 非難 (言葉で) (*with words*) attack, blame

hinan suru V 避難する to take refuge/shelter, to escape (a) disaster

hinata N 日なた sunshine

hineru V ひねる to twist; to turn

hiniku na ADJ 皮肉な sarcastic, cynical

hinin N 避妊 contraception

hiningu N 避妊具 contraceptive

hinmoku N 品目 item, individual thing

hinode N 日の出 sunrise

hinoiri N 日の入 sunset

hinoki N ひのき cypress

hinpan ni ADV 頻繁に frequently

hinshi N 品詞 part of speech

hinshitsu N 品質 quality

hinto N ヒント hint, reminder

hipparu V 引っ張る to pull, to drag, to tug (at), to take/bring

hiragana N ひらがな (*the Japanese letters*) hiragana

hiraku V 開く to open up; (*a party*) to have, to hold

hiraoyogi N 平泳ぎ breast stroke

hiratai ADJ 平たい flat

hire N ひれ fin

hirei suru V 比例する to be proportionate

hiroba N 広場 square, town square, (*public*) open space

hirōen N 披露宴 reception, (*wedding, etc.*) banquet

hirogaru V 広がる to spread, to widen

hirogeru V 広げる to spread/widen it

hiroi ADJ 広い broad, spacious, large, wide

hiroma N 広間 hall

hirou V 拾う to pick it up

hiru N 昼 daytime, noon

hirugohan N 昼ご飯 lunch

hiruma N 昼間 daytime

hirune N 昼寝 nap

hisashiburi ni ADV 久しぶりに (*absence*) after a long time

hisho N 秘書 secretary

hissu no ADJ 必須の compulsory

hītā N ヒーター heater

hitai N 額 forehead, brow

hitaru V 浸る to soak

hitei N 否定 denial

hito N 人 a person

hitobito N, PL 人々 people

hitogoroshi N 人殺し murder

hitogomi N 人ごみ crowd

hitokire no 一切れの a piece of

hitokoto N 一言 a word

hitokuchi N 一口 one mouthful; one bite; one drink, sip

hitori de ADV 一人で alone, on one's own

hitosaji N 一匙 one spoonful

hitosashiyubi N 人差し指 forefinger, index finger

hitoshi'i ADJ 等しい equal, identical

hitotsu N 一つ one

hitsuji N 羊 sheep

hitsujuhin N 必需品 necessity article: *seikatsu hitsujuhin* 生活必需品 daily necessities

hitsuyō de aru V 必要である to need

51

hitsuyō na ADJ 必要な necessary, essential

hitsuyōsei N 必要性 necessity, occasion

hiyake N 日焼け sunburn

hiyasu V 冷やす to cool it off, to refrigerate, to chill

hiyō N 費用 (*expense*) cost

hiyoku na ADJ 肥沃な fertile

hiza N 膝 knee

hizamazuku V ひざまずく to fall on one's knees, to kneel down

hizashi N 日差し sunlight

hizuke N 日付 (*of the month*) date

hizume N 蹄 hoof

ho N 帆 sail

hō N 法 law; rule; method

hō, hoho N 頬 cheek

hobo ADV ほぼ nearly; roughly

hōbō N, ADV 方々 everywhere, all over

hōchi N 放置 neglect

hochikisu N ホチキス stapler: *hochikisu no hari* ホチキスの針 strip of staples

hōchō N 包丁 (*big*) knife, cleaver

hochōki N 補聴器 hearing aids

hodō N 歩道 walk(way), pavement, sidewalk

hōdō N 報道 news report

hodoku V 解く to undo, to untie

hodōkyō N 歩道橋 crossover/pedestrian bridge

hoeru V 吠える (*dog*) to bark

hōgaku N 方角 direction

hōgaku(-bu) N 法学(部) (*science/study of*) law; School of Law

hōgen N 方言 dialect

hogo N 保護 protection

hogoku N 保護区 (動物) (*for animals*) reserve

hogosha N 保護者 guardian

hōhō N 方法 method, process, way

hohoemi N ほほ笑み smile

hohoemu V ほほ笑む to smile

hoikuen 保育園 nursery school

hoikushi N 保育士 nursery teacher

hoippu kurīmu N ホイップクリーム whipping cream

hōjin N 法人 corporation

hōjinzei N 法人税 corporation tax

hojo N 補助 help, assistance

hoka no ADJ ほかの different, other, another

hokan suru v 保管する to leave behind for safekeeping

hoken N insurance 保険

hoken N 保健 healthcare, preservation of health

hōki N ほうき broom

hōki N 放棄 abandonment, neglect

hokkyoku N 北極 North Pole, Arctic

hokkyoku-ken N 北極圏 Arctic Circle

hokkyoku-sei N 北極星 North Star

hōkō N 方向 direction

hōkoku N 報告 report

hōkokusho N 報告書 report, statement

hokorashi'i ADJ 誇らしい be proud

hokori N ほこり dust

hokori N 誇り pride, boast

hokōsha N 歩行者 pedestrian: *hokōsha tengoku* 歩行者天国 pedestrian mall

hokubu N 北部 the north, the northern part

hokui N 北緯 north latitude

Hokuō N 北欧 Northern Europe

hokuro N ほくろ (*on skin*) mole

hokusei N 北西 north-west

hokutō N 北東 north-east

hokyō suru v 補強する to reinforce, to corroborate

hokyū suru v 補給する to supply

homeru v 褒める to praise, to admire

hōmon suru v 訪問する to visit, to call on

hōmudorama N ホームドラマ soap opera

hōmuresu N ホームレス homeless

hōmushikku N ホームシック homesick

hōmusutei N ホームステイ homestay

hon N 本 book

-hon (-pon, -bon) SUFFIX 本 (*counts long (thin) objects*)

honba no ADJ 本場の authentic

honbako N 本箱 bookcase

honban N 本番 real part, real thing

honbu N 本部 central office, headquarters

hondai N 本題 main issue

hondana 本棚 bookshelf

hone N 骨 bone

honki no/de ADJ, ADV 本気の/で serious(ly), (in) earnest

honkon N 香港 Hong Kong

honmono N 本物 the real thing

hon'ne N 本音 true (inner) feeling, real intention

hon'nin N 本人 self, himself, herself, myself

hon no sukoshi/chotto ほんの少し/ちょっと … just a little; just a minute

honō N 炎 flame

honomekasu V ほのめかす to hint

honten N 本店 head office, main store

hontō N 本当 really, truth

hontō ni ADV 本当に really, truly, indeed, absolutely

hontō no ADJ 本当の true, real, genuine

hon-ya N 本屋 bookshop

hon'yaku N 翻訳 translation

hon'yakusha N 翻訳者 translator

hora'ana N 洞穴 cave

horafuki N ほら吹き liar

hōrensō ほうれん草 spinach

hōritsu 法律 laws, legislation

hōrō suru V 放浪する to wander, to stroll

horu V 彫る to carve

horu V 掘る to dig

hōsekirui 宝石類 jewelry

hōshanō N 放射能 radioactivity

hōshasen N 放射線 (*nuclear*) radiation

hoshi N 星 star

hōshi N 奉仕 service

hoshigaru V 欲しがる to want it

hoshī V 欲しい to be desired/desirable; to desire, to wish

hōshin N 方針 policy, (*action*) course, (*direction*) line

hoshiuranai N 星占い astrology

hoshōkin N 補償金 (*money*) compensation, indemnity

hoshōsho N 保証書 guarantee

hoshu-teki na ADJ 保守的な conservative

hōsō N 放送 broadcast, program

hōsō N 包装 packing, wrapping

hōsōbutsu N 包装物 package, packet: *kogata hōsō-butsu* 小型包装物 small packet

hosoi ADJ 細い slender, slim, narrow

hōsoku N 法則 rule(s), law(s)

hōsōkyoku N 放送局 broadcasting station

hosonagai ADJ 細長い long and slender/narrow

hōsōmō N 放送網 network

hossa N 発作 attack, seizure: *shinzō hossa* 心臓発作 heart attack

hosu V 干す to dry it; to air it

hōsu N ホース hose

hōtai N 包帯 bandage

hotategai N 帆立貝 scallop(s)

hōteishiki N 方程式 equation

hoteru N ホテル hotel

Hotoke(-sama) N 仏(様) Buddha

hotondo ADV ほとんど almost, most, nearly

hotondo... nai ADV ほとんど〜ない hardly, seldom

hōtte oku V 放っておく to leave alone, to let alone: *Hottoite!* 放っといて! Leave me alone!

hotto doggu N ホットドッグ hot dog

hotto kēki N ホットケーキ pancake

hottosuru V ほっとする to breathe a sigh of relief

hoyō N 保養 rest, recuperation

hozonsareta ADJ 保存された cured, preserved

hyakka jiten N 百科事典 encyclopedia

hyakkaten N 百貨店 department store

hyaku NUM 百 hundred

hyakuman NUM 百万 million

hyō N 表 list

hyō N ヒョウ (*animal*) leopard

hyō N 票 vote

hyoban no warui 評判の悪い have a bad reputation

hyōgen N 表現 (*words*) expression

hyōjō N 表情 (*on face*) expression

hyōjun N 標準 standard

hyōjungo N 標準語 (*language*) standard Japanese

hyōka N 評価 grade, opinion, appraisal

hyōkin na ADJ ひょうきんな funny, comical

hyōmen N 表面 surface

hyōron-ka N 評論家 critic, commentator, reviewer

hyōshi N 表紙 (*book, magazine, etc.*) cover

hyōshiki N 標識 sign, signpost

hyōshōshiki N 表彰式 awarding ceremony

hyūzu N ヒューズ fuse: *hyūzu ga tobu* ヒューズがとぶ to blow out

I

i N 胃 stomach

ibaru v 威張る to act arrogant; swagger, haughty

ibiki N いびき snore

ibusu v いぶす to smoke, to fumigate, to fume

ibutsu N 遺物 relics, artifact

ichi NUM 一 one

ichi N 位置 position, location, situation

ichiba N 市場 market

ichiban no ADJ 一番の first

ichibu ADV 一部 (not whole) part

ichido ADV 一度 once

ichi-gatsu N 一月 January

ichigo N いちご strawberry

ichi'ichi ADV いちいち one by one, each time

ichijiku N イチジク fig

ichijirushi'i ADJ 著しい conspicuous, prominent, remarkable

ichiji-teki na ADJ 一時的な temporary

ichimai no kami 一枚の紙 a sheet of paper

ichiman NUM 一万 ten thousand

ichi-mei N 一名 one person

ichi-nen N 一年 the year one; one year

ichinensei N 一年生 first-year student, freshman

ichiō ADV 一応 as far as it goes, just in case, tentatively

ichiryū no ADJ 一流の first-rate, topflight, elite, superb

ichiwari N 一割 ten percent

ichō N いちょう (tree) gingko

ichō N 胃腸 stomach and intestines

idai na ADJ 偉大な great

idaku v 抱く to embrace

iden N 遺伝 heredity

idenshi N 遺伝子 gene

ido N 井戸 (for water) well

ido N 緯度 latitude

idō suru v 移動する to move

ie N 家 home, house

igai na (ni) ADJ (ADV) 意外な(に) unexpected(ly)

igaku no ADJ 医学の medical

igan N 胃がん stomach cancer

Igirisu N イギリス England, UK

Igirisu(-jin) no ADJ イギリス (人)の English, British

igo N 囲碁 the board game Go

igokochi ga ii PHR 居心地が いい (while staying) to feel comfortable

igokochi ga warui PHR 居心地
が悪い to feel ill at ease

ihan N 違反 violation, offense

ii ADJ いい good; OK, right,
correct

iie ADV いいえ no

ii'kagen na ADJ いい加減な
random, perfunctory, half-
hearted, indifferent, vague

i'in N 委員 committee member(s)

i'inkai N 委員会 committee

i'itaihōdai 言いたい放題 to say
whatever one wants/feels

i'itsukeru V 言い付ける
to command, to order;
to tattle on

i'iwake N 言い訳 explanation,
excuse

iji ga warui, ijiwaru na
ADJ 意地が悪い, 意地悪な
(*cruel*) mean

ijihi N 維持費 (*expense*) upkeep

ijimeru V いじめる to tease,
to torment

ijō N, SUFFIX 以上 above, over,
upwards of; the above; (*end
of message/speech*) thank
you (*for your attention*)

ijō N 異状/異常 (*the matter*)
something unusual/wrong,
abnormality

ijō na ADJ 異常な abnormal;
unusual; remarkable

ijū N 移住 emigration,
immigration

ijūsha N 移住者 emigrant,
immigrant

...ika N, SUFFIX 〜以下 below
(...), less than ...

ika N イカ squid, cuttlefish

ikada N 筏 raft

ikaga ADV いかが how (*about
it*)?

ikagawashi'i ADJ いかがわしい
suspicious, questionable,
shady

ika no tōri 以下の通り as
(*described*) below, as
follows

ikaiyō N 胃かいよう (*gastric*)
ulcer

ikari N 怒り anger

ikari N 錨 anchor

ike N 池 pond

ikebana N 生け花 flower
arrangement

iken N 意見 opinion

ikeru V 生ける (*flowers*)
to arrange

iki N 息 breath

iki na ADJ 粋な smart, stylish,
cool, chic

iki o hikitoru v 息を引き取る to die, to pass away

iki o suru v 息をする to breathe

ikigai N 生き甲斐 (*livable*) something to live for

ikigurushi'i ADJ 息苦しい stuffy

ikimono N 生き物 living thing; animal

ikinobiru N 生延びる to survive

ikioi N 勢い energy

ikiru v 生きる to live

ikisatsu N いきさつ details, circumstances, complexities

ikite N 生きて alive

ikiteiru N 生きている living

ikizumaru v 行き詰まる to get bogged down

ikkai N 一階 one floor/story; first floor, ground floor

ikkai no N, ADJ 一回の one time, once

ikko no ADJ 一個の a piece of

ikkyū N 一級 first class

ikotsu N 遺骨 (*of person*) remains

iku v 行く to go

ikuji N 育児 child care

ikujinashi N 意気地なし coward, chicken

ikura N イクラ (*caviar*) salmon roe

ikura desu ka いくらですか (価格) (*price*) how much?

ikutsu desu ka いくつです か (*age*) how old?; (*things*) how many?

ikutsuka no ADJ いくつかの several, some

ima N 今 now, this time

ima N 居間 living room

ima da ni ADV 未だに still

ima goro wa 今ごろは about this time

ima made ADV 今まで until now, up to the present (*time*)

ima ni ADV 今に before long, soon, by and by, presently

ima ni mo 今にも at any moment

ima sara ADV 今さら at this point

ima wa 今は at present

imēji N イメージ (*social/ psychological*) image

imēru N Eメール e-mail

imi N 意味 meaning

imin N 移民 immigrant(s)/ emigrant(s)

imōto N 妹 younger sister: **imōto-san** 妹さん (*your*) younger sister

inaka N 田舎 (*rural area*) coun- try (side); one's hometown

inazuma N 稲妻 lightning

inchiki na ADJ いんちきな fake, fraud(ulent)

Indo N インド India

Indo(-jin) no N インド(人)の Indian

Indoneshia N インドネシア Indonesia

Indoneshia(-jin) no ADJ インドネシア(人)の Indonesian

ine N 稲 (*plant*) rice

inekari N 稲刈り harvesting rice

inemuri N 居眠り snooze

inemuri suru V 居眠りするto doze off

infure N インフレ inflation

infuruenza N インフルエンザ flu, influenza

inkan N 印鑑 seal, stamp

inki na ADJ 陰気な gloomy, glum

inku, inki N インク, インキ ink

inkujetto purintā N インクジェットプリンター ink-jet printer

inochi N 命 one's life

inoru V 祈る to pray; to hope for

inreki N 陰暦 the lunar calendar

inryoku N 引力 attractive force, gravity

inryōsui N 飲料水 drinking water

insatsu suru V 印刷するto print

insatsubutsu N 印刷物 printed matter

inshi N 印紙 revenue stamp

inshokuten N 飲食店 restaurant(s)

inshō-teki na ADJ 印象的な impressive

inshōzukeru V 印象づけるto make an impression

inshu N 飲酒 drinking

insutanto N インスタント instant

insutanto kōhī N インスタントコーヒー instant coffee

insutanto rāmen N インスタントラーメン instant noodles

insutorakutā N インストラクター instructor

insutōru N インストール install, installation (*computer*)

intabyū N インタビュー interview

intāhon N インターホン intercom

intai suru V 引退するto retire

intānetto N インターネット Internet

intānetto ginkō N インターネット銀行 Internet bank, web bank

intānetto kafe N インターネットカフェ Internet café

intānetto ōkushon N インターネットオークション Internet auction

intānetto shoppingu N インターネットショッピング Internet shopping

intānetto shoppu N インターネットショップ Internet shopping site

interi N インテリ intellectual; highbrow

interia N インテリア *(accessory)* interior

intoranetto N イントラネット intranet

inu N 犬 dog

inugoya N 犬小屋 kennel, doghouse

in'yō suru V 引用する to quote

inzei N 印税 *(from one's book(s))* royalties

ippai N 一杯 a cupful, a glassful; a drink

ippai no ADJ いっぱいの full, filled

ippaku suru V 一泊する to stay overnight

ippan ni ADV 一般に generally

ippan-teki na ADJ 一般的な general, all-purpose

ippōtsūkō N 一方通行 *(traffic, argument)* one-way

ippun N 一分 one minute

irai N 依頼 request; dependence, reliance; trust, commission

irai N 以来 since

irasshai(mase) INTERJ いらっしゃい(ませ) Welcome!

irekawaru V 入れ替わる to replace

iremono N 入れ物 container

ireru V 入れる to put in, to let in, to admit; to include

irezumi N 入れ墨・刺青 tattoo

iriguchi N 入り口 entrance

iro N 色 color

iroiro na, iron'na ADJ いろいろな、いろんな various

iru V 要る to be necessary; to need, to want

iru V いる to be; to stay

iru V 射る to shoot

irui N 衣類 garment

isamashi'i ADJ 勇ましい brave, daring

ise'ebi N 伊勢エビ lobster

isei N 異性 (*person of*) the opposite sex

iseki N 遺跡 (*historical*) remains

isha N 医者 doctor

isharyō N 慰謝料 damages/ compensation for mental suffering

ishi N 石 rock, stone

ishi N 意志 will, determination

ishi N 意思 intention

ishiatama N 石頭 stubborn, hardheaded

ishiki N 意識 consciousness

ishiki fumei no ADJ 意識不明の unconscious

isho N 遺書 will

ishō N 衣装 costume

isogashi'i ADJ 忙しい (*doing something*) busy

isogi no ADJ 急ぎの hasty, hurried, urgent

isogu V 急ぐ to hurry, to rush

issai ADJ, ADV 一切 all, everything, without exception

issai N 一歳 one year old

issaku-jitsu 一昨日 day before yesterday

issaku-nen 一昨年 year before last

issei ni ADV 一斉に all together

isseki-nichō N 一石二鳥 [IDIOM] Kill two birds with one stone.

isshō N 一生 lifetime

isshō kenmei ni ADV 一生懸命 に desperately; very hard

issho ni ADV 一緒に together

īshoppingu イーショッピング e-shopping, Internet shopping

issō ADV いっそう (*also*) even; all the more…, still/much more …

isu N 椅子 chair, seat

Isuramukyō no ADJ イスラム教 (徒) の Muslim

ita N 板 board, plank

itadaki N 頂 peak, summit

itadakimasu いただきます Let's eat!

itadaku V いただく [HUMBLY] to receive, to eat, to drink

itai ADJ 痛い sore, painful, hurting

itamae N 板前 (*Japanese food*) chef

itameru V 痛める to hurt, to injure

itameru V 傷める to damage, to spoil it

itameru V 炒める to (pan-)fry, to saute

61

itami N 痛み ache, pain

itamu V 痛む to ache

itamu V 傷む to spoil, to rot

Itaria N イタリア Italy

Itaria(-jin) no ADJ イタリア(人)の Italian

itazura N いたずら mischief, prank

itazurakko N いたずらっ子 naughty child

ito N 意図 intention

ito N 糸 thread; yarn; string

itoko N いとこ cousin

itoshi'i ADJ 愛しい (*beloved*) dear

itsu PRON いつ when

itsu de mo ADV いつでも whenever; any time (at all)

itsugoro N いつ頃 about when

itsu ka ADV いつか sometime

itsu made ADV いつまで until when, how long

itsu made mo ADV いつまでも forever

itsu made ni ADV いつまでに by when

itsu mo N, ADV いつも always, everytime, usually

itsumo no ADJ いつもの usual

ittekimasu INTERJ いってきます (*said to those staying home*)

Goodbye!

itterasshai INTERJ いってらしゃい (*said to those leaving home*) Goodbye!

iu V 言う to say, to tell

iwa N 岩 rock, crag

iwashi N イワシ sardine

iwau V 祝う to celebrate

iya na ADJ 嫌な unpleasant; disliked; disagreeable; nasty

iyagaru V 嫌がる to dislike, to hate

iyakuhin N 医薬品 medicine

iyashi'i ADJ いやしい lowly, vulgar

izen ni ADV 以前に (*in time*) before

izumi N 泉 fountain, spring

izure ADV いずれ some other time; someday

J

ja, jā INTERJ, ADV じゃ、じゃあ well, well then; in that case; (*well*) now

jagaimo N ジャガイモ potato

jaguchi N 蛇口 faucet, tap

jaketto N ジャケット coat, jacket

jakuten N 弱点 weak point

jama N 邪魔 hindrance, disturbance

jamu N ジャム jam

jānarisuto N ジャーナリスト journalist

janguru N ジャングル jungle

janku mēru N ジャンクメール junk e-mail, junk mail

janpā N ジャンパー windbreaker, jacket

janpu suru V ジャンプする to jump

jari N 砂利 gravel, pebbles

jettoki N ジェット機 jet (*plane*)

ji N 字 (*symbol*) a letter

-ji SUFFIX 時 o'clock (*counts time*)

jibiki N 字引き dictionary

jibun N 自分 oneself; myself

jidai N 時代 age, period, era, time

jidō N 児童 (*elementary school student*) child

jidō N 自動 automatic

jidō-doa N 自動ドア auto(matic) door

jidō-hanbaiki N 自動販売機 vending machine

jidōsha N 自動車 automobile, car

jidōsha shūrikōjō N 自動車修理工場 (*for repairs*) garage

Jieitai N 自衛隊 the Self-Defense Forces

jigoku N 地獄 hell

jigyō N 事業 enterprise, business, undertaking

ji'in N 寺院 temple

jijitsu N 事実 fact, truth

jijō N 事情 circumstances; conditions

jikaku N 自覚 awareness

jikan N 時間 hour, time

-jikan SUFFIX 時間 (*counts hours or times*)

jikan ga kakaru V 時間がかかる to take time

jika ni ADV 直に directly; personally

jikanwari (hyō) N 時間割(表) (*table*) school time-table

jiken N 事件 happening, incident, event, affair, case

jiki N 時期 time; season

jikken N 実験 experiment

jikkō N 実行 performance; practice; realization, running

jiko N 事故 accident

jiko N 自己 (one)self

jikokuhyō N 時刻表 timetable, schedule

jikoshōkai suru v 自己紹介する to introduce oneself

jiman suru v 自慢する to boast, to brag about

jimen N 地面 ground, earth

jimi na ADJ 地味な simple, (*modest*) plain

jimu N ジム gym(nasium)

jimusho N 事務所 office

jinbutsu N 人物 personage

jingū N 神宮 (*large*) Shinto shrine

jinji N 人事 personnel/human affairs

jinken N 人権 human rights

jinkō N 人口 population

jinkōeisei N 人工衛星 artificial satellite

jinkō no ADJ 人工の artificial

jinrui N 人類 the human race

jinsei N 人生 (*one's*) life

jinshu sabetsu N 人種差別 racial discrimination

jinushi N 地主 landowner

jinzō N 腎臓 kidney

jippā N ジッパー zipper

jisa N 時差 difference in time

jisaboke N 時差ぼけ jet lag

jisan suru v 持参する to bring/ take along

jisatsu suru v 自殺する to commit suicide

jishin N 自信 (self-)confidence, self-assurance

jishin N 自身 self

jishin N 地震 earthquake

jisho N 辞書 dictionary

jishoku N 辞職 (*a position*) resignation

jisoku N 時速 (*per hour*) speed

jissai ni ADV 実際に actually, (*in fact*) really

jitai N 事態 situation, state of affairs

jitai suru v 辞退する to decline, to refuse

jitaku N 自宅 one's home, one's residence

jiten N 時点 (時間) (*in time*) point

jiten N 辞典 dictionary: *kokugo-jiten* 国語辞典 Japanese dictionary; *eiwa-jiten* 英和辞典 English-Japanese dictionary

jiten N 事典 dictionary, subject book: *hyakka-jiten* 百科事典 encyclopedia

jitensha N 自転車 bicycle

jitsubutsu N 実物 the real thing; the actual person: *jitsubutsu-saizu/-dai*

実物サイズ/大 actual size, original size

jitsu ni ADV 実に actually, indeed

jitsu no 実の true, real

jitsu wa 実は to tell the truth, actually, in fact

jitsugyō-ka N 実業家 businessperson

jitsuryoku N 実力 (*real*) strength, ability, proficiency; force, power

jitsuyō-teki na ADJ 実用的な practical

jitto ADV じっと intently, steadily, (*staring*) fixedly; quietly

jiyū N 自由 freedom, liberty

jiyū na (ni) ADJ (ADV) 自由な(に) free(ly); fluent(ly), at ease

jiyūseki N 自由席 unreserved seat

jō N 錠 lock

jōbu na ADJ 丈夫な sturdy, firm, healthy; safe

jōdan N 冗談 joke

jōei N 上映 (*movie*) showing

jōen N 上演 performance

jogakusei, joshigakusei N 女学生, 女子学生 female student

jōge N 上下 top and bottom, high and row, up and down

jogen N 助言 advice

jōgi N 定規 (*measure*) ruler

jogingu N ジョギング jog(ging)

jōgo N じょうご funnel

jōhin na ADJ 上品な elegant, refined

jōhō N 情報 information

jōkai e ADV 上階へ upstairs

jōken N 条件 (*pre-condition*) condition; term, stipulation, provision

jōki N 蒸気 steam

jokki N ジョッキ jug, (*beer*) mug

jōku N ジョーク joke

jōkyaku N 乗客 passenger

jōkyō N 状況 (*status*) condition, situation, circumstances

jōkyū N 上級 high/upper class: *jōkyū kōsu* 上級コース advanced course

jōmuin N 乗務員 crew: *kya-kushitsu jōmuin* 客室乗務員 (*airplane*) flight attendant

jōnetsu-teki na ADJ 情熱的な passionate

joō N 女王 queen

jōryū no ADJ 上流の classy, upper; upstream

jōryūshu N 蒸留酒 spirits, hard liquor

josei N 女性 female, woman

jōsha suru V 乗車する to get on, to ride, to board

jōsharyōkin N 乗車料金 fare

joshi N 女子 girl, woman

joshi-daisei N 女子大生 woman college student

joshikōsei N 女子高生 female (*senior*) high school student

jōshi N 上司 boss

jōshiki N 常識 common sense

jōshō N 上昇 rise, ascendancy

joshu N 助手 helper, assistant

josō N 女装 drag

jōtai N 状態 condition, situation, circumstances

jōtō no ADJ 上等の high-grade, superior, rich

jōyaku N 条約 treaty, agreement

joyū N 女優 actress

jōzai N 錠剤 pills, tablets

jōzu na ADJ 上手な skilled, clever, good at

jū NUM 十 ten

jūatsu N 重圧 pressure

jūbun na ADJ 十分な enough, sufficient

jūdai na ADJ 重大な (*heavy, grave*) serious; important

jūdō N 柔道 (*an art of weaponless defense*) judo, jujitsu

jūendama N 十円玉 ten-yen coin

jū-gatsu N 十月 October

jūgo NUM 十五 fifteen

jugyō N 授業 lesson, class, instruction: *jugyō o ukeru* 授業を受ける to attend a class

jūgyōin N 従業員 employee

jūhachi NUM 十八 eighteen

jūichi NUM 十一 eleven

jūichi-gatsu N 十一月 November

jūjika N 十字架 a cross

jūjiro N 十字路 crossroad(s)

jūjun na ADJ 従順な obedient, tame

juku N 塾 a cram/tutoring school

jukurenshita ADJ 熟練した skillful

jukushita ADJ 熟した ripe

jukusui N 熟睡 sound sleep

Jukyō N 儒教 Confucianism

jukyū N 需給 supply and demand

jūkyū NUM 十九 nineteen

jūman NUM 十万 hundred thousand

jūmin N 住民 resident

jūnana NUM 十七 seventeen

junban N 順番 (*place in*) order, turn; sequence

junban ni ADV 順番に in order

junbi N 準備 preparation(s), arrangements

junchō na ADJ 順調な smooth, normal

jūni NUM 十二 twelve

jūni-gatsu N 十二月 December

jūnin N 住人 resident, inhabitant

junjo N 順序 sequence, order

junkan N 循環 circulation; cycle

junsui na ADJ 純粋な pure

jūoku NUM 十億 billion

jūrai no ADJ 従来の traditional, accustomed, customary

juritsu suru V 樹立する to establish, to set up

jūroku NUM 十六 sixteen

jūryō N 重量 weight

jūryōage N 重量挙げ weight-lifting

jūsan NUM 十三 thirteen

jūsei N 銃声 gunshot(s)

jūshichi NUM 十七 seventeen

jushō N 受賞 winning an award

jūsho N 住所 address

jūsu N ジュース juice

jūtai N 渋滞 congestion

jūtaku N 住宅 residence, house

jūtan N じゅうたん carpet

juwaki N 受話器 (*telephone*) receiver

jūyaku N 重役 (会社の) (*company*) director

jūyō na ADJ 重要な major, important

jūyon NUM 十四 fourteen

K

ka N 蚊 mosquito

ka N 課 section; lesson

ka N 科 (*biological taxonomy*) family; (*university, hospital*) department

... ka ... CONJ 〜か〜 or

kaba N かば hippopotamus

kabā N カバー cover, covering

kaban N 鞄 bag, briefcase

kabau V 庇う to protect, to defend

kabe N 壁 wall

kabegami N 壁紙 wallpaper

kabin N 花瓶 vase

kabocha N カボチャ pumpkin

kabu N 株 (*in a company*) stock

kabu N カブ turnip

kabuki N 歌舞伎 a traditional style of Japanese theater

kaburu V 被る (*on head*) to wear; (*hat, etc.*) to put on

kabushiki shijō N 株式市場 stock market

kachi N 勝ち victory, win

kachi N 価値 (*cost*) value

kachō N 課長 section manager

kadai N 課題 problem, difficult matter; assignment, homework; subject, theme

kādigan N カーディガン cardigan

kado N 角 corner

kadō N 華道 flower arrangement

kādo N カード card

kaeru V 変える to change

kaeru V 換える・替える to exchange, to replace

kaeru V 帰る to go home, to go back, to return, to leave

kaeru N 蛙 frog

kaesu V 返す to return, to give back

kafusu N カフス cuff

kagai N 課外 extracurriculum: *kagai katsudō* 課外活動 extracurricular activity

kagaku N 科学 science

kagaku N 化学 chemistry

kagakusha N 科学者 scientist

kagakusha N 化学者 chemist

kagami N 鏡 mirror

kagayaku V 輝く to shine, to gleam, to glitter

kage N 陰 shade

kage N 影 shadow

kageki-ha N 過激派 the radicals, the extremists

kageki na ADJ 過激な excessive, extreme, radical

kagen N 加減 (*state of*) one's health; allowance; degree, extent; adjustment, moderation

-kagetsu SUFFIX か月 (*counts months*)

kagi N 鍵 (部屋) (*room*) key

kago N かご basket; (*bird*) cage

kagu N 家具 furniture

kagu V 嗅ぐ to smell

kai N 貝 shellfish

-kai SUFFIX 回 (*counts times or occasions*)

-kai SUFFIX 階 (*counts floors or stories*)

kaibō N 解剖 autopsy:
　kaibō-gaku 解剖学 anatomy
kaibutsu N 怪物 monster
kaichō N 会長 chairperson
kaichūdentō N 懐中電灯
　flashlight, (*electrical*) torch
kaidan N 階段 steps, stairs
kaiga N 絵画 painting
kaigai ryokō N 海外旅行
　overseas travel
kaigan N 海岸 seashore, coast,
　beach
kaigi N 会議 meeting, (*formal*)
　conference
kaigi-shitsu N 会議室
　conference room
kaigō N 会合 meeting
kaigun N 海軍 navy
kaihatsu N 開発 development
kaihi N 会費 membership fee,
　dues
kaihō suru V 開放する to open,
　(*windows, etc.*) to leave open
kai'in N 会員 member
kaijō N 会場 hall
kaika ni ADV 階下に downstairs
kaikei N 会計 accounts; bill,
　check
kaikei-gakari, kaikeishi 会計
　係, 会計士 N accountant
kaiketsu suru V 解決する(問題)

(*problem*) to resolve, to solve
kaiko suru V 解雇する to fire,
　to dismiss, to discharge
kaikyō N 海峡 strait
kaikyū N 階級 rank, station
　in life
kaimono N 買い物 shopping
kairi N 海里 nautical mile
kairyō N 改良 improvement,
　modification
kaisai suru V 開催する to hold,
　to open
kaisan suru V 解散する
　to break up, to disperse
kaisanbutsu N 海産物 seafood
kaisatsuguchi N 改札口
　(*ticket*) wicket
kaisetsu N 解説 explanation,
　comment
kaisetsusha N 解説者
　commentator
kaisha N 会社 company
kaishain N 会社員 company
　employee
kaishaku N 解釈 interpretation,
　explanation, exposition
kaisō N 回想 recollection
kaisū N 回数 (*counts number*
　of times)
kaisuiyoku N 海水浴 sea
　bathing

kaisūken N 回数券 (*for commuting*) ticket book, coupon ticket

kaitei N 改訂 (*documents, books, etc.*) revision

kaitei N 海底 bottom of the sea

kaiten suru N 回転する to revolve, to rotate

kaiten suru N 開店する to open shop/business

kaitō N 回答 reply

kaitō N 解答 answer

kaitoru v 買い取る to buy (up)

kaiwa N 会話 conversation

kaizen suru N 改善する to improve

kaizoku N 海賊 pirate

kaji N 火事 (*accidental*) a fire

kaji N 舵 rudder

kaji N 家事 housework, house-keeping

kajiru v かじる to bite, to gnaw, to nibble

kajō na ADJ 過剰な superfluous, surplus

kajū N 果汁 juice

kakaeru v 抱える to hold in one's arms; to keep, to have; to have a problem(s): *atama o kakaeru* 頭を抱える to tear one's hair out

kakaku N 価格 price

kakari N 係 (*in charge*) attendant

kakaru v 掛かる to hang; to take, to require; to weigh; to begin

kakashi N かかし scarecrow

kakato N 踵 heel

kake N 賭け bet, wager

kakegoto N 賭け事 gamble; a bet

kakehiki N 駆け引き tactics, bargaining

kakei N 家系 one's family line

kakei N 家計 household budget: *kakei o sasaeru* 家計を支る to support a household

kakejiku N 掛け軸 (*hanging*) scroll

kakera N 欠片 fragment

kakeru v 賭ける to bet

kakeru v 掛ける to hang; to multiply; to begin: *denwa o kakeru* 〜に電話を掛ける to telephone; *enjin o kakeru* エンジンを掛ける (*engine*) to start

kaketeiru N 欠けている lacking

kaki N 柿 (*fruits*) persimmon

kaki N 牡蠣 oyster

kaki N 花器 flower vase

kaki N 夏期 (*period/term*) summer

kaki N 火気 fire, flame

kaki-kyūka N 夏季休暇 summer holiday

kakigōri N かき氷 (*eaten with syrup*) shaved ice

kaki no tōri 下記の通り as follows, as below

kakikaeru V 書き換える to rewrite

kakikomu V 書き込む to fill out

kakinaosu V 書き直す to rewrite

kakitome N 書留 registered post

kakitomeru V 書き留める to note down

kakitori N 書き取り dictation

kakkō N 格好 shape, form, appearance

kakko ga ii ADJ 格好がいい shapely, cool, stylish

kakko ga warui ADJ 格好が悪い unsuitable

kako N 過去 the past

kakō N 河口 estuary

kakō N 火口 crater

kakō suru V 下降する to descend, to go/come down

kakō suru V 加工する to process

kakokei N 過去形 the past tense

kakoku na ADJ 過酷な too severe, harsh

kakomu V 囲む to surround

kaku V 書く (手紙, 本) (*letters, books*) to write

kaku V 描く (絵) (*a painting*) to paint, to draw

kaku V 掻く to scratch

kaku N 核 core, heart, stone

kaku... PREFIX 各... each, every

kakuchō suru 拡張する to enlarge

kakudai N 拡大 enlargement

kakudo N 角度 angle

kakuheiki N 核兵器 nuclear weapon

kakuho suru V 確保する to secure, to save

kakujitsu na ADJ 確実な certain, reliable, authentic

kakumau V かくまう (*criminal*) to harbor, to shelter

kakumei N 革命 revolution

kakunin suru V 確認する to confirm

kaku no ADJ 核の nucleus, nuclear

kakū no ADJ 架空の imaginary

kakū no jinbutsu N 架空の人物 fictional character

kakurega N 隠れ家 asylum, shelter, refuge

kakurenbo N かくれんぼ hide-and-seek

kakureru V 隠れる to hide

kakuritsu N 確率 probability

kakushin N 確信 conviction

kakusu V 隠す to hide

kakuteru N カクテル cocktail

kakutōgi N 格闘技 martial art

kakutoku N 獲得 acquisition, gain

kakuyasu N 格安 bargain, discounted

kakuyasu kōkūken N 格安航空券 discounted airline ticket

kakyūsei N 下級生 under-classman

kama N 窯 oven, kiln

kamado N かまど cooker; stove; oven

kamakiri N カマキリ praying mantis

kamawanai V 構わない to make no difference; never mind; not to bother, it's o.k.

kame N カメ tortoise, turtle

kamei N 仮名 an assumed name; a temporary/tentative name

kamei N 加盟 affiliation

kamei N 家名 family name

kamen N 仮面 mask

kamera N カメラ camera

kami N 紙 paper

kami N 神 god

kami N 髪 hair

kamibukuro N 紙袋 paper bag

kamidana N 神棚 (*Shinto*) household altar

kamihikōki N 紙飛行機 paper airplane

kamikazari N 髪飾り headdress

kamikuzu N 紙くず wastepaper

kaminari N 雷 thunder

kami-sama N 神様 God

kamisori N かみそり razor

kamitsuku V かみつく to bite

kamiyasuri N 紙やすり sandpaper

kamo N 鴨 wild duck

kamoku N 科目 subject, (*in school*) course: *hisshū kamoku* 必修科目 required course/subject

... ka mo shirenai VERBAL AUXILIARY 〜かもしれない maybe

kamu V 噛む to bite, to chew

kan N 缶 can, tin

kana N かな (*Japanese syllabic writing*) kana

Kanada N カナダ Canada

Kanada(-jin) no ADJ カナダ(人)の Canadian

kanai N 家内 my wife

kanarazu N 必ず for sure; necessity; inevitably

kanari N かなり (*fairly*) quite

kanari no ADJ かなりの fair

kanashi'i ADJ 悲しい sad, unhappy

kanashimi N 悲しみ sorrow, sadness

kanashimu V 悲しむ to be sad

kanau V 叶う to be accomplished, to attain, to achieve, to realize

kanazuchi N かなづち hammer; a person who cannot swim

kanban N 看板 signboard

kanbīru N 缶ビール canned beer

Kanbojia N カンボジア Cambodia

Kanbojia(-jin) no ADJ カンボジア(人)の Cambodian

kanbu N 幹部 executive

kanbutsu N 乾物 dry food

kanbyō N 看病 nursing

kanchi N 感知 appreciation, sense

kanchi N 完治 complete cure

kanchi suru V 感知する to sense

kanchō N 艦長 (*of warship*) captain

kanchō N 官庁 government office

kanchō N 干潮 ebb, low tide

kandai na ADJ 寛大な generous

kandō suru V 感動する to be impressed; to be touched

kane N 金 money

kane N 鐘 (*of church, temple, etc.*) large bell

kanemochi N 金持ち rich person

kānēshon N カーネーション carnation(s)

kanetsu N 加熱 heat, heating

kangae N 考え idea; thought; opinion

kangaeru V 考える to ponder, to think, to consider

kangei N 歓迎 welcome

kangeikai N 歓迎会 welcome party, reception

kangoshi N 看護師 nurse

kani N 蟹 crab

kanja N 患者 patient

kanji N 感じ feeling

kanji N 漢字 (*symbol*) Chinese character, kanji

kanjiru V 感じる to feel

kanjō N 勘定 bill, check, account: *o-kanjō onegai shimasu* お勘定お願いします Check please.

kanjō N 感情 emotion

kanjōdai N 勘定台 (*for paying, buying tickets*) counter

kankaku N 感覚 sense, feeling, sensibility, sensation

kankaku N 間隔 space, (*of time, space*) interval

kankei N 関係 connection, relationship, interest, concern, relevance

kankin suru V 換金する (*money*) to exchange

kankiri N 缶切り can opener

kankitsurui N かんきつ類 citrus

kankō N 観光 sightseeing

Kankoku N 韓国 South Korea

Kankoku(-jin) no ADJ 韓国 (人) の South Korean

kankōkyaku N 観光客 tourist

kankyaku N 観客 audience, spectator

kankyō N 環境 environment, surroundings

kan'na N かんな (*tool*) plane

kan'ningu N カンニング cheating

kan'nō-teki na ADJ 官能的な sensual, erotic

kan'nushi N 神主 (*Shinto*) priest

kanojo PRON, N 彼女 she/her; girlfriend

kanojo no ADJ 彼女の hers

kanojo o PRON 彼女を her

kanojo wa PRON 彼女は she

kanō na ADJ 可能な possible

kanō ni suru V 可能にする to make possible

kanpai N 乾杯 a toast, bottoms up, cheers!

kanpai N 完敗 complete defeat

kanpan N 甲板 (*ship*) deck

kanpeki na ADJ 完璧な (*thorough*) complete

kanpō(yaku) N 漢方(薬) Chinese medicine

kanranseki N 観覧席 (*seats*) grand-stand

kanren N 関連 relevance

kanri N 管理 control

kanrinin N 管理人 custodian, janitor, manager, (*rental manager*) landlord

kanroku ga aru 貫禄がある to have a presence

kansatsu N 観察 watching, observation

kansei N 完成 completion, perfection

kansha N 感謝 thanks, gratitude

kanshin N 関心 concern, interest

kanshō N 鑑賞 (*art, work, music*) appreciation

kansoku N 観測 observation; opinion

kansō N 感想 impression

kansōbun N 感想文 report: *dokusho-kansōbun* 読書感想文 book report

kansōki N 乾燥機 (*washing machine*) dryer

kansuru V 関する to relate (to), to be connected (with)

kantan na ADJ 簡単な (*easy*) simple, brief

kantei suru V 鑑定する to judge, to authenticate

kantoku N 監督 supervision; supervisor, superintendent, manager, director

kanzei N 関税 (*import tax*) customs duty

kanzen ni suru V 完全にする to make whole

kanzō N 肝臓 liver

kao N 顔 face

kaoiro N 顔色 complexion

kaoiro ga ii ADJ 顔色がいい look well

kaoiro ga warui ADJ 顔色が悪い look sick/green/pale

kaomoji N 顔文字 (*computer*) emoticon, face mark

kao o shikameru V 顔をしかめる to frown

kaori N 香り fragrance

kāpetto N カーペット carpet

kappatsu na ADJ 活発な active, lively

kappu N カップ cup

kappuru N カップル (*of lovers*) a couple

kapuseru hoteru N カプセルホテル capsule hotel

... kara PREP 〜から from

... kara hazureru V 〜からはずれる to come off

... kara ... ni idō suru V 〜から〜に移動する to move from one place to another

... kara okoru V 〜から起こる to originate, to come from

kara N 殻 shell, crust

karā N カラー collar

karā N カラー color

karada N 体 body

karai ADJ 辛い hot, spicy, peppery, pungent; salty

karakau V からかう to tease, to poke fun at

kara no, karappo no ADJ 空の, 空っぽの empty

karaoke N カラオケ karaoke

karashi N からし mustard

karasu N からす crow

karate N 空手 (*weaponless self-defense*) karate

kare PRON, N 彼 he/his; boyfriend

karē N カレー curry

karēraisu N カレーライス rice with curry

kare no ADJ 彼の his

kare o PRON 彼を him

kare wa PRON 彼は he

karendā N カレンダー calendar

karera PRON 彼ら they

karera no ADJ 彼らの their, theirs

karera o PRON 彼らを them

karera wa PRON 彼らは they

kareru V 枯れる to wither, to blight

kareshi N 彼氏 boyfriend

kari N 借り borrowing: *kari ga aru* 借りがある to owe

kari no ADJ 仮の temporary, tentative

karifurawā N カリフラワー cauliflower

kariru V 借りる to borrow, to rent

karō N 過労 overfatigue

karōshi N 過労死 death from overwork

karōjite ADJ かろうじて barely

karu V 刈る to mow, to cut

karui ADJ 軽い light

kasa N 傘 umbrella

kasabaru V かさばる to be bulky, to take up much space

kasai N 火災 (*accidental*) fire

kasai hōchiki N 火災報知器 (*device*) fire alarm, fire bell

kasaneru V 重ねる to pile, to put one on top of another

kasegu V 稼ぐ to earn, (*money*) to work for

kasei N 火星 the Mars

kaseki N 化石 fossil(s)

kasen N 下線 underline

kasetto (tēpu) N カセット(テープ) (*for music*) cassette (*tape*)

kashi N 歌詞 lyrics

kashi N 菓子 confectionery, sweets, candy

kashikoi ADJ 賢い clever, smart, wise

kashitsu N 過失 fault, mistakes, errors

kashiya N 貸家 house for rent; rented/rental house

kashi-ya N 菓子屋 candy store, confectionary; confectioner

-kasho SUFFIX か所 (*counter for places, installations, institutions*)

kashu N 歌手 singer

kasō N 仮装 disguise

kasō N 下層 lower layer

kasō N 火葬 cremation

kasoku N 加速 acceleration

kāsoru N カーソル cursor

kasu V 貸す to lend, to rent

kasu N かす sediment, dregs, grounds; scrap, junk; particles: *moekasu* 燃えかす cinders

kasuka na/ni ADJ (ADV) 微かな/に faint(ly), dim(ly), slight(ly)

kasumetoru V 掠め取る to skim off; to rob (*it of …*), to cheat (*one out of …*)

kasumi N かすみ haze, mist

kasutera N カステラ sponge cake

kata N 肩 shoulder

kata N 型 form, shape, size, mold, pattern

katachi N 形 form, shape, style

katachizukuru V 形作る to form, to shape

katagaki N 肩書き (*of person*) title

katahō, katappo N 片方, 片っぽ one of a pair; (*of a pair*) the other one

katai ADJ 堅い stiff; hard; solid; sound; reliable; formal

katai ADJ 固い (*solid*) hard; tight; strict

katai ADJ 硬い (マットレス) (*mattress*) firm; hard, stiff; stilted upright

katakori N 肩こり stiff shoulder

katamari N 塊 a lump, a clot, a mass; (*bread*) a loaf

katamaru V 固まる to harden, to congeal, to clot, (*mud*) to cake

katameru V 固める to harden it, to congeal it; to strengthen it

katamichikippu N 片道切符 one-way ticket

katamuku V 傾く (*one side*) to lean, to slant

77

katana N 刀 sword

kataru v 語る to relate, to tell

katazukeru v 片付ける to tidy up, to clean up

katei N 家庭 home, household

katei N 課程 (*course, stage*) process

katei N 仮定 hypothesis, supposition

kateiyōhin N 家庭用品 home appliances

kāten N カーテン curtain

kāto N カート (手押し) (*pushcart*) cart

katsu v 勝つ to win

katsudō N 活動 activity

katsuo N カツオ bonito

katsu(o)bushi N 鰹節 dried bonito fish

katsura N かつら wig

katsuryoku N 活力 energy

katsute ADV かつて in the past

katsuyaku N 活躍 activity

katte na/ni ADJ, ADV 勝手な/に selfish(ly), as one wishes

kau v 買う to buy

kau v 飼う to raise, (*pets, farm animals, etc.*) to keep

kaunserā N カウンセラー counselor

kauntā N カウンター (*for paying, buying tickets*) counter

kawa N 川 river

kawa N 皮 skin; (*tree*) bark; crust

kawa N 革 leather

kawaii ADJ かわいい cute, appealing

kawairashi'i ADJ かわいらしい pretty

kawaisō na ADJ かわいそうな pitiful, poor

kawakasu v 乾かす to dry

kawaku v 乾く to get dry

kawaku v 渇く thirsty: *nodo ga kawaku* のどが渇く to get thirsty

kawara N 瓦 (*for roof*) tile

kawari no ADJ 代わりの substitute

kawari ni ADV 代わりに instead of

kawaru v 変わる (状況が) (*conditions*) to change

kawaru v 代わる to act as substitute (for)

kawase N 為替 a money order

kawase sōba N 為替相場 exchange rate

kawaserēto N 為替レート (*currency*) rate of exchange

kayaku N 火薬 gunpowder

ka-yōbi N 火曜日 Tuesday

kayou V 通う to commute, to go back and forth, (*regularly*) to go

kayui ADJ かゆい itchy

kazan N 火山 volcano

kazari N 飾り ornament, decoration

kazaru V 飾る to decorate

kaze N 風 wind

kaze N 風邪 cold, flu: *kaze o hiku* かぜをひく to catch (a) cold

kazegusuri N かぜ薬 medicine for colds

kazoekirenai ADJ 数え切れない countless, innumerable, uncountable

kazoeru V 数える to count, to reckon

kazoku N 家族 family

kazu N 数 number

ke N 毛 hair; wool; feathers

kēburu N ケーブル cable

kēburukā N ケーブルカー cable car

kēburu terebi N ケーブルテレビ cable TV

kechappu N ケチャップ ketchup

kechi na ADJ けちな stingy

kedamono, kemono N 獣 animal; beast

kedo, keredo(-mo) CONJ けど、けれど(も) however, though, but

kega N 怪我 wound, injury

kegawa N 毛皮 fur

keiba N 競馬 horse racing/race

keibetsu suru V 軽蔑する to despise

keibi N 警備 security

keibin N 警備員 security guard

keiei N 経営 management, operation

keieisha N 経営者 manager, operator, proprietor

keihi N 経費 expenses

keihin N 景品 giveaway

keihō N 警報 alarm, alert, warning

keiji N 刑事 (*police*) detective

keijiban N 掲示板 bulletin board

keika N 経過 (*time*) course, progress, development

keikai suru V 警戒する to guard against, to watch out (*for …*), to warn, to caution

keikaku N 計画 plan, schedule, project

keikaku suru V 計画する to plan

keiken N 経験 experience

keiki N 景気 business conditions, prosperity, boom: *keiki no ii* 景気のいい booming

keiko N 稽古 exercise, practice, drill

keikō N 傾向 tendency, trend

keikoku N 警告 warning

keikōtō N 蛍光灯 fluorescent light

keimusho N 刑務所 jail, prison

keireki N 経歴 (*history*) career

keirin N 競輪 bicycle race

keirō-no-hi N 敬老の日 (*3rd Mon. of Sept.*) Respect-for-the-Aged Day

keiryōkappu N 計量カップ measuring cup

keisan N 計算 calculation

keisanki N 計算機 calculator

keisatsu N 警察 police

keisatsukan N 警察官 police officer

keisatsusho N 警察署 police station

keishiki N 形式 form, formality

keishoku N 軽食 snack

keisotsu na ADJ 軽率な hasty, rash

keitai ADJ 携帯 portable

keitai, keitaidenwa N 携帯, 携帯電話 cell phone

keitai suru V 携帯する to carry, to take along

keito N 毛糸 wool; yarn

keiyaku N 契約 contract, agreement

keiyakusho N 契約書 contract sheet

keiyōshi N 形容詞 adjective

keiyu de/no ADV, ADJ …経由で/の (*way of*) by, via

keizai N 経済 economy

keizaigaku N 経済学 (*science of*) economics

keizoku suru V 継続する to continue

kēki N ケーキ (*sweets*) cake

kekka N 結果 result, effect

kekkaku N 結核 tuberculosis

kekkan N 欠陥 defect, deficiency

kekkan N 血管 blood vessel

kekkon N 結婚 marriage

kekkonshiki N 結婚式 wedding

kekkon suru V 結婚する to marry, to get married

kekkyoku ADV 結局 after all, in the long run, eventually

kemui, kemutai ADJ 煙い, 煙たい smoky

kemuri N 煙 smoke

ken N 県 a prefecture

ken N 剣 (*double-edged*) sword

ken N 券 (娯楽) ticket (*for entertainment*)

ken N 腱 tendon

-ken SUFFIX 軒 (*counts small buildings*)

kenbaiki N 券売機 ticket vending machine

kenbikyō N 顕微鏡 microscope

kenbutsu N 見物 sightseeing

kenbutsunin N 見物人 bystander

kenchiku N 建築 architecture

kenchiku-ka N 建築家 architect

kendō N 剣道 (*with bamboo swords*) the Japanese art of fencing, kendo

kengaku N 見学 field study/ trip/work

kengi N 嫌疑 suspicion

kenji N 検事 (*public*) prosecutor

kenjū N 拳銃 pistol

kenka N けんか fight, quarrel

kenkō N 健康 health

kenkō-hoken N 健康保険 health insurance

kenkōshindan N 健康診断 medical examination

kenkyo na ADJ 謙虚な (*modest*) humble

kenkyū 研究 research, study

kenmei na ADJ 賢明な wise

ken'okan N 嫌悪感 hatred

kenpō N 憲法 constitution

kenri N 権利 rights

kenryoku(sha) N 権力(者) (*power*) authority

kensa N 検査 inspection, examination, check-up, test

kensaku suru V 検索する to look up, to search, to retrieve

kensetsu N 建設 (*building*) construction (*work*)

kenshō N 検証 verification

kentō N 見当 aim; direction; estimate, guess: ***kentō ga tsuku*** 見当がつく to get a rough idea (of it)

ken'yaku N 倹約 economy, thrift, economizing

keredo(mo) CONJ けれど(も) however, though, but

keri o tsukeru V けりをつける to wind up

keru V 蹴る to kick

kesa N 今朝 this morning

keshigomu N 消しゴム (*rubber*) eraser

keshiki N 景色 scenery, view, panorama

keshōhin N 化粧品 cosmetics

keshōshitsu N 化粧室 rest room, bathroom

kessaku N 傑作 masterpiece

kesseki N 欠席 (*school, work*) absence

kesshin N 決心 decision

kesshite ... nai ADV 決して～ない never

kesshō N 決勝 finals, title match

kesu V 消す to turn off; to erase; (*fire*) to put out

keta N 桁 (*numerical*) column

kētai denwa N 携帯電話 cell-phone, mobile phone

ketsuatsu N 血圧 blood pressure

ketsueki N 血液 blood

ketsumatsu N 結末 outcome

ketsuron N 結論 conclusion: *ketsuron to shite* 結論として in conclusion

ketten N 欠点 flaw, defect, short-coming

kewashi'i ADJ 険しい steep, precipitous; severe

kezuru V 削る to sharpen,

to shave

ki N 木 tree, wood

kī N キー (コンピューター) (*computer*) key

ki ga mijikai ADJ 気が短い impatient, short-tempered

ki ga omoi ADJ 気が重い depressed

ki ga tsuku V 気が付く to come to one's senses

ki ni iru 気に入る to suit one's taste

ki ni naru 気になる to be anxious; to worry

ki ni shinai de 気にしないで never mind!

ki ni suru V 気にする to worry about, to mind

ki o tsukeru V 気をつける to take care; (be) careful

kibarashi N 気晴らし diversion, recreation

kibin na ADJ 機敏な quick

kibishi'i ADJ きびしい strict, severe

kibō N 希望 hope, desire

kībōdo N キーボード (コンピューター) (*computer*) keyboard

kibōsha N 希望者 candidate, applicant

kibun N 気分 feeling, mood

kichi N 基地 military base

kichi N 機知 wit

kichō N 機長 (*airplane*) captain

kichōhin N 貴重品 valuables

kichōmen na ADJ 几帳面 な meticulous, particular; punctual

kieru V 消える to go out; to fade, to vanish

kiga N 飢餓 famine

kigaeru V 着替える to change clothes

ki no kurutta ADJ 気の狂った (*insane*) crazy, mad

ki ga kuru'u V 気が狂う (*insane*) to go mad

kigaru na ADJ 気軽な casual, lighthearted

kigeki N 喜劇 comedy

kigen N 起源 origin

kigen N 期限 term, period; deadline

kigen ga ii ADJ 機嫌がいい cheerful

kigen ga warui ADJ 機嫌が悪い unhappy, moody

kigō N 記号 sign, mark, symbol

kigu N 器具 fixture, apparatus, instrument

kigyō N 企業 firm, company

kihon N 基本 basic

kihon-teki na ADJ 基本的な basic, fundamental

ki'iroi ADJ 黄色い yellow

kiji N 記事 (*in newspaper*) article, news item, write-up

kiji N 生地 cloth, material, fabric

kijitsu N 期日 appointed day; deadline

kijun N 基準 basis, standard

kika PRON 貴下 (男性への敬称) (*term of address*) sir

kikai N 機会 chance, opportunity

kikai N 機械 machine

kikai na ADJ 奇怪な mysterious, strange

kikaku N 企画 plan(ning), project

kikaku suru V 企画する to plan

kikaku N 規格 norm, standard

kikan N 期間 (*of time*) period, term

kikan N 機関 agency, institution, organization; engine

kikanshi N 季刊誌 quarterly

kiken N 危険 danger

kiken suru v 棄権する to abstain

kiki N 危機 crisis, critical moment, emergency

kikime N 効き目 effect

kikite N 聞き手 hearer, listener

kikite N 利き手 stronger hand

kikkake N きっかけ opportunity, occasion

kikō N 気候 climate

kikō N 機構 system, organization, structure

kiku v 聴く to listen

kiku v 聞く to hear

kiku N 菊 chrysanthemum

kikyō suru v 帰郷する to return to one's hometown

kikyū N 気球 balloon

kimae ga ii ADJ 気前がいい generous

kimari N 決まり rule; settlement, arrangement; order; regulation

kimari ga warui ADJ きまりが悪い is/feels embarrassed

kimaru v 決まる to be settled, to be arranged

kimeru v 決める to decide, to fix

kimi N 君 you

kimi N 黄身 (*of egg*) yolk

kimi ga warui ADJ 気味が悪い nervous, apprehensive, (*feeling*) weird

kimo N きも liver; guts, courage, pluck

kimochi N 気持ち feeling, sensation

kimochi (ga) ii ADJ 気持ち(が)いい it feels good, comfortable

kimochi (ga) warui ADJ 気持ち(が)悪い uncomfortable, feeling bad/unwell

kimono N 着物 clothes; a (*Japanese*) kimono

kimyō na ADJ 奇妙な strange, peculiar

kin N 金 gold

kinai N 機内 on a plane

kinako N きな粉 soybean flour

kinchōshita N 緊張した tense

kinen N 記念 commemoration

kin'en N 禁煙 smoking prohibited, no smoking

kinenbi N 記念日 anniversary

kinenhi N 記念碑 monument

kinenhin N 記念品 souvenir

kinenkitte N 記念切手 commemorative stamp

kin'ensha N 禁煙車 no(n)-smoking car

kingaku N 金額 (*of money*) amount

kingan N 近眼 nearsightedness, myopia

kingyo N 金魚 goldfish

kiniro no ADJ 金色の (*color*) gold, golden

kinjiru V 禁じる to forbid, to prohibit

kinjo N 近所 neighborhood

kinka N 金貨 gold coin

kinko N 金庫 (*strongbox*) safe, (*small*) cash box

kinkyū no ADJ 緊急の urgent

kinkyūjitai 緊急事態 emergency

kinmu N 勤務 duty, service, work

kinmusaki N 勤務先 place of work/employment

kin'niku N 筋肉 muscle

kinō N 昨日 yesterday

kinō N 機能 function

kinodoku na ADJ 気の毒な pitiful, pitiable

kinoko N きのこ mushroom

kinomi N 木の実 nuts

kinō suru V 機能する to function, to work

kinshi suru V 禁止する to forbid

kin-yōbi N 金曜日 Friday

kin'yū N 金融 finance

kin'yūkikan N 金融機関 financial institution

kinyū suru V 記入する to fill in

kinzoku N 金属 metal

kioku N 記憶 memories

kippari to ADV きっぱりと definitely, firmly, flatly

kippu N 切符 (乗り物) (*for transport*) ticket

kippu'uriba N 切符売り場 ticket office

kirai na ADJ 嫌いな dislik(e)able; dislike

kiraku na ADJ 気楽な carefree, comfortable; easy-going

kirasu V 切らす to exhaust the supply of, to run out of

kire N 切れ a piece, (*of cloth*) a cut

kirei na ADJ きれいな clean, beautiful

kireme N 切れめ cut, slice

kireru V 切れる to cut (*well*); to run out; to break (*off*)

kiri N 霧 fog, mist

Kirisutokyō N キリスト教 Christianity

Kirisutokyō(to) no ADJ キリスト教(徒) の Christian

kiritsu N 規律 discipline

kiroku N 記録 (*historic*) record

kiru V 切る to cut

kiru V 着る to get dressed, to wear, (*clothes*) to put on

kisaku na ADJ 気さくな frank, friendly, companionable

kisetsu N 季節 season

kisha N 記者 journalist

kishi N 岸 shore, bank

kishō N 気象 weather

kishōyohō N 気象予報 weather forecast(ing)

kiso N 基礎 base, foundation

kisoku N 規則 rules, regulation

kisou V 競う to compete, to vie

kissaten N 喫茶店 tearoom, coffee house, café

kisu N キス kiss

kita N 北 north

Kitachōsen N 北朝鮮 North Korea

Kitachōsen(-jin) no ADJ 北朝鮮(人)の North Korean

kitaeru V 鍛える to forge, to temper; to drill, to discipline

kitai N 気体 vapor, a gas

kitai N 期待 expectation

kitaku suru V 帰宅する to go home

kitanai ADJ 汚い dirty; untidy, messy; unfair

kitei no ADJ 規定の regular, stipulated, compulsory

kiten N 機転 wit

kiten no kiku ADJ 機転の利く quick-witted

kitsuen N 喫煙 smoking

kitsuensha N 喫煙者 smoker

kitsui ADJ きつい close together, tight

kitsune N きつね fox

kitte N 切手 (郵便) (*postage*) stamp

kitto ADV きっと surely, no doubt, doubtless, undoubtedly

kiwadoi ADJ きわどい delicate, dangerous, ticklish

kiyō na ADJ 器用な skillful, nimble, clever

kiyomeru V 清める to purify

kizamu V 刻む to engrave; to chop

kizashi N 兆し sign(s), hint(s), symptom(s), indication(s), omen(s)

kizu N 傷 wound; scratch, flaw, blemish; fault, defect

kizuiteiru V 気づいている (*sensible*) to be aware

kizukai N 気づかい anxiety, concern, worry, care

kizuku V 気づく to notice; to awake; to occur

kizuku V 築く to build; (*buildings*) to construct

kizutsuku V 傷つく to get hurt/injured

-ko SUFFIX 個 (*counts small objects*)

kōba, kōjō N 工場 factory, plant

kobamu V 拒む to refuse, to reject; to oppose, to resist

kōban N 交番 police box

koboreru V こぼれる to spill

kobosu V こぼす to spill (it);

kobu N こぶ bump, knob, swelling

kobu, konbu N 昆布 kelp

kobun N 子分 henchman, subordinate, follower

kobushi N 拳 fist

kōbutsu N 好物 (*food/drink*) favorite

kōcha N 紅茶 (*black*) tea

kōchi N コーチ (*sports*) coach

kochira PRON こちら (*of two*) this one; here, this way

kochō N 誇張 exaggeration

kōchō N 校長 (*elementary school, junior/senior high school*) principal/head of a school

kōchō na ADJ 好調な favorable, satisfactory, in a good condition

kodai no ADJ 古代の ancient

kodama N こだま echo

kodō N 鼓動 heartbeat, pulse

kōdo N コード (*electricity*) cord; (*sign, symbol, mark*) code

kōdō N 行動 action

kōdō N 講堂 public (*lecture*) hall, auditorium

kōdo na ADJ 高度な advanced, sophisticated

kodoku N 孤独 loneliness

kodomo N 子供 (子孫/若い人) (*offspring/young person*) child

kodomotachi N 子供たち children

kodomo-no-hi N こどもの日 (*5 May*) Children's Day

kodomo no koro 子供の頃 one's early years, as a child

koe N 声 voice

koeda N 小枝 twig

kōen N 公園 garden, park

kōen N 公演 performance

87

kōen N 講演 lecture, speech

kōen N 後援 support, backing

koeru V 越える (*a height, an obstacle*) to cross

kōfuku N 幸福 happiness

kōfuku suru V 降伏する to surrender

kōgai N 公害 (*environmental*) pollution

kōgai N 郊外 suburbs, suburbia

kōgaku N 工学 engineering

kōgaku no ADJ 高額の expensive

kōgan N 睾丸 testicles

kogasu V 焦がす to get burned

kogatabasu N 小型バス minibus

kōgeki N 攻撃 (戦争) (*in war*) attack

kogeru V 焦げる to scorch

kōgi N 講義 lecture

kōgi N 抗議 protest

kogirei na ADJ こぎれいな (場所、物) (*of places, things*) neat

kogitte N 小切手 (*bank*) check

kōgo N 口語 spoken language, (*word*) colloquial

kogoe N 小声 low voice, whisper

kogoto N 小言 scolding, complaint

kogu V 漕ぐ (*a boat*) to row

kōgyō N 工業 industry

kōhai N 後輩 one's junior

kōhei na ADJ 公平な just, fair

kōhī N コーヒー coffee

kōhī-kappu/-jawan N コーヒーカップ/茶碗 coffee cup

kōhī-ten N コーヒー店 coffee shop/house

kohitsuji N 子羊 lamb, small sheep

kōhyō N 好評 favorable criticism

koi ADJ 濃い (*of liquids*) thick; (*color*) deep, (*coffee, tea*) strong

koi N 鯉 carp

koi N 恋 (*affair*) love, romance

kōi N 好意 goodwill, favor

kōi N 行為 act, deed; behavior

koi ni ADV 故意に deliberately

koibito N 恋人 sweetheart, lover, boyfriend/girlfriend

koinrokkā N コインロッカー coin locker

koishii V 恋しい (*loved one*) to miss

kōiu, kōyū ADJ こういう、こうゆう this kind/sort of, such

koji N 孤児 orphan

koji N 古寺 ancient temple

kōji N 工事 construction work

kōji-chū ADJ 工事中 under construction

kojin-teki na ADJ 個人的な private, individual, personal

kojireru V こじれる to get twisted; (*illness*) to worsen

kōjitsu N 口実 excuse, pretext

kōjō N 工場 factory, plant

kōjutsu N 口述 dictation

kōka N 効果 effect

kōka N 硬貨 coin

kōka na ADJ 高価な expensive

kokage N 木陰 (*trees*) shade

kōkai N 後悔 regret

kōkai no ADJ 公開の open to the public, open, public

kōkan N 交換 exchange

kōkeiki N 好景気 prosperity, good business conditions

kōki N 好機 (*favorable*) opportunity, chance, occasion

kōkiatsu N 高気圧 high (*barometric*) pressure

kōkishin N 好奇心 curiosity, inquisitiveness

kokka N 国家 (*nation*) country

kokkai N 国会 Diet, assembly, parliament, congress

kokkei na ADJ こっけいな amusing, funny

kokki N 国旗 (*national*) flag

kokku N コック (*person*) cook

kokkyō N 国境 (*between countries*) border

koko N ここ here, this place

kōkō N 高校 senior high school

kokoa N ココア cocoa

kokochiyoi N 心地良い comfortable

kōkoku N 広告 advertisement

kokonattsu N ココナッツ coconut

kokoro N 心 mind, heart, spirit

kokoroatari N 心当たり idea

kokorokubari N 心配り concern, care

kokoromi N 試み trial, attempt, test

kokoromochi N 心持ち feelings, spirit, mood

kokorozashi N 志 mind; intention; purpose; ambition; hope; goodwill, kindness; gift

kokorozuyoi ADJ 心強い heartening, encouraging

kōkōsei N 高校生 (*senior*) high school student

kokuban N 黒板 blackboard

kōkūbin N 航空便 airmail

kokudō N 国道 National Route

kokumin N 国民 a people, a nation; national(s), citizen(s)

kokunai no ADJ 国内の internal, domestic

kokuritsu no ADJ 国立の national, government-established

kokurui N 穀類 cereal(s), grain

kokusai denwa N 国際電話 international phone call

Kokusai rengō N 国際連合 United Nations

kokusai-teki na ADJ 国際的な international

kokusanhin N 国産品 domestic product

kokuseki N 国籍 nationality

kōkūshokan N 航空書簡 air letter

kokyō N 故郷 hometown, birth-place

kōkyo N 皇居 the Imperial Palace

kōkyō no ADJ 公共の public

kōkyōryōkin N 公共料金 utility bills/charges

kokyū N 呼吸 respiration, breathing

kōkyū na ADJ 高級な high-class/grade, luxury, fancy

koma N こま a toy top

komakai ADJ 細かい fine; detailed, exact; thrifty

komaraseru V 困らせる to bother, to cause inconvenience, to embarrass

komaru V 困る to get perplexed; to be at a loss; to be in need

komāsharu N コマーシャル commercial (*message*)

komatta ADJ 困った troublesome; problematic

komayaka na ADJ 細やかな meticulous, attentive, tender

kome N 米 (*uncooked*) rice

komeru V 込める to include

komichi N 小道 alley, lane

komon N 顧問 consultant, adviser

komon bengoshi N 顧問弁護士 a legal adviser

kōmon N 肛門 anus

kōmon N 校門 school gate

komori N 子守 babysitter

kōmori N コウモリ (*flying mammal*) bat

komoriuta N 子守歌 lullaby, cradle song, nursery song

komu V 混む to get crowded

komugi N 小麦 wheat

komugiko N 小麦粉 flour

kōmuin N 公務員 government worker/employee, official

kona N 粉 powder; flour

konban N 今晩 tonight

konban wa INTERJ こんばんは good evening

konbini(ensu sutoā) N コンビニ (エンス・ストアー) convenience store

konbu N 昆布 (*a kind of seaweed*) kelp

konchū N 昆虫 insect

kondate N 献立 menu

kondo N 今度 this time; next

kondōmu N コンドーム condom, contraceptive

kone N コネ contact, connection

koneko N 子猫 kitten

kongan suru V 懇願する to plead

kongetsu N 今月 this month

kongo N 今後 from now on, in the future

kon'i na/ni ADJ, ADV 懇意な/に friendly, close, intimate

kon'in N 婚姻 marriage

kon'in-todoke 婚姻届 marriage notification

kōnin-kaikeishi N 公認会計士 certified public accountant (*CPA*), chartered accountant

kōnin no ADJ 公認の authorized, certified

konkai N 今回 this time

konki N 根気 patience

konki N 婚期 marriageable age

konkurīto N コンクリート (*cement*) concrete

konkūru N コンクール prize contest, prize competition

konkyo N 根拠 basis, grounds, authority, evidence

konkyo no nai ADJ 根拠のない groundless

kon'na ADJ こんな such as, this kind of

kon'nan N 困難 trouble, difficulty

kon'na ni ADV こんなに to this extent, this much

kon'nan na ADJ 困難な difficult, hard

kon'nichi de wa ADV 今日では nowadays

kon'nichi wa INTERJ こんにちは hello, hi

kono PRON, ADJ この this

kōnō N 効能 (*effectiveness*) effect

konoaida この間 the other day

konogoro ADV この頃 recently, lately

91

konomae この前 last time, the last, previously

konomanai v 好まない to dislike

konomi N 好み liking, taste

konomi no ADJ 好みの that one likes, favorite

konomu v 好む to prefer, to like, to be fond of

konotsugi この次 next time

konpasu N コンパス (*for drafting*) compasses; compass

konpon N 根本 foundation, basis

konpyūtā N コンピューター computer

konran N 混乱 (*disorder*) mess, confusion, jumble

konro N コンロ stove

konsarutanto N コンサルタント consultant

konsento N コンセント (*electricity*) outlet, (*light*) plug

konshinkai N 懇親会 reception, get-together party

konshū N 今週 this week

kontakuto, kontakuto-renzu N コンタクト, コンタクトレンズ contact lenses

kontena N コンテナ (*for transporting goods*) container

kontesuto N コンテスト contest

kon'ya N 今夜 tonight

kon'yaku-chū no ADJ 婚約中の (*be married*) engaged

kon'yakusha N 婚約者 fiancé, fiancée

kopī N コピー photocopy

koppu N コップ cup, glass

kōra N 甲羅 (*tortoise, etc.*) shell

kōra N コーラ cola

koraeru v 堪える to stand, to bear; to control, to restrain, to repress

koramu N コラム column, boxed article(s)

kōrasu N コーラス chorus, choir

kore PRON これ this (one)

kore kara これから from now on

korera no ADJ これらの these

kōri N 氷 ice

koriandā N コリアンダー (香草) (*herbs*) cilantro, coriander

kōritsu no ADJ 公立の public, municipal, prefectural

kōritsuku v 凍りつく to freeze

korobu v 転ぶ to fall over

korogaru v 転がる to roll, to tumble

korogasu v 転がす to roll it

korosu v 殺す to kill, to murder

koru v 凝る to get engrossed/absorbed (in); (*shoulder*) to get stiff

kōru v 凍る to freeze

kōryō n 香料 spice

kōryo suru v 考慮する (*think over*) to consider

kōryū suru v 交流する to exchange, to interchange

kōsai n 交際 social relations, company, association

kōsaihi n 交際費 expense account

kosaji n 小さじ teaspoon

kosame n 小雨 (*rain*) shower, drizzle

kōsan suru v 降参する to surrender

kōsaten n 交差点 intersection

kosei n 個性 personality, individuality, character

kosei-teki na ADJ 個性的な individual, unique

kōsei n 構成 constitution, construction, composition

kōsei n 校正 proofreading

kōsei na ADJ 公正な impartial, fair

kōseibusshitsu n 抗生物質 antibiotic(s)

koseki n 戸籍 family register

kōsen n 光線 ray, (*of light*) beam, light

kōsha n 校舎 school-house

kōsha suru v 降車する (*transport*) to get off

koshi n 腰 loin(s), hips

kōshi n 講師 (大学の) (*at university*) lecturer; instructor

koshikake n 腰掛 stool, seat, chair, bench

koshikakeru v 腰掛ける to sit down

kōshiki no ADJ 公式の official, formal

kōshin n 行進 march(ing)

kōshin n 更新 renewal, update

kōshin suru v 行進する to march

kōshin suru v 更新する to renew, to update

kōshinryō n 香辛料 spices

kosho n 古書 old/secondhand book(s), antique book(s)

koshō n こしょう pepper

kōshō n 交渉 negotiations

koshō suru N 故障する (*car, machine*) to break down

kōshoku na ADJ 好色な erotic; lecherous

kōshū N 公衆 the public, the masses

kōshū(kai) N 講習(会) lecture class, (*not regular classes in school*) course

kōsōbiru N 高層ビル high-rise building, skyscraper

kōsō no ADJ 高層の highrise

kōsoku N 高速 high speed

kōsokudōro N 高速道路 expressway, freeway

kossetsu suru V 骨折する to fracture

kossori to ADV こっそりと secretly, sneakily, on the sly

kosu V 越す to move house

kosu V 超す to go over; to exceed

kosu V 漉す to strain

kosu V 濾す to filter

kōsu N コース course; (*traffic, swim*) lane; a set of chef's choices, a set meal

kōsui N 香水 perfume

kosupure N コスプレ cosplay

kosuru V 擦る to rub, to scrape, to scrub

kotae N 答え・応え answer, response

kotaeru V 答える・応える to answer, to respond: *kitai ni kotaeru* 期待に応える to meet one's expectations/ request

kōtai suru V 交替する to alternate, to shift (with)

Kōtaishi N 皇太子 the Crown Prince

kōtei N 校庭 school grounds

kōtei N 工程 process, progress: *seisaku kōtei* 製作工程 process for forming; *sagyō kōtei* 作業工程 working process

kotei suru V 固定する to fix, to fasten, to stabilize

kōtei suru V 肯定する to affirm

koten N 個展 private exhibition

koten N 古典 (*literature, art, etc.*) classic work

kōtetsu N 鋼鉄 steel

koto N こと (*intangible*) thing, matter; fact

koto N 琴 Japanese harp

kōto N コート coat, overcoat

kotoba N 言葉 word, words; (*spoken*) sentence; speech; language

kōtōgakkō, kōkō N 高等学校、高校 high school

kotonaru V 異なる to be different, to differ

kotori N 小鳥 small bird

kotoshi N 今年 this year

kotowaru V 断る to decline, to refuse

kotozuke N 言付け (*for someone*) message

kotsu N こつ knack, trick, tip

kōtsū N 交通 traffic, transportation

kōtsū hyōshiki N 交通標識 traffic signs

kōtsū jūtai N 交通渋滞 traffic jam

kōtsugō N 好都合 (*convenience*) expediency

kottōhin N 骨董品 antiques, curios

kōun N 幸運 lucky: *kōun o inoru* 幸運を祈る good luck!

kōuriten N 小売店 retail store, retailer

kowagari N こわがり a coward

kowagaru V こわがる to fear, to take flight, to be afraid

kowagatte ADJ 恐がって afraid

kowai ADJ 怖い afraid; terrific; frightful

kowaremono N こわれ物 (*article*) fragile

kowaremono-chūi こわれ物注意 Handle With Care

kowareru V 壊れる to break/smash; to be broken

kowareyasui ADJ 壊れやすい fragile, easily broken, breakable

kowasu V こわす to break/smash it, to destroy

koya N 小屋 hut, shack, cabin

koyō N 雇用 (*hiring*) employment

kōyō N 紅葉 red leaves

kōyō N 効用 (*effectiveness*) effect

kōyō no ADJ 公用の official

kōyōgo N 公用語 official language

koyomi N 暦 calendar

kōyū N 交遊 social relations, company, association

koyū no ADJ 固有の indigenous, peculiar; characteristic

kōza N 口座 (銀行) (*bank*) accountt

kōzan N 鉱山 a mine

kōzan N 高山 high mountain

kozeni N 小銭 small change

kōzō N 構造 structure, makeup, organization

kōzu N 構図 (*picture*) composition

kōzui N 洪水 flood

kozukai N 小遣い pin money, pocket money

kozutsumi N 小包 package, parcel

kubaru V 配る to distribute, to allot; (*cards*) to deal

kubetsu N 区別 difference, differentiation; discrimination

kubi N 首 neck

kubi ni naru V クビになる to be fired

kubiwa N 首輪 (*dog*) collar

kuchi N 口 mouth

kuchibiru N 唇 lips

kuchibue o fuku V 口笛を吹く to whistle

kuchigenka N 口げんか[喧嘩] argument

kuchihige N 口ひげ mustache

kuchikomi N 口コミ word of mouth

kuchi o hasamu V 口をはさむ to interrupt

kuda N 管 pipe, rube

kudaku V 砕く to break it, to smash it, to crumble it

kudamono N 果物 fruit

kudaru V 下る to come/go down, to descend; to fall/drop

kudasai V 下さい to give; please (*do*)

kufū N 工夫 device, scheme, idea, invention, artifice, ingenuity

kūfuku no ADJ 空腹の hungry

ku-gatsu N 九月 September

kugi N 釘 (*spike*) nail

kugiru V 区切る to divide

kuguru V くぐる to pass under

kūhaku N 空白 (*space*) a blank

kui N 杭 post, stake, pile

kuichigai N 食い違い discrepancy

kujaku N クジャク peacock

kujikeru V 挫ける (*a plan*) to get frustrated

kujiku V 挫く to sprain

kujira N クジラ whale

kujō N 苦情 complaint

kūkan N 空間 room, space

kuki N 茎 stalk, stem

kūki N 空気 air

kukkī N クッキー (*cookie*) biscuit

kūkō N 空港 airport

kuma N 熊 (*animal*) bear

kumi N 組 a set, suit, pack; a class, band, company

-kumi SUFFIX 組 (*counts sets or pairs*)

kumiai N 組合 association, guild, union

kumiawase N 組み合わせ assortment, mixture

kumiawaseru V 組み合わせる to assemble, to put together, to combine

kumitateru V 組み立てる to set up, to organize; to assemble

kumo N 雲 cloud

kumo N 蜘蛛 spider

kumo-no-su N 蜘蛛の巣 spiderweb, cobweb

kumori N 曇り cloudy weather

kumoru V 曇る to get cloudy

kumu V 汲む to scoop, to draw, to ladle

kumu V 組む to braid; to set up; (*arms*) to fold, (*hands*) to clasp, (*legs*) to cross; to team up (with)

kuni N 国 nation, country

kuni no ADJ 国の national

kunren N 訓練 training

kura N 倉・蔵 warehouse, storehouse, cellar, godown

kūrā N クーラー air conditioner

kuraberu V 比べる to compare, to contrast

kurage N クラゲ jellyfish

kurai ADJ 暗い (*light*) dark, gloomy; dim

kuraianto N クライアント (*computer*) client

kurakkā N クラッカー cracker

kurasu V 暮らす to live, to get by; to make a living

kurasu N クラス (*group*) class

kuratchi N クラッチ (*car*) clutch

kuraudo(konpyūtingu) N クラウド（コンピューティング） cloud computing

kurēn N クレーン (*machine*) crane

kureru V くれる (*me/us; he to you*) to give

kureru V 暮れる to get dark

kuri N 栗 chestnut

kurīmu N クリーム cream

kurīningu-ya N クリーニング屋 (*dry*) cleaner(s); laundry

kurikaesu V 繰り返す to repeat

kurippu N クリップ clip

Kurisumasu N クリスマス Christmas

kurō N 苦労 difficulties, hardships

97

kurō suru v 苦労する to have a lot of trouble

kuroi ADJ 黒い black

kurokoshō N 黒こしょう black pepper

kuromame N 黒豆 black beans

kuru v 来る to come

kurubushi N くるぶし ankle

kuruma N 車 car; taxi; vehicle, (hand) cart

kuruma ni noseru v 車に乗せる(人を) (someone) to pick up

kurushi'i ADJ 苦しい painful; hard; heavy

kurushimeru v 苦しめる to afflict, to cause pain, to distress, to embarrass

kurushimi N 苦しみ affliction, agony, suffering, distress

kurushimu v 苦しむ to suffer; to get afflicted/distressed/embarrassed

kuru'u v 狂う to get warped; to get out of order

kusa N 草 grass

kusai ADJ 臭い smelly, stinking; fishy, questionable

kusari N 鎖 chain

kusaru v 腐る to go bad, to rot, to decay, to spoil, to sour

kuse N 癖 (bad) habit, quirk

kushami N くしゃみ sneeze

kushi N 櫛 comb

kushi N 串 skewer, spit

kuso N くそ shit

kūsō N 空想 fancy, fantasy

kusuguru v くすぐる to tickle

kusuri N 薬 (medicine) drug

kusuri-ya N 薬屋 drugstore; pharmacy

kutabireru v くたびれる to get tired

kutōten N 句読点 (end of a sentence) period

kutsu N 靴 shoes

kutsubera N 靴べら shoehorn

kutsuhimo N 靴ひも shoelace

kutsurogu v くつろぐ to relax, to get comfortable

kutsushita N 靴下 socks, stockings

kutsuzure N 靴ずれ (from shoe rubbing) foot sore

kuttsuku v くっつく to stick to

kuwaeru v 加える to add (on); to impose

kuwaete ADV 加えて in addition, moreover

kuwashi'i ADJ 詳しい detailed, exact

kuyakusho N 区役所 ward office

kuyamu v 悔やむ to regret

kuyashi'i ADJ 悔しい humiliating, mortifying, vexatious

kuzu N くず waste, scum, trash

kuzukago N くずかご waste-basket

kuzureru v 崩れる to crumble, to break (down); (*weather*) to deteriorate

kuzusu v くずす to cash, to change, (*into small money*) to break; to demolish

kyabarē N キャバレー cabaret, night club

kyabetsu N キャベツ cabbage

kyaku N 客 guest, customer

kyakuma N 客間 guest room

kyakusha N 客車 (*railroad*) passenger car, coach

kyanbasu N キャンバス canvas

kyandī, kyandē N キャンディ, キャンデー candy

kyanpasu N キャンパス campus

kyanpu N キャンプ camp(ing)

kyanseru N キャンセル cancellation

kyappu N キャップ cap

kyaputen N キャプテン captain

kyō N 今日 today

kyōbai N 競売 auction

kyōchō suru v 強調する to emphasize

kyōdai N きょうだい sibling, brothers and/or sisters; brother(s); sister(s)

kyodai na ADJ 巨大な huge

kyōdōkeieisha N 共同経営者 (*in business*) partner

kyōfu N 恐怖 fear, terror

kyōgen N 狂言 traditional Noh farce

kyōgi N 協議 conference, discussion

kyōgi N 競技 (*athletic*) game, match, contest, (*game*) event

kyōgijō N 競技場 stadium

kyōhaku suru v 脅迫する to threaten

kyōhan(sha) N 共犯(者) accomplice

kyohi suru v 拒否する to refuse, to reject, to veto

kyōiku N 教育 education

kyōin N 教員 teacher

kyōju N 教授 professor

kyoka N 許可 permit, license

kyōkai N 教会 church

kyōkai N 協会 society, association

kyōkaisen N 境界線 boundary, border

kyōkasho N 教科書 text(book)

kyōki N 狂気 insanity, madness, lunacy

kyōkun N 教訓 lesson, teaching, moral

kyokutan ni ADV 極端に extremely

kyōkyū suru V 供給する to supply

kyōmibukai ADJ 興味深い interesting

kyonen N 去年 last year

kyori N 距離 distance

kyōryoku N 協力 cooperation

kyōryoku na ADJ 強力な strong, powerful

kyōshi N 教師 teacher, instructor

kyōshitsu N 教室 classroom

kyoshoku-shō N 拒食症 anorexia

kyōshuku suru V 恐縮する to feel grateful/obliged/ashamed; to feel sorry/ashamed

kyōsō N 競争 competition, rivalry, contest, race

kyōsōaite N 競争相手 rival

kyōtsū no ADJ 共通の common, general

kyōyō N 教養 culture, education, refinement

kyōyō suru V 強要する to force, to compel

kyozetsu N 拒絶 refusal

kyū NUM 九 nine

kyū ni ADV 急に suddenly

kyūji N 給仕 waiter, waitress

kyūjitsu N 休日 day off, holiday

kyūjo suru V 救助する to rescue

kyūjū NUM 九十 ninety

kyūka N 休暇 holiday

kyūkei N 休憩 rest, recess, break

kyūkō N 急行 (*train, etc.*) express

kyūkyū no ADJ 救急の for emergencies

kyūkyūbako N 救急箱 first-aid kit

kyūkyūsha N 救急車 ambulance

kyūri N キュウリ cucumber

kyūryō N 給料 salary

kyūryōbi N 給料日 payday

kyūshi N 急死 sudden death

kyūshoku N 給食 school lunch

kyūsu N 急須 teapot

kyūtei N 宮廷 (*imperial/royal*) court

kyūyo N 給与 allowance, grant, compensation

kyūyō N 急用 urgent business

kyūyō N 休養 (*time out*) rest

M

ma N 間 room; (*available*) space; time, interval

mā まあ INTERJ oh well; I should say; perhaps, I guess; (*mostly female*) dear me!; good heavens/grief!

mabushi'i ADJ まぶしい dazzling, glaring

mabuta N まぶた eyelid

macchi N マッチ match

machi N 町 town

machiawase suru, machia-waseru V 待ち合わせする, 待ち合わせる to make an appointment

machibuse N 待ち伏せ ambush

machidōshi'i ADJ 待ち遠しい long-awaited; waiting for a long time

machigaeru V 間違える to mistake

machigai N 間違い error, mistake

machigau V 間違う to be mistaken, to be in error

machi no ADJ 町の local

mada ADV まだ (not) yet, still,

even now: **mada... nai** まだ～ない not yet

... made PREP ～まで until, till; to

... made ni SUFFIX, CONJ ～までに by, no later than, (*it gets to be time*) before

... made ni wa SUFFIX, CONJ ～までには by ... at the latest

mado N 窓 window

madoguchi N 窓口 (*opening*) window, wicket

mae N ADV 前に before, in the past; front; in front of

mae no ADJ 前の previous, former

maebarai N 前払い advance, advanced payment

maemotte ADV 前もって (*beforehand*) (in) advance

maemuki no/na ADJ 前向き の/な (*forward-looking*) far-sighted; positive, constructive, affirmative

maemuki ni ADJ 前向きに facing front; positively

maeoki N 前置き introduction

maeuri N 前売り advanced sale

maeuriken N 前売り券 advanced-sale ticket

mafuyu N 真冬 the midwinter

mahiru N 真昼 midday

magaru v 曲がる to turn; to bend, to curve

mageru v 曲げる to bend it, to curve it

magirawashi'i ADJ 紛らわしい confusing

mago N 孫 grandchild; grandson

magokoro N 真心 sincerity

magomusume N 孫娘 granddaughter

magonote N 孫の手 back-scratcher

magukappu N マグカップ mug

magure (atari) N まぐれ(当たり) fluke, *(dumb/good)* luck, accident, fortuity

maguro N まぐろ tuna

mahi N 麻痺 paralysis

-mai SUFFIX 枚 *(counts flat things)*

maiasa N 毎朝 every morning

maiban N 毎晩 every night

maido N, ADV 毎度 every time

maido arigatō gozaimasu 毎度ありがとうございます。 We appreciate your *(continuing)* patronage.

maigo N 迷子 a lost child:

maigo ni naru 迷子になる to get lost, to lose one's way

maikai N 毎回 every time, each time

maikurobasu N マイクロバス minibus

mainen, maitoshi N, ADV 毎年 every year; annually

mainichi N 毎日 every day; all the time

mainichi no ADJ 毎日の daily

maishū N 毎週 every week

maishū no ADJ 毎週の weekly

maitsuki, maigetsu N 毎月 every month

majime na ADJ まじめな *(not funny)* serious, sober, conscientious, honest

majiru v 混じる to mix (with)

majiwaru v 交わる to associate with

majo N 魔女 witch

makeru v 負ける to lose, to be defeated; to be inferior

maki N 薪 firewood

maku v 巻く to roll up; to wind; to wrap

maku v 蒔く *(seed)* to sow

makura N 枕 pillow

mā mā ADV まあまあ *(just)* so-so

mama N ママ (*baby talk*) mommy, mom

… mama no ADJ …ままの intact, undisturbed

mame na ADJ まめな (*person*) diligent/dedicated

mamonaku ADV 間もなく soon, before long, shortly

mamoru V 守る to guard, to protect, to defend

man NUM 万 ten thousand (*10,000*)

manabu V 学ぶ to learn, to study

manchō N 満潮 high tide

manbiki N 万引き shoplifting, shoplifter

mane N 真似 imitation, mimicry

manekineko N 招き猫 beckoning cat

maneku V 招く to invite

maneru, mane o suru V 真似る, 真似をする to imitate, to mimic

manga N 漫画 cartoon, comics, manga

mangetsu N 満月 full moon

maniau V 間に合う to be in time (*for …*)

maniawaseru V 間に合わせる to make do (with …)

man'ichi, man ga ichi 万一, 万が一 if by any chance

man'in N 満員 (*people*) full

manjū N 饅頭 a steamed bun stuffed with sweet bean paste

manmae ni/de ADV 真ん前 に/で right in front

manmaru no/na ADJ 真ん丸 の/な perfectly round

man'naka no ADJ 真ん中の central, middle

man'nenhitsu N 万年筆 fountain pen

manpuku N 満腹 full stomach

manshon N マンション (*house*) a luxury apartment

manten N 満点 perfect score

manugareru V まぬがれる to escape from, to be exempt from, to avoid

manzoku saseru V 満足させる to satisfy

marason N マラソン jog(ging); marathon

mare ni ADV まれに rarely, occasionally

Marēshia N マレーシア Malaysia

Marēshia(-jin) no ADJ マレーシ ア(人)の Malaysian

mari N まり ball

maru de ADV まるで completely [+ NEGATIVE]: *maru de ... no yō na* まるで〜のような as if, just like

maruanki N 丸暗記 rote learning

marui ADJ 丸い (*shape*) round

maruta N 丸太 log

masaka ADV まさか surely [+ NEGATIVE]

masaka! INTERJ まさか! no kidding!; you don't say!; impossible!; No!

masani ADV まさに exactly, just; certainly, really

masaru V 勝る to surpass, to be superior

masatsu N 摩擦 friction

massāji N マッサージ massage

masshiro na ADJ 真っ白な snow white

massugu na ADJ 真っ直ぐな (*not crooked*) straight

masu V 増す to increase, to raise, to swell

masu N マス trout

masukomi N マスコミ (*media*) mass communication

masuku N マスク mask

masumasu ADV ますます more and more, increasingly

masutādo N マスタード mustard

mata ADV また again; moreover: *Mata dōzo* またどうぞ Please (*come, etc.*) again.

mata N 股 crotch

mata wa CONJ または or, or else, on the other hand; also; and

matagaru V 跨がる to straddle, to sit astride, to mount, to ride; to extend over; to span

matagu V 跨ぐ to stride over

matcha N 抹茶 (*for tea ceremony*) powdered green tea

matchi N マッチ matches

mato N 的 target, aim

matomeru V まとめる to settle, to arrange, to finish

matsu V 待つ to wait for

matsu N 松 pine tree

matsubazue N 松葉杖 crutch(es)

matsuri N 祭り festival

mattaku ADV まったく quite, completely, exactly

mattoresu N マットレス mattress

mausu N マウス (コンピュータ ー) (*for computer*) mouse

mawarikudoi ADJ 回りくどい roundabout

mawarimichi N 回り道 detour

mawaru V 回る to go around; to turn, to revolve, to circulate

mawasu V 回す to turn it around, to pass it around, to circulate it

mayaku N 麻薬 drug, narcotic

mayonaka N 真夜中 midnight

mayonēzu N マヨネーズ mayonnaise

mayotta ADJ 迷った (道に) (*can't find way*) lost

mayou V 迷う to get lost; to get perplexed

mayu N マユ cocoon

mazaru V 混ざる to mix

mazeru V 混ぜる to mix it

mazu ADV まず first of all, before anything else

mazui ADJ まずい untasty, bad-tasting; poor

mazushi'i ADJ 貧しい poor

me N 目 eye

me N 芽 (*plant's*) bud

meate N 目当て (*for the eye*) a guide; aim

mechamecha ADJ めちゃめちゃ in pieces, all confused, in disorder

medamayaki N 目玉焼き fried egg(s)

medaru N メダル medal

medatsu V 目立つ to stand out, to become conspicuous

medetai ADJ めでたい happy, auspicious

megami N 女神 goddess

megane N めがね eyeglasses, spectacles

megumareru V 恵まれる to get blessed

megumi N 恵み blessing, mercy, charity

megumu V 恵む to bless with, (*in charity*) to give mercifully

meguru V 巡る to center on, to surround, to concern

megusuri N 目薬 eye lotion, eye drops

mei N 姪 niece

-mei SUFFIX 名 (*counts people*)

meibo N 名簿 list of names, directory, register, roll

meibutsu N 名物 local specialty, famous product

meijin N 名人 expert

meirei N 命令 command, order

meiro N 迷路 labyrinth, maze

meisha N 眼医者 eye doctor, oculist

meishi N 名刺 calling card, visiting card, name card

meisho N 名所 famous place

meiwaku N 迷惑 bother, trouble, nuisance

meiwaku mēru N 迷惑メール e-mail spam, junk mail

meiwaku na ADJ 迷惑な troublesome

meiwaku o kakeru V 迷惑をかける to bother, to trouble

meiyo N 名誉 prestige, honor, glory

mēkyappu N メーキャップ makeup

memo N メモ (*written*) note, memo(randum)

memochō N メモ帳 note pad, tablet

memorī N メモリー (*computer*) memory

men N 綿 cotton

men N めん noodles

menbā N メンバー member

mendō N 面倒 trouble, bother, nuisance

menkyo N 免許 permit, licence

menkyoshō N 免許証 (運転) (*for driving*) licence

menseki N 面積 area

menyū N メニュー menu

menzeihin N 免税品 tax-free goods

meron N メロン melon

mēru N メール e-mail

meshi N 飯 cooked rice; a meal

meshiagaru V 召し上がる (*honorific*) to eat; to drink

messēji N メッセージ message

mesu N 雌 (*animal*) female

mētā N メーター (*device*) meter

mētoru N メートル (*length*) meter(s)

metsuki ga/no warui 目付きが/の悪い have evil eyes

metta ni ADV 滅多に [+ NEGATIVE VERB] seldom

metta ni nai ADJ 滅多にない rare, not too/very often

meyasu N 目安 a standard; guide

mezamashi dokei N 目覚まし時計 alarm clock

mezameru V 目覚める to wake up

mezasu V 目指す (*a destination*) to head for

mezurashi'i ADJ 珍しい (*scarce*) rare, uncommon, unusual, novel, curious

mi N 実 fruit, nut

mi N 身 body

mi ni shimiru v 身に染みる to sink in, to go straight to one's heart; to pierce (*pain, coldness*)

miai N 見合い (*broker-arranged*) meeting of prospective bride and groom

mibōjin N 未亡人 widow

mibun N 身分 social standing

mibunshōmeisho N 身分証明書 identification card

miburi N 身振り gesture, movement

michi N 道 road, street; way, path

michi no ADJ 未知の unknown

michibiku v 導く to lead, to guide

michijun N 道順 the way, (*on the road*) the route

michiru v 満ちる to get complete, full

michizure N 道連れ traveling companion, fellow traveler

midareru v 乱れる to get disturbed, to be confused

midashi N 見出し heading, caption, headline; contents

midashigo N 見出し語 dictionary entry; headword

midasu v 乱す to throw into disorder, to upset, to disturb

midori no ADJ 緑の green

mie o haru v 見栄を張る to show off, to put on airs, to try to make oneself look good

mieppari na ADJ 見栄っぱりな shanty, showy

mieru v 見える visible; can be seen; to appear; to seem

migaku v 磨く to brush, to polish, (*shoes, etc.*) to shine

migi N 右 right

migigawa N 右側 right-hand side

migimawari ni ADV 右回りに clockwise

migite N 右手 right hand

migoto na ADJ 見事な great, impressive, splendid, admirable, beautiful

migurushi'i ADJ 見苦しい ugly, unseemly, unsightly

miharu v 見張る to watch over, to guard

mihattatsu no ADJ 未発達の undeveloped

mihon N 見本 sample

mi'ira N ミイラ mummy

mijikai ADJ 短い brief, short

mikake N 見かけ appearance, looks

mikaku N 味覚 sense of taste

mikakunin hikōbuttai N 未確認飛行物体 unidentified flying object (UFO)

mikakunin no ADJ 未確認の unidentified, unconfirmed

mikan N みかん tangerine, mandarin (orange)

mikata N 味方 friend, side, accomplice, supporter

mikata N 見方 viewpoint

miki N 幹 (of tree) trunk

mikisā N ミキサー blender

mikomi N 見込み promise, hope; outlook, expectation; opinion, view

mikon no haha N 未婚の母 unmarried mother

mikoshi N みこし (for festival parades) portable shrine

mikosu N 見越す to allow, to foresee

mimai N 見舞い (solicitude) visit

miman SUFFIX 未満 less than, (a quantity, an age) below

mimi N 耳 ear

mimi ga tōi ADJ 耳が遠い hard of hearing

mimiuchi N 耳打ち whisper(ing)

mimoto N 身元 one's identity

minami N 南 south

minamiguchi N 南口 the south exit/entrance

minarai N 見習い apprentice

minarau V 見習う (learn from) to follow the example of

mina-san, mina-sama N 皆さん, 皆様 you all, everybody; ladies and gentlemen

minato N 港 harbor, port

mingeihin N 民芸品 folkcraft

minikui ADJ 醜い ugly

minkan no ADJ 民間の civil(ian), (non-government) private

min'na, mina N みんな, 皆 everybody, all; everything, all, completely

min'na de ADV みんなで altogether

minori N 実り crop, harvest

minoru V 実る to bear fruit; to ripen

minoshirokin N 身代金 ransom

minoue N 身の上 one's station in life

minoue banashi N 身の上話 one's life story

minshū N 民衆 the masses, the people

minshuku N 民宿 family inn, guest house, bed and breakfast (B&B)

minshushugi N 民主主義 democracy

min'yō N 民謡 folk song, ballad

minzoku N 民族 race

mirai N 未来 future

mirin N ミリン (*for cooking*) sweet rice wine

miru V 観る (*movie*) to watch

miru V 見る to watch, to look, to see

miruku N ミルク milk

miryoku-teki na ADJ 魅力的な charming, appealing, attractive

misairu N ミサイル missile

misaki N 岬 cape, promontory, headland

mise N 店 shop, store

misekake no ADJ 見せかけの sham, make-believe

misemono N 見せ物 show, exhibition, exhibit

miseru V 見せる to show

miso N 味噌 (*fermented*) bean paste

missetsu na ADJ 密接な thick, dense; close, intimate

misu N ミス miss, mistake

mitai V 見たい to want to see

... mitai V ～みたい (*like*) to seem/look

mitame N 見た目 physical appearance

mitasu V 満たす to fill

mitei N 未定 to be determined

mītingu N ミーティング meeting, conference

mitomeru V 認める to recognize, to acknowledge, to admit

mitorizu N 見取り図 blueprint, sketch

mitōshi N 見通し prospect, outlook

mitsubachi N ミツバチ (honey-)bee

mitsugo N 三つ子 triplets

mitsukaru V 見つかる to be found; to turn up

mitsukeru V 見つける to find, to discover

mitsumeru V 見つめる to gaze at, to stare at

mitsumoru V 見積もる to estimate

mitsurin N 密林 jungle

miuchi N 身内 family, close relatives and close friends

miwakeru v 見分ける to discriminate, to distinguish

miwaku-teki na ADJ 魅惑的な enchanting

miyagemono N みやげ物 souvenir

miyako N 都 capital city

mizo N 溝 drain, ditch, gutter

mizō no ADJ 未曾有の unprecedented, unheard-of, unparalleled

mizore N みぞれ sleet

mizu N 水 (*cold*) water

mizubusoku N 水不足 water shortage

mizugi N 水着 swimming costume, swimsuit

mizuiro N 水色 (*color*) light blue, aqua

mizusashi N 水差し jug, pitcher

mizushibuki N 水しぶき splash

mizutama(moyō) no ADJ 水玉 (模様)の (*pattern*) spotted

mizu'umi N 湖 lake

mizuwari N 水割り (*highball*) whisky and water

mō ADV もう already; now; ADJ more; (not) … any more

mō hitotsu PRON もう一つ another, the other one

mō ichido/ikkai ADV もう一度/ 一回 one more time, again

mō sugu ADV もうすぐ right away

mō sukoshi もう少し (*a bit*) more

... mo mata ADV ～もまた as well, too, also

mochi N 餅 rice cake

mochiageru v 持ち上げる (物 を) (*something*) to pick up, to lift

mochidasu v 持ち出す (話題を) (*topic*) to bring up

mochi'iru v 用いる uses

mochimono N 持ち物 belongings

mochinushi N 持ち主 owner

mochiron ADV もちろん certainly, of course, surely

mōchō N 盲腸 appendix

modemu N モデム modem

moderu N モデル model

mōdōken N 盲導犬 seeing-eye dog

modoru v 戻る to return, to go back, to revert

modosu v 戻す to send back, to return

moeru v 燃える (*fire*) to burn

mōfu N 毛布 blanket

mogishiken N 模擬試験 trial test, mock examination

moguru V 潜る to dive (under); to go under(ground)

mohan N 模範 model, pattern, example: *mohan o shimesu* 模範を示す to gives an example

mōhitotsu no ADJ もうひとつの another, one more

moji N 文字 (*written*) character, letter, writing

mojidōri ADV 文字どおり literally

mōkaru V 儲かる to be profitable, to make money

mokei N 模型 model, mold

mōkeru V 儲ける to make money, profits

mōkeru V 設ける to prepare, to set up

mokugeki suru V 目撃する to witness

mokuhyō N 目標 goal, target

mokuji N 目次 (*table of*) contents

mokuroku N 目録 catalog, list

mokusei no ADJ 木製の wooden

mokutan N 木炭 charcoal

mokuteki N 目的 purpose, aim, objective; end, goal

mokutekichi N 目的地 destination

mokutekigo N 目的語 (*grammar*) object

moku-yōbi N 木曜日 Thursday

mokuzen no ADJ 目前の immediate

momegoto N 揉め事 discord, tiff, trouble

momen N 木綿 cotton

momeru V 揉める to be in discord/trouble

mominoki N モミの木 fir tree

... mo ... mo ... nai ~も~も~ない neither... nor

momo N 桃 peach

momo N もも thigh

momoiro no ADJ 桃色の pink, rosy

mōmoku N 盲目 blindness

mōmoku no N 盲目の blind

mon N 門 gate

mondai N 問題 matter, problem; question; topic, subject, issue

mondainai ADJ 問題ない no problem

mongen N 門限 curfew

monitā N モニター (コンピューター) (*computer*) monitor

monku N 文句 phrase; complaint: *monku o iu* 文句を言う to make a fuss

mono N 物 thing, object, article, something, stuff

-mono N -者 person, fellow

mono sugoi ADJ もの凄い terrible, awesome

mono sugoku ADV もの凄く terribly, extremely

monogatari N 物語 tale, legend

monomane N ものまね mimic(ry), impersonation

mono'oboe ga ii/warui ADJ 物覚えがいい/悪い quick /slow to learn

monosashi N 物差し ruler; measure

monozuki na ADJ 物好きな curious, inquisitive

moppara ADV もっぱら principally, chiefly

moppu N モップ mop

morasu V 漏らす to let leak; to reveal

morau V もらう to receive, to get

moreru V 漏れる to leak out; to be omitted; to leak

mori N 森 forest, woods

moroi ADJ もろい brittle, frail

moru V 漏る to leak

moru V 盛る to pile it up; to serve on a plate; (*poison*) to put

moshi ADV もし if

moshi ka shita ra/suru to ADV もしかしたら/すると perhaps

mōshikomu V 申し込む to apply; to propose; to offer

moshimoshi もしもし (*on phone*) hello

mōshiwake arimasen/ gozaimasen 申し訳ありません/ございません I am very sorry.

mōtā N モーター motor, engine

mōtābōto N モーターボート motorboat

motareru V もたれる (*against*) to lean

motenashi N もてなし hospitality

moto N 元・本 origin, source; (*of an effect*) cause

moto kara 元から from the beginning, always, all along

moto no ADJ 元の former, earlier, original

motomeru V 求める to seek, to demand; to look for; to buy, to get

motomoto N 元々 from the start, originally; by nature, naturally

motsu V 持つ to have, to hold, to carry

motsureru V もつれる to get entangled/complicated

mottainai ADJ もったいない wasteful; undeserving

motteiku V 持って行く to take, to carry; to bring (*you, there*)

mottekuru V 持ってくる to bring

motto ADV もっと more, still more; longer, further

motto ii ADJ もっといい better

motto warui/hidoi ADJ もっと 悪い/ひどい worse

mottomo ADV, CONJ もっとも indeed, of course; but, however, to be sure

mottomo ADV 最も (*superlative*) most; exceedingly

mottomo warui/hidoi ADJ 最も悪い/ひどい worst

moya N もや mist, haze

moyō N 模様 pattern, design

moyōshi N 催し (*live performance*) show

moyōsu V 催す to hold, (*an event*) to give; to feel

mozō N 模造 imitation, fake

mubō na ADJ 無謀な reckless

mucha na ADJ 無茶な reckless; unreasonable; disorderly

muchi no ADJ 無知の ignorant

muchū N 夢中 trance, ecstasy: *... ni muchū ni naru* ...に夢中になる (*engrossed in*) to get entranced with ...

muda N 無駄 waste

muda na ADJ 無駄な futile, no good, wasteful; useless

mudabanashi N 無駄話 idle talk, hot air, bull

mudazukai N 無駄使い waste, extravagance

mueki na ADJ 無益な useless

mugi N 麦 wheat, barley

mugoi ADJ むごい cruel, brutal

mugon no ADJ 無言の silent

muimi na ADJ 無意味な nonsense

muishiki no/na ADJ 無意識の/な unconscious, involuntary

mujaki na ADJ 無邪気な naive, innocent, unsophisticated

mujōken ni/de ADV 無条件に/で unconditionally

113

mujun N 矛盾 inconsistency, contradiction

mukaeru V 迎える to meet; to welcome; to invite

mukankei no/na ADJ 無関係の/な unrelated

mukanshin na ADJ 無関心な indifferent to, unconcerned with

mukashi N 昔 old times, past, long ago; ancient days

mukatsuku V, ADJ むかつく to be queasy, to feel nauseated; disgusting

mukau V 向かう to oppose; to head for

mukigen no/ni ADJ, ADV 無期限の/に indefinite(ly)

muko N 婿 son-in-law; bridegroom

mukō PREP, ADV 向こう beyond; across the way, over there

mukō no ADV 向こうの opposite, facing

mukōgawa N 向こう側 the other side/party, the opposite side

muku V 剥く to peel

muku V 向く to face

mumei no ADJ 無名の nameless, anonymous; obscure

mune N 胸 chest (*breast*)

mura N 村 village

muragaru V 群がる to flock/huddle together, to swarm

murasaki no ADJ 紫の purple

mure N 群れ group, throng, flock

muri mo nai 無理もない no wonder

muri na ADJ 無理な forced, unreasonable; violent; overdoing; (*over-*)demanding

muri o saseru V 無理をさせる to overtax someone's strength

muryō de ADV 無料で free of charge, free

museigen ni ADV 無制限に free of restraints

musekinin na ADJ 無責任な irresponsible

musen N 無線 radio; wireless

mushi N 虫 insect; moth; worm

mushi atsui ADJ 蒸し暑い muggy, close, sultry, humid

mushi suru V 無視する to ignore

mushimegane N 虫眼鏡 magnifying glass

mushiro ADV むしろ rather; preferably

mushoku no ADJ 無職の jobless

mushoku no ADJ 無色の achroma, colorless(ness)

mushoku tōmei no ADJ 無色透明の colorless and transparent

musu V 蒸す to steam; to be sultry, to be humid

musū no ADJ 無数の countless, innumerable

musubu V 結ぶ to tie, ties up

musuko N 息子 son: *musuko-san* 息子さん (*your/someone else's*) son

musume N 娘 daughter: *musume-san* 娘さん (*your/someone else's*) daughter, lady

mutonchaku na ADJ 無頓着 careless

muyō no ADJ 無用の unnecessary, useless; having no business

muzai no ADJ 無罪の innocent, not guilty

muzōsa na ADJ 無造作な easy, effortless

muzukashi'i ADJ 難しい difficult, hard

muzumuzu suru ADJ むずむずする itchy, crawly, creepy

myaku, myakuhaku N 脈、脈拍 pulse

myōji N 苗字 surname, family name

myōnichi N, ADV 明日 tomorrow

myūjikaru N ミュージカル musical

N

na N 名 given name

na N 菜 greens, vegetables; rape

nabe N 鍋 pan, pot

nabemono N 鍋物 food cooked and served in a pan

nadakai ADJ 名高い famous

nadameru V なだめる to sooth, to pacify

nadare N なだれ avalanche; snowslide

naderu V 撫でる to stroke, to smooth; to pat, to pet

nado SUFFIX など and so forth/on, and what-not, and the like

nae N 苗 seedling

naeru V 萎える to droop, to wither

nagai ADJ 長い (距離、時間) (*length, time*) long

nagaiki N 長生き longevity, long life

nagaisu N 長いす couch, sofa

nagame N 眺め view, scenery

nagameru V 眺める to gaze/stare at, to view

nagare N 流れ a stream, a flow

nagareboshi N 流れ星 shooting star

nagareru V 流れる to flow

nagasa N 長さ length

nagasu V 流す to let it flow, to wash away

nageki N 嘆き grief, lamentation

nageku V 嘆く to grieve, to weep, to moan, to lament

nageru V 投げる to throw

naguru V 殴る to knock, to beat, to strike

nagusameru V 慰める to comfort, to console

naibu N 内部 inside

naibu no ADJ 内部の internal, inside

naifu N ナイフ knife

naifukuyaku N 内服薬 oral medicine

naika N 内科 internal medicine

naikaku N 内閣 government cabinet

naikaku sōridaijin N 内閣総理大臣 prime minister

naimen N 内面 inner face, interior surface

naimitsu no ADJ 内密の confidential, secret, private

nairan N 内乱 civil strife

nairiku N 内陸 inland

nairon N ナイロン nylon

naisen N 内線 (*phone line, inside*) extension

naisen N 内戦 civil war, internal fighting

naisho no ADJ 内緒の confidential, secret, private: *naishobanashi* 内緒話 a private talk

naishukketsu N 内出血 internal bleeding

naitei N 内定 unofficial decision, informal appointment

naiyō N 内容 contents

naizō N 内臓 internal organs

naka (ni/de) N (ADV) 中 (に/で) inside

naka ga ii 仲がいい be on good terms (*with* ...)

nakama N 仲間 friend, pal, companion

nakami N 中身・中味 contents

nakayubi N 中指 middle finger

nakigoe N 泣き声 (*person*) cry, sob

nakigoe N (*animals, birds, insects, etc*) 鳴き声 chirp, song, chirping

nakimushi N 泣き虫 crybaby

nakōdo N 仲人 (*matchmaker*) go-between

naku V 泣く to cry, to weep

naku V 鳴く to make an animal sound

nakunaru V 亡くなる to die

nakunaru V なくなる (*from existence*) to vanish; to get lost

nama no ADJ 生の raw, rare, uncooked

namachūkei N 生中継 live coverage

namae N 名前 name

namagomi N 生ごみ (*kitchen waste*) garbage

namahōsō N 生放送 live program, live broadcast

namaiki na ADJ 生意気な impertinent

namari N 訛り dialect, accent

namari N 鉛 (*metal*) lead

namayake no ADJ 生焼けの (*half-cooked*) rare, underdone

nameraka na ADJ なめらかな smooth, glassy

nameru V 舐める to lick, to taste

nami N 波 (*in sea*) wave

nami no ADJ 並の ordinary, common, average, regular

namida N 涙 tears

namida-moroi ADJ 涙もろい easily moved to tears

naminori N 波乗り surfing

nan, nani N 何 what

nan no ADJ 何の what (*kind of*); of what

nan no tame ni 何のために what for

nan to ka shite ADV 何とかして by some means (*or other*), somehow or other

nana NUM 七 seven

nanajū NUM 七十 seventy

nanbāpurēto N ナンバープレート (*car*) license plate

Nanbei N 南米 South America

nanboku N 南北 north and south

nanbu N 南部 the south, the southern part

nani PRON 何 what

nani ga okita 何が起きた what happened

117

nani ka PRON 何か anything, something

nani mo... nai PRON 何も～ない nothing

nani mo, nan ni mo ADV 何も、何にも [+ NEGATIVE] nothing, (*not*) anything

nanjaku na ADJ 軟弱な weak, soft, flaccid [IN NEGATIVE SENSE]

nanji 何時 what time

nankan N 難関 difficulty, obstacle, challenge

nankyoku N 南極 South Pole

nankyoku N 難局 difficult situation

nanmin N 難民 refugee

nansei N 南西 south-west

nantō N 南東 south-east

nanzan N 難産 difficult delivery

naoru V 直る to be righted, fixed, repaired

naoru V 治る cured, to get well, to recover; to improve

naosara ADV なおさら all the more, still more

naosu V 直す to mend, to make it right, to fix

naosu V 治す to cure, to alter; to improve it

naraberu V 並べる to arrange, to line them up

narabu V 並ぶ to line up

narasu V 鳴らす (ベルを) (*bell*) to ring; to sound

narau V 習う to learn

narenareshi'i ADJ 馴れ馴れしい too friendly, overly familiar

nareru V 慣れる to get used to, to grow familiar with

narēshon N ナレーション narration

nareteiru V 慣れている to be used to, to be accustomed to

nariyuki V 成り行き process, course, development; result

naru V なる to become, to get to be, turns into; to be done

naru V 鳴る to sound, to ring

narubeku ADV なるべく ... as ... as possible, preferably

naruhodo INTERJ なるほど I see; quite so; you are so right; how true

nasakenai ADJ 情けない wretched, shameful

nashi N ナシ pear

... nashi ni ADV ～なしに without

nasu N ナス aubergine, eggplant

natsu N 夏 summer

natsukashi'i ADJ 懐かしい (*dearly remembered*) dear

natsuyasumi N 夏休み summer vacation/holiday

nattō N 納豆 fermented soy beans

nattoku N 納得 understanding, compliance, assent

nawa N 縄 rope, cord

nawabari N 縄張り one's territory

nayami N 悩み suffering, distress, torment

nayamu V 悩む to suffer

naze ADV なぜ why

nazenara CONJ なぜなら because

nazo N 謎 riddle, mystery

nazonazo N なぞなぞ (*game*) riddle

nazukeoya N 名付け親 godparent

nazukeru V 名付ける to name, to dub

ne N 音 sound

ne N 根 (植物) (*plant*) root

ne N 値 price

neage N 値上げ price rise; raising the cost

nebarizuyoi ADJ 粘り強い persevering

nebaru V 粘る to hang on

nebiki N 値引き (*price*) discount

nebumi o suru V 値踏みをする to value

nebusoku N 寝不足 having not enough sleep

nedan N 値段 price

negau V 願う to ask for, to request, to beg

nejimawashi N ねじ回し screw-driver

nejiru V ねじる to twist

neisu N 寝椅子 (*chair*) couch, lounge

nekkyō suru V 熱狂する to get excited

neko N 猫 cat: *neko ni koban* 猫に小判 [SAYING] Casting pearls before swine.

nekoze N 猫背 (*like that of cat*) slouch, slight stoop, rounded back

nekutai N ネクタイ tie, necktie: *nekutai o musubu* V ネクタイを結ぶ to put on/wear a necktie

nemaki N 寝巻き nightclothes, nightdress, pajamas

nemui N 眠い sleepy

nemuru V 眠る to sleep

nen N 年 year

-nen SUFFIX 年 (*counts years*)

nen no tame v 念のため to make sure, just in case, just to be sure, as a precaution

nen o osu v 念を押す to double-check

nendo N 粘土 clay

nendo N 年度 year period, fiscal year

nenga N 年賀 New Year's greetings

nengajō N 年賀状 New Year's card

nenkan N 年鑑 yearbook, almanac

nenkan no ADJ 年間の for a year; annual

nenkin N 年金 pension

nenmatsu N 年末 the end of the year

nenrei N 年齢 (*one's*) age

nenryō N 燃料 fuel

nenshō N 年商 annual turnover

nenza N 捻挫 sprain

nerau v ねらう to aim at, to watch for, to seek

neru v 寝る to go to bed, to sleep

neru v 練る to knead; to plan

nē-san N 姉さん older sister

nesoberu v 寝そべる to lie down

nesshin na ADJ 熱心な enthusiastic

nessuru v 熱する to get hot, to get excited; to warm it

netamu v 妬む to envy, to grudge

netsu N 熱 fever; heat

nettai no ADJ 熱帯の tropical

nettō N 熱湯 boiling water

netto banku ネットバンク Internet bank

netto gēmu N ネットゲーム online game

netto kafe ネットカフェ Internet café

netto ōkushon N ネットオークション Internet auction

netto shoppu ネットショップ Internet shopping site

netto tsūhan ネット通販 online shopping, Internet shopping

nettowāku N ネットワーク network

nettowāku-adoresu ネットワークアドレス (*computer*) network address

neuchi N 値打ち value, worth: *neuchi ga aru* 値打ちがある worth

nezumi N ねずみ mouse, rat

nezumi iro N ねずみ色 (*color*) gray

ni NUM 二 two

... ni VERBAL AUXILIARY 〜に on, at, in

... ni fureru V 〜に触れる to touch

... ni hairu V 〜に入る to come in, to enter

... ni hanshite ADV 〜に反して contrary to

... ni haru V 〜に貼る to stick to

... ni ichi suru V 〜に位置する to be located

... ni ittakoto ga aru 〜に行ったことがある have been somewhere

... ni kakeru V 〜に掛ける to hang

... ni kanshite PREP 〜に関して concerning, regarding

... ni kuwaete 〜に加えて in addition to

... ni kyōmi ga aru 〜に興味がある interested in

... ni mo kakawarazu 〜にもかかわらず in spite of

... ni naru V 〜になる to become

... ni shiraseru V 〜に知らせる to let someone know

... ni tsuite PREP 〜について (*regarding*) about

... ni tsuite hanasu 〜について話す to talk about

... ni tsuite wasureru V 〜について忘れる to forget about

... ni tsuzuku V 〜に続く to follow along

... ni yoruto 〜によると according to

... ni yotte PREP 〜によって (作者、芸術家) (*author, artist*) by

niau V 似合う becoming; to suit, to fit

nibai no ADJ 二倍の double

nibanme no ADJ 二番目の second

nibui ADJ 鈍い dull, blunt

nichibotsu N 日没 (*time of*) sunset

nichi-yōbi N 日曜日 Sunday

nigai ADJ 苦い bitter

ni-gatsu N 二月 February

nigeru V 逃げる to run away, to escape

nigirizushi N にぎり寿司 hand formed sushi with a topping of tuna, salmon, etc.

nigiru v 握る to grasp, to grip, to clutch

nigiyaka na ADJ にぎやかな busy, (*crowded*) lively, cheerful, bustling, flourishing

nigoru v にごる to get muddy

Nihon N 日本 Japan

Nihongo N 日本語 (*language*) Japanese

Nihon(-jin) no ADJ 日本 (人) の Japanese

ni'i-san N 兄さん older brother

niji N 虹 rainbow

nijū NUM 二十 twenty

nijū no ADJ 二重の double, duplicate

nikai N 二階 second floor; upstairs

nikei no ADJ 日系の (*of*) Japanese ancestry

nikki N 日記 diary, journal

nikkō N 日光 sunshine

Nikkō 日光 Nikko (*place in Tochigi Prefecture*)

nikkyū N 日給 daily wage

nikomi N 煮込み stew

nikoniko suru v にこにこする to smile

niku N 肉 meat

nikudango N 肉団子 meatball

nikui, nikurashi'i ADJ 憎い, 憎ら

しい disliked, hated

nikumu v 憎む to hate, to detest

nikutai N 肉体 flesh, the body

niku-ya N 肉屋 (*shop*) butcher

nimotsu N 荷物 baggage, load

-nin SUFFIX 人 (*counts people*)

ninau v 担う to carry on shoulders

ningen N 人間 human being

ningyo N 人魚 mermaid

ningyō N 人形 doll

ninja N 忍者 Ninja

ninjin N 人参 carrot

ninjō N 人情 human nature, human feelings, warm-heartedness

ninki N 人気 popularity

ninki no aru ADJ 人気のある popular

ninmei suru v 任命する to appoint

ninmu N 任務 duty, assignment, task, mission

nin'niku N にんにく garlic

Nippon, Nihon N 日本 Japan

nise no ADJ にせの false, phony, fake, imitation

ninshin suru v 妊娠する to get pregnant

nintai N 忍耐 endurance

nioi N 臭い・匂い smell

niou V 臭う・匂う to smell, to be fragrant

niramu V 睨む to glare, to stare

niru V 煮る to boil, to cook

nise no ADJ にせの false, phony, fake, imitation

nisemono N 偽物 a fake, an imitation, a forgery

nisesatsu N にせ札 (*currency*) counterfeit bill

nishi N 西 west

nisshi N 日誌 (*business, nursing, etc.*) diary, journal

nitchū N 日中 daytime

nittei N 日程 schedule, program, itinerary

niwa N 庭 garden, yard

niwatori N ニワトリ chicken, rooster

nizukuri N 荷造り packing

... no PREP ～の of, from

... no aida PRE ～の間 (時間、年) (*time, years*) in, during

... no aida ni CONJ ～の間 に among, while, during, between

... no ato de PREP ～のあとで after

... no hō e PREP ～の方へ toward

... no hōhō ～の方法 the way of

... no hōhō de ～の方法で by means of

... no jōtai ni aru ～の状態に ある to be in a ... situation/ condition

... no kachi ga aru ～の価値が ある to be worth

... no kawari ni ～の代わりに instead of

... no kekkatoshite ～の結果と して as a result of

... no mae ni PREP ～の前に before; in front of

... no mukai ni PREP ～の向かい に across from

... no naka ni PREP ～の中に inside of, into

... no saichū ～の最中 in the middle of

... no shita ni PREP ～の下に under, underneath

... no soba ni PREP ～のそば に near

... no soto ni PREP ～の外に outside of

... no ue ni PREP ～の上に on, above

... no ushiro ni PREP ～の後ろ に behind

123

... no yō na PREP 〜のような like, as, such

... no yō ni mieru V 〜のように見える to look like

... no yō ni omowareru V 〜のように思われる to look, to seem, to appear

nō N 脳 brain

nobasu V 伸ばす・延ばす (*lengthens, stretches*) to extend

noberu V 述べる to express, to state, to mention

nobiru V 伸びる to extend, to reach; to spread

noboru V 登る to go up, to climb

noboru V 昇る to rise

nochihodo ADV のち程 later

nodo N のど throat

nodo ga kawaita ADJ のどが渇いた thirsty

nodoka na ADJ のどかな tranquil, peaceful, quiet, calm

nōgyō N 農業 agriculture, farming

nohara N 野原 field

nōjō N 農場 farm

nōkō na ADJ 濃厚な thick, rich; dense, passionate

nokori N 残り left, remaining, rest, remainder

nokorimono N 残り物 remainder, leftover

nokoru V 残る to stay, to remain

nokosu V 残す to leave, to leave behind/over

nomi N のみ chisel

...nomi SUFFIX, ADJ ...のみ only

nomikomu V 飲み込む to swallow

nomimizu N 飲み水 drinking water

nomimono N 飲み物 drink, beverage, refreshments

nōmin N 農民 the farmers

nomi-ya N 飲み屋 tavern, drinking place

nomu V 飲む to drink, (*medicine*) to take

nonbiri suru V のんびりする to relax

nonki na ADJ のん気な easy-going, happy-go-lucky

nonoshiru V ののしる to revile, to abuse, to curse

noren N のれん shop curtain; goodwill

nori N 海苔 seaweed

nori N のり glue, paste; starch

norikaeru v 乗り換える to change, (*of vehicle*) to transfer

norimaki N のり巻き sushi rice in a seaweed roll

norimono N 乗り物 vehicle

noriokureru v 乗り遅れる (バス、飛行機) (*bus, flight*) to miss

noroi N 呪い a curse

noroi N のろい slow, dull, sluggish

noronoro to ADV のろのろと slowly, sluggishly

noru v 乗る (乗り物) to get aboard, to ride; (*vehicle*) to be carried

noruma N ノルマ norm, quota

nōryoku N 能力 ability

noseru v 乗せる (車に) (*car*) to give a lift

noseru v 載せる (*in book, magazine, etc.*) to publish, (*an article, etc.*) to post

nōto N ノート notebook

nōtopasokon N ノートパソコン notebook computer

nottoru v 乗っ取る to hijack; (*illegally*) to take over, to seize

nōzei N 納税 payment of taxes

nozoite CONJ 除いて except

nozoku v 覗く to peek, to peep

nozoku v 除く to eliminate, to remove; to omit

nozomi N 望み desire, hope, expectation

nozomu v 望む to desire, to look to, to hope for

nozomu v 臨む to look out on

nūdo N ヌード a nude

nugu v 脱ぐ (服、靴) (*clothes, shoes*) to take off

nugu'u v 拭う to wipe it away

nuime N 縫い目 seam

nukeru v 抜ける to come off; to escape; to be omitted

…nuki de/no SUFFIX, ADJ, ADV … 抜きで/の (*omitting*) without

nuku v 抜く to uncork; to remove; to surpass; to select

numa N 沼 pond

nurasu v 濡らす to wet, to dampen

nureru v 濡れる to get wet

nurigusuri N 塗り薬 ointment

nuru v 塗る to paint; to spread

nurui ADJ ぬるい lukewarm, tepid

nushi N 主 master, owner

nusumi N 盗み theft

nusumu v 盗む to steal, to swipe, to rob, to rip off

nu'u v 縫う to sew

nyō N 尿 urine, urinating

nyōbō, nyōbo N 女房 my wife

nyūeki N 乳液 latex; milky lotion, (*cosmetic*) milky liquid

nyūgakushiken N 入学試験 entrance exam

nyūgakushiki 入学式 school entrance ceremony

nyūgaku suru v 入学する (*in school*) to enroll

nyūgan N 乳がん breast cancer

nyūin suru v 入院する to enter a hospital

nyūji N 乳児 infant

Nyūjīlando N ニュージーランド New Zealand

Nyūjīlando(-jin) no ニ ュージーランド(人)の New Zealander

nyūjō suru v 入場する to be admitted, to enter

nyūjōken N 入場券 admission ticket

nyūjōryō N 入場料 admission fee

nyūka suru v 入荷する (*goods*) to receive

nyūkai suru v 入会する to

become a member

nyūkoku kanrikyoku N 入国管理局 Immigration Bureau of Japan

nyūseki suru v 入籍する to register one's marriage

nyūsen suru v 入選する to win a prize

nyūsha suru v 入社する to enter/join a company

nyūsu N ニュース news

nyūsu bangumi N ニュース番組 news program

nyūyoku N 入浴 bath, taking a bath

Nyūyōku N ニューヨーク New York

O

o N 尾 tail

ō-ame N 大雨 heavy rain

oba N おば aunt

ōbā N オーバー overcoat

obake N お化け ghost

oba-san N おばさん aunt; (*middle-aged*) woman

obā-san N おばあさん grandmother; old lady/woman

Ōbei N 欧米 Europe and America

o-bentō N お弁当 box lunch

obi N 帯 girdle, sash, belt, (*Japanese*) obi

obieta ADJ おびえた scared

oboegaki N 覚え書き memo (-randum), note

oboeru V 覚える to remember, to keep in mind; to learn

obon N お盆 tray

oboreru V おぼれる to drown

obō-san N お坊さん Buddhist monk

ōbun N オーブン oven

o-cha N お茶 tea; the tea ceremony

ochiru V 落ちる to fall

ō-daiko N 大太鼓 large drum

odayaka na ADJ 穏やかな calm, (*not severe*) mild

odeko N おでこ forehead

odori N 踊り dance

ō-dōri N 大通り main street, avenue

odorokasu V 驚かす to surprise, to scare, to astonish

odorokubeki ADJ 驚くべき surprising

odoru V 踊る to dance

ōesu N オーエス(OS) operating system, OS (*computer*)

ofisu N オフィス office

ofukai N オフ会 meet-up, off-line meeting

ōfuku N 往復 round trip

ōfukukippu N 往復キップ return ticket

o-furo N お風呂 bath

ogakuzu N おがくず sawdust

ogamu V 拝む to worship, to look at with respect

ogawa N 小川 brook, stream

oginau V 補う to complete; to complement, to make good, to make up for

ōgon N 黄金 gold

ogoru V おごる to be extravagant; to treat

o-hashi N お箸 chopsticks

O-hayō (gozaimasu) INTERJ おはよう(ございます) Good morning!

ō-hi N 王妃 queen

ohina-sama N おひな様 (*Dolls Festival*) dolls

o-hiya N お冷や cold water

oi N 甥 nephew

oi INTERJ おい hey! (*mostly male, very informal*)

ōi ADJ 多い many, numerous; lots

oiharau V 追い払う to chase away, to chase out

oikakeru V 追いかける to chase

oikosu v 追い越す to pass

oiru v 老いる to grow old

oisha-san N お医者さん doctor

oishi'i ADJ おいしい delicious, tasty, nice, yummy

oishisō ADJ おいしそう looks tasty/nice/delicious/ yummy

ō-isogi no/de ADJ, ADV 大急ぎの/で (in) a great rush, a big hurry

oiteiku v 置いていく to leave behind on purpose; drop off

oitsuku v 追い付く to catch up (with), to overtake

o-iwai N お祝い celebration

ōja N 王者 king; champion; ruler

O-jama shimashita お邪魔しました。(*when you leave someone's home*) Excuse me for having interrupted/ bothered you

oji N おじ uncle

ō-ji N 王子 prince

o-jigi N お辞儀 bow

oji'i-san N おじいさん grandfather; old (gentle)man

ōjiru v 応じる to respond (to), to accede (to), to comply (with)

oji-san N おじさん uncle; gentleman, (*middle-aged*) man

ō-jo N 王女 princess

ojō-san N お嬢さん a young lady; (*your/someone else's*) daughter; Miss

oka N 丘 hill

O-kaerinasai! INTERJ お帰りなさい！Welcome back!

okage-sama de おかげさまで thanks to your solicitude; thank you (*I'm very well or it's going very nicely*)

O-kamainaku INTERJ お構いなく Don't go to any trouble.

ōkami N オオカミ wolf

ō-kan N 王冠 crown; bottle cap

o-kane N お金 money

okā-san N おかあさん mother

o-kashi N お菓子 cakes, sweets, candy

okashi'i ADJ おかしい funny; queer

okasu v 犯す to commit, to perpetrate; to violate

okasu v 侵す to encroach upon, to invade

ōkata ADV おおかた for the most part; probably

o-kayu N おかゆ (*rice*) gruel

okazu N おかず main/side dish

o-keiko N お稽古 (*artistic*) practice

okidokei N 置き時計 clock

ōki'i ADJ 大きい big, large; loud

ōkikunaru V 大きくなる to grow larger

okimono N 置き物 ornament; bric-a-brac

okini'iri N お気に入り favorite; (*web browser*) bookmarks

okiru V 起きる to get up

ōkisa N 大きさ size

okite N 掟 law, rule, regulation

okiwasureru V 置き忘れる to leave behind by accident, to lose, to misplace

o-kō N お香 incense

ō-koku N 王国 kingdom

o-kome N お米 rice

okonai N 行い act(ion), deed, conduct

okonau V 行う to act, to do, to carry out, to perform

okoru V 起こる to happen, to occur

okoru V 怒る to get angry

oko-san N お子さん (*your/ someone else's*) child

okosu V 起こす to wake someone up

okotaru V 怠る to neglect, to

shirk; to be lazy about

oku V 置く to place, to put, to set

oku NUM 億 hundred million

oku N 奥 the back or inside part

okubyō na ADJ 臆病な cowardly, timid

okubyōmono N 臆病者 a coward

okugai N 屋外 outdoor

okujō N 屋上 roof (top), rooftop floor

okuman chōja N 億万長者 a billionaire

okunai N 屋内 inside, interior

okure N 遅れ delay

okureru V 遅れる to be late, to get delayed; to lag, to fall behind; to run late

okurimono N 贈り物 (*gift*) present

okuru V 送る to send

okuru V 贈る to present, to award

oku-san N 奥さん wife, your wife

okuyami N お悔やみ condolences

okyaku-san/-sama N お客さん/様 visitor; customer, patron

o-kyō N お経 (*Buddhist scripture*) sutra

ōkyūshochi N 応急処置 first aid

omae PRON お前 you (*mostly male; familiar or rude*)

omake N おまけ extra, bonus, premium

omamori N お守り amulet, charm

o-matsuri N お祭り festival

omawari-san N おまわりさん policeman, (*police*) officer

omedetō (gozaimasu) INTERJ おめでとう(ございます) congratulations!

o-mikoshi N おみこし portable shrine

o-mikuji N おみくじ (*written*) fortune

ō-misoka N 大晦日 last day of a year; New Year's eve

o-miyage N おみやげ gift, souvenir

omo na ADJ 主な principal, main

omocha N おもちゃ toy

omoi ADJ 重い heavy; grave, serious; important

omoi N 思い thought, idea; feeling, mind; desire, will

omoidasaseru V 思い出させる to remind

omoidasu V 思い出す to recall, to remember

omoigakenai V 思いがけない unexpected, surprising

omoiyari N 思いやり (*being kind*) consideration, solicitude

ō-moji N 大文字 capital letter

omoni N 重荷 (*on one's mind*) burden

ō-mono N 大物 a big shot

omosa N 重さ weight

omoshiroi ADJ おもしろい humorous, interesting, pleasant, amusing, fun

omote N 表 front, surface, outer side/surface

omotedōri N 表通り main street

omotemuki no/wa ADJ, ADV 表向きの/は ostensible, on the surface, official(ly)

omou V 思う (*have an opinion*) to consider, to think; to feel

omuraisu N オムライス omelet wrapped around rice

omutsu N おむつ diapers

onaji N 同じ same

onaji yō ni ADV 同じように

likewise

onajitakasa no ADJ 同じ高さの (*height*) of the same level

onaka N おなか stomach: *onaka no guai ga warui* おなかの具合が悪い has an upset stomach

onaka ga suku V おなかがすく to be hungry

onaka ga ippai no ADJ おなかがいっぱいの full, eaten one's fill

onanī N オナニー masturbation

onara N おなら flatulence, fart

ondo N 温度 (*temperature*) degrees

ondokei N 温度計 thermometer

ondori N オンドリ rooster

onegaishimasu ADV お願いします (*request for something*) please

onē-san N お姉さん older sister

ongaku N 音楽 music

ongak(u)-ka N 音楽家 musician

ongak(u)kai N 音楽会 concert

oni N 鬼 demon, devil, ogre

oniai no ADJ お似合いの suitable, fitting, compatible

onī-san N お兄さん older brother

onjin N 恩人 benefactor

onkyō N 音響 sound

on'nanohito/kata N 女の人/方 woman, female

on'nanoko N 女の子 girl

ono N 斧 ax, hatchet

ono'ono ADJ, ADV 各々 each, respectively, severally

onpa N 音波 sound wave

onrain gēmu N オンラインゲーム an online game, online gaming

onrain ginkō N オンライン銀行 online banking

onrain sutoa N オンラインストア online store

onryō N 音量 sound volume

onsen N 温泉 hot spring; spa

onshi N 恩師 former teacher

onshitsu N 温室 greenhouse

ontei N 音程 musical interval

oppai N おっぱい (*baby talk, slang*) breast; milk

ōraka na ADJ おおらかな generous, big-hearted, easygoing

Oranda N オランダ Holland

ore PRON 俺 (*male, unrefined*) I/me

o-rei N お礼 acknowledgment, thank-you, (*of appreciation*) present

orenji N オレンジ (*citrus*) orange

oreru V 折れる (骨など) (*of bones, etc.*) to be broken, snapped

ori N おり cage; jail

origami N おりがみ origami, paper-folding

orimono N 織り物 weaving, cloth, textile, fabric

oriru V 下りる・降りる to get down, (*a ship/plane*) to get off, (*of a car*) to get out

oritatamu V 折りたたむ to fold up

oroka na ADJ 愚かな stupid, foolish

oroshiuri N 卸し売り (*selling*) wholesale

orosu V 下ろす to take down, to lower; to unload; to invest

orosu V 降ろす (*a ship/plane*) to let one off, (*from a car*) to drop off, (*of a car*) to let out

oru V 織る to weave

oru V 折る to fold, to bend; to break

orugōru N オルゴール music box

ōryō N 横領 embezzlement

osaeru V 抑える to restrain

osaeru V 押さえる to repress;

ō-saji N 大さじ tablespoon

o-sake N お酒 (*Japanese rice wine*) sake; liquor

osaki ni dōzo お先にどうぞ Please go first

osaki ni shitsurei shimasu お先に失礼します Goodbye.., Excuse me for going before you.

ō(-sama) N 王(様) king

osameru V 納める (*tax, premium, etc.*) to pay

osameru V 治める to govern; to pacify

osan N お産 childbirth

osanai ADJ 幼い infant(ile), very young; childish, (*inexperienced*) green

ō-sawagi N 大騒ぎ fuss, disturbance

ōsawagi suru V 大騒ぎする to make a fuss

o-seibo N お歳暮 year-end present, winter gift

o-seji N お世辞 compliment, flattery

osekkai N お節介 meddling

osen N 汚染 contamination, pollution

o-senbei N お煎餅 rice crackers

o-sewa N お世話 care, assistance, help

oshaberi N おしゃべり chatterbox, gossip

oshare na ADJ おしゃれな dandy, smart, sophisticated

oshiego N 教え子 (*of a teacher's*) a student

oshieru V 教える to teach, to tell, to let know; to inform

oshi'i ADJ 惜しい regrettable; precious

oshi'ire N 押し入れ (*traditional Japanese*) closet

ōshin N 往診 house call

oshinko N お新香 pickles

oshirase N お知らせ report, information, notice

oshiri N お尻 buttock, hip, bottom

oshiroi N おしろい face powder

ō-shitsu N 王室 royal family

oshitsukeru V 押し付ける to push, to press; to intrude

O-shōgatsu N お正月 New Year; January

Ōshū N 欧州 Europe

osoi ADJ 遅い late, slow

ō-sōji N 大掃除 great cleaning

osoraku ADV おそらく perhaps, probably

osore N 恐れ fear

osoreru V 恐れる to fear

osoroshi'i ADJ 恐ろしい fearful, dreadful, terrible, horrible

o-sōshiki N お葬式 funeral

osou V 襲う to attack, to assault; to strike, to hit

osowaru V 教わる to be taught, to study, to learn

ossharu V おっしゃる (*someone honored*) to say; to be called

osu V 押す to press, to push

osu N お酢 vinegar

osu N 雄 (*animal*) male

osushi N お鮨[寿司] sushi

Ōsutoraria N オーストラリア Australia

Ōsutoraria(-jin) no ADJ オーストラリア(人) の Australian

otagai no ADJ お互いの mutual, reciprocal

otearai N お手洗い washroom, toilet, restroom

o-tenki N お天気 fair weather

oto N 音 sound, noise

ōtobai N オートバイ motorcycle

otokonohito/kata N 男の人/方 man, male

otokonoko N 男の子 boy

otokui(-sama) N お得意(さま) good customer(s), regular customer(s)

otona N 大人 adult

otonashi'i ADJ おとなしい gentle, well-behaved, polite

otori N おとり decoy; lure

otoroeru V 衰える to decline, to fade, to grow weak

otō-san N お父さん father

otōto N 弟 younger brother

ototoi N 一昨日 day before yesterday

ototoshi N 一昨年 year before last

o-tsuri N おつり (*money returned*) change

otto N 夫 husband

ou V 追う to chase, to pursue

ōu V 覆う to cover

ō-uridashi N 大売出し big sale

oushi N 雄牛 bull, ox

o-wakare N お別れ parting, farewell

owari N 終わり (*finish*) end

owaru V 終る to end

oya N 親 parent

oyako 親子 parent and child

oyakōkō N 親孝行 (*honoring one's parents*) filial piety

ōya(-san) N 大家(さん) landlord

oyashirazu N 親知らず wisdom tooth

o-yasumi N お休み rest; holiday; recess; time off

O-yasuminasai INTERJ おやすみなさい. Good night.

oyayubi N 親指 thumb

oyogu V 泳ぐ to bathe, to swim

oyome-san N お嫁さん bride

ōyō N 応用 application, putting to use

ōyō suru 応用する to apply it, to put it to use

ōyoso ADV おおよそ approximately, roughly

ōyoso no ADJ おおよその approximate, rough

o-yu N お湯 hot water

ōzappa na ADJ おおざっぱな rough

ōzei no ADJ 大勢の (*people*) many

o-zōni N お雑煮 (*eat on the New Year's Day*) rice cakes boiled with vegetable soup

P

pachinko(-ya) N パチンコ (屋) (*Japanese*) pinball (*machine*), pachinko (*parlor*)

pai N パイ (*food*) pie; a mahjong tile

painappuru N パイナップル pineapple

pairotto N パイロット pilot

pajama N パジャマ pajamas, pyjamas

pāma N パーマ permanent wave

pan N パン bread

panko N パン粉 bread crumbs

panda N パンダ (*animal*) panda

panfuretto N パンフレット pamphlet, brochure

pankēki N パンケーキ pancake

pansuto, pantīsutokkingu N パンスト, パンティーストッキング panty hose

pantī N パンティー panties, (*for woman*) underwear

pantsu N パンツ (下着) (*underpants*) shorts

pan-ya N パン屋 bakeshop, bakery; baker

papa N パパ daddy, dad

Pari N パリ Paris

pāsento N パーセント percent, percentage

pasokon N パソコン personal computer

pasupōto N パスポート passport

pātī N パーティー (*event*) party

patokā N パトカー patrol car, police car

pātotaimu N パートタイム part-time work

pazuru N パズル puzzle

pedaru N ペダル pedal

pēji N ページ page

Pekin N 北京 Peking, Beijing

pen N ペン pen

penchi N ペンチ pliers, pincers

penisu N ペニス penis

penki N ペンキ paint

perapera no ADJ ペラペラの (*speak*) fluently; (*clothes*) thin

petto N ペット pet animal

piano N ピアノ piano

pikapika no ADJ ピカピカの shiny, cleanly, sparkly clean

pikunikku N ピクニック picnic

pīnattsu N ピーナッツ peanut

pinboke N ピンぼけ out-of-focus

pinchi N ピンチ pinch
pinku no ADJ ピンクの pink
pinsetto N ピンセット tweezers
pinto N ピント focus
pisutoru N ピストル revolver, pistol
pōtarusaito N ポータルサイト a portal website (*MSN, Yahoo!, Google*)
piza N ピザ pizza
poketto N ポケット pocket
ponpu N ポンプ pump
poppukōn N ポップコーン popcorn
poppusu N ポップス pops, popular music
poribukuro N ポリ袋 plastic bag
poruno N ポルノ pornography
posuto N ポスト mail box
potto N ポット pot
puragu N プラグ (*electric*) plug
puran N プラン plan
puranetariumu N プラネタリウム planetarium
purasuchikku N プラスチック plastic
purattohōmu N プラットホーム (*station*) platform
purezento N プレゼント present, gift

purintā N プリンター printer
puro N プロ pro(fessional)
puroguramu N プログラム program
pūru N プール swimming pool

R

rabel N ラベル label
raibaru N ライバル rival
raigetsu N 来月 next month
raikyaku N 来客 guest, caller, visitor, company
raimu N ライム (*citrus*) lime
rainen N 来年 next year
raion N ライオン lion
raisensu N ライセンス license, permit
raishū N 来週 next week
raitā N ライター lighter; writer
rajio N ラジオ radio
rakuda N ラクダ camel
rakudai N 落第 (*in a test*) failure
rakuen N 楽園 paradise
rakugaki N 落書き scribbling; doodling
rakugo N 落語 (*traditional Japanese*) comic storytelling
raku na ADJ 楽な comfortable

rāmen N ラーメン Chinese noodles

ramu N ラム lamb

ramune N ラムネ lemon soda

ran N 欄 column, field

ranbō na ADJ 乱暴な violent, wild, rough, disorderly

ranchi N ランチ lunch

ranpu N ランプ lamp

Raosu N ラオス Laos

Raosu(-jin) no ADJ ラオス(人)の Laotian

rappa N ラッパ trumpet, bugle

rasenjō no ADJ らせん状の spiral

...rashi'i SUFFIX, ADJ 〜らしい (*seems*) like, apparent, seems to be

rashinban N 羅針盤 (*for directions*) compass

rasshuawā N ラッシュアワー rush hour

Ratengo N ラテン語 (*language*) Latin

rebā N レバー liver; lever

regyurā N レギュラー regular

rei N 例 example

rei N 礼 thanks, gift greeting; bow

rei N 零 zero

reibō N 冷房 (*cooling*) air conditioning

reigai N 例外 (*the rule*) exception

reigi N 礼儀 courtesy, etiquette

reigitadashi'i ADJ 礼儀正しい polite

reihai, raihai N 礼拝 worship

reinen no ADJ 例年の annual

reisei na ADJ 冷静な calm, cool, composed

reitōko N 冷凍庫 freezer

reitōshokuhin N 冷凍食品 frozen food

reizōko N 冷蔵庫 refrigerator, icebox

rejā N レジャー leisure, recreation

reji N レジ cashier; checkout counter

rekishi N 歴史 history

rekōdo N レコード (*phonograph*) a record

rekuriēshon N レクリエーション recreation

remon N レモン (*citrus*) lemon

remonēdo N レモネード lemonade

ren'ai N 恋愛 love

rengō N 連合 union, alliance, Allied

renji N レンジ cooking stove, kitchen range

renketsu suru v 連結する to connect together

renmei n 連盟 union, federation

renraku suru v 連絡する to contact, to get in touch with

renshū n 練習 training, practice, drill

rentakā n レンタカー rental car

rentogen(-sen) n レントゲン (線) X-ray

renzoku n 連続 continuity; series

renzu n レンズ lens

repōtā n レポーター reporter

repōto n レポート report

rēsā n レーサー racing driver

reshipi n レシピ recipe

reshīto n レシート receipt

ressha de 列車で by rail

ressun n レッスン lesson

rēsu n レース (*fabric*) lace; race

resuringu n レスリング wrestling

resutoran n レストラン restaurant

retasu n レタス lettuce

retsu n 列 queue, line

rettō n 列島 archipelago, chain of islands

ribon n リボン ribbon

rieki n 利益 profit, benefit, advantage

rihabiri n リハビリ rehabilitation

rihāsaru n リハーサル rehearsal

rika n 理科 science

rikai suru v 理解する to understand

rikō na ADJ 利口な clever, sharp, smart, intelligent

rikon suru v 離婚する to divorce

riku(chi) n 陸(地) land, dry land

rikugame n 陸亀 (*land*) tortoise

rikugun n 陸軍 army

rikutsu n 理屈 reason, argument

rimokon n リモコン remote control

ringo n りんご apple

rinji no ADJ 臨時の extra-ordinary, special; temporary

rinjin n 隣人 neighbor

rinkaku n 輪郭 border, edge

rinri n 倫理 ethics

rippa na ADJ 立派な fine, splendid, admirable

ririku n 離陸 (*plane*) take-off

riron n 理論 theory

rishi, risoku N 利子, 利息 interest

risō-teki na ADJ 理想的な ideal

risu N リス squirrel

ritsu N 率 rate, proportion; average; a cut, a percentage

rittai N 立体 solid; 3-D

riyō suru V 利用する to utilize, to make use of

riyōsha N 利用者 user

riyū N 理由 reason, cause

rizaya N 利ざや margin

rizumu N リズム rhythm

rō N ロウ wax

roba N ロバ donkey

robī N ロビー lobby

rōdōkumiai N 労働組合 labor union

rōdōsha N 労働者 worker, laborer

roguauto N ログアウト log-out

roguin N ログイン login

rōhi N 浪費 extravagance

roji N 路地 alley

rōjin N 老人 old person

rōka N 廊下 corridor

roketto N ロケット rocket

rokkā N ロッカー locker

rokku N ロック (*music*) rock, rock'n'roll

roku NUM 六 six

roku-gatsu N 六月 June

rokuga suru V 録画する to videotape, to record

rokujū NUM 六十 sixty

rokuon suru V 録音する (*sound*) to record

Rōma N ローマ Rome

rōmaji N ローマ字 romanization, Latin letters

romendensha N 路面電車 streetcar

ronbun N 論文 treatise; essay

Rondon N ロンドン London

ronri-teki na ADJ 論理的な logical

ronsō N 論争 controversy, dispute, argument, debate, discussion

rōpu N ロープ rope

rōrā sukēto N ローラースケート roller-skates/-skating

rōrupan N ロールパン (*bread*) roll

rosen N 路線 (*bus, train*) route

Roshia N ロシア Russia

Roshiago N ロシア語 (*language*) Russian

rōsoku N ろうそく candle

Rosu, Rosanzerusu N ロス, ロサンゼルス Los Angeles

rōsutobīfu N ローストビーフ roast beef

rōto N ろうと funnel

ruijin'en N 類人猿 ape

rūmusābisu N ルームサービス (*at hotel, etc.*) room service

rūru N ルール rule

rusu no ADJ 留守の absent, away from home

rusubandenwa N 留守番電話 answering machine, voicemail

rūtā N ルーター router (*computer*)

ryaku-go N 略語 abbreviation

ryō N 量 amount

ryō N 猟 hunting

ryō N 漁 fishing

ryō N 寮 dormitory, boarding house

ryōchi N 領地 territory

ryōgae suru V 両替する to exchange

ryōgawa N 両側 both sides

ryōhō N 両方 both

ryokan N 旅館 (*traditional*) inn

ryoken N 旅券 passport

ryōkin N 料金 rate, tariff, fare

ryokō N 旅行 travel, trip

ryokō an'naisho N 旅行案内書 guidebook

ryokō gaisha N 旅行会社 travel agency

ryokō o suru V 旅行をする to travel, to take a trip

ryokōsha N 旅行者 traveler

ryokucha N 緑茶 green tea

ryōri 料理 cooking, cuisine, (*particular food*) dish

ryōriten N 料理店 restaurant

ryōshi N 猟師 hunter

ryōshi N 漁師 fisherman

ryōshiki N 良識 good/common sense

ryōshin N 両親 parents

ryōshin-teki na ADJ 良心的な conscientious

ryōshūsho N 領収書 receipt

ryū N 竜・龍 dragon

ryūchō na ADJ 流暢な fluent

ryūgakusei N 留学生 foreign student(s)

ryukku, ryukkusakku N リュック, リュックサック knapsack

ryūkō no ADJ 流行の fashionable

ryūtsū N 流通 circulation, distribution

S

sa N 差 difference, discrepancy

saba N 鯖 mackerel

sābā N サーバー (*computer*) server

sabaku N 砂漠 (*arid land*) desert

sabetsu N 差別 discrimination

sabi N さび rust

sabiru V さびる to rust

sabishi'i ADJ 寂しい lonely

sābisu N サービス service

sābisueria N サービスエリア highway service area; (*mobile phone, etc.*) coverage

sabita ADJ さびた rusty

saboru V サボる to bunk it, (*class*) to play hookey, to skip, to stay away

saboten N サボテン cactus

sadō N 茶道 tea ceremony

sāfin N サーフィン surf

sagaku N 差額 (*in price*) the difference, the balance

sagaru V 下がる to hang down; to go down

sagasu V 探す to look for, to search for

sageru V 下げる to hang it, to

lower it, to bring it down

sagyō N 作業 work, operations

agyō kōtei N 作業工程 working process

sagyōin N 作業員 laborer

sahō N 作法 manners, etiquette

-sai SUFFIX 歳・才 (*counts years of age*)

sai N 差異 (*discrepancy in figures*) difference

saiaku no ADJ 最悪の worst

saibā-kōgeki N サイバー攻撃 cyber attack, cyber terrorism

saiban N 裁判 trial

saibankan N 裁判官 judge

saibansho N 裁判所 court

saichū N 最中 midst

saidai no ADJ 最大の largest, most; maximal, maximum

saidaigen no ADJ 最大限の maximal, maximum, utmost

saidan N 祭壇 altar

saidoburēki N サイドブレーキ handbrake

saifu N 財布 wallet, purse

saigai N 災害 disaster

saigen suru V 再現する to reappear

saigo N 最後 last

saigo ni ADV 最後に finally

saigo no ADJ 最後の final, last

saihō N 裁縫 sewing

saihōsō N 再放送 rebroadcast

saijōi N 最上位 (*position, rank, etc.*) top-level

saijōkai N 最上階 the top floor

saijitsu N 祭日 (*festival*) holiday

saikai N 最下位 (*position, rank, etc.*) last place

saikakunin N 再確認 reconfirmation

saikentō suru V 再検討する to review

saikin N 細菌 germ

saikin no ADJ 最近の recent, last, latest

saikō no ADJ 最高の best

saikon N 再婚 remarriage

saikuringu N サイクリング cycling

saikutsu suru V 採掘する to mine

saiminjutsu N 催眠術 hypnotism

sain N サイン signature; autograph; sign

sainan N 災難 disaster

sain'in N サインイン sign in

sainō N 才能 talent

sainofu N サインオフ sign off

sairen N サイレン (*sound*) siren

saisei N 再生 reproduction, (*audio*) playback, replay; (*button*) play

saisen N さい銭 (*at a shrine*) money offering

saishi N 妻子 wife and child(ren)

saishin no ADJ 最新の newest, up-to-date, latest

saishin no chūi N 細心の注意 close attention

saisho N 最初 at first, first

saisho no ADJ 最初の first, beginning, primary

saishō no ADJ 最小の smallest, least, minimal, minimum

saishū N 採集 collection, (*as specimen, data, etc.*) picking and gathering

saisoku suru V 催促する to remind, to urge

saitei no ADJ 最低の lowest, worst; minimum

saiten N 採点 rating, grading, marking

saiwai ni mo ADV 幸いにも fortunately

saiyō siru V 採用する to employs, to adopt

saizen N 最善 the best; one's best/utmost

saizu N サイズ size

saka N 坂 slope, hill

sakaeru V 栄える to thrive, to flourish, to prosper

sakai N 境 boundary, border

sakana N 魚 fish

sakana-ya N 魚屋 fish dealer/market

sakanoboru V さかのぼる (*the stream*) to go against, to go upstream; to go back (*in time*) to

sakarau V 逆らう to defy, to oppose, to go against

sakariba N 盛り場 downtown area

sakasama no ADJ 逆さまの reversed, backwards, upside down

sākasu N サーカス circus

saka-ya N 酒屋 liquor shop

sake N 酒 alcohol, liquor, sake

sake, shake N さけ, しゃけ salmon

sakebu V 叫ぶ to cry out, to shout, to yell

sakeru V 避ける to avoid

saki N 先 front; future; ahead; point, tip

sakihodo 先程 a little while ago

sakka N 作家 writer

sakkā N サッカー soccer

sakkaku N 錯覚 illusion

sakki さっき a little while ago

sakkin N 殺菌 sterilization

sakkyoku N 作曲 music composition

saku V 咲く to bloom, to blossom

saku V 裂く to split it; to tear it

sakubun N 作文 writing essay, (*a theme*) composition

sakugen N 削減 cut, reduction

sakugen suru V 削減する to reduce: *kosuto sakugen* コスト削減 cost reduction

sakuhin N 作品 composition, writings

sakuin N 索引 index

sakujitsu N, ADV 昨日 yesterday

sakumotsu N 作物 crops

sakunen N 昨年 last year

sakura N 桜 cherry tree

sakusen N 作戦 tactics

sakusha N 作者 author

sakushi-ka N 作詞家 songwriter

sakuya N 昨夜 last night

sakyū N 砂丘 sand dune

··· -sama SUFFIX ...様 Mr., Ms., Mrs., Miss [HONORIFIC]

samasu v 覚ます to awake, to wake up

samasu v 冷ます to cool

samatageru v 妨げる to disturb, to hinder, to prevent

samayou v さまよう to wander about

samazama na/no ADJ 様々な/の diverse, all kinds of

same N 鮫 shark

sameru v 覚める to awake, to wake up

samui ADJ 寒い cold, chilly

samurai N 侍 (*warrior*) samurai

… -san SUFFIX …さん Mr., Ms., Mrs., Miss

san NUM 三 three

san N 酸 acid

sanbashi N 桟橋 pier

sanbika N 賛美歌 hymn

sanbutsu N 産物 product, produce; fruit, outcome

sanchi N 産地 (*of a product/ crop*) production area

sanchō N 山頂 peak, summit, mountaintop

sandaru N サンダル sandals

sandoitchi N サンドイッチ sandwich

Sanfuranshisuko N サンフラン

shisuko San Francisco

san-gatsu N 三月 March

sangi'in N 参議院 House of Councilors

sangoshō N さんご礁 coral

sangurasu N サングラス sunglasses

sangyō N 産業 industry

sanjū NUM 三十 thirty

sanka suru N 参加する to join in, to participate

sankaku N 三角 triangle

sankō N 参考 reference

sankō(to)sho N 参考(図)書 reference book

sanmyaku N 山脈 mountain range

sanma N サンマ mackerel pike

san'ninshō N 三人称 third person

sanpo N 散歩 walk, stroll

sanpuru N サンプル sample

sanrinsha N 三輪車 tricycle

sansai N 山菜 edible wild plants

sansei N 賛成 approval, support

sansei no ADJ 酸性の acid

sanso N 酸素 oxygen

sansū N 算数 (*elementary school*) mathematics

sao N さお pole, rod

sappari wakaranai さっぱり分からない I have no idea.

sara N 皿 dish, platter, plate; saucer

sara ni ADV 更に also; (*some*) more; further

sarada N サラダ salad

sarai-getsu N 再来月 month after next

sarai-nen N 再来年 year after next

sarai-shū N 再来週 week after next

sararīman N サラリーマン business-person, company employee, salaried worker

sarasu V さらす to expose; to bleach; to dry under the sun

sāroinsutēki N サーロイン・ステーキ sirloin steak

saru N 猿 monkey

saru V 去る to leave, to go away; to remove it

sasaeru V 支える to support, to prop (up)

sasai na ADJ ささいな petty, trivial, not a big deal at all

sasayaka na ADJ ささやかな small(-scale), petty

sasayaku V ささやく to whisper

sashie N 挿絵 (*book, magazine, newspaper, etc.*) illustration

sashikomi N 差し込み (電気) (*electric*) plug

sashikomu V 差し込む to insert

sashizu N 指図 directions, instructions, commands

sashō N 査証 visa

sasou V 誘う (*ask along*) to invite

sasshi N 冊子 brochure

sasshi ga tsuku V 察しがつく to perceive, (*correctly*) to guess

sassoku N 早速 immediately, at once, right away, promptly

sasu V 指す to indicate

sasu V 差す(傘) (*umbrella*) to hold

sasu V 刺す to stab, to sting

sate INTERJ さて well now/then, and now/then, as to the matter at hand

satei N 査定 (*decide the rank, salary, etc.*) assessment

satō N 砂糖 sugar

satōkibi N サトウキビ sugarcane

sato'oya N 里親 foster parent

satoru V 悟る to realize, to be aware of

145

satsu N 札 folding money, currency bill/note

-satsu SUFFIX 冊 copy (*counts bound things*)

satsuei N 撮影 shooting a film, filming, taking a photograph

satsujin N 殺人 murder

satsumaimo N さつま芋 sweet potato

sauna N サウナ steam bath

sawagashi'i ADJ 騒がしい boisterous; noisy

sawagu V 騒ぐ to make lots of noise, to clamor

sawaru V 触る to touch

sawayaka na ADJ さわやかな refreshing, bracing; fluent

sayōnara INTERJ さようなら goodbye

sayū N 左右 right and left

se N 背 height

sei N 姓 family name, last name

seibetsu N 性別 sex, gender

seibun N 成分 ingredient, component

seibutsu N 生物 living thing, creature

seibutsu-gaku N 生物学 biology

seibyō N 性病 venereal disease

seichō suru V 成長する to grow; to grow up

seido N 制度 system

seifu N 政府 government

seifuku N 制服 (*attire*) uniform

seigaku N 声楽 vocal music

seigen N 制限 limit, restriction

seihin N 製品 product, manufactured goods

sei'i N 誠意 sincerity

sei'iki N 聖域 sanctuary

seiji N 政治 politics

seijin-no-hi N 成人の日 Coming-of-Age Day (*honoring 20-year-olds, on 2nd Mon. of Jan.*)

seijitsu na ADJ 誠実な sincere

seijukushita ADJ 成熟した ripe, mature

seika N 成果 good result, outcome

seikaku N 性格 (*personality*) character

seikaku na ADJ 正確な correct, exact

seikatsu N 生活 life, (*daily*) living

seikatsuhi N 生活費 living costs

seiketsu na ADJ 清潔な clean, pure

seiki N 世紀 century

seikō N 性交 sex, sexual

intercourse

seikō N 成功 success

seikyū suru V 請求する to demand, to request

seimei N 生命 life

seimei hoken N 生命保険 life insurance

seimitsu na ADJ 精密な precise, detailed, minute, thorough

seimon N 正門 the front (*main*) gate

seinen N 青年 young person, youth, adolescent

seinen-gappi N 生年月日 date of birth

seireki N 西暦 the Western/ Christian calendar, A.D.

seiri N 生理 (*menstrual*) period

seiri suru V 整理する to adjust, to arrange, to (re)order, to (re)organize

seiritsu suru V 成立する (*organized*) to come into being, to get finalized/ concluded

seiryō-inryōsui N 清涼飲料 soft drink

seiryoku N 勢力 power, energy; influence

seisaku N 政策 policy

seisaku N 制作・製作 manufacture, production

seisaku kōtei N 製作工程 process for forming

seisan suru V 生産する to produce

seisan suru V 清算する to clear, to liquidate

seiseki N 成績 results, marks, grades, record

seishiki no/na ADJ 正式の/な formal, formality

seishin no ADJ 精神の mental

seisho N 聖書 Bible

seishun N 青春 adolescence

seisō N 清掃 cleaning

sei-teki na ADJ 性的の sexual

seito N 生徒 pupil, student

seitō N 政党 political party

seitō na ADJ 正当な fair, just, justifiable

seitō na ADJ 正統な legitimate, orthodox

seiton suru V 整頓する to tidy up

seiyō N 西洋 the West, Europe

seiyōjin N 西洋人 westerner

seiza N 星座 constellation

seizon-ritsu N 生存率 survival rate

seizō suru v 製造する to produce, to manufacture

seji N 世辞 compliment, flattery

sekai N 世界 world

seken N 世間 the public, people, the world, society

sekentei N 世間体 appearance, reputation, decency

seki N 咳 cough

seki N 席 seat

sekidō N 赤道 equator

sekigaisen N 赤外線 infrared rays

sekihan N 赤飯 (commonly for celebration) steaming rice with red beans

sekijūji N 赤十字 Red Cross

sekikomu v 咳きこむ to cough

sekimen suru v 赤面する to blush

sekinin N 責任 responsibility: *sekinin o toru* 責任を取る to take responsibility

sekiri N 赤痢 dysentery

sekitan N 石炭 coal

sekkai N 石灰 (mineral) lime

sekkaku ADV せっかく [+ NEGATIVE VERB] with much effort/devotion; on purpose, taking the trouble

sekkei N 設計 (of machine, etc.) designing, planning

sekkezu N 設計図 draft, blueprint

sekken N 石っけん soap

sekkin suru v 接近する to approach, to draw near

sekkō N 石こう plaster

sekkusu N セックス sex, sexual intercourse

sekkyō N 説教 sermon: *o-sekkyo* お説教 lecture

sekkyō suru v 説教する to preach, to lecture

sekkyoku-teki na ADJ 積極的な positive, energetic, vigorous

sekyuritī N セキュリティー (computer) security

semai ADJ 狭い narrow, tight

semeru v 責める to blame, to censure, to criticize

semeru v 攻める to attack, to assault

semete ADV せめて at least; at most

semi N セミ cicada, locust

sen N 千 thousand

sen N 線 (mark) line

senaka N 背中 (part of body) back

senbei N せんべい rice crackers

senchō N 船長 (*ship*) captain

senden N 宣伝 propaganda, publicity

sengetsu N 先月 last month

sengo no ADJ 戦後の postwar, after/since the war

sen'i N 繊維 fiber

senji-chū N 戦時中 during the war

senjitsu N 先日 the other day

senjōzai N 洗浄剤 detergent

senkō N 線香 incense, joss stick

senkō N 専攻 (*study*) major

senkyo N 選挙 election

senmenjo N 洗面所 lavatory, bathroom

senmenki N 洗面器 wash basin

senmon N 専門 specialty, (*line/field/study*) major

senmon-ka N 専門家 expert

sen'nyūkan N 先入観 preconceived idea, prejudice

senobi N 背伸び standing on tiptoe; trying to do more than one is able to do

senpai N 先輩 (*colleague, fellow student*) one's senior

senpūki N 扇風機 (*for cooling*) fan

senritsu N 旋律 melody

senro N 線路 (*track*) railroad, railway

senryō suru V 占領する to occupy

sensai na ADJ 繊細な delicate, sensitive

sensei N 先生 teacher; doctor; (*artisan/artist*) master

senshu N 選手 athlete; player

senshū N 先週 last week

sensō N 戦争 war

sensu N 扇子 (*folding*) fan

sensu N センス sense

sensuikan N 潜水艦 submarine

sentaku N 選択 choice, selection

sentakuki N 洗濯機 (*washing machine*) washer

sentan N 先端 tip, (*pointed*) end; forefront

sentangijutsu N 先端技術 high-technology

sentō N 先頭 lead, head, front, top

sentō N 戦闘 battle

sentō N 銭湯 public bath

senzen no ADJ 戦前の prewar, before the war

senzo N 先祖 ancestor

seou V 背負う to carry on the back

seppuku N 切腹 *harakiri*

seri N 競り auction

sero(han)-tēpu N セロ(ハン)・テープ cellophane tape, scotch tape

serori N セロリ celery

sesseto ADV せっせと diligently, (*laboriously*) hard; often

sesshoku N 接触 contact, touch

sessuru V 接する to come in contact (with), to border (on), to be adjacent (to); to encounter, to receive, to handle

sētā N セーター sweater

setai N 世帯 a household

setsubi N 設備 equipment, facilities, accommodations

setsudan suru V 切断する to cut off

setsuden N 節電 save electricity/power

setsumei suru V 説明する to explain, to describe

setsuritsu suru V 設立する to establish, to found

setsuyaku suru V 節約する (*economize on*) to save, to conserve

setsuzoku suru V 接続する to

join together

settai N 接待 business entertainment

settei suru V 設定する to set up

settōhan N 窃盗犯 thief

settoku suru V 説得する to persuade, to convince

sewa o suru V 世話をする to take care of, to look after

sewashinai ADJ 忙しない busy, hectic

shaberu V しゃべる to chatter

shaburu V しゃぶる to suck

shachō N 社長 president of a company, boss

shadō N 車道 road(way), drive(way), street

shagamu V しゃがむ to squat, to crouch on heels

shageki N 射撃 (*firing a rifle, shotgun, etc*) shooting

shain N 社員 (*company*) employee

shajitsu-teki na ADJ 写実的な realistic

shakai N 社会 society

shakaishugi N 社会主義 socialism

shakkin N 借金 debt

shakkuri N しゃっくり hiccup

shako N 車庫 *(for parking)* garage

shanai de ADV 社内で within the office/company, internal, in-house

shanpū N シャンプー shampoo

share N しゃれ pun

sharin N 車輪 wheel

shasei N 写生 sketching, sketch

shasen N 車線 (高速道路) *(highway)* lane

shashin N 写真 photograph, picture

shashin-ki N 写真機 camera

shashō N 車掌 *(train)* conductor

shatsu N シャツ shirt, undershirt

shawā N シャワー *(for bathing)* shower: *shawā o abiru* シャワーを浴びる to take a shower

shi N 市 city

shi N 死 death

shi N 詩 poetry, poem, verse

shiage N 仕上げ the finish(ing touch)

shiageru V 仕上げる to finish up

shiai N 試合 match, game

shiasatte N, ADV しあさって three days from now

shiawase N 幸せ happiness

shibai N 芝居 *(drama)* play

shibaraku ADV しばらく (for) a while, after a while

shibaru V 縛る to tie up

shibashiba ADV しばしば often, repeatedly

shibireru V 痺れる to get numb, *(a leg, etc.)* to go to sleep

shibō N 志望 desire, wish

shiboru V 絞る to wring (out), to squeeze, *(through cloth)* to strain

shibu N 支部 branch office

shibui ADJ 渋い astringent, *(taste)* bitter; wry, *(face)* sour; cool, *(appearance)* elegant

shichaku suru V 試着する (服) *(clothes)* to try on

shichi NUM 七 seven

shichi-gatsu N 七月 July

shichi-ya N 質屋 pawnbroker, pawnshop

shichō N 市長 mayor

shichū N シチュー stew

shidashi-ya N 仕出し屋 caterer, catering shop

shī-dī N シーディー CD

shī-dī romu N シーディーロム CD-ROM

shidō suru V 指導する to guide, to direct, to lead, to counsel, to coach

shidōsha N 指導者 leader

shīemu N シーエム・CM TV commercial, CM

shifuku N 私服 plain clothes; civilian clothes

shigai N 市外 outskirts of city, suburbs

shi-gatsu N 四月 April

shigeki-teki na ADJ 刺激的な exciting, provocative, stimulating

shigeru V 茂る to grow thick(ly)/luxuriant(ly)

shigoto N 仕事 job, work, occupation

shihai suru V 支配する to rule, to control

shihainin N 支配人 manager

shihaisha N 支配者 ruler

shiharai N 支払い payment

shihei N 紙幣 note (currency)

shihon N 資本 capital, funds

shihonshugi N 資本主義 capitalism

shi-in N 死因 cause of death

shi-in N 子音 consonant

shiiru V 強いる to force, to compel

shi'itake N 椎茸 shi'itake mushrooms

shiji suru V 支持する to back up, to support, to endorse

shiji suru V 指示する to instruct, to tell someone to do something

shijin N 詩人 poet

shijō N 市場 market

shijū N 始終 all the time

shika N 鹿 deer

shikai N 歯科医 dentist

shikaku N 資格 qualification

shikakui ADJ 四角い (shape) square

shikamo ADV しかも moreover; and yet

shikaru V 叱る to scold

shikashi CONJ しかし although, but

shikashi nagara ADV しかしながら however, nevertheless

shiken N 試験 exam, test

shiki N 式 expression; ceremony

shiki N 指揮 command; (orchestra) conducting

shikichi N 敷地 building lot; (house) site

shikifu N 敷布 (*bed*)sheet

shikin N 資金 funds, funding

shikiri N 仕切り partition

shikiri ni ADV しきりに incessantly; intently, hard

shikisha N 指揮者 (オーケストラ) (*orchestra*) conductor

shikkari ADV しっかり firmly, resolutely

shikke N 湿気 dampness, humidity

shikki N 漆器 lacquer(ware)

shikō N 思考 thoughts

shikō N 嗜好 liking, fancy, taste

shiku V 敷く (*a quilt, etc.*) to spread

shikyōhin N 試供品 tester, free sample

shikyū N 至急 urgency

shima N 島 island

shima N 縞 (模様) (*pattern*) stripes

shimai N 姉妹 sister

shimaru V 閉まる to close, to shut, to lock

shimatsu suru V 始末する to deal with, to settle

shimatta INTERJ しまった! Damn!, Good heavens

shimau V しまう to put away, to house

shimauma N シマウマ zebra

shimei N 氏名 (*one's*) full name

shimei N 使命 mission

shimei suru V 指名する to nominate

shimeitehai N 指名手配 listing a person (*criminal*) on the wanted list

shimekiri N 締め切り closing; deadline

shimeppoi ADJ 湿っぽい damp; humid

shimeraseru V 湿らせる to moisten/dampen it, to wet it

shimeru V 閉める to shut, to close, to lock

shimeru V 締める to tie, to fasten, to tighten; to put on, (*necktie, belt*) to wear

shimesu V 示す to show, to indicate

shimikomu V 染み込む to penetrate, to soak

shimin N 市民 citizen

shimiru V しみる to smart, to sting

shimo N 霜 frost

shimon N 指紋 fingerprint

shin N 芯 core, pith

shin N 心 heart, spirit

shinagara しながら while doing

... shinai VERBAL AUXILIARY 〜しない (*with verbs and adjectives*) no, not

shinai N 市内 within the city; urban, city, municipal

shina(mono) N 品(物) articles, goods; quality

shinbō suru V 辛抱する to endure, to put up with

shinbun N 新聞 newspaper

shinchō N 身長 height, stature

shinchū N 真ちゅう brass

shindō N 振動 vibration

Shingapōru N シンガポール Singapore

shingō N 信号 signal; (*trafic*) light

shinin N 死人 dead person

shinja N 信者 believer

shinjiru V 信じる to believe, to trust

shinjitsu N 真実 truth

shinju N 真珠 pearl

Shinkansen N 新幹線 bullet train, Shinkansen

shinkei-shitsu na ADJ 神経質な nervous

shinkoku na ADJ 深刻な serious, grave

shinkō suru V 信仰する to worship

shin'nen N 信念 belief, faith

shin'nen N 新年 new year

shinpai suru V 心配する to worry

shinpi-teki na ADJ 神秘的な mysterious, esoteric, miraculous

shinpo N 進歩 progress

shinpo suru V 進歩する to make progress

shinpu N 神父 (*Christian*) priest, Father, Reverend

shinrai-sei N 信頼性 reliability

shinri-gaku N 心理学 (*science/ study of*) psychology

shinsatsu N 診察 medical examination

shinsei na ADJ 神聖な holy, sacred

shinseki N 親戚 relatives

shinseisho N 申請書 application

shinsen na ADJ 新鮮な fresh

shinsetsu na ADJ 親切な kind, cordial

shinshi N 紳士 gentleman

shinshitsu N 寝室 bedroom

Shintō N 神道 Shinto

shinu V 死ぬ to die

shinwa N 神話 myth

shin'ya N 深夜 late at night

Shin'yaku seisho N 新約聖書 the New Testament

shin'yō N 信用 trust, confidence; credit

shinzō N 心臓 heart

shio N 塩 salt

shiokarai ADJ 塩辛い salty

shippai N 失敗 failure

shippo N しっぽ tail

shiraberu V 調べる to investigate, to examine, to check

shiraga N 白髪 gray hair

shiranai hito N 知らない人 stranger

shiraseru V 知らせる to inform, to notify, (*informs of*) to announce

shirei N 指令 command

shiri N 尻 (*buttocks*) bottom

shiriai N 知り合い acquaintance

shiro N 城 castle

shiro(i) ADJ 白(い) white

shiroppu N シロップ syrup

shirōto N 素人 amateur, novice

shiru V 知る to learn, to realize

shiru N 汁 juice, gravy; soup

shirushi N 印 indication, sign, symptom; effect(iveness)

shiryō N 資料 materials; data

shiryo no aru ADJ 思慮のある sensible

shiryoku N 視力 vision, eyesight, visual acuity

shisai N 司祭 priest

shisan N 資産 property, assets

shisei N 姿勢 posture; attitude

shisen N 視線 eye direction

shisetsu N 施設 facility, institution, installation

shisha N 支社 branch office

shishoku o suru V 試食をする (*sample*) to taste

shishōsha N 死傷者 (*dead and wounded*) casualties

shishunki N 思春期 adolescence

shisō N 思想 thought, concept

shison N 子孫 descendant

shisso na ADJ 質素な simple, plain, frugal, rustic

shissoku saseru V 失速させる (車) (*car*) to stall

shita (ni) N (PREP, ADV) 下(に) below, under, bottom, lower

shita 舌 tongue

shita no ADJ 下の under

shitagaru V したがる (*be eager*) to want to do

shitagatte ADV, CONJ したがって accordingly, therefore

shitagau v 従う to obey, to conform, to accord

shitagi N 下着 underwear

shitai N 死体 corpse

... shitai v 〜したい to want

... shitakoto ga aru 〜したことがある have done something

shitamachi N 下町 downtown

shitashi'i ADJ 親しい intimate, familiar

shitate-ya N 仕立屋 tailor

shitei suru v 指定する to designate, to point out

shiteiseki N 指定席 reserved seat(s)

shiteki suru v 指摘する to indicate, to point out

... shitemoyoi VERBAL AUXILIARY 〜してもよい can, may

shiten N 支店 (office, shop) branch

shitetsu N 私鉄 private railroad

shitsu N 質 quality, nature

shītsu N シーツ bedsheet, sheet

shitsudo N 湿度 humidity

shitsugyō-chū no ADJ 失業中の unemployed

shitsuke N しつけ (manner, etiquette) training, discipline, upbringing

shitsumon N 質問 question

shitsurei N 失礼 impoliteness

shitsurei desu ga 失礼ですが Pardon me.

shitsurei na ADJ 失礼な rude, impolite

shitsuren N 失恋 disappointment in love, broken heart, lost love

shitteiru v 知っている to know

shitto N 嫉妬 jealousy

shiwaza N 仕業 (evil doing) act, deed

shiyakusho N 市役所 city office, city hall

... shiyō 〜しよう (提案) (suggestion) let's

shiyō N 私用 private use/business

shiyō N 仕様 spec(ification)

shiyō-chū no ADJ 使用中の (toilet, etc.) in use, occupied

shiyōdekiru ADJ 使用できる available

shiyōnin N 使用人 servant

shizen N 自然 nature

shizuka na ADJ 静かな still, quiet

shizumaru v 静まる to quiet/calm down

shizumeru v 沈める to sink it

shizumu v 沈む to sink

shō N ショー (*live performance*) show

shō N 賞 prize, reward

shōbai N 商売 trade, business

shōben o suru V 小便をする to urinate

shōbōsha N 消防車 fire engine

shōbōshi N 消防士 fire fighter

shobu N 勝負 match, contest

shobun suru V 処分する to dispose of, to deal with

shochi suru V 処置する to deal with

shōchishita ADJ 承知した OK, all right!

shōchō N 象徴 symbol

shōdaku suru V 承諾する to consent, to accept

shodō N 書道 calligraphy

shōgai N 障害 handicap, obstacle

shōgai N 生涯 life(long), for all one's life(time)

shōgaisha N 障害者 handicapped person

shōgakkō N 小学校 primary/elementary school

Shōgatsu N 正月 January; New Year

shōgi N 将棋 Japanese chess, shogi

shōgo N 正午 midday, noon

shōgyō N 商業 commerce, trade, business

shōhin N 商品 goods, (*sales*) product

shōhin N 賞品 (*object*) prize

shōhisha N 消費者 consumer

shōhizei N 消費税 consumption tax

shohō suru V 処方する (*medicine*) to prescribe

shohōsen N 処方箋 prescription

shōji N 障子 translucent sliding door, paper screen, shoji

shoji suru V 所持する to own

shōjiki na ADJ 正直な honest

shojo N 処女 (*female*) virgin

shōjo N 少女 young girl

shōkafuryō N 消化不良 indigestion

shōkai suru V 紹介する to introduce someone

shōkaki N 消火器 fire extinguisher

shōken N 証券 (*stock, bond*) security

shoki N 書記 secretary

shōkin N 賞金 prize money; reward

shokken N 食券 meal ticket

157

shokkidana N 食器棚 dish rack; cupboard

shōko N 証拠 proof, evidence

shokubutsu N 植物 plant

shokubutsuen N 植物園 botanic gardens

shokudō N 食堂 dining room; diner, eatery

shokudō-sha N 食堂車 dining car, diner

shokuen N 食塩 table salt

shokugo ni ADV 食後に after a meal

shokugyō N 職業 occupation, profession, job

shokuhin N 食品 food, foodstuffs, groceries

shokuji N 食事 meal

shokuminchi N 植民地 colony

shokumotsu N 食物 food(s)

shokuniku N 食肉 meat

shokupan N 食パン bread

shokureki N 職歴 professional experience

shokuryōhin N 食料品 food, foodstuffs, groceries

shokutaku N 食卓 dining table

shokuyoku N 食欲 appetite

shokuzen ni ADV 食前に before a meal

shōkyoku-teki na ADJ 消極的な negative; conservative

shomei N 署名 signature

shōmei N 照明 lighting

shōmeisho N 証明書 certificate

shōmei suru V 証明する to prove, to verify, to attest

shōmen N 正面 (*front side*) front, facade

shomotsu N 書物 book

shōnen N 少年 young boy

shōnika N 小児科 pediatrics

shōnin N 商人 merchant, trader

shōnin N 証人 witness

shōrai N 将来 in future

shori N 処理 managing, transacting, dealing with

shōri N 勝利 victory

shōron N 小論 essay

shorui N 書類 document

shōryaku suru V 省略する to abbreviate, to omit

shosai N 書斎 (*room*) study, library

shōsai N 詳細 details

shōsan suru V 賞賛する to admire, to praise

shoseki N 書籍 books, publications

shōsetsu N 小説 novel

shōsha N 勝者 winner, victor

shōsho N 証書 certificate

shōshō N, ADV 少々 a little

shōshō omachi kudasai 少々 お待ちください Please wait for a moment

shōshūzai N 消臭剤 deodorant

shōsoku N 消息 news, word (*from/of ...*)

shōtai suru V 招待する (*formally*) to invite

shōtaijō N 招待状 (*card*) invitation

shoten N 書店 bookshop, bookstore

shōten N 焦点 focus, focal point

shōten N 商店 shop, store

shōtengai N 商店街 shopping street(s), shopping area

shotoku N 所得 income

shōtotsu suru V 衝突する to collide

shōtsu N ショーツ (*short trousers*) shorts

shōyo N 賞与 bonus

shōyu N しょう油 (*salty*) soy sauce

shoyū suru V 所有する to have, to own, to possess

shoyūsha N 所有者 owner

shozai N 所在 whereabouts

shōzōga N 肖像画 portrait

shozoku suru V 所属する to belong to

shū N 週 week

shūbun-no-hi N 秋分の日 Autumnal Equinox Day

shuchō suru V 主張する to assert, to claim, to maintain

shūchū suru V 集中する to concentrate, to center (on)

shudan N 手段 ways, means, measures, steps

shūdan N 集団 group, collective body

shūdōin N 修道院 convent

shufu N 主婦 housewife

shūgeki suru V 襲撃する to attack, to charge, to raid

shugi N 主義 principle, doctrine, -ism

shūgi'in N 衆議院 House of Representatives

shūgō suru V 集合する (*as a group*) to congregate

shugyō N 修行・修業 (*getting one's*) training, ascetic practices

shūgyō jikan N 就業時間 working hours

shūha N 宗派 sect

shūhen N 周辺 circumference; environs

shuhin N 主賓 guest of honor

shūi N 周囲 circumference; surroundings

shūji N 習字 calligraphy

shujin N 主人 husband; host; master, owner

shujutsu N 手術 surgical operation, surgery

shūkaku suru V 収穫する to harvest, to reap

shūkan N 習慣 custom, practice

-shūkan SUFFIX 週間 (*counts weeks*)

shūki N 周期 (*length*) cycle

shūkin suru N 集金する to collect money

shukkin suru V 出勤する to go to work

shukōgei N 手工芸 handicraft

shukudai N 宿題 homework

shukuhakujo N 宿泊所 accommodation

shukujitsu, shukusaijitsu N 祝日, 祝祭日 national holiday

shūkyō N 宗教 religion

shūmatsu N 週末 weekend

shumi N 趣味 hobby, taste, interest, liking

shumoku N 種目 item, (*competition*) event

shunbun-no-hi N 春分の日 Vernal Equinox Day

shuniku N 朱肉 red ink pad

shunkan N 瞬間 (*instant*) moment

shūnyū N 収入 earnings, income

shuppan N 出版 publishing

shuppatsu N 出発 departure

shuppin suru V 出品する to exhibit; (*net auctions*) to sell

shūri suru V 修理する to fix, to repair

shurui N 種類 kind, type, sort

shūsen N 終戦 the end of a war

shūshi(-gō) N 修士(号) master's degree

shūshifu N 終止符 period, (*punctuation*) full stop

shūshinkei N 終身刑 life imprisonment

shushō N 首相 prime minister

shūshoku N 就職 getting a job, finding employment

shūshū N 収集 (*trash, etc.*) collecting; (*as one's hobby, for research, etc.*) collection

shūshū-ka N 収集家 collector

shusse N 出世 making a success in life

shusseki suru v 出席する to attend, to be present

shusshinchi N 出身地 (*one's*) hometown

shutchō suru v 出張する to make a business trip

shūten N 終点 terminus, last stop, destination

shuto N 首都 capital city

shutoken N 首都圏 Tokyo metropolitan area

shūtome N 姑 one's mother-in-law

shuyō na ADJ 主要な main, most important

shūzen N 修繕 repair

sō N 層 layer

sō desu そうです That's right, yes

soba N 側 near/close(-by), (be)side

soba N そば buckwheat noodles

soba-ya N そば屋 noodle shop

sōbetsukai N 送別会 (*reception*) farewell party

sobo N 祖母 grandmother

soboku na ADJ 素朴な simple, naive

sōchi N 装置 equipment, apparatus

sochira PRON そちら there, that way; that one (*of two*)

sōchō ni ADV 早朝に early in the morning

sodachi ga yoi/ii ADJ 育ちが良い well-bred

sodachi ga warui ADJ 育ちが悪い ill-bred

sōdai na ADJ 壮大な grand, great

sōdan suru v 相談する to consult, to talk over with

sodateru v 育てる (子供) (*child*) to raise, to bring up

sodatsu v 育つ (子供) (*child*) to grow up

sofā N ソファー couch, sofa

sofu N 祖父 grandfather

sofubo N 祖父母 grandparents

sofuto(wea) N ソフト(ウェア) (*computer*) software, application

sōgo no ADJ 相互の mutual, reciprocal

sōgō-teki na ADJ 総合的な composite, comprehensive, overall, synthesized

sōi N 相違 discrepancy, difference

sōji suru v 掃除する to clean, to sweep

sōjū suru v 操縦する to manipulate, to handle, to control, to operate

sōkan N 壮観 spectacles

soketto N ソケット (電気の) (*electric*) socket

sōkin suru v 送金する to remit

sokkuri no ADJ そっくりの exactly like

sokkusu N ソックス anklets, socks

soko N そこ there, that place

soko N 底 bottom

soko de ADV そこで there

soko ni ADV そこに there

sōko N 倉庫 warehouse

sokoku N 祖国 homeland, mother country

sokonau v 損なう to damage

-soku SUFFIX 足 (*counts footwear*)

sokudo N 速度 speed

sokutatsu N 速達 special delivery, express (*mail*)

somatsu na ADJ 粗末な crude, coarse, poor

sōmen N そうめん thin white wheat-flour noodles

someru v 染める to dye

son, songai N 損, 損害 damage, harm, loss; disadvantage

son (o) suru v 損(を)する to lose, to suffer a loss

sonaeru v 備える to prepare, to fix, to furnish; to possess

sōnan suru v 遭難する (*a disaster*) to have an accident; (*a ship/train*) to be wrecked

sonkei N 尊敬 respect

son'na ADJ そんな such, that kind of

sono aida ni ADV その間に meanwhile

sono go ADV その後 afterwards, later, after that, since then

sono hito その人 that person

sono kekka ADV その結果 therefore

sono koro wa ADV その頃は (at) that time, then, (in) those days

sono mama no ADJ そのまま の intact

sono ta no ADJ その他の the other

sono toki ADV その時 at that time

sono tōri ADV その通り exactly! just so!

sono uchi ADV そのうち soon, before long, sometime in the future

sono ue ADV その上 besides, further, additional, moreover

sono yō ni ADV そのように like that, that way

sonshitsu N 損失 a loss

sonzai suru V 存在する to exist

sora N 空 sky

sorasu V 逸らす to dodge, to turn aside; to warp it

sore PRON それ that one/matter, it

sore de CONJ それで and (*then/so/also*)

sore demo CONJ それでも still, yet, even so

sore dewa mata それではまた see you later!

sore hodo CONJ それほど to that extent, so

sore kara CONJ それから and (*then*); after that, since then

sore made ni CONJ それまでに by them

sore nano ni ADV それなのに nevertheless, and yet

sore ni ADV それに moreover, in addition

sore ni mo kakawarazu ADV それにもかかわらず nevertheless

sore to mo CON それとも or, or else

sore yue ni ADV それゆえに therefore

sorezore PRON, ADV それぞれ each, respectively, severally

sōridaijin N 総理大臣 prime minister

sōritsu N 創立 establishment

soroeru V 揃える to put in order; to collect; to complete a set

soru V 剃る to shave

sōryo N 僧侶 Buddhist priest

sōsa suru V 操作する to operate, to handle

sōsaku N 創作 creation

sōsaku suru V 捜索する to search, to investigate

sosen N 祖先 ancestor

sōsharu nettowāku sābisu (SNS) N ソーシャルネットワークサービス (SNS) Social Network Services

soshiki N 組織 system, setup, structure, organization

sōshiki N 葬式 funeral

soshite N そして and then

soshō N 訴訟 lawsuit

sosogu V 注ぐ to pour

soto N 外 outside, outdoors

sotogawa N 外側 outside

sotsugyō suru V 卒業する to graduate

sou v 沿う to run along, to follow

sōzō suru v 想像する to imagine

sōzōshi'i ADJ 騒々しい noisy

su N 酢 vinegar

su N 巣 nest

subarashi'i ADJ すばらしい wonderful, splendid

... subeki de aru VERBAL AUXILIARY 〜すべきである ought to, should

suberu v すべる to slide, to slip, to skate

subesubeshita ADJ すべすべした (*surfaces*) smooth, glossy, slippery

subete PRON 全て all

subete no ADJ 全ての every, whole, all of

sude ni ADV すでに already; long before/ago

sūgaku N 数学 mathematics

sugata N 姿 form, figure, shape

sugi N 杉 cryptomeria, Japanese cedar

sugiru v 過ぎる to pass, to exceed

sugoi ADJ すごい wonderful, swell, terrific; fierce, ghastly, uncanny

sugosu v 過ごす (*time*) to pass

sugu ni ADV すぐに in a moment, right away, immediately, soon; directly

sugu soba no すぐそばの ADJ close to, nearby

suidō N 水道 water system, water service, plumbing

suiei N 水泳 swimming

suigyū N 水牛 (*water*) buffalo

suiheisen N 水平線 (*sea*) horizon

suijun N 水準 (*standard*) level

suika N スイカ watermelon

suimasen, sumimasen すいません, すみません excuse me; sorry; thank you

suisei N 彗星 comet

suisei no ADJ 水性の water-based

suisen N 推薦 recommendation

suisen-toire N 水洗トイレ flush toilet

suisō N 水槽 water tank

suisoku suru v 推測する to guess, to surmise

Suisu N スイス Switzerland

suitchi N スイッチ switch

suitchi o ireru/kiru v スイッチを入れる/切る to turn/ switch it on/off

sui-yōbi N 水曜日 Wednesday

suizokukan N 水族館 aquarium

sūji N 数字 figure, number

sukāfu N スカーフ scarf

sukāto N スカート skirt

sukēto N スケート skate(s); skating

suki V 好き is liked; to like

sukī N スキー ski, skiing

sukima N すき間 crack; opening; opportunity

sukkari ADV すっかり completely, all

sukoshi ADV 少し (*slightly*) bit

sukoshizutsu 少しずつ bit by bit, little by little, gradually

Sukottorando N スコットランド Scotland

Sukottorando(-jin) no ADJ スコットランド(人)の Scottish, Scot

suku V 空く to get empty/clear

sukunai ADJ 少ない (*not much*) few, little

sukunakunaru V 少なくなる to lessen, to reduce

sukunakutomo ADV 少なくとも at least

sukurīn N スクリーン(映画) (*movie*) screen

suku'u V 救う to help, to rescue, to save

suku'u V すくう to scoop

sumai N 住まい residence

sumasu V 済ます to finish off

sumāto na ADJ スマートな slender; smart, stylish, fashionable

sumātofon N スマートフォン smartphone

sumi N 墨 ink

sumi N 炭 charcoal

sumimasen INTERJ すみません Thank you.; Excuse me.; Sorry.

sumō N 相撲 (*traditional Japanese wrestling*) sumo

sumu V 住む (*stay in a place*) to live

suna N 砂 sand

sunao na ADJ 素直な docile, gentle, obedient, meek

sune N すね shin, leg

supaisu N スパイス spice

supaiwea N スパイウェア (*computer*) spyware

sūpāmāketto N スーパーマーケット supermarket

supamu mēru N スパムメール junk mail, spam, e-mail spam

Supein N スペイン Spain

Supein(-jin) no ADJ スペイン(人)の Spanish
supīchi N スピーチ speech
supīdo N スピード speed
supīkā N スピーカー (loud) speaker
suponjikēki N スポンジケーキ sponge cake
supōtsu N スポーツ sports
suppai ADJ すっぱい sour
sūpu N スープ broth, soup
supūn N スプーン spoon
supuringu N スプリング (metal part) spring
suri N すり pickpocket
surippa N スリッパ slippers
surippu N スリップ (petticoat, underskirt) slip
suru V する to do, to perform an action, to play
suru V 擦る to rub
suru V 刷る to print
... suru koto ga dekiru ～することができる to be able to
... suru koto o kyokasareru ～することを許可される to be allowed to
... suru koto o shōdaku suru ～することを承諾する to agree to do something
... suru tame no/ni PREP ～するための/に for
... suru toki ni/wa CONJ ～する時に/は when, at the time
... suru tsumori V ～するつもり (intend) to mean
... suru yoyū ga aru V ～する余裕がある to afford
surudoi ADJ 鋭い sharp
sushi N 寿司 sushi
suso N 裾 hem
susumeru V 勧める to recommend, to encourage, to counsel; to persuade
susumu V 進む to go forward, to progress; to go too fast, to get ahead
sutā N スター (actor, pop star) star
sutaffu N スタッフ staff
sutajio N スタジオ studio
sutanpu N スタンプ (ink) stamp
sutēki N ステーキ steak
suteki na ADJ 素敵な lovely, nice, fine, swell
sutekki N ステッキ walking stick, cane
sutereo N ステレオ (sound/player) stereo
suteru V 捨てる to throw away/out, to dump
sutōbu N ストーブ stove, heater

sutōkā N ストーカー stalker

sutoraiki N ストライキ (*industrial action*) strike

sutoresu N ストレス stress, tension

sutoretchi N ストレッチ (*exercises*) stretch

sutorō N ストロー (*drink with*) straw

sūtsu N スーツ business suit

sūtsukēsu N スーツケース suitcase

su'u V 吸う to suck, to smoke, to sip, to breathe in

suwaru V 座る to sit (down)

suzume N 雀 sparrow

suzushi'i ADJ 涼しい cool

T

ta N 他 other(s)

ta, tanbo N 田, 田んぼ rice field

taba N 束 bundle, bunch

tabako N タバコ cigarette: *tabako o su'u* タバコをすう (*tobacco*) to smoke

tabemono N 食べ物 food

taberu V 食べる to eat

tabesaseru V 食べさせる to feed

tabi N 旅 trip, journey

tabitabi ADV たびたび often

tabō na ADJ 多忙な busy

tabun ADV 多分 perhaps; probably, likely

taburetto N タブレット tablet (PC)

tachiagaru V 立ち上がる to stand up, to rise

tachiba N 立場 viewpoint, standpoint, situation

tachidomaru V 立ち止まる to stop, to stand still

tachi'iri kinshi 立ち入り禁止 No Trespassing. Off Limits.

tachimachi ADV たちまち instantly, immediately, suddenly

tada no ADJ ただの only, just; (*for*) free, gratis, no fee/ charge; ordinary

tadaima ただいま I'm back!

tadashi CONJ ただし however; provided

tadashi'i ADJ 正しい right, proper, correct; honest

tadotadoshi'i ADJ たどたどしい halting, not smooth

taga N たが a barrel hoop

tagai ni ADV 互いに mutually, reciprocally, with each other

Tagarogu(-jin) no ADJ タガログ (人)の Tagalog

tagayasu V 耕す to plow

tāgetto N ターゲット object, target

tai N 鯛 sea bream, red snapper

Tai N タイ Thailand

Tai(-jin) no ADJ タイ(人)の Thai

taichō N 体調 (*physical condition*) tone

taichō ga ii/warui ADJ 体調 がいい/悪い is in good/poor health condition

taidan suru V 対談する to have a talk

taido N 態度 attitude, disposition, behavior

taifū N 台風 typhoon

taigaku suru V 退学する to leave school

taigū N 待遇 treatment, reception; pay, working conditions; official position

Taiheiyō N 太平洋 Pacific Ocean

taihen ADV 大変 terribly, very, exceedingly; seriously

taihen na ADJ 大変な serious; disastrous; enormous

taiho suru V 逮捕する to arrest

tai'iku N 体育 physical education, athletics

tai'ikukan N 体育館 gymnasium

tai'in suru V 退院する to leave hospital

taiji suru V 退治する to exterminate

taijū N 体重 body weight

taika N 退化 degeneration

taikai N 大会 mass meeting; convention; tournament

taikaku N 体格 body build, physique

taikakusen no ADJ 対角線の diagonal

taiken N 体験 personal experience

taiko N 太鼓 drum

taikō suru V 対抗する to oppose, to confront

taikutsu na ADJ 退屈な dull, boring

taiman na ADJ 怠慢な lazy, neglectful

taimatsu N たいまつ torch

taimingu N タイミング timing

taionkei N 体温計 (*clinical*) thermometer

taipu suru V タイプする to type

taira na ADJ 平らな level, (*even, flat*) plain

tairiku N 大陸 continent

tairyoku N 体力 stamina

tairyōseisan N 大量生産 mass production

taisho N 対処 dealing

taishō N 対象 object, target

taishō N 対称 symmetry

taishokkin N 退職金 retirement allowance

taishoku suru V 退職する to retire

taishokunegai N 退職願 letter of resignation

taishū N 体臭 body odor

taishū N 大衆 the general public, the masses

taisō N 体操 physical exercises

taisō ADJ, ADV たいそう very

taitei ADV たいてい usually

taitō no ADJ 対等の equal, equivalent

taitoru N タイトル title; (title) championship; caption, subtitle

taiwa N 対話 conversation, dialogue

taiya N タイヤ (for car) tire

taiyō N 太陽 sun

taizai N 滞在 visit

takai ADJ 高い high, tall; costly, expensive

takameru V 高める to lift, to raise

takarakuji N 宝くじ lottery

takaramono N 宝物 treasure

takasa N 高さ height

take N 竹 bamboo

taki N 滝 waterfall

takibi N 焚き火 bonfire

takkyū N 卓球 table tennis

tako N たこ octopus; callus, corn

tako N 凧 kite

takoage N 凧揚げ kite-flying

takokuseki no ADJ 多国籍の multinational

takoyaki N たこ焼き griddled dumplings with octopus bits

taku V 炊く(米) (rice) to cook

takuhaibin N 宅配便 delivery service

takumashi'i ADJ たくましい (body) strong, robust; (will) strong

takumi na ADJ 巧みな skillful

takuramu V 企む to plan, to scheme, to plot

takusan no ADJ たくさんの lots of, many, much

takushī N タクシー taxi

takuwae N 蓄え store, reserve, savings, stock

takuwaeru v 蓄える to save up, to hoard, to amass

tama n 玉/球 ball

tama n 弾 bullet

tamago n 卵 egg

tamanegi n 玉ねぎ onion

tamashi'i n 魂 soul, spirit

tamatama ADV たまたま occasionally

tamerau v ためらう to hold back, to hesitate

tameru v 貯める (*money*) to save

tameshi ni ADV 試しに as a trial/test

tamesu v 試す to test, to try

tāminaru n ターミナル terminal

taminzoku no ADJ 多民族の multiracial

tamotsu v 保つ to keep, to save

tana n 棚 shelf, rack

Tanabata n 七夕 (*7 July*) the Festival of the Weaver Star

tanbo n 田んぼ rice fields

tandoku n 単独 alone

tane n 種 seed

tango n 単語 word(s), vocabulary

Tango-no-sekku n 端午の節句 (*5 May*) Boys' Festival

tani, tanima n 谷, 谷間 valley

tan'i n 単位 unit

tanin n 他人 outsider, stranger; others

tanjikan n 短時間 short time, a moment

tanjōbi n 誕生日 birthday, date of birth: *Tanjōbi Omedetō* 誕生日おめでとう Happy Birthday!

tanjun na ADJ 単純な simple; simplehearted, simpleminded

tanka n 単価 unit cost, unit price

tanka n 担架 stretcher, litter

tanki n 短期 short period

tankidaigaku n 短期大学 junior college, two-year college

tanmatsu n 端末 (*computer*) terminal

tan ni ADV 単に merely

tan'nin n 担任 (*teacher*) in charge

tanomu v 頼む (非公式に) (*informally*) to request, to beg; to rely on, entrust with

tanoshi'i ADJ 楽しい pleasant, enjoyable

tanoshimi n 楽しみ pleasure, delight

tanoshimu v 楽しむ to enjoy oneself, to have fun

tanpan N 短パン (*short trousers*) shorts

tanpenshōsetsu N 短編小説 (*novel*) short story

tansha N 単車 motorcycle

tansho N 短所 shortcoming, fault, weak point

tansu N たんす chest of drawers

tantei N 探偵 detective

tantō suru V 担当する to take charge of

tantōsha N 担当者 person in charge, responsible person

tanuki N タヌキ raccoon dog

taoreru V 倒れる to fall down, to tumble, to collapse

taoru N タオル towel

taosu V 倒す to knock down, to overthrow

tappuri ADV たっぷり fully, more than enough

tara N タラ (*fish*) cod

tarasu V 垂らす to dangle, to drop, to spill

tareru V 垂れる to hang down, to dangle; to drip

tariru V 足りる to be enough/ sufficient, to suffice

taru N 樽 barrel, keg, cask

tashika na ADV 確かな safe, sure, certain

tashika ni ADV 確かに indeed, surely; for sure, undoubtedly

tashikameru V 確かめる to check, to verify

tassei suru V 達成する to attain, to reach, to accomplish

tassha na ADJ 達者な healthy; skillful, expert, good at

tashō ADJ 多少 (*large and/ or small*) number, quantity, amount

tashō no ADV 多少の more or less; somewhat; some

tasu V 足す to add

tasū N 多数 large number; majority

tasukaru V 助かる to be saved; to be relieved

tasukeru V 助ける to assist, to help; to save

tasukete INTERJ 助けて help!

tatakau V 戦う to fight; to make war/game

tataku V 叩く to strike, to hit; to knock

tatami N 畳 tatami (mat)

tatamu V たたむ to fold up

tatchipaneru N タッチパネル touch panel, touchscreen

tate no ADJ 縦の vertical

tatekaeru V 建替える to rebuild

tatemae N 建て前 principle, policy

tatemono N 建物 building

tateru V 建てる to build, to erect, to rise; to establish

tatoe CONJ たとえ even if

tatoe 例え N an example, an instance; a simile, an analogy

tatoeba ADV 例えば such as, for example

tatsu V 立つ to stand (up)

tatsu V 発つ (*for a far place*) to leave

tatsu V 断つ to stop; to cut off

tatta ADJ たった just, merely, only

tatta hitotsu no ADJ たった一つ の sole, only

tatta ima ADV たった今 just now; in (*just*) a minute

tatta no ADJ たったの just, only, merely

tatta...dake ADJ たった〜だ け only

tayori N 便り communication, correspondence, a letter, news

tayori nai ADJ 頼りない undependable, unreliable

tayoru V 頼る to rely on, to depend on

tazuna N 手綱 reins

tazuneru V 尋ねる to ask about, to enquire

tazuneru V 訪ねる to go around, to visit, to stop by

te N 手 hand

tearai N 手洗い toilet, restroom

teate N 手当て treatment; reparation, provision; allowance

tebukuro N 手袋 gloves

tēburu N テーブル table

tegakari N 手掛かり a hold, a place to hold on; a clue

tegami N 手紙 letter

tegata N 手形 note, bill

tegoro na ADJ 手ごろな (値段) (*price*) reasonable

teguchi N 手口 (*doing bad things*) way, trick

tehai N 手配 arrangements, planning

tehon N 手本 model, example

teian N 提案 suggestion

teian suru V 提案する to suggest

teiden N 停電 power failure/ outage

teido N 程度 degree, level

teika N 定価 fixed/set price

teiketsuatsu N 低血圧 low blood pressure

teikiatsu N 低気圧 (*barometric*) low pressure

teikiken N 定期券 (*commuter ticket*) pass, season ticket

teikō N 抵抗 resistance

teikyō N 提供 offering

teinei na ADJ ていねいな polite; careful

teiryūjo N 停留所 (バス, 電車) (*bus, train*) stop

teisai N 体裁 appearance, get-up, form, format, layout

teisei suru V 訂正する to correct

teisha suru V 停車する (*a vehicle*) to stop

teishi suru V 停止する to suspend

teishoku N 定食 set meal

teishu N 亭主 (*my*) husband

teishutsu N 提出 handing out, submission

tejina N 手品 (*tricks*) jugglery, magic

tejun N 手順 order, procedure, program

teki N 敵 enemy

tekido na ADJ 適度な reasonable, moderate

tekikaku na ADJ 適格な qualified, eligible

tekisetsu na ADJ 適切な appropriate, fitting, suitable

tekisuto N テキスト textbook

tekisutofairu N テキストファイル (*computer*) text file

tekitō na ADJ 適当な suitable, proper; irresponsible, haphazard, random, half-hearted

tekkyō N 鉄橋 iron bridge

tekubi N 手首 wrist

tema N 手間 (*taken up*) time; one's trouble

tēma N テーマ theme, topic

temae N 手前 this side (*of …*)

temaneki N 手招き beckoning

ten N 点 point, dot

ten N 天 sky, heaven

tenbōdai N 展望台 (*sightseeing*) observatory

tendon N 天丼 bowl of rice with tenpura on top

tengoku N 天国 paradise, heaven

tenimotsu N 手荷物 baggage, luggage

ten'in N 店員 sales assistant, shopkeeper; salesperson

tenisu N テニス tennis

tenji N 展示 display

tenjikai N 展示会 exhibition

tenjō N 天井 ceiling

tenkei-teki na ADJ 典型的な typical

tenken suru V 点検する to inspect

tenki N 天気 weather

tenkin N 転勤 job transfer, relocation

tenkiyohō N 天気予報 weather forecast

tenkō suru V 転校する to transfer to another school

tenmondai N 天文台 (*astronomical*) observatory

tenmongaku N 天文学 astronomy

ten'nen no ADJ 天然の natural

ten'nengasu N 天然ガス natural gas

ten'nō (heika) N 天皇 (陛下) (*His Majesty*) the Emperor

tenpo N 店舗 store, shop

tenpu fairu N 添付ファイル attached file/document

tenpura N 天ぷら deep-fried food, fritter, tempura

tenrankai N 展覧会 (*art*) exhibition

tensai N 天才 genius

tensei no ADJ 天性の natural, natural-born, instinctive

tenshi N 天使 angel

tenshu N 店主 shopkeeper

tensū N 点数 score, points

tento N テント tent

tentō N 店頭 store front

teppen N てっぺん top, highest part

teppō N 鉄砲 gun, rifle

tera N 寺 Buddhist temple

terasu V 照らす to illuminate, to light it up, to shine on

terebi N テレビ TV, television

terebi-bangumi N テレビ番組 TV show

teriyaki N 照り焼き (*fish, chicken, etc.*) teriyaki

tero N テロ terrorism

terorisuto N テロリスト terrorist

tesei no ADJ 手製の homemade, hand-crafted

tesūryō N 手数料 fee

tesuto N テスト test

tetsu N 鉄 iron, steel

tetsu no ADJ 鉄の iron, steel

tetsudau V 手伝う to help

tetsudō N 鉄道 railroad, railway

tetsugaku N 哲学 philosophy

tetsuya N 徹夜 staying up all night

tetsuzuki N 手続き formalities, procedure

tettei-teki ni ADV 徹底的に thoroughly

tezawari N 手ざわり texture

tezukuri no ADJ 手作りの homemade, made by hand

tī-shatsu N ティーシャツ T-shirt

... to CONJ 〜と and, with

... to hikaku suru V 〜と比較する compared with ...

... to omowareru V 〜と思われる to seem

... to onaji 〜と同じ same as ...

... to ... ryōhō 〜と〜両方 both ... and

to N 戸 door

tō N 党 (政治的な) (political) party

tō N 塔 tower

-tō SUFFIX 頭 (counts large animals)

tobaku N 賭博 gambling

tobasu V 飛ばす to let fly; to skip, to omit; to hurry

tobidasu V 跳び出す to jump out

tobidasu V 飛び出す to run/burst out; to protrude

toboshi'i ADJ 乏しい scarce, meager, scanty

tobu V 跳ぶ to jump

tobu V 飛ぶ to fly

tōbun N 当分 for the time being

tōchaku N 到着 arrival

tochi N 土地 land; ground, earth, soil

tochū de ADV 途中で on the way, halfway

tochūgesha 途中下車 (train) stopover

tōdai N 燈台 lighthouse

todana N 戸棚 cupboard, enclosed shelves

todokeru V 届ける to deliver

todoku V 届く to reach; to arrive

tōfu N 豆腐 beancurd, tofu

toge N とげ thorn

tōge N 峠 mountain pass

tōgei N 陶芸 ceramic art, ceramics

togu V 研ぐ to sharpen, to grind, (blade) to polish; (rice) to wash

toho N ADV 徒歩で on foot

tōhyō suru V 投票する to vote

tōi ADJ 遠い far-off, distant

toire N トイレ toilet, restroom

tōitsu suru v 統一する to unify, to standardize

tōji ADV 当時 at that time, then, in those days

tojiru v 閉じる to shut, to close

tōjitsu N 当日 the day in question, that very day, on the day

tōjō suru v 搭乗する to board

tōjō suru v 登場する to appear on stage

tōjōken N 搭乗券 boarding pass

tokage N トカゲ lizard

tokai N 都会 city, town

tokasu v 溶かす to melt/thaw/dissolve it

tokasu v とかす (*hair*) to comb

tokei N 時計 clock; watch

tokeru v 溶ける to melt, to thaw, to dissolve

toki N 時 time

tōki N 陶器 pottery, ceramics

tokidoki ADV 時々 from time to time, sometimes

tokku ni ADV とっくに long before

tokkyo N 特許 patent

tokkyū N 特急 (*train*) limited express

tokoro de CONJ ところで by the way, now

tokoro ga CONJ ところが but, however

toko-ya N 床屋 barber

tōku ADV 遠く the distance, far off; so as to be far/distant

tokui na ADJ 得意な proud, exultant

toku ni ADV 特に particularly, especially

tokubetsu na ADJ 特別な special

tokubetsu ni ADV 特別に especially

tokubetsu no ADJ 特別の extra, special, particular

tokuchō, tokushoku N 特徴, 特色 characteristics, special feature

tokushu na ADJ 特殊な special, particular

tokuten N 得点 points obtained, score

tomaru v 止まる to stop

tomaru v 泊まる to stay overnight

tomato N トマト tomato

tōmawari N 遠回り detour

tōmei na ADJ 透明な transparent, clear

tomeru v 止める to stop, to halt

tomeru v 留める (*firmly attaches*) to fasten

tōmin N 冬眠 hibernation

tomo, tomodachi N 友、友達 friend

tomo ni ADV 共に together

tomokaku ADV ともかく anyway, anyhow, at any rate

tomonau V 伴う to involve, to escort, to accompany

tōnan N 盗難 (*suffering*) theft

Tōnan Ajia N 東南アジア Southeast Asia

tonari ni ADV 隣に next to

tonbo N トンボ dragonfly

tondemonai ADJ とんでもない no way

tonikaku ADV とにかく anyway, anyhow

tonkatsu N とんかつ pork cutlet

ton-ya N 問屋 wholesale store

tōnyō-byō N 糖尿病 diabetes

tōnyū N 豆乳 soybean milk

tora N トラ tiger

toraeru V 捕らえる to capture

torakku N トラック truck

toranpu N トランプ cards

torēnā N トレーナー sweatshirt

torēningu N トレーニング (*exercise, etc.*) training, workout

tori N 鳥 bird

tōri N 通り street, avenue; passage

toriageru V 取り上げる to take up; to take away

toriatsukau V 取り扱う to handle, to deal with

torihiki N 取り引き transaction, deal, business, trade

tori'i N 鳥居 the gate to a Shinto shrine

torikaeru V 取り替える to replace

torikesu V 取り消す to cancel; to delete, to erase

tōrikosu V 通り越す to pass, to go past

toriniku N 鶏肉 (*meat*) chicken

torinozoku V 取り除く to rid, to get rid of

tōrinukete ADV 通り抜けて through, past

torishimariyaku N 取締役 managing director

torishimaru V 取り締まる to control, to manage, to supervise, to direct

tōroku suru V 登録する to register, to enroll

tōron N 討論 debate, discussion, dispute

toru v 取る to take; to take away, to remove; (*salt, sugar, etc.*) to pass

toru v 撮る (*a picture*) to take, to shoot

tōru v 通る to pass by/through

toryō N 塗料 paint

tōsaku N 盗作 plagiarism

tōsan N 倒産 bankruptcy

toshi N 都市 city

toshi N 年 age, year

tōshi N 投資 investment, investing

tōshi N 凍死 freezing to death, frost-killing

toshi no ADJ 都市の urban

toshi o totta 年を取った(人) (*person*) old

toshokan N 図書館 library

toshoshitsu N 図書室 (*room*) library

tōshu N 投手 (*baseball, etc.*) a pitcher

tōsō N 逃走 escape

tossa ni ADV とっさに in an instant, immediately

tōsutā N トースター toaster

tōsuto N トースト toast

totemo N とても very

totemo chīsana ADJ とても小さな tiny

totemo takusan no ADJ とてもたくさんの a large number of

totonoeru v 整える to arrange; to adjust; to prepare

totsuzen ADV 突然 suddenly

totte N 取っ手 handle

tōtte ADJ 通って via

Tōyō N 東洋 the East, the Orient

tozan N 登山 mountain-climbing

tōzayokin N 当座預金 current deposit, checking account

tōzen ADV 当然 naturally

tsuba N つば spit, saliva

tsubame N ツバメ (*bird*) swallow

tsubasa N 翼 wing

tsubo N つぼ jar, crock

tsubusu v つぶす to smash, to crush, to squish; to grind, to grate: **jikan o tsubusu** 時間をつぶす to kill time

tsubuyaku v つぶやく to murmur; (*Twitter*) to tweet

tsuchi N 土 earth, ground

tsūchi N 通知 report, notice

tsūchō N 通帳 passbook, bankbook

tsūgaku suru v 通学する to commute to school

tsugeguchi suru v 告げ口する
to tattle

tsugeru v 告げる to tell,
to inform

tsugi ni ADV 次に next, secondly

tsugi no ADJ 次の (*in line*)
next, the following

tsugō N 都合 circumstances,
convenience, opportunity

tsugō ga ii/warui ADJ 都合
がいい/悪い convenient/
inconvenient

tsugu v 注ぐ to pour it

tsui ni ADV ついに at last,
finally

tsuiraku suru v 墜落する (*a
plane*) to crash

tsuishi N 追試 makeup exam

tsuitachi N 一日 first day of
a month

tsuitate N 衝立 partition

tsuittā N ツイッター Twitter

tsuiyasu v 費やす to spend

tsūjiru v 通じる to get
through, to communicate;
to transmit; to connect;
to be understood

tsūjō no ADJ 通常の regular,
normal, usual, ordinary

tsūka N 通貨 currency

tsukaeru v 仕える to serve

tsukamaeru v 捕まえる to
catch, to seize, to arrest

tsukamu v つかむ to hold, to
grasp, to seize, to clutch

tsukareru v 疲れる to get
tired

tsukau v 使う to use; to spend
to employ; to handle

tsukeru v 点ける to switch on,
to turn (*something*) on

tsukeru v 漬ける to pickle;
to soak

tsukeru v 付ける to attach, to
stick on, to add; to apply

tsukeru v 着ける to put on,
to wear

tsuki N 月 moon

tsukiai 付き合い N association,
social company, friendship

tsūkin N 通勤 commuting to
work

tsukiru v 尽きる to come to an
end, to run out

tsuku v 着く to arrive

tsuku v 突く to stab, to thrust,
to poke, to push

tsukue N 机 table, desk

tsukue o naraberu v 机を並べ
る to lay the table

tsukuri-banashi N 作り話
(*stories*) fiction

tsukurou v 繕う to mend, to repair

tsukuru v 作る to create, to make, to produce, to prepare

tsuma N 妻 wife

tsumaranai ADJ つまらない boring, no good, trivial

tsumari ADV つまり after all; in short

tsumasaki N つま先 toe

tsumazuku v つまずく to stumble

tsume N 爪 (手、足) (*finger, toe*) nail; claw

tsumetai ADJ 冷たい (*the touch*) cold

tsumi N 罪 crime, sin, guilt, fault

tsumitatekin N 積立金 reserve fund

tsumu v 積む to pile it up, to accumulate it; to deposit

tsumu v 摘む to gather, to pluck, to clip, to pick

tsuna N 綱 rope, cord, cable

tsunagaru v つながる to be connected, to link

tsunagu v つなぐ to connect, to link, to tie

tsunami N 津波 tsunami

tsuneru v つねる to pinch

tsunezune N つねづね all the time, usually

tsuno N 角 (*of an animal*) horn

tsurai ADJ 辛い painful, cruel, hard, trying

tsurara N つらら icicle

tsuri N 釣り fishing

tsuri, tsurisen N つり、つり銭 (*small*) change

tsuribashi N つり橋 suspension bridge

tsurigane N つり鐘 (*temple, etc.*) big bell

tsurikawa N つり革 (*train, bus, etc.*) strap to hang on to

tsūro N 通路 passage(way), aisle, thoroughfare

tsuru v 釣る to fish

tsuru v 吊る (*by a line*) to hang it, to suspend, to string up

tsuru N つる vine

tsuru N 鶴 (*bird*) crane

tsurugi N 剣 sword

tsūshin N 通信 correspondence

tsūshinhanbai N 通信販売 mail order

tsūshinkōza N 通信講座 correspondence course

tsuta N つた ivy

tsutaeru v 伝える to report, to communicate; to transmit; to hand down

tsutanai ADJ つたない halting, unskillful, poor

tsutawaru v 伝わる to be passed on; to be communicated/transmitted; to be handed down

tsutome N 務め duty, role

tsutomeru v 勤める to be employed, to work; to work as

tsutomesaki N 勤め先 place of employment, one's office

tsutsumi N 包み pack, wrap

tsutsumu v 包む to wrap

tsutsushimu v 慎む to be discreet, to be careful; to refrain from

tsūyakusha N 通訳者 interpreter

tsuyoi ADJ 強い strong; brave

tsuyu N 梅雨 (*in Japan*) rainy season

tsuyu N 露 dew

tsuyu N つゆ (*clear*) soup

tsuzukeru v 続ける to continue it, to go on (with it)

tsuzukete ADV 続けて continuously, in succession

tsuzuki N 続き continuation, series, sequel

tsuzuku v 続く (*will continue*) to continue; to adjoin

tsuzuri N 綴り spelling

tsuzuru v 綴る to spell

U

uba N 乳母 nanny

ubau v 奪う to seize, to plunder

uchi N 家 house, home; family

uchiakeru v 打ち明ける to admit, to confess

uchiawase N 打ち合わせ prior arrangement, consultation, meeting

uchiawaseru v 打ち合わせる to hold a meeting/consultation

uchigawa N 内側 inside

uchikatsu v 打ち勝つ to overcome

uchiki na ADJ 内気な shy, timid

uchiwa N うちわ (*for cooling*) fan

uchū N 宇宙 universe, (*outer*) space

uchūhikōshi N 宇宙飛行士 astronaut

uchūsen N 宇宙船 spaceship

ude N 腕 arm

udedokei N 腕時計 wristwatch
udemae N 腕前 prowess, skill, ability
udon N うどん Japanese noodles
ue no ADJ 上の top
ue no hō e ADV 上のほうへ up, upward
ueru V 植える to plant, to grow
ueru V 飢える (*hunger*) to starve
ugoki N 動き movement, motion
ugoku V 動く to move
uirusu N ウイルス virus
uirusutaisaku-sofuto N ウイルス対策ソフト antivirus software
uisukī N ウイスキー whisky
ukabu V 浮かぶ to float
ukagau V 伺う [HUMBLE] to visit; to inquire; to hear
ukaru V 受かる to pass, to succeed
ukeireru V 受け入れる to accept
ukeru V 受ける to accept; to receive; to take; to get; to suffer, to incur
ukemotsu V 受け持つ to take/accept/have charge of
uketoru V 受け取る to accept, to get, to receive
uketsuke N 受付 acceptance;

information desk; receptionist
uketsukeru V 受け付ける to accept, to receive
ukiwa N 浮輪 (*swimming*) inner tube, float
ukiyo-e N 浮世絵 Japanese woodblock prints, Ukiyoe
uku V 浮く to float
uma N 馬 horse
umai ADJ うまい tasty, delicious
umai ADJ 上手い skillful, good
umareru V 生まれる to be born
umi N 海 ocean, sea
umibe N 海辺 (sea)shore, seaside
umu V 産む to give birth, to bear
un N 運 luck, fate
unagasu V 促す to stimulate, to urge (on)
unagi N うなぎ eel
unazuku V うなずく to nod
unchin N 運賃 (*transportation*) fare
undō N 運動 movement; exercise; sports; athletics
undōjō N 運動場 athletic field, playground
un'ei suru V 運営する to manage, to run
unga N 運河 canal

un ga ii/warui ADJ 運がいい/悪い lucky, unlucky

uni N ウニ *(roe)* sea urchin

unmei N 運命 destiny

unomi ni suru N 鵜呑みにする *(someone's words, talk, etc.)* to swallow, to believe every word someone says

unpan/unsō suru N 運搬/運送する *(goods)* to transport

unten suru V 運転する(車) *(a car)* to drive

untenshu N 運転手 driver

unwaruku ADV 運悪く unluckily

unyoku ADV 運良く luckily

uppun N うっぷん frustration, pent-up anger/discontent

ura N 裏 *(side)* reverse, back; lining; *(of foot/shoe)* sole

uragaeshi no ADJ 裏返しの inside-out

uragaesu V 裏返す to flip over, to turn over

uragiru V 裏切る to betray, to double-cross

uramu V 恨む to begrudge, to resent

uranai N 占い fortune-telling

urayamashi'i ADJ うらやましい enviable; envious

urayamashisō na ADJ うらやましそうな envious

ureru V 売れる to sell, to be in demand; to thrive; to be popular; saleable

ureshi'i ADJ うれしい delightful, pleasant, wonderful

ureshiku omou V うれしく思う to be glad

uriba N 売り場 *(shop)* counter, stand; shop, store

urikire N 売り切れ sold out

urimono N 売りもの for sale

uroko N うろこ *(on a fish)* scales

urotsuku V うろつく to hang around

uru V 売る to sell

urūdoshi N うるう年 leap year

urusai ADJ うるさい noisy, annoying

usagi N うさぎ rabbit, hare

ushi N 牛 ox, oxen; cow, cattle

ushiro N 後ろ back, rear, tail

ushiro kara tsuitekuru 後ろからついてくる to follow behind

ushiromuki ni ADV 後ろ向きに backward

uso o tsuku V 嘘をつく to lie, to tell a falsehood

usotsuki N 嘘つき liar

183

usui ADJ 薄い thin, pale, weak

uta N 歌 song

utagau V 疑う to doubt, to suspect

utau V 歌う to sing, to chant

utouto suru V うとうとする to drowse, to doze

utsu V 撃つ to shoot, to fire

utsu V 打つ to strike, to hit, to hammer; (*keyboard*) to type

utsukushi'i ADJ 美しい beautiful

utsumuku V うつむく to look down, to hang one's head

utsushi N 写し copy

utsusu V 写す to copy; to take a picture of; to project a picture

uttaeru V 訴える to accuse, to sue

uttori suru V うっとりする to be fascinated/spellbound, to be enchanted

uttōshi'i ADJ うっとうしい gloomy, dismal, dreary

uwagaki suru V 上書きする to overwrite

uwagi N 上着 coat, jacket

uwaki o suru V 浮気をする to be unfaithful, to have an (*extramarital*) affair

uwamawaru V 上回る to exceed

uwasa N うわさ rumor, gossip

uyamau V 敬う to revere, to respect

uzu, uzumaki N うず, うず巻き whirlpool

uzura N ウズラ quail

W

wa N 輪 circle; wheel; link; ring; loop

-wa (-pa) SUFFIX 羽 (*counts birds or rabbits*)

wadai N 話題 topic, subject

wafū N 和風 Japanese style

wafuku N 和服 Japanese clothes; kimono

wagamama na ADJ わがまま な selfish

wagashi N 和菓子 Japanese cakes/sweets

waifai N ワイファイ Wi-Fi

wairo N わいろ bribe(ry); graft

waishatsu N ワイシャツ shirt

wakai ADJ 若い young

wakai suru V 和解する to be reconciled

wakamono N 若者 (*young person*) youth

wakareru v 別れる to have a breakup (with), to separate

wakariyasui ADJ 分かりやすい clear, easy to understand

wakaru v 分かる to clear; to understand; to find out; to have good sense

wakasa N 若さ (*state of being young*) youth

wakasu v 沸かす (*water*) to boil

wake N 訳 reason; meaning

wakemae N 分け前 portion, share

wakeme N 分け目 dividing line, (*in hair*) part(ing)

wakeru v 分ける (*split*) to separate, to divide

waki N 脇 side

wakimizu N 湧き水 (*water*) spring

wakkusu N ワックス wax

waku v 沸く (*water*) to boil

waku v 湧く to gush, (*courage, hope*) to spring forth

waku N 枠 frame, framework

wakuchin N ワクチン vaccine

wakusei N 惑星 planet

wākusuteshon N ワークステーション workstation

wakuwaku suru v わくわくする to be thrilled/excited

wan N 湾 bay

wan N 碗 bowl

wani N ワニ crocodile, alligator

wanpaku na ADJ わんぱくな naughty

wanpīsu N ワンピース (*one-piece*) dress

warau v 笑う to laugh, to smile

wareme N 割れ目 crack, crevice, gap

waremono N われ物 fragile

wareru v 割れる to crack; to split

wareware no PRON 我々の our

wari to ADV わりと relatively, comparatively

wariai N 割合 rate, percentage

waribiki N 割引 discount

waru v 割る to divide, to split; to break; to dilute

warui ADJ 悪い bad, wicked, (*morally*) wrong

warujie N 悪知恵 cunning, craft

warukuchi, waruguchi N 悪口 (*verbal*) abuse, slander

185

warumono N 悪者 bad guy/ fellow, villain, scoundrel

wasabi N ワサビ horse radish

washi N ワシ eagle

washi N 和紙 Japanese paper

washitsu N 和室 Japanese-style room

washoku N 和食 Japanese food

wasuremono N 忘れ物 leaving something behind; (*forgetfully*) a thing left behind

wasureppoi ADJ 忘れっぽい forgetful

wasureru V 忘れる to forget

wata N 綿 cotton

watashi no PRON 私の my, mine

watashi o PRON 私を me

watashi wa PRON 私は I

watashitachi o PRON 私たち を us

watashitachi wa PRON 私た ちは we

watasu V 渡す to hand over; to ferry

wayaku N 和訳 translation into Japanese

wazato ADV わざと deliberately, on purpose

wazawai N 災い misfortune, mishap, disaster, calamity

wazawaza ADV わざわざ especially; purposely

wazuka ADV わずか bit; a few, a little

wazuka ni ADV わずかに slightly

wazuka no ADV わずかの a little, slight

wazurawashi'i ADJ わずらわし い troublesome; complicated

webuburauza N ウェブブラウザ (*Internet*) web browser

weburogu N ウェブログ weblog

webusaito N ウェブサイト website

webu shoppingu N ウェブシ ョッピング (*Internet*) web shopping

Y

ya N 矢 arrow

yabai ADJ やばい [VERY INFORMAL] (*will get you into trouble*) dangerous; awesome

yaban na ADJ 野蛮な barbarous, barbarian, savage

yabō N 野望 ambition

yabo na ADJ 野暮な rustic, inelegant

yabuisha N ヤブ医者 quack doctor

yabuku V 破く (*bursts*) to tear; to frustrate; to violate; to defeat

yaburu V 破る to tear, to rip

yachin N 家賃 house rent

yado, yado-ya N 宿, 宿屋 inn

yagai N 野外 outdoors, in the field

yagate ADV やがて before long; in time

yagi N 山羊 goat

yahari, yappari ADV やはり, やっぱり also; either; after all; just as we/I thought!

yakamashii ADJ やかましい noisy, boisterous; annoying; overly strict, demanding

yakan ni ADV 夜間に at night

yake ni ADV やけに excessively, unbearably, terribly

yake(kuso) N やけ(くそ) desperation

yakedo N 火傷 (*injury*) burn

yakeru V 焼ける to burn; to be baked

yakeru V やける to be jealous, to envy

yakimochi N やきもち jealousy

yakin N 夜勤 nightwork

yakiniku N 焼肉 grilled meat

yakisoba N 焼きそば fried Chinese noodle

yakitori N 焼き鳥 skewered grilled chicken, yakitori

yakkai na ADJ 厄介な troublesome, annoying

yakkyoku N 薬局 drugstore, pharmacy

yaku V 焼く to bake, to fry, to grill, to roast, to toast

yaku N 約 (*approximately*) about

yaku N 訳 translation

yaku ni tatanai 役に立たない useless, not useful

yakudatsu, yaku ni tatsu 役立つ, 役に立つ V to be useful

yakuhin N 薬品 drugs; chemicals

yakume N 役目 duty, function, role, part

yakunin N 役人 (政府) (*government*) officials

yakusha N 役者 actor

yakusho N 役所 government office

yakusoku N 約束 promise, agreement, appointment, engagement, date

yakuwari N 役割 role

yakuza N やくざ gangster, hoodlum

yakyū N 野球 baseball

yakyūjō N 野球場 ball park, (*baseball*) stadium

yama N 山 mountain; pile

yamabiko N やまびこ echo

yamanobori N 山登り mountain-climbing

yamashi'i ADJ やましい ashamed of oneself; has guilty feeling

yameru V やめる to stop, to cease; to quit

yameru V 辞める to resign, to quit

yamete やめて don't! stop it!

yamu V 止む to stop

yamu-o-enai ADJ やむを得ない unavoidable

yane N 屋根 roof

yanushi N 家主 landlord, landlady

yao-ya N 八百屋 greengrocer, vegetable market

yarikata N やり方 way, method, process, manner

yarinaosu V やり直す to redo it, to do it over (*again*)

yaru V やる to give; to send; to do

yasai N 野菜 vegetable

yasashi'i ADJ やさしい gentle, kind; easy, simple

yasei no ADJ 野性の wild, not cultivated

yashinau V 養う to grow, to cultivate

yasui ADJ 安い cheap, low(-*priced*)

yasumi N 休み rest, break, pause; vacation, holiday

yasumono N 安物 cheap stuff

yasumu V 休む to rest, to relax; to go to bed, to sleep

yasuri N やすり file, rasp

yasu'uri N 安売り (*reduced prices*) sale

yatou V 雇う to hire, to employ

yatsuatari suru V 八つ当たりし する to take out on

yattekuru V やってくる to come, to come along

yatto ADV やっと at last; barely, with difficulty

yawarakai ADJ やわらかい soft; mild

yaya ADJ やや a little, slightly

yayakoshi'i ADJ ややこしい complicated; puzzling; tangled; troublesome

yō na SUFFIX, ADJ 様な seem(ing) to be

yō ni SUFFIX, ADJ 様に (*so as to be*) like

yoake N 夜明け dawn

yobareteiru V 呼ばれている to be called, named

yōbi N 曜日 day of the week

yobi no ADJ 予備の reserve, spare

yobidasu V 呼び出す to call, to summon

yobikō N 予備校 prep school, cram school

yobō N 予防 precaution, prevention

yōbō N 要望 strong desire

yobōsesshu N 予防接種 vaccination

yobu V 呼ぶ to call; to name; to summon; to invite

yobun no ADJ 余分の extra

yōchi na ADJ 幼稚な childish

yōchien N 幼稚園 kindergarten

yōdai N 容態 (*patient*) health condition

yodare N よだれ drool

yofukashi suru N 夜更かしする to stay up late

yōfuku N 洋服 (*Western-style*) clothes

yōgaku N 洋楽 Western-style music

yōgashi N 洋菓子 western cakes/sweets

yogen N 予言 prediction

yōgisha N 容疑者 a suspect

yōgo N 用語 (*technical word, etc.*) (*special*) term

yogore N 汚れ dirt, smudge, blot, blotch

yogoreru V 汚れる to get soiled, to be smudged

yogosu V 汚す to soil, to dirty, to stain

yōgu N 用具 tools, implements, instruments, kit

yōguruto N ヨーグルト yogurt

yohaku N 余白 (*space*) margin, blank

yōhin N 用品 utensils, appliances, supplies, necessities

yohō N 予報 forecast, prediction

yohodo, yoppodo ADV よほど、よっぽど considerably, a good deal

yoi ADJ 良い well, good

yōi N 用意 preparation; caution

yōi suru V 用意する to arrange, to prepare

yōji N 用事 (*something to do*) business, errand

yōji N 楊枝 toothpick

yōji N 幼児 infant

yōjin suru V 用心する to take care, to use caution

yōjinbukai ADJ 用心深い cautious, careful

yojinoboru V よじ登る to climb onto

yōjo N 養女 adopted daughter

yokan N 予感 premonition, foreboding

yokei na ADJ 余計な superfluous, uncalled-for

yōken N 用件 (*something to tell*) business

yokeru V 避ける to avoid, to keep away from

yōki N 容器 container, receptacle

yōki na ADJ 陽気な cheerful, bright, lively

yokin suru V 預金する (*put money in the bank*) to deposit

yokinkōza N 預金口座 bank account

yokintsūchō N 預金通帳 bankbook

yokkyūfuman N 欲求不満 frustration

yoko N 横 side

yoko ni naru V 横になる to lie down

yokogiru V 横切る to cross, to go over

yokoku N 予告 advance notice

yōkoso INTERJ ようこそ welcome!

yoku dekimashita INTERJ よくできました well done!

yokuaru ADJ よくある common, frequent

yokubari na ADJ 欲張りな greedy

yokubaru V 欲張る to be greedy

yokubō N 欲望 greed; desire, want

yoku-getsu N 翌月 the following month, the next month

yoku-jitsu N 翌日 the following day, the next day

yokushitsu N 浴室 bathroom

yoku-shū N 翌週 the following week, the next week

yokusō N 浴槽 bathtub

yoku-toshi N 翌年 the following year, the next year

yōkyū suru V 要求する to demand, to request, to require

yome N 嫁 bride

yomu V 読む to read

yon NUM 四 four

yonaka N 夜中 middle of the night

yonbun no ichi 四分の一 quarter

yonjū NUM 四十 forty

yo-no-naka N 世の中 the world at large, society

yopparai N 酔っ払い (*person*) drunk

... yori ADV 〜より than

... yori mushiro ADV 〜よりむしろ rather than

... yori ōku ADV 〜より多く more than

yori sukunaku ADV より少なく (*smaller amount*) less than

... yori ue ni ADV, PREP 〜より上に above

yori warui ADJ より悪い worse

yori yoi ADJ よりよい better

yorokobu V 喜ぶ to be glad/happy, to delight; to rejoice

yoron N 世論 public opinion

Yōroppa N ヨーロッパ Europe

yoroshiku (onegai-shimasu) よろしく(お願いします) Kind/Best regards; Thank you

yoru N 夜 night

yoruosoku ADV 夜遅く late at night

yosan N 予算 budget

yosen N 予選 preliminary; primary

yōshi N 用紙 (*fill out*) form

yōshi N 養子 adopted child

yōshoku N 洋食 foreign/Western food

yōshoku N 養殖 raising, farming, culture

yoshū N 予習 preparatory study

yosō suru V 予想する to expect, to anticipate, to presume

yoso'ou V 装う to pretend

yōsu N 様子 circumstances; aspect; appearance, look

yōsuru ni V 要するに in summary, to sum it up, in short; in effect; after all

yotei N 予定 program, schedule, plan

yōten N 要点 gist, point

you V 酔う to get drunk/seasick/airsick

yowai ADJ 弱い weak; frail; poor at

yowami N 弱み weakness, weak point

yoyaku N 予約 reservation, booking; subscription, appointment

yōyaku N 要約 a summary

191

yūbe N ゆうべ last night

yubi N 指 finger

yūbin N 郵便 post, mail

yūbinbangō N 郵便番号 zip code; ZIP Code

yūbinbutsu N 郵便物 mail, post

yūbinkyoku N 郵便局 post office

yūbō na ADJ 有望な promising

yubune N 湯船 bathtub

yūdachi N 夕立 (*during evening*) sudden shower

yudan suru V 油断する to let one's guard down

yudaneru V 委ねる to entrust, to commit

yuderu V 茹でる (*food*) to boil

yūenchi N 遊園地 amusement park

yūfuku na ADJ 裕福な well off, wealthy

yūga na ADJ 優雅な elegant

yugamu V 歪む to get distorted/warped

yūgata N 夕方 evening, twilight

yūguredoki N 夕暮れ時 dusk

yūhan, yūmeshi N 夕飯 supper, dinner

yūhi N 夕日 setting sun

yūhodō N 遊歩道 promenade

yuigon, yuigon-jō/-sho N 遺言, 遺言状/書 a will, testament

yui'itsu no ADJ 唯一の (*only one*) single

yūjin N 友人 friend

yūjō N 友情 friendship

yuka N 床 floor

yūkai N 誘拐 kidnap(ping)

yukai na ADJ 愉快な amusing, comical

yūkan N 夕刊 evening paper

yukata N 浴衣 (*in Japanese inn*) bathrobe, (*for summer*) cotton kimono

yuketsu N 輸血 blood transfusion

yuki N 雪 snow

yūki no aru ADJ 勇気のある brave, valiant

yūkiyasai N 有機野菜 organic vegetables

yukkuri ADV ゆっくり slowly

yūkō na ADJ 有効な valid, effective

yukuefumei N 行方不明 (*lost person*) missing

yūkyū no ADJ 有給の paid

yume N 夢 dream

yūmei na ADJ 有名な famous, well-known

yumi N 弓 (*violin*) bow

yūmoa N ユーモア humor, wit

yunifōmu N ユニフォーム (*of athlete, etc.*) uniform

yūnō na ADJ 有能な capable

yunyū N 輸入 import

yūrei N 幽霊 ghost

yureru V 揺れる to shake, to sway, to swing, to roll

yuri N ユリ lily

yūri na ADJ 有利な profitable, advantageous

yuri ugokasu V 揺り動かす to swing

yurui ADJ ゆるい loose, not tight

yurusu V 許す to forgive; to allow, to permit

yūryō no ADJ 有料の (*not free*) paid, charged

yūryoku na ADJ 有力な strong, powerful, influential

yūsen N 優先 priority

yūshi N 有志 volunteer, supporter, interested person

yūshi suru V 融資する to finance

yūshoku N 夕食 dinner, evening meal

yūshō suru V 優勝する (*the victory*) to win

yūshōsha N 優勝者 champion

yūshū na ADJ 優秀な excellent, superior

yushutsu N 輸出 export

yūsō N 郵送 mailing

yūsō seru V 郵送する to mail

yusō seru V 輸送する to transport

yūsōryō N 郵送料 postage

yutori ADJ ゆとり leeway, breadth of mind, space

yūzā-aidī N ユーザーID (*computer*) user ID

yūzai N 有罪 (*a crime*) guilty

yūzāmei N ユーザー名 user name

yūzū no/ga kiku ADV 融通の/が きく adaptable, versatile

yuzuru V 譲る to give up/in; to yield; to be inferior

Z

zabuton N 座布団 cushion

zaidan N 財団 a foundation

zaigen N 財源 financial resources

zaihō N 財宝 (*money, jewels, etc.*) treasures, riches

zaiko N 在庫 inventory

zaimoku N 材木 lumber, wood

zairyō N 材料 material, ingredient

zaisan N 財産 wealth, property, fortune

zakka N 雑貨 miscellaneous goods, sundries

zandaka N 残高 (*remaining money*) balance

zangyō N 残業 (*work*) overtime

zankoku na ADJ 残酷な cruel, brutal, harsh

zan'nen da 残念だ what a pity/shame!

zappi N 雑費 miscellaneous expenses

zaseki N 座席 seat

zasetsu suru V 挫折する to get frustrated, to fail

zashiki N 座敷 (*parlor*) tatami room, drawing room

zasshi N 雑誌 magazine

zassō N 雑草 weeds

zatsudan N 雑談 chat

zatsuon N 雑音 noise(s), static

zehi ADV ぜひ without fail, for sure

zeikan N 税関 customs

zeikin N 税金 tax

zeitaku na ADJ ぜいたくな luxurious

zekkōchō N 絶好調 best condition

Zen N 禅 (*Buddhism*) Zen

zenbu de ADV 全部で altogether, in total

zenchō N 前兆 omen, sign

zengo N 前後 before and after; ahead and behind; back and forth

zenhan N 前半 the first half

zen'i N 善意 goodwill

zen'in N, PRON 全員 everyone, all

zenmen N 前面 front

zenpō ni ADV 前方に forward, in front

zenrei N 前例 precedent, prior example

zenshin N 全身 the whole body, body as a whole

zenshin suru V 前進する to advance, to go forward

zenshu no ADJ 全種の every kind of

zentai ni ADV 全体に wholly, generally

zentai no ADJ 全体の entire, whole

zentei N 前提 premise

zenzen ADV 全然 completely, utterly, entirely, altogether; (*not*) at all, (*not*) ever

zero N 零 zero

zettai ni ADV 絶対に totally, absolutely

zō N 象 elephant

zō N 像 statue

zōka N 増加 raise, increase

zokugo N 俗語 slang

zonbun ni ADV 存分に as much as one likes

zōryō N 増量 (*quantity*) increase

zōsatsu suru V 増刷する (*publishing*) to reprint

zōsho N 蔵書 book collection, library

zuan N 図案 sketch, design

zubon N ズボン pants, trousers

zuga N 図画 drawing

zukai N 図解 illustration, diagram

zuibun ADV ずいぶん quite (*very*), awfully

zuiji ADV 随時 as needed, at any time as one likes

zunō N 頭脳 brains, head

zurugashikoi ADJ ずる賢い cunning, wily

zuruyasumi N ずる休み skipping school, playing hookey

zutsū N 頭痛 headache

zutto ADV ずっと directly; by far, much (*more*); all the way through, all the time

zūzūshi'i ADJ 図々しい brazen, shameless, pushy

English–Japanese

A

abacus N soroban そろばん

abalone N awabi あわび

abandon V suteru 捨てる

abbreviate V ryakusu 略す

abbreviation N ryakugo 略語, shōryaku 省略

abdomen N fukubu 腹部

abduct V yūkai suru 誘拐する

ability N nōryoku 能力, kiryō 器量, udemae 腕前; (*talent*) sainō 才能; (*proficiency*) jitsu-ryoku 実力

abject ADJ mijime na 惨めな, hisan na 悲惨な, zetsubō-teki na 絶望的な

able to ADJ ... suru koto ga dekiru 〜することができる

abnormal ADJ ijō na 異常な

aboard V *get aboard* noru 乗る; *put aboard* noseru 乗せる

abolish V haishi suru 廃止する; yameru 止める; (*destroy*) ... o horobosu 〜を滅ぼす

abolition N haiki 廃棄

abortion N datai 堕胎, (ninshin) chūzetsu (妊娠)中絶; ryūzan 流産

about PREP (*approximately*) yaku 約, ōso おおよそ, gúrai 位, hodo 程; (*a time*) ... goro (ni) 〜頃(に); (*concerning*) ... ni tsuite no 〜 ついての; (*regarding*) ... ni tsuite 〜について

above PREP ... yori ue ni 〜より 上に; (*the above*) ijō 以上

abrade V (*wear down*) suriherasu すり減らす; (*chafe*) iraira saseru イライラさせる

abridge V (*shorten*) tanshuku suru 短縮する; (*abate*) herasu 減らす

abroad ADV gaikoku de 外国で; káigai de 海外で

abrupt(ly) ADJ (ADV) totsuzen no (ni) 突然の(に); jōki no 上記 の, zenki no 前記の

absence N kesseki 欠席; (*from home*) rusu 留守

absent V kesseki suru 欠席する

197

absolute N (ADJ) zettaiteki (na) 絶対的(な); zettai (no) 絶対の

abstain v (stop) yameru 止める、(refrain from) tsutsushimu 慎む; (do not vote) kiken suru 棄権する、tatsu 断つ

abstention N kiken 棄権

abstract N (ADJ) chūshōteki (na) 抽象的(な); (summary) yōshi 要旨

absurd ADJ bakarashi'i 馬鹿らしい

abundant ADJ yutaka na 豊かな

abuse N warukuchi/guchi 悪口

abusive ADJ ranbō na 乱暴な、kuchigitanai 口汚い

AC, alternating current N kōryū 交流

academic ADJ akademikku アカデミック、gakumon 学問

academic ability N gakuryoku 学力

academy N gakkō 学校

accede v tsugu 継ぐ、dōi suru 同意する; accede to ... ni ō-jiru ～に応じる

accelerate v kasoku suru 加速する

accelerator N akuseru アクセル

accent N akusento アクセント

accept v ukeru 受ける、uketoru 受け取る、uketsukeru 受け付ける; (consent) shōdaku suru 承諾する

access N akusesu アクセス; kōtsūshudan 交通手段; v (computer) akusesu suru アクセスする、setsuzoku suru 接続する

accessory N akusesarī アクセサリー

accident N jiko 事故; dekigoto 出来事; (disaster) sōnan 遭難; *have an accident* jiko ni au 事故にあう; sōnan suru 遭難する

accidental(ly) ADJ (ADV) gūzen no (ni) 偶然の(に)

acclaim N shōsan 称賛; v shōsan suru 称賛する

accommodate v shukuhaku saseru 宿泊させる; tekiō suru 適応する; wakaisaseru 和解させる

accommodation N shuku-hakujo 宿泊所、shukuhaku shisetsu 宿泊施設; (facilities) setsubi 設備

accompany v dōhan suru 同伴する、issho ni iku 一緒に

行く; o-tomo suru お供する

accomplice N kyōhansha 共犯者, ichimi 一味

accomplish V (shite)shimau (して)しまう; hatasu 果たす; togeru 遂げる; *(attain)* ... ni tassuru ～に達する; ... ga kanau ～がかなう

accord (with) V itchi suru 一致する

according to ... ni yori ～により; *(relying on)* ... ni yoru to ～によると, ... no hanashi de (wa) ～の話で (は); *(in conformity with)* ... ni shitagatte ～に従って

account N *(bill)* (o-)kanjō (お)勘定; *(credit)* tsuke つけ; *(bank account)* (yokin) kōza (預金)口座

accountable ADJ sekinin ga aru 責任がある, setsumei dekiru 説明できる

accountant N kaikei(gakari) 会計(係), kaikeishi 会計士

accumulate VI tsumoru 積もる, tamaru たまる; tsumeru つめる; atsumaru 集まる; VT tsumu 積む, tameru ためる; atsumeru 集める

accurate ADJ seikaku na 正確な

accuse V uttaeru 訴える; *(criticize)* hinan suru 非難する

accustomed ADJ jūrai no 従来の

ache V itamu 痛む; N itami 痛み

achievements N gyōseki 業績

acknowledge V mitomeru 認める; kansha suru 感謝する

acquaintance N shiriai 知り合い, chijin 知人

acrobat N akurobatto アクロバット, kyokugei 曲芸

acronym N kashira moji 頭文字

across PREP ... no mukō ni ～の向こうに; ADV yokogitte 横切って: *across from* ... no mukaini ～の向かいに; *go across* ōdan suru 横断する

act N *(deed)* okonai 行い, kōi 行為, furumai 振る舞い; V furumau 振る舞う: *act like a baby* amaeru 甘える, dada suru 駄々をこねる

action N kōdō 行動, akushon N アクション; katsudō 活動; *(conduct)* okonai 行い

activate V ugokasu 動かす

active ADJ kappatsu na 活発な

activity N katsudō 活動, katsuyaku 活躍, kōdō 行動; *(work)* hataraki 働き, torikumi 取り組み

actor N yakusha 役者, haiyū 俳優

actress N joyū 女優

actual ADJ jissai no 実際の, genjitsu no 現実の

actual conditions N genjitsu 現実

actually ADV jitsu wa/ni 実は/に; jissai wa/ni 実際は/に

acute ADJ *(sharp)* surudoi 鋭い; *(severe)* hageshi'i 激しい; *(sudden)* kyūsei no 急性の

adapt V tekigō saseru 適合させる, ... ni tsukurikaeru 〜に作り替える

adapter N adaputā アダプター

add V kuwaeru 加える; soeru 添える; yoseru 寄せる; kuwaete 加えて; *(attach)* tsukeru 付ける

addict N jōyōsha 常用者, chūdoku(-sha) 中毒(者), izon-sha 依存者: *drug addict* mayaku jōyō/chūdoku(-sha) 麻薬常用者/中毒(者)

addition N tsuika 追加, tenka 添加: *in addition to* ...no hoka (ni) ...の他(に)

address N jūsho 住所, banchi 番地 *(house number)*; *(destination)* todokesaki 届け先, atesaki 宛て先; V torikumu 取り組む: *e-mail address* mēru adoresu (meru-ado) メールアドレス (メルアド); *address book* adoresu-chō アドレス帳

addressee N uketori-nin 受取人, jushin-sha 受信者

adhesive plaster/tape N bansōkō ばんそうこう

adjust V totonoeru 整える, chōsei/seiri/kagen suru 調整/整理/加減する

adjustment N chōsei 調整, kagen 加減, chōsetsu 調節

administer V *(government)* osameru 治める, kanri suru 管理する

administration N *(of government)* gyōsei 行政; *(of business)* keiei 経営, kanri 管理

admire V kanshin suru 感心する; homeru 褒める, shōsan suru 賞賛する

admission N *(hospital)* nyūin 入院; *(school)* nyūgaku 入学; *(a place)* nyūjō 入場: *admis-*

sion fee nyūjōryō 入場料, haikanryō 拝観料

admit v *(let in)* ireru 入れる, tōsu 通す; *(acknowledge)* mitomeru 認める; *(confess)* uchiakeru 打ち明ける

adopt v *(a boy or girl)* yōshi ni suru 養子にする; *(a girl)* yōjo ni suru 養女にする

adorable ADJ kawaii かわいい, airashi'i 愛らしい

adore v akogareru 憧れる

adult N (ADJ) seijin 成人 (の), otona (no) 大人(の)

adultery N furin 不倫

advance N zenshin 前進; v *(go forward)* susumu 進む, zenshin suru 前進する; susumeru 進める; *(deposit)* maebarai suru 前払する: *in advance* arakajime あらかじめ, *(beforehand)* maemotte 前もって, jizen ni 事前に

advance money N *(deposit)* maebarai(kin) 前払(金)

advantage N toku 得, *(benefit)* rieki 利益; *(merit)* chōsho 長所

adventure N bōken 冒険

adverse ADJ furi na 不利な, gyaku no 逆の

advertisement N kōkoku 広告

advice N chūkoku 忠告; jogen 助言, adobaisu アドバイス; *(consultation)* sōdan 相談

advise v jogen suru 助言する

adviser N *(consultant)* komon 顧問, sōdan-aite 相談相手

advocate v tonaeru 唱える, shuchō suru 主張する

aerobics N earobikusu エアロビクス

affable ADJ aiso/aisō ga ii あいそ/愛想がいい, hitoatari no ii 人当たりのいい, shita-shimiyasui 親しみやすい

affair N koto 事, jiken 事件; *(extramarital affair)* uwaki 浮気

affect v eikyō o ataeru 影響を与える

affiliate v kamei suru 加盟する; N kogaisha 子会社, shiten 支店

afford v ... suru yoyū ga aru ～する余裕がある; jūbun na (...) ga aru 十分な(～)がある

affront v bujoku suru 侮辱する; N bujoku 侮辱

afraid ADJ kowagaru 怖がる, kowagatte 恐がって

after PREP ... no atode ～のあと

で; ... kara ～から, ... no ato de ～の後で: *after all* kekkyoku 結局, tōtō とうとう, tsuini ついに; yappari やっぱり; tsumari つまり, yōsuru ni 要するに; *after a long time (of absence)* hisashiburi ni 久しぶりに; *after a while* shibaraku shite しばらくして; *after that* sonogo その後; ... shita ato ni/de ～した後に/で

afternoon N *(3 p.m. to dusk)* gogo 午後; *(midday)* shōgo 正午

afterwards ADV *(then)* sonogo その後, ato de 後で

again ADV mō ichido もう一度, mō ikkai もう一回, futatabi 再び, mata また

against PREP *(in contrast to)* ... ni taishite ～に対して; *(contrary to)* ... ni hanshite ～に反して; *(opposing)* ... ni hantai/taikōshite ～に反対/対抗して

age N toshi 年, nenrei 年齢; *(era)* jidai 時代; V toshi o toru 年を取る, fukeru 老ける

agent N dairi 代理, dairinin 代理人; *(proxy)* daikōsha 代行者

ago ADV mae ni 前に

agree V *(approve)* sansei suru 賛成する; *(concur)* dōi suru 同意する; shōdaku suru 承諾する; *(promise)* yakusoku suru 約束する: *agree with* ... to chōwa suru ～と調和する; ... ni dōi suru ～に同意する

agreement N *(promise)* yakusoku 約束; *(contract)* keiyaku 契約, *(treaty)* jōyaku 条約; *(understanding)* shōdaku 承諾, *(consensus)* itchi 一致, dōi 同意, gōi 合意

agriculture N nōgyō 農業

ahead ADV zenpo ni 前方に; saki ni 先に(に)

AIDS N eizu エイズ, AIDS

aim N nerai 狙い, meate 目当て, medo 目処, meyasu 目安; *(goal)* mokuteki 目的; *(direction)* hōshin 方針; *(target)* mato 的; V kentō o tsukeru 見当をつける

air N kūki 空気; V *(be dry)* hosu 干す

air conditioning N eakon エアコン; reibō 冷房

airmail N kōkū(yū)bin 航空(郵)便, eameru エアメール

airplane N hikōki 飛行機

airport N kūkō 空港, hikōjō 飛行場

airy ADJ kaze tōshi no yoi 風通しのよい; keikai na 軽快な; keihaku na 軽薄な

aisle N tsūro 通路

alarm N keihō (sōchi) 警報 (装置)

alarm clock N mezamashi (dokei) 目覚し(時計)

album N (photograph) arubamu アルバム

alcohol N arukōru アルコール; (liquor) sake 酒

alcoholic N arukōru izonshō アルコール依存症

alert N (alarm) keihō 警報

alien ADJ yoso no よその; N (an alien) gaikoku(-jin) no 外国(人)の

alike ADJ, ADV onaji (yō na) 同じ(様な), niteiru 似ている; dōyō ni 同様に

alive ADJ ikiteiru 生きている

all PRON (everything) min'na みんな, zenbu 全部, subete no 全ての, arayuru あらゆる, issai 一切; (completely) sukkari すっかり; all day (long) ichinichi-jū 一日中; all kinds of samazama na 様々な,

iroiro (na/no) いろいろ (な/の), shuju no 種々の; all the time zutto ずっと, shotchū しょっちゅう, shijū 始終; (usually) tsunezune 常々; all together issei ni 一斉に合わせて, issei ni 一斉に; not at all dōitashima shite どういたしまして

all right ADJ (OK) daijōbu na 大丈夫な; (permissible) ii いい, yoroshi'i よろしい

allergy N arerugī アレルギー

alley N roji 路地, komichi 小道; (back street) uradōri 裏通り; (side street) yokochō 横町・丁

alliance N rengō 連合

allocate V wariateru 割り当てる, haibun suru 配分する

allow V (permit) yurusu 許す, kyoka suru 許可する

allowance N (bonus) teate 手当

almond N āmondo アーモンド

almost ADV hotondo ほとんど, daitai 大体; itsumo いつも

alone ADJ, ADV hitori de ひとりで: Leave me alone. Hottoite. 放っといて, Hōtte oite. 放っておいて

along PREP, ADV ... ni sotte 〜に

沿って; *(somewhere)* ...no doko ka (de) のどこか(で)

a lot ADJ akusan たくさん

already ADV mō もう, sudeni すでに

also CONJ ... mo (mata) ～も(また), sono ue その上, mata また, dōyō ni 同様に; yahari やはり, yappari やっぱり

alternative ADJ kawari no 代わりの; N sentakushi 選択肢

although CONJ ... no ni ～のに, ... daga ～だが, ... towae ～とはいえ

altogether ADV zenbu de 全部で, min'na de みんなで; *(completely)* mattaku まったく

alumni N dōsōkai 同窓会

always ADV itsumo いつも, *(usually)* fudan 普段; *(from the beginning)* moto kara 元から

a.m. ADV *(morning)* gozen 午前

amalgamate V gappei suru 合併する, heigō suru 併合する; yūgō suru 融合する, mazeru 混ぜる

amateur N amachua アマチュア; *(novice)* shirōto 素人

amaze V bikkuri saseru びっくりさせる

ambassador N taishi 大使

amber N kohaku (iro) 琥珀(色)

ambition N *(hope)* netsubō 熱望, yashin 野心

ambivalent ADJ aimaina na 曖昧な, anbibarento na アンビバレントな, mayotteiru 迷っている

ambulance N kyūkyūsha 救急車

amend V shūsei suru 修正する, kaisei suru 改正する

amenity N kokochiyosa 心地よさ, kaitekisa 快適さ; reigi 礼儀; benri na shisetsu 便利な施設

America N Amerika アメリカ, Beikoku 米国

American N Amerika-jin アメリカ人; ADJ Amerika(-jin) no アメリカ(人)の

amiable ADJ aiso/aisō ga ii 愛想がいい, shakō-teki na 社交的な, hitozukiai no yoi 人付き合いのよい, kanji no yoi 感じのよい

among PREP ... no naka/uchi/aida (ni) ～の中/内/間(に)

amount N *(sum)* (sō)gaku (総)額, kingaku 金額; *(large and/or small)* tashō 多少

amplifier N anpu アンプ

amulet N o-mamori お守り

amuse V warawaseru 笑わせる, tanoshimaseru 楽しませる

amusement N asobi 遊び; *(recreation)* goraku 娯楽

amusement park N yūenchi 遊園地

amusing ADJ omoshiroi 面白い; *(funny)* okashi'i おかしい, kokkei na こっけいな

analysis N bunseki 分析

ancestor N sosen 祖先, senzo 先祖

anchor N ikari 錨

anchor man N nyūsu kyasutā ニュースキャスター

ancient ADJ mukashi no 昔の, kodai no 古代の

and CONJ *(including each item)* ... to 〜と; *(choosing typical items)* ... ya 〜や; *(or)* mata wa または: *and now/then* sate さて; *and others* nado など; sonohoka/ta その他

anesthetic N masui(-yaku/zai) 麻酔(薬/剤)

anew ADV atarashiku 新しく, aratamete 改めて, sara ni さらに

angel N tenshi 天使

anger N ikari 怒り

angle N kakudo 角度; kado 角; *(viewpoint)* kenchi 見地

angry ADJ okotte 怒って, hara o tatete 腹を立てて: *be angry with* atama ni kuru 頭にくる

animal N dōbutsu 動物, ikimono 生き物, ke(da)mono 獣

animation N dōga 動画, animēshon アニメーション, anime アニメ

ankle N ashikubi 足首

annex N *(building)* bekkan 別館, *(new)* shinkan 新館, *(addition)* tatemashi 建て増し

anniversary N *(day)* kinenbi 記念日

announce V *(inform)* shiraseru 知らせる; *(publish)* happyō suru 発表する; *(wedding, etc.)* hirō suru 披露する

announcer N anaunsā アナウンサー

annoyance N *(trouble)* meiwaku 迷惑

annoying ADJ urusai うるさい, yakamashi'i やかましい, meiwaku na 迷惑な

annual ADJ ichinen no 一年の; N nenkan 年刊, nenpō 年報

anonymous ADJ mumei no 無名の

another PRON mō hitotsu もう一つ, hoka no ほかの

answer N *(an answer)* kotae 答え, kaitō 解答, *(a reply)* henji 返事; v kotaeru 答える, kaitō suru 解答する; *(telephone)* (denwa ni) deru (電話に)出る

ant N ari あり

Antarctica N nankyoku (tairiku) 南極(大陸)

antenna N antena アンテナ

anthropology N jinruigaku 人類学

antibiotic(s) N kōseibusshitsu 抗生物質

anticipate v matsu 待つ, kitai suru 期待する; *(presume)* yosō suru 予想する

anti-diarrhetic N geridome 下痢止め

antihistamine N kōhisutamin-zai 抗ヒスタミン剤

antique N jidaimono 時代物; *(curio)* kottōhin 骨董品

antiseptic N bōfuzai 防腐剤

antivirus software N *(computer)* anchi uirusu sofuto アンチウイルスソフト

antiwar ADJ hansen no 反戦の

antonym N hantaigo 反対語, hanigo 反意語

anus N kōmon 肛門

anxious ADJ harahara suru はらはらする, shinpai suru 心配する, ki o momu 気をもむ

any PRON, ADJ *(at all)* dore (de) mo どれ(でも, don'na どんな; *(not ...)* sukoshi mo 少しも, ikuraka (no) いくらか(の)

anybody PRON hito 人, dare ka 誰か; *(not ...)* dare mo 誰も; *(at all)* dare demo 誰でも

anyhow → anyway

anyone → anybody

anyplace → anywhere

anything PRON *(something)* nani ka 何か *(but often omitted)*; *(not ...)* nani mo 何も; *(at all)* nan demo 何でも

anytime, any time ADV itsu demo いつでも

anyway ADV *(nevertheless)* tonikaku とにかく; *(in any case)* tomokaku ともかく, nanibun なにぶん, nanishiro 何しろ; *(at all)* dō demo どうでも

anywhere ADV *(somewhere)* doko ka どこか; *(at all)* doko

demo どこでも

apart ADV barabara ni バラバラ に, betsu betsu ni 別々に

apartment N apāto アパート, *(luxury)* manshon マンション

ape N saru 猿; noroma na hito のろまな人

apologize V wabiru 詫びる, ayamaru 謝る

apology N (o-)wabi (お)詫び, shazai 謝罪

apparatus N sōchi 装置; kigu 器具

apparel N (i)fuku (衣)服

appeal V ki ni iru 気に入る; uttaeru 訴える

appear *(look, seem)* mieru 見える; *(show up)* deru 出る, arawareru 現れる, tōjō suru 登場する, *(occur)* hassei suru 発生する

appearance N yōsu 様子, gaiken 外見; *(air, manner)* ...-fū ～風; *(get-up, form)* teisai 体裁; *(shape)* kakkō 格好・恰好

append V fuka suru 付加する, tsuketasu 付け足す, soeru 添える

appendicitis N mōchōen 盲腸炎

appetite N shokuyoku 食欲

appetizers N zensai 前菜; *(go with drinks)* (o-)tsumami (お)つまみ

applause N hakushu 拍手

apple N ringo りんご

appliance N kateiyōhin 家庭用品; *(electric)* denki-yōhin 電気用品, kaden (katei-yō denkikigu) 家電(家庭用電気用具)

applicant N mōshikomisha 申し込み者, kibōsha 希望者

application N *(for a job, etc.)* mōshikomi 申し込み, gansho 願書; *(for a permit)* shinseisho 申請書; *(putting to use)* ōyō 応用, jitsuyō 実用; *(for computer)* sofutowea ソフトウェア

apply VI ataru 当たる; VT ateru 当てる, tsukeru 付ける; ōyō suru 応用する; *(apply for)* mōshikomu 申し込む, ōbo suru 応募する; *(claim)* mōshideru 申し出る

appoint V *(nominate)* meijiru 命じる; *(designate)* shitei suru 指定する

appointment N yakusoku 約束; yoyaku 予約

appraisal N hyōka 評価

appreciation N kansha 感謝, hyōka 評価

apprehensive ADJ kimi ga warui 気味が悪い

apprentice N deshi 弟子

approach V (... ni) chikazuku (〜に)近付く, yoru 寄る; sekkin 接近する

appropriate ADJ (suitable) tekisetsu na 適切な, tekitō na 適当な

approval N dōi 同意

approve V sansei suru 賛成する

approximate ADJ daitai no 大体の, gaisan no 概算の, chikai 近い; VI chikazuku 近づく; VT chikazukeru 近づける

approximately ADV daitai 大体, yaku 約, gurai 位, ... zengo 〜前後

April N shi-gatsu 四月

apron N epuron エプロン

aquarium N suizokukan 水族館

Arab N Arabu アラブ, (people) Arabu-jin アラブ人

Arabian N (ADJ) Arabia-jin (no) アラビア人 (の)

Arabic N (language) Arabia-go アラビア語

arcade N ākēdo アーケード

archaeologist N kōko gakusha 考古学者

archery N ācherī アーチェリー, (Japanese traditional art) kyūdō 弓道

archipelago N ... rettō 〜列島

architect N kenchikuka 建築家

architecture N kenchiku 建築

archive N kiroku 記録

Arctic N Hokkyoku 北極 : **Arctic Circle** N hokkyoku-ken 北極圏

area N menseki 面積; (district) chihō 地方, chi'iki 地域, chitai 地帯; fukin 付近

argue V kenka suru けんかする, arasou 争う; (discuss, debate) ronjiru 論じる

argument N kenka けんか, kuchigenka 口げんか; (discussion) ronsō 論争; (logic) rikutsu 理屈

arise V (happen) okiru 起きる, shōjiru 生じる

arm N te 手; (strictly) ude 腕

armor N yoroi 鎧

arms N heiki 兵器, buki 武器

army N guntai 軍隊; (vs. navy) rikugun 陸軍

around ADV (... no) mawari ni

(～の)周りに; oyoso およそ、daitai 大体、yaku 約、gurai 位

arrange v *(line them up)* naraberu 並べる; *(decide, set)* kimeru 決める、*(a meeting/consultation)* uchiawaseru 打ち合わせる; *(put together)* matomeru まとめる; *(arrange flowers)* (hana o) ikeru (花を)生ける

arrangement N *(settlement)* kimari 決まり; *(adjustment)* seiri 整理

array N hairetsu 配列、narabi 並び; v ... o haichi suru ～を配置する、narabaseru 並ばせる

arrest v toraeru 捕える、tsukamaeru 捕まえる、taiho suru 逮捕する

arrive (at) v *(... ni)* tsuku (～に)着く、tōchaku suru 到着する、itaru 至る

arrogant ADJ gōman na 傲慢な、ibatta 威張った

arrow N ya 矢; *(sign)* yajirushi 矢印

art N bijutsu 美術、geijutsu 芸術

article N *(thing)* mono 物、*(goods)* shina(mono) 品(物); *(writeup)* kiji 記事; *(scholarly)* ronbun 論文

artifact N ibutsu 遺物

artificial ADJ jinkō no 人工の、jinkō-teki na 人工的な

artisan N *(master)* shokunin 職人、meijin 名人

artist N geijutsuka 芸術家、āchisuto アーチスト; *(painter)* gaka 画家

arts N gei 芸、waza 技

as CONJ *(like)* ... no yō (ni) ～の様 (に); *(so as to be)* ... ni ～に; *(in the role of)* ... to shite ～として; **as always/usual/ever** aikawarazu 相変わらず; **as (described) below** ika no tōri 以下の通り、**as follows** ika no tōri 以下の通り; **as for** ... ni tsuite wa ～については; **as much as** ... gurai ～位; ... hodo ～程; **as possible** dekirudake 出来るだけ; ... ni tsuite ～について; **as soon as** ... suru to sugu ni ～するとすぐに

ascertain v tashikameru 確かめる

ascetic practices N shugyō 修行、gyō 行

ashamed ADJ hazukashi'i 恥ずかしい; *(guilty feeling)* yamashi'i やましい

ash(es) N hai 灰

ashtray N haizara 灰皿

Asia N Ajia アジア

Asian N *(people)* Ajia-jin アジア人; ADJ Ajia no アジアの

ask V *(a favor of a person)* tanomu 頼む, negairu 願う; *(require)* motomeru 求める; *(a person a question)* (... ni) kiku (〜に)聞く, tazuneru 尋ねる, ukagairu 伺う

asleep ADV, ADJ nemutte (iru) 眠って(いる)

asparagus N asupara (gasu) アスパラ(ガス)

aspect N yōsu 様子; jōkyō 状況

asphalt N asufaruto アスファルト

aspirin N asupirin アスピリン

assemble VI atsumaru 集まる, shūgō suru 集合する; VT atsumeru 集める; *(fit parts together to make a whole)* kumiawaseru 組み合わせる, kumitateru 組み立てる

assembly N *(gathering)* shūgō 集合; *(parliament)* kokkai 国会

assist V ōen suru 応援する; tasukeru 助ける

assistance N sewa 世話; tetsudai 手伝い; hojo 補助,

enjo 援助; ōen 応援

assistant N joshu 助手, ashisutanto アシスタント

associate V *(...with)* ... to tsukiau 〜と付き合う; ... to majiwaru 〜と交わる; ... o chikazukeru 〜を近付ける; N nakama 仲間

association N kyōkai 協会; *(academic)* gakkai 学会; *(guild, union)* kumiai 組合; *(social company)* tsukiai 付き合い

assortment N kumiawase 組み合わせ, toriawase 取り合わせ

asterisk N hoshijirushi 星印, asutarisuku アスタリスク

asthma N zensoku 喘息

astringent ADJ shibui 渋い; N asutorinzen アストリンゼン

astronomy N tenmongaku 天文学

at PREP ... de 〜で; *(being located at)* ... ni 〜に: *at any moment* ima ni mo 今にも; *at last* iyoiyo いよいよ, yōyaku ようやく, tsui ni ついに; *(after difficulty)* yatto やっと; *at least* sukunaku to mo 少なくとも, semete せめて; *at most* semete せめて,

210

seizei せいぜい; *at once* sassoku 早速

atelier N atorie アトリエ

athlete N (undō) senshu (運動)選手

athletics N undō 運動, supōtsu スポーツ; *(physical education)* tai'iku 体育

Atlantic Ocean N Taiseiyō 大西洋

atmosphere *(of a place)* N fun'iki 雰囲気

atom N genshi 原子

atomic ADJ genshi(ryoku) no 原子(力)の: *atomic energy* genshiryoku 原子力

atmosphere N fun'iki 雰囲気

attach V *(stick on)* tsukeru 付ける; *(add)* soeru 添える

attachment N fuzoku 付属・附属, fuzokuhin 付属品・附属品; *(computer)* tenpu fairu 添付ファイル

attack N *(an attack)* kōgeki 攻撃, shūgeki 襲撃; hossa 発作; V *(make an attack)* osoiru 襲う; semeru 攻める; kōgeki/shūgeki suru 攻撃/襲撃する

attempt N tameshi 試し, kokoromi 試み; *(plot, scheme)* kuwadate 企て;

V *(attempt it)* tamesu 試す, kokoromiru 試みる; kuwadateru 企てる

attend V deru 出る; shusseki suru 出席する

attendance N shusseki 出席; *(office)* shukkin 出勤

attendant N *(in charge)* kakari 係, kakari'in 係員

attention N chūi 注意, nen 念

attest V shōmei suru 証明する

attitude N taido 態度, shisei 姿勢

attract V hiku 引く; VT *(charming)* miryō suru 魅了する

attraction N atorakushon アトラクション; inryoku 引力

attractive ADJ *(nice-looking)* kirei na きれいな, *(charming)* miryoku-teki na 魅力的な, miryoku ga aru 魅力がある, aikyō ga aru 愛きょうがある, chāmingu na チャーミングな

auction N seri 競り, kyōbai 競売, ōkushon オークション

audience N chōshū 聴衆, kankyaku 観客

audio ADJ onsei no 音声の; N ōdio オーディオ; onsei 音声

audition N ōdishon オーディション, shinsa 審査

auditorium N kaidō 会堂, kōdō 講堂, hōru ホール

August N hachi-gatsu 八月

aunt N oba(-san) おば(さん)

auspicious ADJ medetai めでたい, engi no yoi 縁起の良い

Australia N Ōsutoraria オーストラリア

Australian N (people) Ōsutoraria-jin オーストラリア人; ADJ Ōsutoraria no オーストラリアの

authentic ADJ kakujitsu na 確実な, honba no 本場の, honkakuteki na 本格的な

authentication N (certificate) shōmeisho 証明書

author N chosha 著者, sakka 作家

authority N (expert) taika 大家, tsū 通; (power) ken'i 権威; (basis) konkyo 根拠

automatic ADJ jidōteki na 自動的な

automatically ADV jidōteki ni 自動的に; (spontaneously) hitoride ni 独りでに, onozukara 自ずから

automation N ōtomēshon オートメーション, jidō (ka) 自動(化)

automobile N jidōsha 自動車, kuruma 車

autumn N aki 秋

Autumnal Equinox Day N shūbun-no-hi 秋分の日

available ADJ riyō dekiru 利用できる; (room(s)) akibeya/shitsu 空き部屋/室, (taxi) kūsha 空車

avalanche N nadare 雪崩; (snowslide) yukinadare 雪なだれ

avenue N tōri 通り, ōdōri 大通り, kaidō 街道; michi 道

average N (on the average) heikin 平均; ADJ (ordinary) nami no 並の, heibon na 平凡な; V narasu ならす

aversion N daikirai na 大嫌いな

avoid V sakeru 避ける, yokeru よける

awake V (come awake) mezameru 目覚める; (not asleep) nemuranai 眠らない

award N shō 賞; V (give) (shō) o juyo suru (賞)を授与する; okuru 贈る

awarding ceremony N hyōshōshiki 表彰式

away ADV hanarete 離れて;

atchi he あっちへ; tōku (ni) 遠く(に): *go away* iku 行く, tachisaru 立ち去る, dekakeru 出掛ける, nigeru 逃げる, naoru 治る; *right away* sugu すぐ; *take away* toru 取る; tsureteiku 連れて行く

awful ADJ osoroshi'i 恐ろしい; hidoi ひどい

awkward ADJ mazui まずい, gikochinai ぎこちない

ax N ono 斧

axis, axle N jiku 軸

B

babble N oshaberi おしゃべり

baby N akachan 赤ちゃん

babysitter N bebīshittā ベビーシッター, *(professional)* komori 子守

bachelor N dokushin 独身, hitorimono 独り者; gakushi 学士

back N *(part of body)* senaka 背中; *(lower part)* koshi 腰; *(rear)* ushiro 後ろ, ura 裏; *back and forth* zengo (ni) 前後(に); *back up* shiji suru 支持する; *I'm back.* Tadaima. ただいま.

backbone N sebone 背骨

background N haikei 背景, bakku バック; *(one's career)* keireki 経歴, bakku gura(u) ndo バックグラ(ウンド); *(background information)* yobi chishiki 予備知識

back issue/number N *(magazines, etc.)* bakku nanbā バックナンバー

back-order N toriyose chūmon 取り寄せ注文

backpack N ryukku-sakku リュックサック

backside N ushiro 後ろ

backstage ADJ, ADV butai ura (no/de) 舞台裏(の/で), gakuya (no/de) 楽屋(の/で)

backup N *(computer)* bakku appu バックアップ, yobi 予備, hikae 控え

backward ADV *(contrariwise)* gyaku (ni) 逆(に), ushiromuki ni 後ろ向きに

bad ADJ warui 悪い, dame na 駄目な; furyō no 不良の; *(inept)* heta na 下手な

bad guy N furyō 不良, warumono 悪者

bad luck N fu'un 不運

bad taste N akushumi 悪趣味

213

bad-tasting ADJ mazui まずい

badge N bajji バッジ

badly ADV waruku 悪く; *(very)* totemo とても

bag N fukuro 袋; kaban 鞄, baggu バッグ

baggage N (te)nimotsu (手)荷物

baggy ADJ dabudabu no だぶだぶの

bait N esa えさ

bake V yaku 焼く

baker N *(bakery, bakeshop)* pan-ya パン屋

baking powder N bēkingu paudā ベーキングパウダー

balance N *(equilibrium)* tsuriai 釣り合い; *(remaining money)* zandaka 残高

bald ADJ hageta 禿げた

baldness N hage はげ

bale N tawara 俵

ball N bōru ボール; tama 玉, mari まり

ballad N *(Japanese traditional music)* min'yō 民謡; *(Western-style)* barādo バラード

balloon N fūsen 風船

ballpoint pen N bōrupen ボールペン

bamboo N take 竹

bamboo blind N *(Japanese traditional)* sudare すだれ

banana N banana バナナ

band N *(watch-band, etc.)* bando バンド, beruto ベルト; *(music)* bando バンド, gakudan 楽団

bandage N hōtai 包帯

bank N *(finance)* ginkō 銀行; *(of river)* dote 土手; *(river bank)* kishi 岸

bank account N yokinkoza 預金口座

bankbook N tsūchō 通帳, yokin-tsūchō 預金通帳

bankrupt V hasan suru 破産する

banner N *(flag)* hata 旗; *(hanging cloth)* taremaku 垂れ幕; *(Internet)* banā (kōkoku) バナー (広告)

banquet N enkai 宴会, bansankai 晩餐会

bar N *(lattice)* kōshi 格子; *(serving drinks)* bā バー, sakaba 酒場; *(stick/pole)* bō 棒

barbecue N bābekyū バーベキュー

barber N toko-ya 床屋

bar-code N bākōdo バーコード

barefoot ADJ, ADV hadashi (no/de) 裸足(の/で)

barely ADV yatto やっと, yōyaku ようやく, karōjite かろうじて

bargain N yasu'uri 安売り; bāgensēru バーゲンセール

bark N (of tree) juhi 樹皮; v (of animals) hoeru 吠える

barley N mugi 麦, ō-mugi 大麦

barn N naya 納屋

barometer N baromētā バロメーター; (atmospheric pressure) kiatsu-kei 気圧計

barrier N (fence) saku 柵; (obstacle) shōgai(butsu) 障害(物); (limit) kyōkai 境界

barter N butsubutsu kōkan 物々交換

base N (military) kichi 基地; (of a tree) nemoto 根元; (foundation) kiso 基礎

baseball N yakyū 野球

basement N (floor) chikai 地階; (room) chika(shitsu) 地下(室)

bashful, be v hanikamu はにかむ

bashing N ...tataki 〜叩き, basshingu バッシング

basic N kihon 基本; ADJ kihonteki na 基本的な, konponteki na 根本的な

basin N (for washing face) senmenki 洗面器, senmendai 洗面台

basis N dodai 土台, kihon 基本, konpon 根本, kijun 基準, bēsu ベース; (grounds) konkyo 根拠

basket N kago かご, basuketto バスケット

basketball basukettobōru バスケットボール

bat N kōmori こうもり, (baseball) batto バット

bath N furo 風呂; nyūyoku 入浴: **take a bath** furo ni hairu 風呂に入る, nyūyoku suru 入浴する

bathe v (swim) oyogu 泳ぐ; nyūyoku suru 入浴する

bathroom N (for bathing) yokushitsu 浴室, basurūmu バスルーム, furoba 風呂場; (toilet) toire トイレ, keshō-shitsu 化粧室, (o-)tearai (お)手洗い

bathtub N yubune 湯舟, yokusō 浴そう

battery N denchi 電池, batterī バッテリー

battle N sentō 戦闘, tatakai 戦い, arasoi 争い; v tatakairu 戦う

bay N wan 湾

BBS, Bulletin Board (System) N (Internet) denshi keijiban 電子掲示板

be v (exist) sonzai suru 存在する: *be able to* ...dekiru ～できる

beach N bīchi ビーチ, hamabe 浜辺, kaigan 海岸

bead N tama 玉, bīzu ビーズ; (for praying) juzu 数珠

beak N kuchibashi くちばし

bean N mame 豆

beancurd N tōfu 豆腐

bear N (animal) kuma 熊; v (put up with) taeru 耐える, shinbō suru 辛抱する; (fruit) minoru 実る

beard N agohige あごひげ

beat v (defeat) uchimakasu 打ち負かす; (strike) hageshiku utsu 激しく打つ; naguru 殴る; (heart throbs) dokidoki suru どきどきする

beautiful ADJ kirei na きれいな, utsukushi'i 美しい, migoto na 見事な

beauty parlor N biyōin 美容院

because CONJ nazenara なぜ なら

become v ...ni naru ～になる

bed N beddo ベッド, shindai 寝台; *go to bed* neru 寝る

bedroom N shinshitsu 寝室

bedsheet N shītsu シーツ, shikifu 敷布

bee N mitsubachi 蜜蜂, hachi 蜂

beef N gyūniku 牛肉

beefsteak N sutēki ステーキ

beer N bīru ビール: *draft beer* nama-bīru 生ビール

before CONJ, PREP (in front of) ... no mae ni ～の前に; ADV (previously) mae ni 前に, izen ni 以前に: *before a meal* shokuzen 食前

beg v tanomu 頼む, negairu 願う

begin vt hajimeru 始める; vi hajimaru 始まる

beginner N shoshin-sha 初心 者, biginā ビギナー

beginning hajime 始め, (outset) saisho 最初, hajimari 始まり; *(in) the beginning* hajime 初め

behalf N (support) shiji 支持; (benefit) rieki 利益

behave v furumau 振る舞う

behavior N *(actions)* kōdō 行動, *(act)* kōi 行為; *(manners)* gyōgi 行儀; *(attitude)* taido 態度

behind PREP, ADV ... no ushiro ni ～の後ろに; *(the other side)* ... no uragawa ～の裏側; **leave behind** nokosu 残す; *(forgets)* wasuremono o suru 忘れ物をする

Beijing N pekin 北京

belch N geppu げっぷ

belief N *(faith)* shin'nen 信念

believe v shinjiru 信じる

bell N *(large)* kane 鐘; *(small)* rin/suzu 鈴; *(doorbell)* yobirin 呼び鈴

belly N hara 腹, onaka お腹

belong to v shozoku suru 所属する

belongings N shoyūbutsu 所有物

beloved N itoshii 愛しい, saiai no 最愛の; *(thing)* aiyō no 愛用の, okini'iri no お気に入りの, daisuki na 大好きな

below PREP ... no shita ni ～(の)下に; *(less than)* ... ika no ～以下の, ... miman (o) ～未満(の); *(downstairs)*

kaika ni 階下に

belt N *(watch-band, etc.)* beruto ベルト, bando バンド; *(zone)* (chi)tai 地帯

bend VI oreru 折れる, *(curve)* magaru 曲がる, *(warp)* soru 反る; VT oru 折る, mageru 曲げる, sorasu 反らす

benefit N rieki 利益; *(benefits)* teate 手当; v (... no) tame ni naru (～の)ためになる

beside PREP ... no soba ni ～のそばに, ... no tonari ni ～の隣りに, ... no waki ni ～のわきでに, ... no toko ni ～の横に

besides PREP sonoue その上, (sono) hoka (その)他

best ADJ *(highest)* saikō no 最高の, ichiban ii 一番いい; sairyō no 最良の, besuto no ベストの; *Best wishes* gotakō o inorimasu ご多幸を祈ります

bet v kakeru 賭ける, kake o suru 賭けをする; N kake 賭け; *(money)* kakekin 賭け金

better ADJ yoriyoi よりよい, *(improve)* genki ni naru 元気になる, yoku naru よくなる; *(preferable)* ... (no hō) ga ii/yoi ～(の方)がいい/良い

between PREP ... no aida ni ～ の間に, ... (no) chūkan ni ... (の)中間に

beverage N nomimono 飲み物

beware V chūi suru 注意する, ki o tsukeru 気をつける

beyond PREP (... no) muko (ni) (～の)向こう(に)

bias N (prejudice) henken 偏見, sen'nyū-kan 先入観; (statistics) baiasu バイアス

bible N seisho 聖書

bicycle, bike N jitensha 自転車

big ADJ ōki'i 大きい; (spacious) hiroi 広い

bill N seikyūsho 請求書; (pay) (o-)kanjō (お)勘定; denpyō 伝票; daikin 代金, ... dai ～代; (currency note) (o-)satsu (お)札; (handbill) bira ビラ

billion NUM jūoku 十億; ADJ jūoku no 十億の

binder N baindā バインダー

binding N (book) seihon 製本

binoculars N sōgan-kyō 双眼鏡

biography N denki 伝記

biology N seibutsugaku 生物学

biotechnology N baio

tekunorojī バイオテクノロジー, seibutsu kōgaku 生物工学

bird N tori 鳥

birth N (being born) umare 生れ; V (give birth to) umu 産む, shussan suru 出産する

birthday N tanjōbi 誕生日

biscuit N (cookie) bisuketto ビスケット, kukkī クッキー; (cracker) kurakkā クラッカー

bit N (a little) sukoshi 少し, chotto ちょっと, (part) wazuka わずか

bite V kamu 噛む, kami-tsuku かみつく; N (hurt) kamikizu かみ傷: **one bite** hito-kuchi ひと口

bitter ADJ nigai 苦い, hidoi ひどい

black ADJ kuroi 黒い

blackmail N yusuri ゆすり, kyōkatsu 恐喝

blade N (razor) (kamisori no) ha (かみそりの)刃

blame N hinan 非難; V (rebuke one) togameru とがめる, hinan suru 非難する; semeru 責める

bland ADJ aji ga usui 味が薄い; heibon na 平凡な, onwa na 温和な

blank N yohaku 余白; *(form)* yōshi 用紙; ADJ hakushi no 白紙の; *(vacant look)* utsuro na 虚ろな

blanket N mōfu 毛布

bleach V *(color)* aseru 褪せる; N hyōhaku-zai 漂白剤

bleed V chi ga deru 血が出る, shukketsu suru 出血する

blend N burendo ブレンド, kongō 混合; V mazeru 混ぜる, mazeawaseru 混ぜ合わせる

blender N mikisā ミキサー

blessed ADJ megumareta 恵まれた, shukufuku sareta 祝福された; *(holy)* shinsei na 神聖な, seinaru 聖なる

Bless you. INTERJ *(sneezer)* Odaiji ni お大事に

blind ADJ mōmoku no 盲目の; N *(sun-shade)* hiyoke 日よけ, buraindo ブラインド

block N *(city block)* chōme 丁目; *(block of wood)* kakuzai 角材; VI *(clog, impede)* fusagu ふさぐ; VT fusagaru ふさがる

blog N burogu ブログ, weburogu ウェブログ

blond ADJ kinpatsu no 金髪の, burondo no ブロンドの

blood N chi 血, ketsueki 血液: *blood pressure* ketsuatsu 血圧; *blood type* ketsueki-gata 血液型

bloom V saku 咲く

blouse N burausu ブラウス

blow N dageki 打撃; V fuku 吹く; *(blow nose)* hana o kamu 鼻をかむ

blowup N bakuhatsu 爆発, bakuha 爆破

blue ADJ aoi 青い; *(feel blue)* burū ブルー, yūutsu 憂うつ

blueprint N aojashin 青写真

blunt ADJ bukkirabō na ぶっきらぼうな, busahō na 不作法な

blush V kao ga akaku naru 顔が赤くなる, sekimen suru 赤面する

board N *(plank)* ita 板, *(art)* daishi 台紙; V *(get on a train/bus)* jōsha suru 乗車する, *(a plane)* tōjō suru 搭乗する

boarding house N geshuku (-ya) 下宿(屋); *(dormitory)* kishukusha 寄宿舎, ryō 寮

boarding pass N tōjō-ken 搭乗券

boat N fune 舟・船, bōto ボート, *(small)* kobune 小船

body N karada 体

bogged down v ikizumaru 行き詰まる

boil vt *(water)* o-yu o wakasu お湯を沸かす; *(food)* niru 煮る, yuderu ゆでる; *(rice)* taku 炊く; vi o-yu ga waku お湯が沸く, futtō suru 沸騰する; n dekimono できもの, o-deki おでき

boiler n boirā ボイラー; yuwakashiki 湯沸かし器

bold adj daitan na 大胆な, yūkan na 勇敢な

bomb n bakudan 爆弾; v bakugeki suru 爆撃する

bone n hone 骨

bonito n katsuo かつお; *(dried bonito)* katsuobushi かつお節

bonus n *(wage)* bōnasu ボーナス, shōyo 賞与; *(extra)* omake おまけ

book n *(publications)* hon 本, shoseki 書籍; *(account)* chōbo 帳簿; v yoyaku suru 予約する

bookcase n honbako 本箱

booking n yoyaku 予約

bookkeeper n bokigakari 簿記係

bookmark n shiori しおり

bookshelf n hondana 本棚

bookshop, bookstore n hon-ya 本屋, shoten 書店

boom n *(prosperity)* keiki 景気; *(fad)* būmu ブーム

booth n *(stall)* baiten 売店; *(theater, etc.)* bokkususeki ボックス席; *(telephone booth)* denwabokkusu 電話ボックス

boot(s) n nagagutsu 長靴, būtsu ブーツ, *(rubber)* gomunaga ゴム長

border n *(boundary)* sakai 境, kyōkaisen 境界線; *(between countries)* kokkyō 国境

borderline n kyōkaisen 境界線, bōdārain ボーダーライン; adj girigiri no ぎりぎりの

bore v *(drill a hole)* unzari saseru うんざりさせる

bored adj taikutsushita 退屈した

boring adj *(dull)* taikutsu na 退屈な, tsumaranai つまらない

born v *(born in/of)* ... no umare 〜の生まれ, ... umare no 〜生まれの

borrow v kariru 借りる

boss n jōshi 上司

botanic garden n shokubutsu-en 植物園

both pron ryōhō 両方; adv

ryōhō no 両方の, **dochira mo** どちらも: *both ... and* ... to ... ryōhō 〜と 〜両方; *both sides* ryōmen 両面

bother N mendō 面倒, meiwaku 迷惑; *(intrusion)* jama 邪魔; *(care)* sewa 世話, yakkai 厄介; v jama o suru 邪魔をする

bothersome ADJ mendōkusai 面倒くさい, yakkai na 厄介な; jama na 邪魔な

bottle N bin 瓶

bottom N soko 底; *(underneath)* shita 下; *(base)* kontē 根底; *(buttocks)* shiri 尻

bottoms up kanpai 乾杯

bounce v hazumu 弾む

bound for ... -iki no 〜行きの

boundary N kyōkaisen 境界線

bouquet N hanataba 花束

bow N *(archery or violin)* yumi 弓; *(shape)* yumigata 弓形; *(of ribbon)* chōmusubi 蝶結び; o-jigi お辞儀; v *(bow one's head)* o-jigi o suru お辞儀をする

bowel(s) N chō 腸; naizō 内臓

bowl N donburi どんぶり; *(ricebowl)* chawan 茶碗

bowling N bōringu ボーリング

box N hako 箱; *(cardboard)* danbōrubako 段ボール箱

boxing N bokushingu ボクシング

box lunch N bentō 弁当

box office N kippu'uriba 切符売り場

boy N otoko no ko 男の子, danshi 男子, botchan 坊ちゃん; shōnen 少年

boyfriend N kareshi 彼氏, kare 彼, bōifurendo ボーイフレンド

Boys' Festival N *(5 May)* Tango no sekku 端午の節句

bra N burajā ブラジャー

braid v amu 編む

brain N nō 脳, nōmiso 脳みそ, atama 頭, zunō 頭脳; *(mind)* chiryoku 知力

brake N burēki ブレーキ; v burēki o kakeru ブレーキをかける

branch N *(tree)* eda 枝; *(store/office)* shiten 支店, shisha 支社, bumon 部門

brand N burando ブランド

brandy N burandē ブランデー

brave ADJ *(daring)* yūkan na 勇敢な, isamashi'i 勇ましい; tsuyoi 強い

bread N pan パン

break N (*rift or pause*) kireme 切れ目, (*rest*) yasumi 休み, kyūkei 休憩; VI kowareru 壊れる, (*in two*) oreru 折れる, (*split*) wareru 割れる, (*smash*) kudakeru 砕ける; VT kowasu 壊す, oru 折る; (*split it*) waru 割る, (*smash it*) kudaku 砕く, konagona ni suru 粉々にする: *break down* (*car, machine*) koshō suru 故障する; *break out* (*appear*) hassei suru 発生する; (*happen*) okoru 起こる

breakdown N (*crash*) koshō 故障, (*item by item*) meisai 明細, uchiwake 内訳

breakfast N chōshoku 朝食, asagohan 朝ご飯, asameshi 朝飯

breast N mune 胸

breath N iki 息

breathe V iki o suru 息をする, kokyū suru 呼吸する

breed N (*species of plant, etc.*) hinshu 品種; (*kind*) shurui 種類; (*lineage*) kettō 血統

breeze N (soyo)kaze (そよ)風

brick N renga 煉瓦

bride N hanayome 花嫁, oyome-san お嫁さん

bridegroom N hanamuko 花婿, omuko-san お婿さん

bridge N hashi 橋

brief ADJ (*short*) mijikai 短い; (*simple*) kantan na 簡単な

briefing N jōkyō setsumei 状況説明

briefs N burīfu ブリーフ (下着)

bright ADJ (*sunny*) akarui 明るい, hogaraka na ほがらかな, (*colorful*) hanayaka na 華やかな, (*gaudy*) hade na 派手な; (*cheerful*) yōki na 陽気な

brilliant ADJ subarashi'i 素晴らしい, sugoi すごい

bring V mottekuru 持ってくる, tottekuru 取って来る

bring up V (*children*) (kodomo o) sodateru (子供を)育てる, yashinau 養う, yōiku suru 養育する; (*trains*) shitsukeru しつける; (*topic*) (wadai o) mochidasu (話題を)持ち出す

British N Eikoku-jin 英国人, Igirisu-jin イギリス人; ADJ Eikoku/Igirisu (-jin) no 英国/イギリス(人)の

broad ADJ (*spacious*) hiroi 広い

222

broadband N burōdobando ブロードバンド

broadcast N hōsō 放送; v hōsō suru 放送する

broadcasting station N hōsōkyoku 放送局

brochure N panfuretto パンフレット, katarogu カタログ

broil v yaku 焼く

broken ADJ (does not work) kowareta 壊れた, koshōshita 故障した; (of bones, etc.) oreta 折れた (骨など)

bronze N dō 銅

brooch N burōchi ブローチ

broom N hōki ほうき

broth N sūpu スープ

brother N (older) ani 兄; (younger) otōto 弟

brother-in-law N (older) giri no ani 義理の兄; (younger) giri no otōto 義理の弟

brothers and sisters N kyōdai 兄弟

brown N(ADJ) chairo(i) 茶色(い)

browser N (computer) burauza ブラウザ

bruise N aza あざ, uchimi 打ち身, dabokushō 打撲傷

brush N burashi ブラシ, (for teeth) haburashi 歯ブラシ; (for painting) hake はけ; (for writing) fude 筆; v burashi o kakeru ブラシをかける; miagku 磨く

bubble gum N fūsengamu 風船ガム

bucket N baketsu バケツ

buckwheat (noodles) N soba そば

bud N (leaf) me 芽; (flower) tsubomi つぼみ

Buddha N hotoke-sama 仏様, (sakyamuni) shaka 釈迦, o-shaka-sama お釈迦様

Buddhist N bukkyōto 仏教徒

budget N yosan 予算

buffalo N baffarō バッファロー, suigyū 水牛

bug N mushi 虫, konchū 昆虫

build v tateru 建てる; (creates) tsukuru 造る

building N tatemono 建物, birudingu ビルディング

bulge v fukuramu 膨らむ

bullet N tama 弾, dangan 弾丸

bullet train N shinkansen 新幹線

bulletin board N keiji-ban 掲示板

bump into ... v ... ni butsukaru

~にぶつかる; *(happens to meet)* deau 出会う

bunch N *(cluster)* fusa 房; *(pile)* yama 山; *(bundle)* taba 束; *(group)* mure 群れ

bureau N *(department)* ...-kyoku ―局

burglar N dorobō 泥棒

burial N maisō 埋葬, sōshiki 葬式, haka 墓

burn VI yakeru 焼ける; moeru 燃える; VT yaku 焼く; *(fire, wood, coal)* taku 焚く, *(light)* tomosu 灯す; N *(injury)* yakedo 火傷

Burma N biruma ビルマ

Burmese N *(language)* biruma-go ビルマ語; *(people)* biruma-jin ビルマ人; ADJ biruma(-jin) no ビルマ(人)の

burst VI yabureru 破れる, *(explodes)* bakuhatsu suru 爆発する; VT yaburu 破る; *burst out* tobidasu 飛び出す

bus N basu バス: *bus station/stop* basutei バス停

bush N shigemi 茂み

business N *(job)* shigoto 仕事, shōbai 商売, gyōmu 業務; *(transaction)* torihiki 取引;

(errand) yōji 用事, yō 用; *(enterprise)* jigyō 事業; *(commerce)* shōgyō 商業: *business hours* eigyōjikan 営業時間, gyōmu jikan 業務時間; *business trip* shutchō 出張

busy ADJ *(doing something)* isogashi'i 忙しい, sewashinai せわしない; tabō na 多忙な; *(crowded)* nigiyaka na にぎやかな; *(in the midst of work)* shigoto-chū 仕事中, *(in conference)* kaigi-chū 会議中; *(telephone)* hanashi-chū 話し中

but CONJ shikashi しかし, demo でも, da ga だが, datte だって, tokoro ga ところが; keredo(mo) けれど(も)

butcher N *(shop)* niku-ya 肉屋

butter N batā バター

butterfly N chō 蝶, chōchō 蝶々

buttocks N (o-)shiri (お)尻

button N botan ボタン

buy V kau 買う

buyer N kaite 買い手; *(professional)* baiyā バイヤー

by PREP *(no later than)* ... made ni ~までに; *by ... (means of)* ... de ... で; ADV *(way of)* ... o tōtte ～を通って; *(via)* ... keiyu (de) ～経由(で); *(author, artist)* ... ni yotte ～によって (作者, 芸術家): *by the way* tokorode ところで

bypass N baipasu バイパス

by-product N fukusanbutsu 副産物

bystander N kenbutsu-nin 見物人

byte N *(computer)* baito バイト

C

cab N takushī タクシー

cabbage N kyabetsu キャベツ

cabin N koya 小屋

cabinet N *(government)* naikaku 内閣; *(cupboard)* todana 戸棚

cable N tsuna 綱, kēburu ケーブル; *(cable television)* kēburu terebi ケーブルテレビ

cafe N *(coffee shop)* kōhīten コーヒー店, kissaten 喫茶店; kafe カフェ

cafeteria N kafeteria カフェテリア, shokudō 食堂

cage N *(for bird)* kago かご, torikago 鳥かご; *(for animal)* ori 檻

cake N *(pastry)* kēki ケーキ

calculate V keisan suru 計算する

calculation N keisan 計算; *(estimate)* mitsumori 見積もり

calculator N keisanki 計算機

calendar N koyomi 暦; karendā カレンダー

call N *(phone ...)* denwa 電話; V yobu 呼ぶ; yobidasu 呼び出す

calligraphy N shodō 書道, (o-)shūji (お)習字

calm ADJ *(quiet)* shizuka na 静かな, odayaka na 穏やかな, reisei na 冷静な; nodoka na のどかな; VI shizumaru 静まる; VT shizumeru 静める

calorie N karorī カロリー

Cambodia N Kanbojia カンボジア

Cambodian N *(language)* Kanbojia-go カンボジア語; *(people)* Kanbojia-jin カンボジア人; ADJ Kanbojia(-jin) no カンボジア(人)の

camel N rakuda らくだ

camera N kamera カメラ, shashin-ki 写真機

camp N kyanpu キャンプ; *(bivouac)* yaei 野営; V kyanpu suru キャンプする

campaign N kyanpēn キャンペーン, undō 運動

campsite N kyanpu-jō キャンプ場; yaeichi 野営地

campus N kyanpasu キャンパス, *(within the university)* daigaku-kōnai 大学構内; kōtei 校庭

can N *(tin can)* kan 缶; V *(kan ni)* tsumeru (缶に)詰める; MODAL V *(can do it)* dekiru 出来る, ... suru koto ga dekiru 〜する事が出来る; kanau 叶う; *(may)* ... shitemoyoi 〜してもよい

can opener N kankiri 缶切り

Canada N Kanada カナダ

Canadian N *(people)* Kanada-jin カナダ人; ADJ Kanada(-jin) no カナダ(人)の

canal N unga 運河

cancel V torikesu 取り消す

cancellation N torikeshi 取り消し; kyanseru キャンセル

cancer N gan がん

candidate N kōho-sha 候補者

candle N rōsoku ろうそく

candy N (o-)kashi (お)菓子,

kyandī キャンディー, ame あめ

canyon N kyōkoku 峡谷

cap N bōshi 帽子; kyappu キャップ, *(of a bottle)* ōkan 王冠; *(of a mushroom)* kasa 笠

capable of ADJ yūnō na 有能な

capacity N kyapa(sitī) キャパ(シティー); *(ability)* nōryoku 能力; *(contents)* yōseki 容積

cape N *(promontory)* misaki 岬

capital N *(city)* shufu 首府, shuto 首都, miyako 都; *(money)* shihon 資本

capital letter N ōmoji 大文字

capricious ADJ kimagure na 気まぐれな

capsule N kapuseru カプセル

captain N *(army)* tai'i 大尉; *(navy)* taisa 大佐; *(airplane)* kichō 機長; *(ship)* senchō 船長, *(warship)* kanchō 艦長; *(team)* kyaputen キャプテン

caption N kyapushon キャプション, *(situation)* midashi 見出し; *(movie, etc)* jimaku 字幕; *(explanation)* setsumei bun 説明文

captive N horyo 捕虜

capture V toraeru 捕らえる

226

car N kuruma 車, jidōsha 自動車

carbohydrate N tansuikabutsu 炭水化物

card N fuda 札, kādo カード: *cards (game)* toranpu トランプ

cardboard N bōrugami ボール紙; *(corrugated)* danbōru 段ボール

care N *(caution)* yōjin 用心; *(upkeep)* teire 手入れ; sewa 世話: *care for* konomu 好む; *take care of* sewa o suru 世話をする, ... no mendō o miru 〜の面倒を見る

career N *(occupation)* shokugyō 職業; *(history)* keireki 経歴, *(summary, resume)* rireki 履歴

careful ADJ chūibukai 注意深い; neniri na 念入りな; *(be ~)* ki o tsukete 気をつけて

careless ADJ taiman na 怠慢な, fuchūi na 不注意な, zusan na ずさんな

carnival N kānibaru カーニバル, shaniku-sai 謝肉祭

carp N *(fish)* koi 鯉

carpenter N daiku 大工

carpet N jūtan じゅうたん, kāpetto カーペット

carrot N ninjin にんじん

carry V motte/totte iku 持って/取って行く; *(load aboard)* noseru 載せる; *(convey)* hakobu 運ぶ; *(dangling from the hand)* sageru 提げる; *carry on (one's back/ shoulders)* shou/seou 背負う, katsugu かつぐ; *carry out (perform)* okonau 行う; *(bring about)* jikkō suru 実行する

cart N *(horsecart)* basha 馬車; *(pushcart)* kāto カート (手押し車), daisha 台車

cartoon N manga まんが

carve V horu 彫る, kizamu 刻む

case N *(situation)* ba'ai 場合; *(matter)* jiken 事件, kēsu ケース, mondai 問題; *(box)* hako 箱, kēsu ケース

cash N genkin 現金; V *(a check)* kankin suru 換金する

cash dispenser N genkin jidō shiharai-ki 現金自動支払機

cashier N kaikeigakari 会計係, rejigakari レジ係

cassette N kasetto カセット

castle N shiro 城

casual ADJ nanigenai 何気ない; kigaru na 気軽な; kajuaru na カジュアルな

casualty N higai 被害; *(victim)* higai-sha 被害者; *(dead and injured)* shishō-sha 死傷者

cat N neko 猫

catalog N katarogu カタログ; mokuroku 目録

catastrophe N dai-sanji 大惨事, dai-saigai 大災害, katasutorofi カタストロフィ

catch V *(seize)* tsukamaeru 捕まえる; toru 取る; *(attract)* hiku 引く; *(a disease)* (byōki ni) naru (病気に)なる: *catch a cold* kaze o hiku 風邪をひく

catering N demae 出前, kētaringu ケータリング, shidashi 仕出し

caterpillar N kemushi 毛虫

Catholic N Katorikku カトリック, *(person)* Katorikku kyōto カトリック教徒

cause N *(of an effect)* moto 元, gen'in 原因; *(reason)* wake 訳, riyū 理由

caution N yōjin 用心, chūi 注意; *(precaution)* yōi 用意

cave N hora'ana ほら穴; dōkutsu 洞窟

CD N shī-dī シーディー

CD-ROM N shī-dī romu シーディーロム

ceiling N tenjō 天井

celebrate V iwau 祝う

celebration N *(party)* o-iwai お祝い

cell phone N keitai denwa 携帯電話

cellar N *(storehouse)* kura 倉・蔵; *(basement)* chikashitsu 地下室

cemetery N hakaba 墓場, bochi 墓地

censure N *(blame)* hinan 非難; V *(blame)* hinan suru 非難する, semeru 責める

center N man'naka 真ん中, chūō 中央, chūshin 中心

central ADJ man'naka no 真ん中の, chūshin no 中心の, chūō no 中央の

century N seiki 世紀

ceramics N *(ceramic art)* tōgei 陶芸; *(ceramic ware)* tōki 陶器; *(pottery)* yakimono 焼き物

ceremony N gishiki 儀式

certain ADJ tashika na 確かな; kakujitsu na 確実な

certainly ADV mochiron もち

ろん; tashika ni 確かに; masani まさに

certificate N shōsho 証書; shōmei-sho 証明書

chain N kusari 鎖、chēn チェーン

chair N isu 椅子

chairperson N kaichō 会長、gichō 議長

chalk N chōku チョーク

challenge N chōsen 挑戦、charenji チャレンジ; V (try) chōsen suru 挑戦する、charenji suru チャレンジする; (test) tamesu 試す

challenger N charenjā チャレンジャー、chōsen-sha 挑戦者

champion N yūshōsha 優勝者、chanpion チャンピオン

championship N senshu-ken 選手権

chance N kikai 機会、chansu チャンス: by chance gūzen ni 偶然に

change N kozeni 小銭; (money returned) otsuri おつり、tsurisen つり銭、henka 変化; (abnormality) ijō 異常; (of trains) norikae 乗り換え; VT (clothes) kigaeru 着替える; kaeru 変える; aratameru

改める; (train, bus, plane) norikaeru 乗り換える; VI (conditions, situations) (jōkyō ga) kawaru (状況が)変わる、henka suru 変化する; (money) kankin suru 換金する; henkan suru 変換する: change one's mind ki ga kawaru 気が変わる

channel N chan'neru チャンネル (TV); kaikyō 海峡

chant V utau 歌う

chapel N chaperu チャペル、reihai-dō 礼拝堂

chapter N (book) shō 章、chaputā チャプター

character N (quality) seishitsu 性質; (personality) seikaku 性格、kosei 個性; (written) ji 字、moji 文字

characteristic N (an earmark) tokushoku 特色、tokuchō 特徴; ADJ (specific) koyū no 固有の、dokutoku no 独特の

charcoal N sumi 炭、mokutan 木炭

charge N (fee) ryōkin 料金、daikin 代金; (battery) jūden 充電; (an attack) shūgeki 襲撃; V seikyū suru 請求する; (attack) shūgeki suru 襲撃

する、kōgeki suru 攻撃する；
(battery) jūden suru 充電する

charity N jizen 慈善、charitī
チャリティー

charm N *(amulet)* o-mamori
お守り；*(attraction)* miryoku
魅力、aikyō 愛きょう；v *(... o)*
uttorisaseru （〜を）うっとり
させる

chart N zuhyō 図表、zu 図、
chāto チャート

chase v oikakeru 追いかける、
ou 追う、tsuiseki suru 追跡する

chat N (v) oshaberi (o suru) おし
ゃべり(をする)

cheap ADJ yasui 安い

cheat N peten ペてん、ikasama
いかさま、sagi 詐欺；v
(deceive) damasu だます、
gomakasu ごまかす

check v *(confirm)* tashikameru 確かめる；*(baggage)*
azukeru 預ける；*(investigate)*
shiraberu 調べる、chekku
suru チェックする；*(inspect)*
kensa suru 検査する；N
(inspection) chekku チェッ
ク、*(bank)* kogitte 小切手、
(restaurant bill) denpyō 伝票

check in v *(register)* chekkuin
suru チェックインする

check out v *(of hotel)*
chekkuauto suru チェックア
ウトする

checkbook N *(bank)* kogitte
chō 小切手帳

check-up N kensa 検査

cheek N hō/hoho 頬、hoppeta
ほっぺた

cheerful ADJ kigen ga ii 機嫌が
いい、genki ga ii 元気がいい、
hogaraka na ほがらかな、yōki
na 陽気な

cheers N kanpai 乾杯

cheese N chīzu チーズ

chef N *(Japanese food)* itamae
板前、ryōrichō 料理長、shefu
シェフ

chemicals N kagakuseihin
化学製品；*(pharmaceuti-
cals)* (kagaku)yakuhin
(化学)薬品

chemist N kagaku-sha 化学者；
(pharmacist) yakuzai-shi
薬剤師

chemistry N kagaku 化学

cherish v chōhō suru 重宝する、
daiji ni suru 大事にする

cherry N *(tree)* sakura 桜；
(fruit) sakuranbo さくらんぼ

chess N chesu チェス；
(Japanese chess) shōgi 将棋

chest N *(box)* seiridansu 整理だんす; *(breast)* mune 胸

chew V kamu 噛む

chewing gum N gamu ガム, chūingamu チューインガム

chic ADJ shikku na シックな, *(cool)* iki na 粋な, jōhin na 上品な

chicken N niwatori 鶏, niwatori ニワトリ; ikujinashi 意気地なし

chief N *(head)* chō 長, chōkan 長官, chīfu チーフ, *(ringleader)* oya-bun 親分; ADJ *(main)* shuyō na 主要な, omo na 主な.

child N SING kodomo 子供

childish ADJ chisetsu na 稚拙な, kodomoppoi 子どもっぽい, yōchi na 幼稚な

childlike ADJ adokenai あどけない

children N kodomotachi 子供達; *Children's Day (5 May)* Kodomo no hi こどもの日

chill V hiyasu 冷やす

chilli pepper N tōgarashi 唐辛子

chilli sauce N chiri sōsu チリソース

chilly ADJ samui 寒い, hieru 冷える

chime N chaimu チャイム

chimney N entotsu 煙突

chin N ago あご

China N chūgoku 中国

chinaware N *(porcelain)* setomono 瀬戸物

Chinese N *(language)* Chūgokugo 中国語; *(people)* Chūgoku-jin 中国人; ADJ Chūgoku(-jin) no 中国(人)の: *Chinese character* kanji 漢字; *Chinese cooking* chūkaryōri 中華料理

chip N kirehashi 切れ端; *(crack)* kizu 傷

chocolate N chokorēto チョコレート: *chocolate bar* itachoko 板チョコ

choice N *(selection)* sentaku 選択; ADJ *(best-quality)* jōtō na 上等な

choose V erabu 選ぶ, sentaku suru 選択する

chop V kizamu 刻む; *(firewood)* (takigi o) waru (薪を) 割る

chopsticks N hashi 箸

Christian N Kirisutokyōto キリスト教徒; ADJ Kirisutokyōto no キリスト教(徒)の

Christianity N Kirisutokyō キリスト教

Christmas N Kurisumasu クリスマス

chronicle N nendai-ki 年代記

chrysanthemum N kiku 菊

church N kyōkai 教会

cider N *(fizzy lemon soda)* saidā サイダー、ringoshu リンゴ酒

cigar N hamaki 葉巻

cigarette N tabako タバコ: *cigarette/cigar butt* suigara 吸い殻

cinema N eigakan 映画館

circle N en 円、maru 丸、wa 輪

circulate vt mawaru 回る; vT mawasu 回す、haifu suru 配布します

circumstance N ba'ai 場合; koto 事; wake 訳; jijō 事情、ikisatsu いきさつ; jōtai 状態、jōkyō 状況、yōsu 様子

citizen N shimin 市民

citizenship N shimin-ken 市民権

citrus N kankitsurui かんきつ類

city N shi 市、*(town)* machi 町、*(metropolis)* toshi 都市、tokai 都会

city office N shiyakusho 市役所

civilization N bunmei 文明、bunka 文化

claim N *(demand)* yōkyū 要求、seikyū 請求; v *(maintain)* shuchō suru 主張する、*(demand)* yōkyū/seikyū suru 要求/請求する

clamor N sawagi 騒ぎ; v sawagu 騒ぐ

clan N ichizoku 一族、ikka 一家

clap *(one's hands)* v te o tataku 手を叩く; hakushu suru 拍手する

clarification N setsumei 説明

clarify vT *(make clear)* akiraka ni suru 明らかにする; vI *(become clear)* akiraka ni naru 明らかになる、hakkiri suru はっきりする

class N *(category)* bumon 部門; *(degree)* kaikyū 階級; *(rank)* kyū 級; *(in school)* gakkyū 学級、kurasu クラス

classic N kurashikku クラシック、koten 古典

classical ADJ koten no 古典の、koten-teki na 古典的な; *classical music* kurashikku ongaku クラシック音楽、koten ongaku 古典音楽

classmate N dōkyūsei 同級生, kurasumeito クラスメイト

classroom N kyōshitsu 教室

claw N tsume 爪; *(of crab)* hasami はさみ; *(animal)* kagitsume かぎ爪

clean ADJ kirei na きれいな, seiketsu na 清潔な; *(fresh)* sapparishita さっぱりした; V kirei ni suru きれいにする, *(clean)* katazukeru 片付ける, *(sweep)* sōji suru 掃除する

cleaning N *(dry)* (dorai) kurīningu (ドライ)クリーニング; *(sweeping up)* sōji 掃除

cleanliness N seiketsu 清潔

clear ADJ *(bright)* akarui 明るい; *(sunny)* hareteiru 晴れている, hareta 晴れた; *(transparent)* tōmei na 透明な; *(evident)* akiraka na 明らかな; *(understood)* wakatta 分かった; *(easy to see)* miyasui 見やすい; *(easy to understand)* wakariyasui 分かりやすい; V *(clean)* katazukeru 片付ける; *(weather)* hareru 晴れる

clerk N *(in shop)* ten'in 店員, *(in office)* jimuin 事務員; *(in bank)* ginkōin 銀行員

clever ADJ kashikoi かしこ

い; rikō na 利口な; *(nimble with fingers)* kiyō na 器用な; *(skilled)* jōzu na 上手な

client N *(computer)* kuraianto クライアント; *(customer)* kokyaku 顧客; irainin 依頼人

cliff N gake 崖

climate N kikō 気候

climax N chōten 頂点; *(upshot)* ketsumatsu 結末

climb (up) V *(hills, etc)* noboru 登る (丘、山)

clinic N byōin 病院

clip V *(pluck)* tsumu 摘む; *(cut)* kiru 切る; N *(paperclip)* kurippu クリップ

clippers N hasami はさみ; *(for nail)* tsumekiri 爪切り

clock N tokei 時計, okidokei 置き時計: *alarm clock* mezamashi dokei 目覚まし時計

clockwise N (ADJ, ADV) migimawari (no/ni) 右回り(の/に), tokeimawari (ni) 時計回りに

clog V tsumaru 詰まる, tsukaeru つかえる

clogs N *(Japanese wooden sandal)* geta 下駄

close VT *(shut)* shimeru 閉める, *(a book, etc.)* tojiru 閉じる; *(close one's eyes)* me

o tsuburu/tojiru 目をつぶ
る/閉じる; *(end)* owaru 終
わる; vi shimaru 閉まる; adj
(near) chikai 近い; *(familiar)*
shitashi'i 親しい, shinmitsu
na 親密な; chimitsu na 緻密
な; adv chikaku ni 近くに; n
(the end) owari 終わり

closet n oshi'ire 押し入れ,
kurōsetto クローゼット

cloth n orimono 織物, kiji 生
地, nuno 布; *(a piece of)* kire
きれ, nunokire 布切れ

clothes, clothing n fuku 服,
fukusō 服装

cloud n kumo 雲

cloud computing n *(Internet)*
kuraudo (conpyūtingu) クラ
ウド (コンピューティング)

cloudy adj *(overcast)* kumotta
曇った; *(weather)* kumori 曇
り

club n *(group)* kurabu クラブ;
(golf) (gorufu) kurabu (ゴル
フ)クラブ

clumsy adj bukiyō na 不器用
な, heta na 下手な, gikochi-
nai ぎこちない

coach n *(railroad)* kyakusha
客車; *(sports)* kōchi コーチ; v
shidō suru 指導する

coal n sekitan 石炭

coast n engan 沿岸, kaigan
海岸

coat n *(jacket)* jaketto ジャケ
ット, uwagi 上着; *(overcoat)*
kōto コート, ōbā オーバー,
gaitō 外套

cock n ondori 雄鶏

cockroach n gokiburi ごきぶり

cocktail n kakuteru カクテル

cocoa n kokoa ココア

coconut n kokonattsu ココ
ナッツ

cod n *(fish)* tara たら: *cod roe*
tarako たらこ

code n kōdo コード; *(secret)*
angō 暗号

coffee n kōhī コーヒー

coffee shop/house n kōhīten
コーヒー店, kissaten 喫茶店

coin n kōka 硬貨

coin locker n koinrokkā コイ
ンロッカー

cola n kōra コーラ

cold adj samui 寒い; *(touch)*
tsumetai 冷たい; n *(flu)* kaze
風邪]: *catch a cold* kaze o
hiku 風邪をひく; *cold water*
mizu 水, (o-)hiya (お)冷や

collaborate v *(cooperate)*
kyōryoku suru 協力する;

(work with) gassaku suru 合作する

collar N *(of coat)* eri 襟; *(of dog)* kubiwa 首輪

collarbone N sakotsu 鎖骨

colleague N dōryō 同僚

collect VT *(gather up)* atsumeru 集める, shūshū suru 収集する; *(complete a set)* soroeru 揃える; *(reap, bring in)* osameru 納める; *(levy tax etc.)* chōshū suru 徴収する; VI *(come together)* atsumaru 集まる; *(collect on delivery)* daikin hikikae (de) 代金引き換え(で)

collection N *(antiques, etc.)* korekushon コレクション; *(of books)* zōsho 蔵書

college N daigaku 大学

collide V shōtotsu suru 衝突する

collision N shōtotsu 衝突

colloquial N *(language, word)* kōgo 口語; ADJ kōgoteki na 口語的な

color N iro 色

colorful ADJ *(bright)* hanayaka na 華やかな; *(various)* tasai na 多彩な, karafuru na カラフルな

column N ran 欄; *(page column)* dan 段; *(numerical column)* keta 桁; *(pillar)* hashira 柱

comb N kushi くし; V *(hair)* kami o suku/toku/tokasu 髪をすく/とく/とかす

combine VT kumi-awaseru 組み合わせる, awaseru 合わせる; VI gappei/gōdō suru 合併/合同する

come V kuru 来る; *(I come to)* iku 行く; *come along* yatte-kuru やって来る; *come back* fukki 復帰, itte kuru 行って来る; kaeru 帰る; *come down* kudaru 下る; *(on the price)* makeru 負ける; *come in ... ni hairu* 〜に入る; *come on* *(let's go)* sā ikō さあ行こう; *(go for it)* ganbare 頑張れ; *come out* deru 出る, dete kuru 出て来る; *(appear)* arawareru 現れる; *(photograph)* utsuru 写る

comedy N kigeki 喜劇, komedī コメディー

comfort N anraku 安楽, kiraku 気楽; *(consolation)* nagusame 慰め, ian 慰安; V *(console)* nagusameru 慰める

235

comfortable ADJ kokochi yoi 心地良い; raku na 楽な, kiraku na 気楽な; kaiteki na 快適な, kimochi ga ii 気持ちがいい; *(easy to wear)* kiyasui 着やすい, *(easy to sit on)* suwariyasui 座りやすい: **feel comfortable** ADJ igokochi ga ii 居心地がいい

comical ADJ okashi na おかしな, omoshiroi 面白い, hyōkin na ひょうきんな

comics N manga 漫画

Coming-of-Age Day N *(2nd Monday of January)* Seijin no hi 成人の日

command N *(order)* meirei 命令; V meirei suru 命令する, *(order a person)* ii'tsukeru 言い付ける, tsugeguchi suru 告げ口する, meijiru 命じる; *(leads)* hiki'iru 率いる

comment N *(explanation)* kaisetsu 解説, *(critique, opinion)* hyōron 評論

commerce N shōgyō 商業; *(trade)* bōeki 貿易

commercial N *(TV)* komāsharu コマーシャル, shīemu (CM) シーエム; ADJ shōgyō no 商業の

commission N *(handling charge)* tesūryō 手数料; dairi 代理; irai 依頼; V irai suru 依頼する

commit V *(entrust)* yudaneru 委ねる; *(perpetrate)* okasu 犯す; hataraku 働く

committee N i'inkai 委員会

commodities N seikatsu-hitsujuhin 生活必需品

common ADJ yokuaru よくある, futsū no 普通の; *(average)* nami no 並の; ippanteki na 一般的な; arigachi na ありがちな

communicate V tsutaeru 伝える; tsūjiru 通じる

communication N *(message, news)* renraku 連絡, jōhō 情報; tsūshin 通信

Communism N kyōsan-shugi 共産主義

community N komyunitī コミュニティー, *(society)* shakai 社会

commute V *(school, etc.)* kayou 通う; *(business, etc.)* tsūkin shimasu 通勤する

compact ADJ kogata no 小型の, konpakuto na コンパクトな: **compact file** *(computer)*

asshuku fairu 圧縮ファイル

companion N nakama 仲間; tsure 連れ, tomodachi 友達; aite 相手

company N kaisha 会社, kigyō 企業; *(group)* kumi 組, gurūpu グループ, nakama 仲間

compare V hikaku suru 比較する, kuraberu 比べる: *compared with* ... to hikakushite 〜と比較して

compass N *(for directions)* rashinban 羅針盤

compatible ADJ naka ga yoi 仲が良い, ki no au 気の合う: *be compatible with* aishō ga ii 相性がいい; *(computer)* gokansei no aru 互換性のある

compensation N *(indemnity money)* hoshō-kin 補償金, benshō 弁償, baishō 賠償

compel V shi'iru 強いる

compete V kisou 競う, kyōsō suru 競争する

competition N kyōsō 競争

competitive ADJ kyōsō no hageshi'i 競争の激しい; kyōsō-shin no tsuyoi 競争心の強い

competitor N kyōsōaite 競争相手

complain V guchi o kobosu 愚痴をこぼす; fuhei/monku/kujō o iu 不平/文句/苦情を言う; uttaeru 訴える

complaint N fuhei 不平, kujō 苦情, monku 文句, kogoto 小言, guchi 愚痴

complete ADJ *(finished)* kanseishita 完成した, *(thorough)* kanpeki na 完璧な, *(whole)* subete sorotta 全てそろった; V kanryō suru 完了する

completely ADV kanzen ni 完全に, mattaku まったく, to(t)temo と(っ)ても, sukkari すっかり, sokkuri そっくり

complex N konpurekkusu コンプレックス, rettō-kan 劣等感

complicated ADJ fukuzatsu na 複雑な, komi'itta 込み入った, yaya(k)koshi'i やや(っ)こしい, kojireta こじれた

complications N ikisatsu いきさつ

compliment N homekotoba ほめ言葉, o-seji お世辞

component N seibun 成分; yōso 要素

compose V *(letters, books)* kaku 書く; *(music)* sakkyoku suru 作曲する

composition N sakuhin 作品; haigō N 配合

comprehension N rikai 理解; *(comprehension ability)* rikairyoku 理解力

comprehensive ADJ *(composite)* sōgōteki na 総合的な

compress V asshuku suru 圧縮する; *(presses)* appaku suru 圧迫する; *(shorten)* tanshuku suru 短縮する

compromise N dakyō 妥協

compulsory ADJ hissu no 必須の; gimuteki na 義務的な; *(stipulated)* kitei no 規定の

computer N konpyūtā コンピューター

computer game N konpyūtā gēmu コンピューター・ゲーム

comrade N dōshi 同志

concentrate V shūchū suru 集中する

concern N *(relevance)* kankei 関係, *(interest)* kanshin 関心; *(worry)* shinpai 心配; *(business)* kaisha 会社; V *(relate to)* ... ni kansuru ~に関する, *(center on)* ... o meguru ~を巡る

concerning PREP ... ni kanshite

~に関して、... o megutte ~を巡って

concert N ongakukai 音楽会, ensōkai 演奏会

concise ADJ kanketsu na 簡潔な

conclude V *(bring to an end)* sumasu 済ます; *(end a discussion)* ketsuron o dasu 結論を出す; *(finalize)* seiritsu suru 成立する

concrete N *(cement)* konkurīto コンクリート; ADJ *(not abstract)* gutai-teki na 具体的な

condition N *(pre-condition)* jōken 条件; *(status)* jōkyō 状況, jōtai 状態, jijō 事情, guai 具合; chōshi 調子: *be in good (bad) condition* chōshi ga ii (warui) 調子がいい(悪い)

condom N kondōmu コンドーム

condominium N kondominiamu コンドミニアム

conductor N *(train)* shashō 車掌; *(orchestra)* shikisha 指揮者; *(tour guide)* tenjōin 添乗員

confectionery N (o-)kashi (お)菓子

conference N *(personal)*

sōdan 相談; *(formal)* kaigi 会議; *(negotiation)* hanashiai 話し合い

confession N kokuhaku 告白

confidence N shin'yō 信用, shinrai 信頼, tanomi 頼み; *(self-confidence)* jishin 自信; *(secure feeling)* anshin 安心

confidential ADJ naisho no 内緒の

confirm V kakunin suru 確認する

Confucianism N Jukyō 儒教

confuse V konwaku saseru 困惑させる, konran saseru 混乱させる, madowaseru 惑わせる

congratulations N omedetō おめでとう

connect with V (... to) tsunagu (〜と)つなぐ; (... to) renraku suru (〜と)連絡する; tsūjiru 通じる; *(be connected with)* (... to) tsunagaru (〜と)つながる, (... ni) kansuru (〜に)関する

connection N renraku 連絡; *(relevance)* kankei 関係; *(relation)* tsunagari つながり; *(link)* tsunagi つなぎ

conscious of (be ~) jikaku suru 自覚する

consciousness N ishiki 意識

conservative ADJ hoshuteki na 保守的な; shōkyokuteki na 消極的な; *(moderate)* uchiwa no 内輪の

conserve V *(save)* setsuyaku suru 節約する; N *(fruit jam)* jamu ジャム; *(fish or seaweed)* tsukuda-ni つくだ煮

consider V *(have an opinion)* omou 思う; *(think over)* kangaeru 考える; kōryo suru 考慮する; hairyo suru 配慮します

considerable ADJ sōtō na 相当な, yohodo no 余程の, yoppodo no よっぽどの

consideration N *(being kind)* omoiyari 思いやり, hairyo 配慮; *(thought)* kōryo 考慮, shiryo 思慮

consolation N nagusame 慰め, ian 慰安

console V nagusameru 慰める

constant ADJ chakujitsu na 着実な

constipation N benpi 便秘

constitute V kōsei suru 構成する

constitution N *(basic laws)* kenpō 憲法; *(physical)* taishitsu 体質; *(composition)* kōsei 構成

construction N *(work)* kōji 工事

consulate N ryōji-kan 領事館

consult V sōdan suru 相談する

consultant N komon 顧問, konsarutanto コンサルタント

consumer N shōhisha 消費者

contact N sesshoku 接触; V *(~ with)* renraku suru 連絡する; *(... ni) fureru* (〜に)触れる, sesshoku suru 接触する; *(meet)* ... ni au 〜に会う

contact lenses N kontakuto (renzu) コンタクト(レンズ)

contagious disease N densenbyō 伝染病

contain V ... ga haitteiru 〜が入っている; ... o fukumu 〜を含む

container N nakami 中身, yōki 容器; *(box)* hako 箱

contamination N osen 汚染

contend for V arasou 争う

contents N nakami 中身, naiyō 内容; *(table of contents)* mokuji 目次, midashi 見出し

contest N konkūru コンクール, kontesuto コンテスト; *(sports)* kyōgi 競技, *(competition)* kyōsō 競争, *(match)* shiai 試合

continent N tairiku 大陸

continue VI tsuzuku 続く, keizoku suru 継続する; VT tsuzukeru 続ける

continuously ADV taemanaku 絶え間なく, taezu 絶えず; tsuzukete 続けて

contract N *(an agreement)* keiyaku 契約; V *(agree to undertake work)* ukeou 請け負う

contrast N taishō 対照; taihi 対比; V *(compare)* kuraberu 比べる; *(in contrast to/with)* ... ni taishite/hanshite 〜に対して/反して

control N shihai 支配, kanri 管理; *(of prices, etc.)* tōsei 統制; V *(supervise)* torishimaru 取り締まる; *(restrain)* osaeru 抑える; *(operate)* sōjū suru 操縦する

convenience N tsugō 都合, tsuide ついで, benri 便利: *at your convenience* tsuide no toki ni ついでの時に

convenience store N konbini コンビニ

convenient ADJ benri na 便利な, ben ga ii 便がいい; chōhō na 重宝な

conventional ADJ heibon na 平凡な

conversation N kaiwa 会話, hanashi 話, danwa 談話

conversion N henkan 変換

convert V henkan suru 変換する; kōkan suru 交換する

convey V hakobu 運ぶ

cook N (person) kokku コック, ryōrinin 料理人; VT ryōri suru 料理する; (rice, soup) taku 炊く; VI nieru 煮える

cookie N kukkī クッキー, bisuketto ビスケット

cool ADJ suzushi'i 涼しい; (calm) reisei na 冷静な; (chic) iki na 粋な; VI (~ off/down) sameru 冷める, hieru 冷える; VT hiyasu 冷やす; samasu 冷ます

cooperation N kyōryoku 協力; (joint activity) kyōdō 共同

copy N (photocopy) kopī コピー; (reproduction) fukusha 複写, utsushi 写し, fukusei 複製; V utsusu 写す, fukusha/fukusei suru 複写/複製する; (imitate) niseru 似せる; (make a copy) kopī o toru コピーをとる

cord N himo 紐, nawa 縄, kōdo コード

cordial ADJ shinsetsu na 親切な, kokoro no komotta 心のこもった

core N shin 芯

corkscrew N koruku-nuki コルク抜き, sen-nuki 栓抜き

corn N (grain) tōmorokoshi トウモロコシ; (callus) tako たこ, (bunion) mame まめ

corner N (outside) kado 角; (inside) sumi 隅

corporation N kabushiki-gaisha 株式会社, hōjin 法人

correct ADJ tadashi'i 正しい, seikaku na 正確な; V naosu 直す, aratameru 改める; teisei suru 訂正する

correspond V (write letters) buntsū suru 文通する; taiō suru 対応する; tsūshin suru 通信する

correspondence N (messages) tsūshin 通信

corridor N rōka 廊下

cosmetics N keshōhin 化粧品

cost N (expense) hiyō 費用; (price) kakaku 価格

costume N fukusō 服装; ishō 衣装

cotton N men 綿

couch N nagaisu 長いす, neisu 寝椅子

cough N seki 咳き; V seki-komu 咳きこむ, seki o suru 咳をする

could ADV *(possible)* ... suru koto ga dekita ~することが出来た; *(guess)* hyotto shita ra ... ka mo shirenai ひょっとしたら~かもしれない

count V kazoeru 数える

counter N *(for paying, buying tickets)* kauntā カウンター, *(shop)* reji レジ; *(bank)* madoguchi 窓口

counterclockwise ADJ hidari-mawari (ni) 左回り(に)

counterfeit bill N *(currency)* nisesatsu にせ札

countless ADJ kazoe-kirenai 数え切れない, musū no 無数の

country N *(nation)* kokka 国家, kuni 国; *(rural area)* inaka 田舎

county N *(U.S.)* gun 郡; *(Britain)* shū 州

couple N *(husband and wife)* fūfu 夫婦; *(on a date)* kappuru カップル: *a couple (of)* hitokumi (no) 一組の(の)

course N kōsu コース; *(in school)* kamoku 科目; *(of action)* hōshin 方針

court N *(of law)* saibansho 裁判所, hōtei 法廷; *(sports)* kōto コート; *(imperial, royal)* kyūtei 宮廷

courtyard N nakaniwa 中庭

cousin N itoko いとこ

cover N *(lid)* futa ふた; kabā カバー; *(book, magazine, etc.)* hyōshi 表紙, V ōu 覆う

cover charge N *(restaurant)* sekiryō 席料; *(admission)* nyūjōryō 入場料

cow N ushi 牛

coward N ikujinashi 意気地なし, okubyō-mono おくびょう者

co-worker N dōryo 同僚

crab N kani 蟹

crack N sukima すき間; *(wide)* wareme 割れ目; *(fine)* hibi ひび; *(flaw)* kizu 傷; V wareru 割れる

cracker N kurakkā クラッカー

crafts N kōgei 工芸

cramped ADV bisshiri びっしり

crane N *(bird)* tsuru 鶴; *(machine)* kurēn クレーン

crash N *(plane)* tsuiraku 墜落; *(collision)* shōtotsu 衝突

crate N konpōbako 梱包箱

crawl V hau 這う; *(baby)* haihai suru はいはいする

crazy ADJ kurutta 狂った

create V tsukuru 作る・造る

creature N seibutsu 生物

credit N shin'yō 信用

credit card N kurejittokādo クレジットカード

creep V hau 這う; *(baby)* hai hai suru はいはいする

crescent N mikazuki 三日月, shingetsu 新月

crew N *(member)* jōmuin 乗務員, *(ship)* sen'in 船員

crime N tsumi 罪, hanzai 犯罪; hankō 犯行

criminal N hanzaisha 犯罪者

crisis N *(critical moment)* kiki 危機

crisp ADJ paripari no パリパリの, karikari/sakusaku shita カリカリ/サクサクした

critic N hihyōka 批評家, *(commentator)* hyōronka 評論家

criticism N *(bad)* akuhyō 悪評, hihan 批判, hihyō 批評

crocodile N wani ワニ

crop N *(harvest)* minori 実り, shūkaku 収穫; V *(cut out)*

cross N *(symbol)* jūji 十字; jūjika十字架; V *(go across)* wataru 渡る, yokogiru 横切る; *(go over a height)* koeru 越える; ADJ *(angry)* okotta 怒った

crossing N *(street intersection)* kōsaten 交差点

crouch V shagamu しゃがむ, kagamu かがむ

crow N karasu からす

crowd N gunshū 群衆, renjū/renchū 連中

crown N ōkan 王冠

Crown Prince N kōtaishi (-sama) 皇太子(様)

Crown Princess N kōtaishi-hi 皇太子妃

crude ADJ somatsu na 粗末な, zatsu na 雑な

cruel ADJ zankoku na 残酷な, mugoi むごい, hakujō na 薄情な

crumble VI kudakeru 砕ける; VT kudaku 砕く

crumb(s) N pankuzu パンくず; panko パン粉

cry N naku 泣く; *cry out* sakebu 叫ぶ

cucumber N kyūri キュウリ

cuisine N *(style of cooking)* ryōri 料理

cultivate V tagayasu 耕す

culture N bunka 文化, *(refinement)* kyōyō 教養; *(farming)* yōshoku 養殖

cunning N *(cheating)* kan'ningu カンニング; ADJ zurui ずるい

cup N koppu コップ, *(with handle)* kappu カップ, chawan 茶わん

cupboard N shokkidana 食器棚, todana 戸棚

cure N *(medical)* chiryō 治療 *(医療)*; V naosu 治す

curios N *(antiques)* kottōhin 骨董品

curiosity N kōkishin 好奇心

curious ADJ *(inquisitive)* monozuki na 物好きな, *(novel)* mezurashi'i 珍しい

currency N tsūka 通貨, *(bill/note)* (o-)satsu (お)札; shihei 紙幣

current ADJ *(present)* genzai no 現在の, ima no 今の

curry N karē カレー; *(with rice)* karēraisu カレーライス

cursor N kāsoru カーソル

curt ADJ bukkirabō na ぶっきらぼうな

curtain N kāten カーテン

curve N kyokusen 曲線; *(road)* kābu カーブ; VI magaru 曲がる; VT mageru 曲げる

cushion N *(seat)* zabuton 座布団, kusshon クッション

custom N shūkan 習慣, dentō 伝統

customer N (o-)kyaku (お)客, o-kyaku-sama お客様; *(patron)* otokui-sama お得意様, tokui-saki 得意先

customs N *(place)* zeikan 税関

cut N *(slice)* kireme 切れめ; V kiru 切る: *cut across* yokogiru 横切る; *cut down (lessen)* herasu 減らす; *(reduce)* chijimeru ちぢめる; *(dilute)* waru 割る; *cut off* kiru 切る; tatsu 断つ; *cut out (eliminates)* habuku 省く; *cut the price (reduce price)* makeru まける, *(reduction)* nesage suru 値下げする

cutlery N hamono 刃物, katorarī カトラリー

cute ADJ *(appealing)* kawaii かわいい, kawai-rashi'i かわいらしい

cutlet N katsu(retsu) カツ(レツ), *(pork)* tonkatsu トンカツ

cuttlefish N *(squid)* ika いか

cyber attack, cyberterrorism N saibā-kōgeki サイバー攻撃, saibā-tero サイバーテロ

cycle V jitensha ni noru 自転車に乗る; N *(circulation)* junkan 循環

cynical ADJ hiniku na 皮肉な, hinekureta ひねくれた

D

daddy, dad N papa パパ

daily ADJ mainichi no 毎日の

daily necessaries N seikatsu-hitsujuhin 生活必需品

dairy N *(shop)* gyūnyū-ya 牛乳屋; ADJ gyūnyū no 牛乳の, nyūseihin no 乳製品の

dam N damu ダム

damage N songai 損害; son sō, gai 害, higai 被害; V itameru 傷める, arasu 荒らす; sokonau 損なう

damp ADJ shikke no aru 湿気のある, himeppoi 湿っぽい

dance N odori 踊り, dansu ダンス; V odoru 踊る

dandy N (ADJ) *(fancy dresser)* oshare (na) おしゃれ(な)

danger N kiken 危険

dangerous ADJ kiken na 危険な, abunai 危ない; yabai やばい; kiwadoi きわどい *(delicate, tricky)*

dark ADJ kurai 暗い; *(color)* koi 濃い; N higure 日暮れ, yami 闇

darkness N (kura)yami (暗)闇

data N dēta データ

database N dētabēsu データベース

date N *(of the month)* hizuke 日付; *(complete)* nengappi 年月日; *(engagement)* yakusoku 約束; V *(a couple)* dēto suru デートする

date of birth N tanjōbi 誕生日

daughter N musume 娘

dawdle V guzuguzu suru ぐずぐずする

dawn N yoake 夜明け

day N hi 日: *day after tomorrow* asatte 明後日; *day before last/yesterday* ototoi 一昨日, issaku-jitsu 一昨日; *day of the week* yōbi 曜日; *day off* kyūjitu 休日

daybreak N akegata 明け方, yoake 夜明け

daydream N kūsō 空想, hakuchūmu 白昼夢; V

245

bon'yari suru ぼんやりする、kūsō suru 空想する

daytime N hiru 昼, hiruma 昼間

dead N shinin 死人; ADJ shinda 死んだ

deadline N shimekiri 締め切り, (saishū-)kigen (最終)期限

deaf ADJ mimi no kikoenai 耳の聞こえない; mimi ga fujiyū na 耳が不自由な

deal N (transaction) torihiki 取引; v (card) kubaru 配る: **deal with** (tori)atsukairu (取り)扱う; (treat a person) ashiraru あしらう; (cope) shori/shobun/shochi suru 処理/処分/処置する; (dispose of a matter) shimatsu suru 始末する

dealer N kouriten 小売店, (retail outlet) hanbaiten 販売店

dean N gakubu-chō 学部長

dear ADJ (beloved) itoshi'i 愛しい; natsukashi'i 懐かしい

death N shi 死

debate N tōron 討論, ronsō 論争, dibēto ディベート; v ronjiru 論じる

debt N shakkin 借金

deceive v damasu だます

December N jūni-gatsu 十二月

decent ADJ (respectable) jōhin na 上品な, rippa na 立派な

decide v kimeru 決める; kettei suru 決定する

decimal N shōsū 小数

decimal point N shōsūten 小数点

decision N kesshin 決心; kettei 決定

deck N (of ship) kanpan 甲板, dekki デッキ

decline v (get less) kakō suru 下降する, (refuse) kotowaru 断る, jitai suru 辞退する; (fade) otoroeru 衰える

decorate v kazaru 飾る

decoration N kazari 飾り, sōshoku 装飾

decoy N otori おとり

decrease N genshō 減少; VI heru 減る, genshō suru 減少する; VT herasu 減らす

dedicate v sasageru 捧げる

dedication N kenshin 献身; kenji 献辞

deduct v ... o sashihiku 〜を差し引く

deep ADJ fukai 深い; (saturated color) koi 濃い

deer N shika 鹿

default N deforuto デフォルト, shoki-settei 初期設定

defeat V uchimakasu 打ち負かす, yaburu 破る; N make 負け, shippai 失敗

defecation N daiben 大便

defect N kekkan 欠陥; *(fault)* ketten 欠点

defend V *(in war)* bōgyo suru 防御する (戦争); mamoru 守る; *(with words)* yōgo suru 擁護する, kabau 庇う

defense N bōei 防衛, bōgyo 防御

deficit N *(figures)* akaji 赤字

definite ADJ kakuteishita 確定した

degree N *(level)* teido 程度; kagen 加減

degrees N *(heat)* ondo 温度; *(higher learning)* gakui 学位

delay N okure 遅れ; VT okuraseru 遅らせる; VI okureru 遅れる, guzuguzu suru ぐずぐずする

delete V torikesu 取り消す

deliberately ADV waza to わざと, wazawaza わざわざ, koi ni 故意に

delicate ADJ *(fine)* bimyō na 微妙な; *(sensitive)* sensai na 繊細な

delicious ADJ oishi'i おいしい

delight N yorokobi 喜び; VI ōyorokobi suru 大喜びする; VT tanoshimaseru 楽しませる

deliver V haitatsu suru 配達する

deluxe ADJ jōtō no 上等の, gōka na 豪華な, derakkusu na デラックスな; ADV gōka ni 豪華に

demand N yōkyū 要求, seikyū 請求; V yōkyū suru 要求する, seikyū suru 請求する; todokeru 届ける

democracy N minshushugi 民主主義

democratic ADJ minshu-shugi no 民主主義の, minshu-teki na 民主的な

demolish V kuzusu 崩す; hakai suru 破壊する

dent N kubomi 窪み

dentist N haisha 歯医者

deodorant N *(personal)* shōshūzai 消臭剤; *(household, etc.)* hōkōzai 芳香剤

depart V shuppatsu suru 出発する

department N *(university, hospital)* ka 科; *(company)*

bumon 部門, busho 部署, bu 部, ka 課

department head N *(division head)* buchō 部長

department store N hyakka-ten 百貨店, depāto デパート

departure N shuppatsu 出発

depend on v izon suru 依存する, (... ni) tayoru (～に)頼る, irai suru 依頼する; (... ni) yoru (～に)よる

deposit v azukeru 預ける; *(money)* yokin/chokin suru 預金/貯金する; N atamakin 頭金

depressed ADJ *(feeling)* ki ga omoi 気が重い; *(concave)* hekomu へこむ

depression N *(hard times)* fukeiki 不景気, fukyō 不況

depth N fukasa 深さ

descendant N shison 子孫

describe v byōsha suru 描写する; *(explains)* setsumei suru 説明する

desert N *(arid land)* sabaku 砂漠; v *(abandon)* hōki suru 放棄する

design N *(sketch)* zuan 図案; dezain デザイン; v *(plan)* sessei suru 設計する; dezain

suru デザインする

desire N kibō 希望, ganbō 願望, nozomi 望み; *(hope)* kibō 希望; v (... ga) hoshi'i (～が) 欲しい; *(wants to do)* ...(shi) tai ～(し)たい; *(hopes for)* nozomu 望む

desk N tsukue 机, desuku デスク

desktop personal computer N *(computer)* desukutoppu pasokon デスクトップ パソコン

desperately ADV *(hard)* hisshi ni 必死に, isshō kenmei ni 一生懸命に; *(out of despair)* yake ni natte やけになって

despite PREP ...ni mo kakawarazu ～にもかかわらず

dessert N dezāto デザート

destination N mokutekichi 目的地; iki saki 行き先; *(last stop)* shūten 終点

destiny N unmei 運命

destroy v kowasu 壊す; hakai suru 破壊する; horobosu 滅ぼす

detach v hanasu 離す

detailed ADJ kuwashi'i 詳しい; bisai na 微細な; seimitsu na 精密な

details N shōsai 詳細; ikisatsu いきさつ

detective N tantei 探偵; *(police)* keiji 刑事; *(investigator)* sōsa-kan 捜査官

detergent N senjōzai 洗浄剤

determine V kettei suru 決定する

detour N mawarimichi 回り道, ukai 迂回, tōmawari 遠回り

develop VI *(happen)* hatten suru 発展する; *(grow)* seichō suru 成長する; VT *(film)* genzō suru 現像する; *(create)* kaihatsu suru 開発する

developing nation N hatten tojōkoku 発展途上国

development N hatten 発展, kaihatsu 開発, hattatsu 発達, *(process)* nariyuki 成り行き, *(course)* keika 経過

device N sōchi 装置, kiki 機器; *(gadget)* shikake 仕掛け

devil N *(ogre)* oni 鬼, *(Satan)* akuma 悪魔

diagonal ADJ taikakusen no 対角線の, naname no 斜めの

diagram N zu 図, zuhyō 図表, zukai 図解

dial N daiyaru ダイヤル; V *(telephone)* denwa o kakeru 電話をかける

dialect N hōgen 方言; *(regional accent)* namari なまり

dialogue N kaiwa 会話, taiwa 対話; *(lines)* serifu せりふ

diamond N daiyamondo ダイヤモンド, daiya ダイヤ

diapers N oshime おしめ, omutsu おむつ

diarrhea N geri 下痢

diary N nikki 日記

dice N *(for game)* saikoro さいころ

dictionary N jisho 辞書, jiten 辞典

die V shinu 死ぬ, nakunaru 亡くなる; iki o hikitoru 息を引き取る

diet N daietto ダイエット

Diet N *(parliament)* kokkai 国会, gikai 議会

difference N *(discrepancy in figures)* sai 差異; *(in quality)* sōi 相違, chigai 違い

different ADJ chigairu 違う; kotonaru 異なる; *(other)* hoka no ほかの

difficult ADJ muzukashi'i 難しい; kon'nan na 困難な

difficulty N kon'nan 困難; *(hardship)* kurō 苦労

diffusion N fukyū 普及

dig V horu 掘る, (dig up) hakkutsu suru 発掘する

digest V konasu こなす, shōka suru 消化する, N yōyaku 要約, daijesuto ダイジェスト

digit N (Arabic figures) (arabia) sūji (アラビア)数字; (digit number) keta 桁

digital ADJ dejitaru デジタル

digital camera N dejitaru-kamera デジタルカメラ, dejikame デジカメ

diligent ADJ kinben na 勤勉な, mame na まめな

dimple N ekubo えくぼ

diner N (dining car) shoku-dōsha 食堂車, shokudō 食堂

dining room N shokudō 食堂, dainingu ダイニング

dinner N (supper) bangohan 晩ご飯, yūshoku 夕食

dinosaur N kyōryū 恐竜

diploma N menjō 免状; (graduation diploma) sotsugyō-shōsho 卒業証書

diplomat N (diplomatic official) gaikōkan 外交官

dipper N hishaku ひしゃく

direct ADJ chokusetsu no 直接の; V (tell the way) (... e no) michi o oshieru (～への) 道を教える; (guide, coach) shidō suru 指導する; (a film) kantoku 監督する; (manage) kanri suru 管理する

direction N hōkō 方向; hōmen 方面; hōgaku 方角

directive N shirei 指令

director N (company) jūyaku 重役; (coach) shidōsha 指導者; (of a film) kantoku 監督

directory N (telephone) denwachō 電話帳; (list of names) meibo 名簿

dirt N yogore 汚れ; (filth) doro 泥; (grime) aka 垢; (soil) tsuchi 土

dirty ADJ kitanai 汚い fuketsu na 不潔な, (dirty-minded) gehin na 下品な, etchi na エッチな

disadvantage N son 損, furi 不利; (shortcoming) ketten 欠点, demeritto デメリット, tansho 短所

disagreement N fuitchi 不一致

disappointment N shitsubō 失望, kitai hazure 期待はずれ, rakutan 落胆; (in love) shitsuren 失恋

disarray N konran 混乱, mu-chitsujo 無秩序

disaster N sōnan 遭難, sainan 災難, wazawai 災い: *disaster area* hisai-chi 被災地

discharge V *(from employment)* kaiko suru 解雇する

disciple N deshi 弟子

discipline N kiritsu 規律, chitsujo 秩序; shitsuke しつけ; V *(drill, train)* kitaeru 鍛える, *(bring up children, ...)* shitsukeru しつける

disclose V *(public)* kōkaishiru 公開する; abaku 暴く

disco N disuko ディスコ

disconnect V hanasu 離す; *(get disconnected)* hazureru 外れる

discontent N *(grumbling)* fuhei 不平, fuman 不満

discount N waribiki 割引, nebiki 値引き

discourage V gakkari saseru がっかりさせる; samatageru 妨げる

discourtesy N burei 無礼, shitsurei 失礼

discover V *(find)* mitsukeru 見つける, hakken suru 発見する

discovery N hakken 発見

discrepancy N sa 差, sōi 相違, kuichigai 食い違い; *(gap)* zure ずれ

discretion N tsutsushimi 慎み, funbetsu 分別

discriminate V *(distinguish them)* miwakeru 見分ける, shikibetsu suru 識別する

discrimination N sabetsu 差別; kubetsu 区別; *(distinguishing)* shiki-betsu 識別

discuss V *(debate, argue)* giron suru 議論する, *(talk it over)* hanashiau 話し合う, sōdan suru 相談する

discussion N hanashiai 話し合い; kyōgi 協議; *(debate)* giron 議論, tōron 討論, ronsō 論争

disease N byōki 病気

disgrace oneself V haji o kaku 恥をかく

disgraceful ADJ hazukashi'i 恥ずかしい

disgusting ADJ mukatsuku yō na むかつくような; iya na 嫌な

dish N sara 皿; *(particular food)* ryōri 料理

dishonest ADJ fuseijitsu na 不誠実な, fushōjiki na 不正直

な、ii'kagen na いいかげんな、fusei no 不正の

diskette N furoppīdisuku フロッピーディスク

dislike V konomanai 好まない、kirau 嫌う

disobey V ... ni somuku、〜に背く

disorder N konran 混乱、sōdō 騒動、fukisoku 不規則

display N tenji 展示；V tenji suru 展示する；*(computer)* disupurē ディスプレー

disposal N haiki 廃棄、shobun 処分

dissatisfied ADJ fuman na 不満な

dissolve VT tokasu 溶かす；VI tokeru 溶ける

distance N kyori 距離

distinctly ADV hakkiri to はっきりと

distinguish V *(discriminate)* miwakeru 見分ける、shikibetsu suru 識別する

distribution N haifu 配布、bunpai 分配；ryūtsū 流通；hanbai 販売

district N chihō 地方、chi'iki 地域

disturb V samatageru 妨げる

disturbance N bōgai 妨害、arasoi 争い、jama 邪魔

disunity N futōitsu 不統一

dive N tobikomi 飛び込み、daibingu ダイビング；V *(under)* moguru 潜る；tobikomu 飛び込む

divide N bunkatsu 分割；VT bunkatsu suru 分割する、wakeru 分ける；VI wakareru 分かれる

diving N tobikomi 飛び込み；sensui 潜水、daibingu ダイビング

division N bu 部；shikiri 仕切り；*(math calculation)* warizan 割り算

division head N buchō 部長

divorce N rikon 離婚；V rikon suru 離婚する

dizzy ADJ me ga mararu 目が回る；baka-geta ばかげた

do V *(perform an action)* ... suru 〜する、yaru やる、okonau 行う：*do one's best* besuto o tsukusu ベストを尽くす；*do one's share* buntan suru 分担する；*do(es) not work (spoiled)* kowareta 壊れた

doctor N isha 医者；sensei

先生; *(Ph.D.)* hakase 博士

document N shorui 書類

dog N inu 犬

doll N ningyō 人形; *Doll's Festival (3 March)* Hinamatsuri ひな祭

dollar N doru ドル

domain-name N *(Internet)* domein mei/nēmu ドメイン名/ネーム

domestic ADJ *(not foreign)* kokunai no 国内の; *(domestically made)* kokusan no 国産の

done ADJ *(cooked)* yoku hi no tōtta よく火の通った; *(finished)* sunda 済んだ; *(ready)* dekita 出来た

donkey N roba ろば

don't shinai しない; dame 駄目, ikenai いけない; ... *(shi)* nai de ～(し)ないで

door N to 戸, doa ドア

doorbell N yobirin 呼び鈴

doorway N deiriguchi 出入り口

dormitory N kishukusha 寄宿舎, ryō 寮, *(for singles)* dokushinryō 独身寮

dot(s) N ten点, mizutama *(moyō)* 水玉(模様)

double N (ni)bai (2)倍; ADJ nibai no 二倍の, *(two-layer)* nijū no 二重の; *(double room)* daburu ダブル; v *(...o)* bai ni suru (～を)倍にする

doubt N *(a doubt)* gimon 疑問, utagai 疑い, giwaku 疑惑; v utagau 疑う, fushin ni omou 不審に思う

dove N hato 鳩

down, downward ADJ shita ni aru 下にある; PREP ... no shita e ～の下へ; ADV shita ni 下に

down payment N atamakin 頭金

download v *(computer)* daunrōdo suru ダウンロードする

downpour N gōu 豪雨, doshaburi 土砂降り

downtown N hankagai 繁華街

doze off v inemuri suru 居眠りする

dozen N dāsu ダース

draft N *(rough)* shitagaki 下書き; *(beer)* namabīru 生ビール; *(military conscription)* shōshū 召集

drag N bōgai 妨害, shōgai 障害, *(drag on)* ashidematoi 足

手まとい; v hipparu 引っ張る、
hiku 引く、hikizuru 引きずる

drain N (kitchen) gesuikan
下水管; (ditch) mizo 溝; vi
(water) (mizu ga) nagareru
(水が)流れる; vt (mizuke o)
kiru (水気を)切る

drama N engeki 演劇, geki 劇,
dorama ドラマ

draw v (a picture) egaku/
kaku 描く; (pull) hiku 引く;
(water etc.) kumu 汲む; N
(game) hikiwake 引き分け

drawer N hikidashi 引き出し

drawing N (picture) e 絵,
zuga 図画; (diagram) zu 図,
chūsen 抽選

dream N yume 夢; v yume o
miru 夢を見る

dreary ADJ ajike no nai 味気
のない, ajikenai 味気ない;
uttōshi'i うっとうしい

dress N yōfuku 洋服, fuku 洋
服, fukusō 服装, (woman's)
wanpīsu ワンピース, doresu
ドレス; v fuku o kiru 服を着る

dried ADJ kawaita 乾いた;
hoshi... 干し～:

drill N (tool) kiri 錐, doriru
ドリル; (practice) keiko
稽古; (study) renshu 練習,

(training) kunren 訓練; vt
(train) kunren suru 訓練する,
(discipline) kitaeru 鍛える

drink N nomimono 飲み物; v
nomu 飲む: **a drink** N ippai
一杯

drinking N (alcoholic
beverage) inshu 飲酒

drip vt shitataru 滴る, tareru
垂れる

drive v (a car) unten suru 運転
する; N doraibu ドライブ

driver N untenshu 運転手

driver license N unten-
menkyo-shō 運転免許証

driveway N shadō 車道

drop vt otosu 落とす, (let it
fall, spill) tarasu 垂らす; vi
ochiru 落ちる; N (a drop)
tsubu 粒, tama 玉: **drop off**
(a person from a vehicle)
orosu 降ろす

drought N kanbatsu 干ばつ

drown v oboreru おぼれる

drug N (medicine) kusuri 薬,
yakuhin 薬品; (narcotic)
mayaku 麻薬

drug addict N mayaku-
chūdoku-sha 麻薬中毒者

drugstore N yakkyoku 薬局,
doraggu sutoa ドラッグストア

drum N taiko 太鼓, doramu ドラム

drunk ADJ yopparatta 酔っ払った; N yopparai 酔っぱらい

dry ADJ kawaita 乾いた; (weather) kansōshita 乾燥した(天気); VI kawaku 乾く, kansō suru 乾燥する; VT kawakasu 乾かす, (foodstuff) hosu 干す

dry cleaning N doraikurīningu ドライクリーニング

dryer, drier N doraiyā ドライヤー

duck N ahiru アヒル

dull ADJ (boring) taikutsu na 退屈な; nibui 鈍い, noroi のろい; (weather) don'yorishita どんよりした (天気)

dumpling N dango 団子

dune N sakyū 砂丘

duplicate ADJ (double) nijū no 二重の; fukusei no 複製の; N fukusei 複製; utsushi 写し; V fukusei suru 複製する; saigen suru 再現する

during ADV ... no aida ni 〜の間に

dusk N yūure doki 夕暮れ時

dust N hokori 埃; (in house) gomi ごみ

duty N (import tax) kanzei 関税; (responsibility) gimu 義務

DVD N dī-bui-dī ディーブイディー

dwindle V heru 減る

dye V someru 染める

dynamic ADJ gōkai na 豪快な

E

each PRON, ADJ ... goto ni 〜毎に

each other PRON o-tagai ni お互いに

each time ADV ichi'ichi いちいち, maikai 毎回

ear N mimi 耳

eardrum N komaku 鼓膜

earlier ADJ (former) mae no/ni 前の/に

early ADJ hayai 早い; ADV hayaku 早く; (ahead of time) hayame ni 早めに

earn V eru 得る, kasegu 稼ぐ

earnings N (income) shūnyū 収入, shotoku 所得

earnest ADJ majime na 真面目な, (serious) honki no 本気の

earphone N iyahon イヤホン, iyahōn イヤホーン

255

earth N dojō 土壌; tsuchi 土、tochi 土地

Earth N chikyū 地球

earthquake N jishin 地震

ease N *(comfort)* raku 楽; V yasumeru 休める

east N higashi 東

Easter N īsutā イースター、fukkatsu-sai 復活祭

easy ADJ kantan na 簡単な、yasashi'i やさしい、tayasui たやすい; *assari (to) shita* あっさり(と)した

easygoing ADJ nonki na のん気な、kiraku na 気楽な

eat V taberu 食べる: *eat out* gaishoku suru 外食する

e-book, electronic book N denshi shoseki 電子書籍

e-cash, e-money N denshi-manē 電子マネー

eccentric N fūgawari na hito 風変わりな人、ekisentorikku エキセントリック; *(freak)* henjin 変人、kijin 奇人

echo N hibiki 響き、kodama こだま、hankyō 反響; V hibiku 響く

ecology N seitai-gaku 生態学、ekorojī エコロジー、seitai-kankyō 生態環境

economic ADJ keizai no 経済の

economical ADJ keizaiteki na 経済的な

economics N keizai 経済; *(science/study)* keizaigaku 経済学

economy N keizai 経済; setsuyaku 節約

economy-class syndrome N ekonomī-kurasu shōkō-gun エコノミークラス症候群

edge N *(rim)* fuchi/heri 縁、*(end)* hashi/ha 端、端、*(brink)* kiwa 際、*(nearby)* soba そば; *(of knife)* ha 刃、hasaki 刃先

edible ADJ shokuyō no 食用の

edit V henshū suru 編集する

editor N henshūsha 編集者

educate V oshieru 教える、kyōiku suru 教育する

education N kyōiku 教育; *(learning)* gakumon 学問、*(culture)* kyōyō 教養

educational background N gakureki 学歴

eel N unagi ウナギ: *broiled eel* kabayaki 蒲焼き

eerie ADJ bukimi na 不気味な

effect N *(effectiveness)* kōka 効果、kikime 効き目; eikyō

影響, *(result)* kekka 結果; v kiku 効く, motarasu もたらす

effective ADJ yūkō na 有効な, kōka-teki na 効果的な

effort N doryoku 努力, kurō 苦労: *make an effort* doryoku suru 努力する

e.g. ADV tatoeba 例えば

egg N tamago 卵

eggplant N nasu ナス

ego N jiga 自我, ego エゴ

eight NUM hachi 八

eighteen NUM jūhachi 十八

eighty NUM hachijū 八十

either ADJ dochiraka ippō no どちらか一方の; CONJ mata wa または, ka ... ka ...〜か〜

elaborate ADJ chimitsu na 緻密な; *(complex)* fukuzatsu na 複雑な; *(diligent)* kinben na 勤勉な; v kuwashiku setsumei suru 詳しく説明する

elbow N hiji ひじ

elder ADJ nenchō no 年長の

eldest son N chōnan 長男

elect VT erabu 選ぶ; VI senkyo suru 選挙する; ADJ erabareta 選ばれた

election N senkyo 選挙

electric ADJ denki no 電気の

electric current N denryū 電流

electrical (appliances) N denkikiki 電気機器; kaden 家電, denkikigu 電気器具, denka-seihin 電化製品

electricity N denki 電気

electronic ADJ denshi no 電子の

elegant ADJ fūryū na 風流な, yūbi na 優美な, yūga na 優雅な; jōhin na 上品な, hin no ii/aru 品のいい/ある

element N yōso 要素, seibun 成分; yōin 要因

elementary school N *(primary school)* shōgakkō 小学校

elephant N zō 象

elevator N erebētā エレベーター

eleven NUM jūichi 十一

elite ADJ ichiryū no 一流の

else ADJ *(anything else)* sono ta/hoka no その他の; ADV hoka ni 他に; *(or else)* mata wa または, soretomo それとも; *(somewhere else)* (doko ka) betsu no basho (no/ni) (どこか)別の場所(の/に)

email N denshi mēru 電子メール, emēru Eメール; v mēru o okuru メールを送る

email address N *(denshi)* mēru adoresu (電子)メールアドレス

embarrass v komaraseru 困らせる, kurushimeru 苦しめる; *embarrass oneself* haji o kaku 恥をかく

embarrassed, embarrassing ADJ komaru 困る; batsu no warui ばつの悪い, kimari ga warui きまりが悪い; tereru 照れる; *(ashamed, shy)* hazukashi'i 恥ずかしい

embassy N taishikan 大使館

embrace v idaku 抱く

emergency N kinkyūjitai 緊急事態; hijōji 非常時, hijō(jitai) 非常(事態); *(in an emergency)* ōkyū 応急; *(for emergencies)* kyūkyū 救急

emergency exit N hijōguchi 非常口

emigrant N ijūsha 移住者, imin 移民

Emoticon N *(computer)* kaomoji 顔文字, emōtikon エモーティコン

emotion N kanjō 感情; *(feeling)* kandō 感動, kangeki 感激

Emperor N *(Japanese)* Ten'nō 天皇; *His Majesty the Emperor* Ten'nō-heika 天皇陛下; kōtei 皇帝

emphasize N kyōchō suru 強調する

employ N koyō 雇用; v yatou 雇う, (hito o) tsukau (人を)使う

employee N jūgyōin 従業員; *(of a company)* shain 社員

employer N koyō-sha 雇用者, koyō-nushi 雇用主

Empress N Kōgō 皇后: *Her Majesty the Empress* Kōgō-heika 皇后陛下

empty ADJ kara no 空の; *(hollow)* utsuro na 虚ろな; *(futile)* munashi'i むなしい; *(is vacant)* aiteiru 空いている; aita 空いた; v akeru 空ける

empty box N aki-bako 空き箱

empty can N aki-kan 空き缶

empty house N aki-ya 空き家

enclose v *(in envelope)* dōfū suru 同封する

encounter v ... ni deau ～に出会う, sōgū suru 遭遇する

encourage v susumeru 勧める, hagemasu 励ます

encyclopedia N hyakka jiten 百科事典

end N *(finish)* owari 終わり, o-shimai おしまい; *(tip)* hashi 端; kiri 切り; ketsumatsu

結末; *(close)* sue 末; *(of street)* tsukiatari 突き当たり; *(purpose)* mokuteki 目的; ADJ saishū no 最終の; v owaru 終わる; sumu 済む; *(run out)* tsukiru 尽きる: **end of the year** (toshi no) kure (年の)暮れ, nenmatsu 年末

ending N owari 終わり, ketsu-matsu 結末: *happy ending* happīendo ハッピーエンド

endless ADJ *(no limit)* owari no nai 終わりのない, kiri ga nai 切りがない; eien no 永遠の

enemy N teki 敵

energetic ADJ genki na 元気な, enerugisshu na エネルギッシュな; *(vigorous)* sekkyokuteki na 積極的な

energy N katsuryoku 活力, enerugī エネルギー; *(pep)* genki 元気; kioi 勢い

engaged ADJ *(telephone)* hanashi-chū 話し中; *(booked up, occupied)* fusagatteiru ふさがっている; siyōchū no 使用中の; *(be married)* kon'yaku-chū no 婚約中の

engine N enjin エンジン

engineer N gishi 技師

England N Igirisu イギリス

English N *(people)* Igirisu-jin イギリス人; *(language)* Eigo 英語; ADJ Igirisu(-jin) no イギリス(人)の, Eigo no 英語の

engrave v kizamu 刻む

enjoy v tanoshimu 楽しむ

enlarge v kakuchō suru 拡張する

enormous ADJ bakudai na 莫大な; taihen na 大変な

enough ADJ jūbun na 十分な, tariru 足りる; akuhodo no 飽きるほどの

enquire v tazuneru 尋ねる

enter v hairu 入る

entertainer N geinō-jin 芸能人

entertainment N oraku 娯楽; moyōshi 催し; settai 接待

entire ADJ zentai no 全体の

entrance N genkan 玄関, iriguchi 入口

entrance exam N *(school)* nyūgaku shiken 入学試験

entrust v azukeru 預ける; makaseru 任せる; tanomu 頼む, irai suru 依頼します

entry N nyujō 入場, nyūkoku 入国, sanka 参加; *(appears on stage)* tōjō 登場; iriguchi 入口; tōroku 登録

envelope N fūtō 封筒

environment N kankyō 環境

environmental pollution N kankyōosen 環境汚染

environmental protection N kankyōhogo 環境保護

envy N shitto 嫉妬; v urayamu 羨む, netamu 妬む

epidemic N densenbyō 伝染病

episode N *(story)* episōdo エピソード, sōwa 挿話: *final episode* saishū-kai 最終回

e-publication, e-publishing N denshi shuppan 電子出版

equal N dōtō 同等; byōdō 平等; ADJ dōtō no 同等の; byōdō na 平等な, *(on a ~ level)* taitō no 対等の; *(equivalent to)* … to hitoshi'i …と等しい; v *(extend to)* … ni tsuriai ～につり合う

equipment N *(apparatus)* sōchi 装置, *(facilities)* setsubi 設備

equivalent N dōtō no mono 同等のもの; ADJ taitō no 対等の; dōtō no 同等の

eraser N *(pencil)* keshigomu 消しゴム

erotic ADJ iroppoi 色っぽい, kōshoku na 好色な

error N machigai 間違い, ayamari 誤り, erā エラー: *to make an error* machigaeru 間違える

escalator N esukarētā エスカレーター

escape N tōbō 逃亡, dasshutsu 脱出; v nigeru 逃げる, *(escape a disaster)* hinan suru 避難する; nukeru 抜ける

e-shopping N īshoppingu イーショッピング, intānetto shoppingu インターネットショッピング

especially ADV toku ni 特に

essay N shōron 小論, essē エッセー; zuihitsu 随筆

essential N yōten 要点; hitsujuhin 必需品; ADJ *(necessary)* hitsuyō na 必要な, fukaketsu na 不可欠な

establish v setsuritsu suru 設立する, juritsu suru 樹立する

estimate N mitsumori(sho) 見積(書); kentō 見当, *(forecast)* yosoku 予測; v mitsumoru 見積もる; *(forecast)* yosoku suru 予測する; *(guess)* kentō o tsukeru 見当をつける

eternal ADJ eien no 永遠の

ethics N rinri 倫理, dōtoku 道徳

ethnic group N minzoku shūdan 民族集団

etiquette N reigi 礼儀, echiketto エチケット

euro N *(currency unit)* yūro ユーロ

Europe N Yōroppa ヨーロッパ

even ADV *(also)* nao issō なおいっそう; ... (de) sae mo (で)さえも; ADJ *(smooth, flat)* nameraka na なめらかな; taira na 平らな; *(equal)* hitoshi'i 等しい, kintō na 均等な

evening N yūgata 夕方

evening meal N yūshoku 夕食

evening paper N yūkan 夕刊

event N dekigoto 出来事; *(incident)* jiken 事件; *(case)* dan 段; *(ceremony)* gyōji 行事; *(game)* kyōgi (shumoku) 競技(種目)

ever ADV *(always)* itsumo いつも; katsute かつて; *ever since* ... irai ～以来

every ADJ *(all)* subete no 全ての, doredemo どれでも, arayuru あらゆる; *(each)* ... goto ni ～ごとに; mai... 毎～: *every day* mainichi 毎日, hibi 日々; *every month* maitsuki 毎月; *every morning*

mai-asa 毎朝; *every night* mai-ban 毎晩; *every time* maido 毎度; itsumo いつも; *every week* mai-shū 毎週; *every year* mai-toshi 毎年, mainen 毎年

everybody, everyone PRON subete no hito 全ての人, zen'in 全員, min'na みんな, minasan 皆さん, dare demo 誰でも

everyday ADJ fudan no 普段; mainichi no 毎日の, nichijō no 日常の, fudan no 普段の; arifureta ありふれた, heibon na 平凡な

everything PRON subete no mono 全ての物, min'na みんな, zenbu 全部, nan demo 何でも, issai 一切

everywhere ADV doko demo どこでも, doko ni mo どこにも, hōbō 方々

evidence N shōko 証拠; *(basis)* konkyo 根拠

exact ADJ *(detailed)* kuwashi'i 詳しい, komakai 細かい; *(correct)* seikaku na 正確な

exactly ADV sonotōri その通り; seikaku ni 正確に; chōdo 丁度, pittari ぴったり;

261

masani まさに; hakkiri to はっきりと

exam, examination N *(test)* shiken 試験; *(inquiry)* chōsa 調査; *(inspection)* kensa 検査, *(medical)* shinsatsu 診察

examine V *(investigate)* chōsa suru 調査する, shiraberu 調べる; kentō suru 検討する

example N rei 例, ichirei 一例, tatoe 例え: *for example* tatoeba 例えば

excavate V hakkutsu suru 発掘する

exceed V koeru 超える, uwa-mawaru 上回る; ... ni masaru ...に勝る

excess ADJ kajō na 過剰な, yobun no 余分の: *be in excess* amaru 余る

excellent ADJ sugureta 優れた, yūshū na 優秀な

except PREP ... o nozoite ～を除いて; ... no hoka ... の他, ... igai ni ～以外に

exchange N *(money, opinions)* ryōgae 両替; kōkan 交換; V *(money)* ryōgae suru 両替する; kankin suru 換金する;

kōkan suru 交換する; *(tori)* kaeru (取り)替える

excite V ki o takaburaseru 気を高ぶらせる, kōfun saseru 興奮させる

exciting ADJ wakuwaku saseru わくわくさせる, shigekiteki na 刺激的な, kōfun saseru 興奮させる, suriru no aru スリルのある, omoshiroi 面白い

exclude V haijo suru 排除する; ... o nozoku ～を除く

excluded ADJ *(not included)* fukumaretenai 含まれてない; ... o nozoita ～を除いた

excuse N ii'wake 言い訳; *(pretext)* kōjitsu 口実

excuse me *(apology)* gomennasai ごめんなさい (謝罪); *(attracting attention, getting past)* sumimasen すみません

exercise N *(physical)* undō 運動, *(calisthenics)* taisō 体操; *(study)* kadai 課題; *(practice)* renshū 練習, keiko 稽古; VI undō suru 運動する; VT kunren suru 訓練する, renshū saseru 練習させる; hatarakaseru 働かせる

exhaust N haiki 排気; *(fumes)* haiki-gasu 排気ガス; V

tsukai-hatasu 使い果たす;
(run out of) kirasu 切らす

exhibition N *(display)* tenjikai
展示会, tenrankai 展覧会,
hakurankai 博覧会

exhibitor N shuppin-sha
出品者

exhumation N hakkutsu 発掘

exist V sonzai suru 存在する

exit N deguchi 出口; V *(go out)*
deru 出る

expand VI hirogaru 広がる;
bōchō suru 膨脹する; VT hiro-
geru 広げる; kakudai suru
拡大する

expect V *(await)* matteiru 待
っている, kitai suru 期待する;
(anticipate) yosō suru 予想す
る; yoki suru 予期する

expense(s) N keihi 経費,
shuppi 出費; hiyō 費用,

expensive ADJ *(nedan ga)*
takai (値段が)高い; kōgaku
no 高額の

experience N keiken 経験,
(personal) taiken 体験;
(professional) shokureki 職
歴; V *(undergoes)* keiken/
taiken suru 経験/体験する

expert N *(veteran,
specialist)* senmonka 専門

家, ekisupāto エキスパート,
meijin 名人

explanation N setsumei 説明;
(interpretation) kaishaku 解
釈; *(excuse)* ii'wake 言い訳

explosion N bakuhatsu 爆発

export N yushutsu 輸出; V
yushutsu suru 輸出する

express N *(train, bus)* kyūkō
急行; *(mail)* sokutatsu 速達;
ADJ meikaku na 明確な;
kyūkō no 急行の; V *(put into
words)* ii'arawasu 言い表す,
(tell) noberu 述べる; sokutatsu
de okuru 速達で送る

express train N kyūkō-ressha
急行列車

expression N *(way of saying)*
ii'kata 言い方, *(phrase)*
hyōgen 表現; *(on face)* hyōjō
表情, kao(tsuki) 顔(つき)

extend VT nobasu 延ばす,
enchō suru 延長する; VI
nobiru 伸びる; *(reach)* oyobu
及ぶ

extension N *(telephone)*
denwa no koki 電話の子機;
naisen 内線 (電話); enchō
延長, kakuchō 拡張

exterior N gaibu 外部,
sotogawa 外側

263

extinguish vt *(fire)* kekesu 消す(火を); vi *(fire)* kieru 消える(火が)

extra N yobun na mono 余分なもの; gōgai 号外; ekisutora エキストラ; *(bonus)* omake おまけ; ADJ yobun na 余分な; tsuika no 追加の; ADV *(special)* tokubetsu ni 特別に

extract N ekisu エキス

extraordinary ADJ rinji no 臨時の; namihazureta 並外れた

extreme ADJ kyokutan na 極端な; *(radical)* kageki na 過激な

extremely ADV kyokutan ni 極端に; hijō ni 非常に, kiwamete 極めて, totemo とても, sugoku すごく

eye N me 目

eyelash N matsuge まつげ

eyelid N mabuta まぶた

eyeglasses N megane めがね

eyesight N shiryoku 視力

F

fable N gūwa 寓話

fabric N *(textile)* nuno 布, orimono 織物, kiji 生地

fabulous ADJ subarashi'i すば

らしい, wakuwaku suru ワクワクする

face N kao 顔; *(one's honor)* taimen 体面; *(front)* shōmen 正面; *(surface)* hyōmen 表面

Facebook N *(Internet)* feisu bukku フェイスブック

facility, facilities N shisetsu 施設, setsubi 設備

facsimile N fakushimiri ファクシミリ, fakkusu ファックス

fact N jijitsu 事実: *in fact* jitsu wa 実は, jissai (wa) 実際(は)

factory N kōjō 工場

fade v *(color)* aseru 褪せる, usureru 薄れる; yowamaru 弱まる; otoroeru 衰える

fail v shippai suru 失敗する; *(exam)* ochiru 落ちる, rakudai suru 落第する; *(engine etc. breaks down)* koshō suru 故障する

fair N *(market)* ichi 市, ichiba 市場; *(street fair)* en'nichi 縁日; ADJ *(just, impartial)* kōhei na 公平な; *(sunny)* hareta 晴れた, tenki no ii 天気のいい

fairly ADV *(equally)* kōhei ni 公平に; *(rather)* kanari かなり, sōtō 相当, zuibun ずいぶん

fairy N yōsei 妖精

264

faithful ADJ seijitsu na 誠実な、chūjitsu na 忠実な、seikaku na 正確な

fake ADJ nise no にせの、inchiki na インチキな; N *(thing)* nisemono にせ物、inchiki インチキ、feiku フェイク; V detchiageru でっちあげる

fall N *(autumn)* aki 秋; rakka 落下; V ochiru 落ちる; sagaru 下がる; *(falls and scatters)* chiru 散る; *(snow, rain)* furu 降る; **fall behind** okureru 遅れる、okure o toru 後れを取る; **fall down** taoreru 倒れる、korobu 転ぶ; **fall in love with** … ni horeru ～に惚れる、koi ni ochiru 恋に落ちる; **fall on one's knees** hizamazuku ひざまずく

falls N *(waterfalls)* taki 滝

false ADJ *(imitation)* nise no にせの; *(not true)* fuseikaku na 不正確な; *(artificial)* jinkō no 人工の

fame N *(reputation)* hyōban 評判; meisei 名声

familiar ADJ shitashi'i 親しい

family N kazoku 家族; *(household)* katei 家庭

family name N *(surname)* sei

姓、*(as written)* myōji 名字・苗字、kamei 家名

famous ADJ yūmei na 有名な、nadakai 名高い、hyōban no 評判の

fan N *(admirer)* fan ファン; *(folding)* sensu 扇子; *(flat)* uchiwa うちわ; *(electric)* senpūki 扇風機

fancy N kūsō 空想、*(dream)* yume 夢; ADJ *(high-grade)* kōkyū na 高級な; *(fashionable)* oshare na おしゃれな

fantastic N subarashi'i 素晴らしい

fantasy N kōsō 空想、fantajī ファンタジー

far ADV tōku e 遠くへ; haruka ni はるかに; ADJ tōi 遠い

fare N *(fee)* (jōsha)ryōkin (乗車)料金、*(transportation)* unchin 運賃

farm N nōjō 農場

fashion N *(way)* ryūkō 流行、fasshon ファッション; *(...)* fū (～)風

fashionable ADJ hayari no はやりの、ryūkō no 流行の、sumāto na スマートな

fast ADJ *(rapid)* hayai 速い; ADV *(speedily)* hayaku 速く

fast food N fāsutofūdo ファーストフード

fasten V *(firmly attaches)* tomeru 留める; *(tightens, secures)* shimeru 締める

fat N *(grease)* shibō 脂肪, abura 脂; ADJ *(plump)* futotta 太った; abrakkoi 油っこい; debu no デブの: *get fat* futoru 太る

fate N un 運, unmei 運命, shukumei 宿命

father N chichi 父; otō-san お父さん, chichioya 父親

father-in-law N giri no chichi 義理の父

fatty N aburakkoi 油っこい・脂っこい

faucet N jaguchi 蛇口

fault N kashitsu 過失; *(defect)* kizu きず; *(shortcoming)* tansho 短所, ketten 欠点; *(guilt)* tsumi 罪; *(cause)* sekinin 責任

favor N *(kindness)* shinsetsu 親切, *(goodwill)* kōi 好意; *(request)* o-negai お願い

favorite N o-kini'iri お気に入り, ADJ daisuki na 大好きな, okini'iri no お気に入りの; konomi no … 好みの…;

tokui (na/no) 得意(な/の)

fax N *(machine)* fakkusu ファックス; V fakkusu o okuru ファックスを送る

fear N osore 恐れ; kyōfu 恐怖, shinpai 心配

feather N hane 羽, umō 羽毛; ke 毛

feature N tokuchō 特徴/特長; *(article)* tokushū-kiji 特集記事

February N ni-gatsu 二月

feces N ben 便, daiben 大便

federation N renmei 連盟

fee N ryōkin 料金, tesūryō 手数料; …ryō 〜料; *(remuneration)* sharei 謝礼

feed N *(for animal)* esa 餌, *(for baby)* shokuji 食事; VI taberu 食べる; VT tabemono o ataeru 食べ物を与える; tabesaseru 食べさせる; *(for animal)* kau 飼う; *(for child)* yashinau 養う

feel N *(touch)* kanshoku 感触; *(atmosphere)* funiki 雰囲気; VI *(by emotion)* kanjiru 感じる; *(body reaction)* … shitakunaru 〜したくなる; VT *(by touch)* sawaru 触る; *(think)* omou 思う

feeling N *(touch)* kanshoku 感触; kimochi 気持ち, kokoro

心, omoi 思い; *(mood)* kanji 感じ, kokoromochi 心持ち, kibun 気分; *(sense)* kansei 感性

fellow N *(person)* hito 人; *(man)* otoko 男

female N josei 女性

fence N saku 柵; kakine 垣根

ferry N *(ferryboat)* ferī フェリー, watashibune 渡し舟; V *(bring over)* watasu 渡す

fertile ADJ hiyoku na 肥沃な

festival N matsuri 祭り

fetch V tottekuru 取ってくる

fever N hatsunetsu 発熱; netsu 熱

few ADJ sukoshi no 少しの; sukunai 少ない: *a few* wazuka わずか, sukoshi 少し

fiancé *(male)* kon'yakusha 婚約者(男性)

fiancée *(female)* kon'yakusha 婚約者(女性)

fiber N sen'i 繊維; suji 筋

fiction N shōsetsu 小説, tsukuri-banashi 作り話, fikushon フィクション: *science fiction* fikushon サイエンスフィクション, esu-efu *(shōsetsu)* SF (小説)

field N *(empty space)* akichi 空き地; *(dry)* hatake 畑; nohara 野原, harappa 原っぱ; *(rice paddy)* ta 田, tanbo 田んぼ

fierce ADJ ara'arashi'i 荒々しい; hageshi'i 激しい, sugoi すごい

fifteen NUM jūgo 十五

fifty NUM gojū 五十

fight N *(physically)* kenka けんか, tatakai 戦い; V kenka suru けんかする, tatakau 戦う; momeru もめる

figure N *(number)* sūji 数字

file N *(nail file, etc.)* yasuri やすり; *(document, computer)* fairu ファイル; VI *(grind)* kezuru 削る; *(apply)* shinsei suru 申請する; VT *(shorui o)* tojiru/hokan suru (書類)をとじる/保管する, fairingu suru ファイリングする

Filipino N *(language)* Firipingo フィリピン語; *(people)* Firipin-jin フィリピン人; ADJ Firipin(-jin) no フィリピン(人)の

fill V mitasu 満たす; ippai ni suru 一杯にする

film N *(camera)* firumu フィルム, *(movie)* eiga 映画

filter N firutā フィルター; V kosu 濾す

fin N hire ひれ

final ADJ saigo no 最後の, saishū no 最終の

finance N kin'yu 金融; zaimu 財務; zaisei 財政

find N hakken 発見; *(bargain)* horidashimono 掘り出し物; V *(find out)* deau 出会う; mitsukeru 見つける; hakken suru 発見する; kizuku 気付く

fine ADJ subarashi'i 素晴らしい, suteki na すてきな; *(good)* yoi 良い, *(fair weather)* hareta 晴れた, *(healthy)* genki na 元気な; *(small/detailed)* komakai 細かい, *(minute)* bisai na 微細な, *(delicate)* bimyō na 微妙な; N *(punishment)* bakkin 罰金

finger N yubi 指

finish N saigo 最後

fire N honō 炎; hi 火, *(accidental)* kaji 火事, kasai 火災; V ... ni hi o tsukeru 〜に火を付ける; *(lay off, disemploy)* kubi ni suru 首にする, kotowaru 断る, *(fire someone)* kaiko suru 解雇する

fire engine N shōbōsha 消防車

fire fighter N shōbōshi 消防士

fireworks N hanabi 花火

firewall N *(Internet security)* faiawōru ファイアウォール

firm ADJ *(definite)* danko to shita 断固とした; *(material)* katai 硬い; jōbu na 丈夫な; N *(company)* kigyo 企業

firmly ADV chanto ちゃんと, shikkari to しっかりと

first N *(number one)* ichiban 一番; saisho 最初; hajimari 始まり; ADJ ichiban(me) no 一番(目)の; hajime no 初めの; dai'ichi no 第一の; saisho no 最初の, hatsu no 初のの; ADV mazu まず; *(ahead of others)* saki (ni) 先(に); *first time* ADJ hajimete no 初めての;

first day N *(of the month)* tsuitachi 一日: *the first day* shonichi 初日

first floor N ikkai 一階

first-year student N ichinensei 一年生

first aid N ōkyūteate 応急手当

first class N ikkyū 一級, ichiryū 一流; *(ticket, seat)* fāsuto kurasu ファーストクラス; ADJ *(hotel, school)* ichiryū no 一流の

fish N sakana 魚; v tsuru 釣る

fish sauce N nanpurā ナンプラー, gyoshō 魚醤

fisherman N ryōshi 漁師, gyofu 魚夫

fishhook N tsuribari 釣り針

fishing N (as sport) (sakana-) tsuri (魚)釣り, ryō 漁; (business) gyogyō 漁業

fist N kobushi 拳, genkotsu 拳骨, genko げんこ

fit N kamiawase かみ合わせ; ADJ (suitable) tekishita 適した; (health) kenkō na 健康な; (fit together well) aishō ga ii 相性がいい; v ... ni hamekomu ～にはめ込む; (clothes) au 合う; (conform) gacchi suru 合致する

five NUM go 五

fix N shūri 修理; v (a time, appointment) kimeru 決める; (repair) shūri suru 修理する, naosu 直す; (make) tsukuru 作る; (prepare) sonaeru 備える; (settle) sadameru 定める

flag N hata 旗

flame N honō 炎; vi moeagaru 燃え上がる; vt moyasu 燃やす

flap N (of envelope, etc.) futa

ふた, furappu フラップ

flat N (apartment) apāto アパート; heimen 平面; ADJ (smooth) heitan na 平坦な, taira na 平らな, hiratai 平たい; (flavorless) aji ga nai 味がない; ADV (just) chōdo ちょうど

flavor N aji 味, fūmi 風味; (seasoning) chōmi 調味, ajitsuke 味付け; teisuto テイスト

flax N asa 麻

flea N nomi ノミ

flea market N nomi no ichi のみの市, furīmāketto フリーマーケット

flesh N nikutai 肉体

flight N hikō 飛行; (flight number) (...)-bin (〜)便

flight attendant N kyaku-shitsu jōmuin 客室乗務員

float N ukabu 浮かぶ, uku 浮く; vt ukaberu 浮かべる

flood N kōzui 洪水; v hanran suru 氾濫する

floor N yuka 床; (...th floor) ...kai 〜階

flour N komugiko 小麦粉

flow N nagareru 流れる vi nagasu 流す; N (outflow) nagare 流れ

flower N hana 花

flower shop, florist N hana-ya 花屋

flower vase N kabin 花瓶

flower viewing N (o-)hanami (お)花見

flu N kaze 風邪, infuruenza インフルエンザ

fluent ADJ ryūchō na 流暢な; sawayaka na さわやかな

fluently ADV (speaking) perapera (to) ぺらぺら(と), ryūchō ni 流暢に

flush V (the toilet) suisen suru 水洗する, (mizu o) nagasu (水を)流す; sekimen suru 赤面する

flute N furūto フルート, fue 笛

fly N (insect) hae 蠅; VI tobu 飛ぶ; (go by plane) hikōki de iku 飛行機で行く; VT tobasu 飛ばす; (a kite) (tako o) ageru (凧)を揚げる

focus N (camera) pinto ピント; (focal point) shōten 焦点

fog N kiri 霧

fold N orime 折り目; VT oru 折る; (ori)tatamu (折り)畳む; VI oreru 折れる

folder N (for filing) forudā フォルダー

follow VI ... ni tsuite iku 〜に ついて行く; VT ... no ato ni tsuite iku 〜の後をついて行く; (follow along) ... ni tsuzuku 〜に続く; ou 追う; tuiseki suru 追跡する; (adhere to) ... ni tsuku 〜に付く, (conform to) ... ni shitagau 〜に従う, (run along) ... ni sou 〜に沿う

following (adherent) shijisha 支持者; fan ファン; ADJ tsugi no 次の, ika no 以下の; PREP ... no ato ni 〜の後に; ... no tsugi no 〜の次の

follower N (adherent) shijisha 支持者; (follower of a stronger person or boss) kobun 子分

food N tabemono 食べ物; (meal) shokuji 食事

fool N baka 馬鹿, aho あほ, manuke まぬけ; fool around fuzakeru ふざける; fool someone karakau からかう

foolish ADJ bakarashi'i 馬鹿らしい, baka na 馬鹿な

foot N ashi 足

football N (American) futto-bōru フットボール, amefuto アメフト

footprint N ashiato 足跡

for CONJ ... dakara だから; PREP ... no tame (ni) 〜のため(に); ... ni totte 〜にとって; *(for the use of)* ... yō no 〜用の, ... suru tame no 〜するための; *(suitable for)* ... muki no 〜向きの; *(bound/intended for)* mukatte 向かって: *for a long time (now)* zutto mae kara ずっと前から; *for a while* shibaraku しばらく; hitomazu ひとまず; *for example/ instance* tatoeba 例えば

forbid V kinshi suru 禁止する

force N chikara 力; V shi'iru 強いる

forecast N yohō 予報, yosoku 予測; V yosoku suru 予測する

foreign ADJ gaikoku no 外国の

foreign language N gaikoku-go 外国語

foreigner N gaikokujin 外国人

forest N mori 森, *(grove)* hayashi 林

for ever, forever ADV eien ni 永遠に; itsu(made) mo いつ(まで)も, eikyū ni 永久に

foreword N jobun 序文, mae-gaki 前書き

forget V wasureru 忘れる

forgive V yurusu 許す

fork N fōku フォーク

form N *(shape)* katachi 形; *(pattern)* kata 型, *(figure)* sugata 姿, kakkō 格好; *(appearance)* teisai 体裁; *(fill out)* yōshi 用紙; *(document)* shorui 書類

formal ADJ seishiki na/no 正式な/の; keishikiteki na 形式的な

format N *(book, magazine)* teisai 体裁, hankei 版型; *(data)* fōmatto フォーマット

former ADJ mae no 前の; moto no 元の

fortunate ADJ saiwai na 幸いな, kōun na 幸運な

fortunately ADV kōun ni mo 幸運にも

fortune-telling N uranai 占い

forty NUM yonjū 四十

forward ADV zenpō ni 前方に

foul N hansoku 反則

foundation N *(base)* kiso 基礎, *(basis)* konpon 根本, kihon 基本; *(non-profit organization)* zaidan 財団

fountain N funsui 噴水, izumi 泉

four NUM yon 四

fourteen NUM jūyon 十四

fox N kitsune きつね

fragile ADJ koware-yasui 壊れやすい; *(thing)* koware-mono こわれもの, waremono 割れ物

fragrance N kaori 香り

frame N waku 枠, fuchi 縁; *(of picture)* gakubuchi 額縁

France N Furansu フランス

frank ADJ assari (to) shita あっさり(と)した, *(casual)* zakkubaran na ざっくばらんな; sotchoku na 率直な

fraud(ulent) ADJ inchiki ないんちきな

free ADJ *(independent)* dokuritsu-shita 独立した; *(gratis)* tada no ただの; *(no fee/charge)* muryō no 無料の; *(unrestrained)* jiyū na 自由な: *free of charge* muryō de 無料で; *free seat (unreserved)* jiyū-seki 自由席

freedom N jiyū 自由

freelance, freelancing ADJ *(work)* jiyū keiyaku no 自由契約の, furī no フリーの

freeze VI kōritsuku 凍りつく; kōru 凍る; *(a thing)* kōraseru 凍らせる, reitō suru 冷凍する

freezer N reitōko 冷凍庫

French N *(language)* Furansu-go フランス語; *(people)* Furansu-jin フランス人; ADJ Furansu(-jin) no フランス(人)の

frequent ADJ hinpan na 頻繁な

fresh ADJ shinsen na 新鮮な; atarashi'i 新しい

freshman N ichinensei 一年生; *(student)* shin'nyu-sei 新入生

Friday N kin-yōbi 金曜日

fried ADJ ageta 揚げた

fried chicken N tori no kara-age 鶏の唐揚げ, furaido chikin フライドチキン

friend N tomodachi 友達; tomo 友, yūjin 友人, *(pal)* nakama 仲間; *(accomplice)* mikata 味方: *close friend* sinyū 親友

friendly ADJ *(outgoing)* shakōteki na 社交的な

friendship N yūjō 友情

frightened ADJ odoroita 驚いた

frog N kaeru カエル

from PREP ... kara 〜から: *from now on* kore kara これから, kongo 今後

front N mae 前, *(ahead)* saki 先; zenpō 前方; *(side)* omote 表, *(surface)* shōmen 正面, zenmen 前面

front desk N furonto フロント

frost N shimo 霜

frown v kao o shikameru 顔をしかめる

frozen ADJ kōtta 凍った

fruit N kudamono くだもの

fry v yaku 焼く; (pan-fry, saute) itameru 炒める

frying pan N furaipan フライパン

ftp N (file transfer protocol) efu-tī-pī, ftp エフ・ティー・ピー

fuel N nenryō 燃料; (gasoline) gasorin ガソリン

fulfill v hatasu 果たす

full ADJ ippai no いっぱいの, takusan no たくさんの, michita 満ちた; zenbu no 全部の; (of people) man'in no 満員の

fully ADV jūbun ni 十分に, kanzen ni 完全に, mattaku 全く, sukkari すっかり, zentai ni 全体に

fumigate v ibusu いぶす

fun N omoshiroi (koto) 面白い(こと); asobi 遊び: *have fun* tanoshimu 楽しむ, asobu 遊ぶ

function N kinō 機能, hataraki 働き; v (work) kinō suru 機能する

funds, funding N shikin 資金, (capital) shihon 資本

funeral N sōshiki 葬式

funny ADJ (comical) okashi'i おかしい, okashi na おかしな, hyōkin na ひょうきんな; (droll) yukai na 愉快な, (strange) hen na 変な, fushigi na 不思議な

fur N kegawa 毛皮

furniture N kagu 家具

further ADJ (additional) sonoue その上; ADV (more) motto saki ni もっと先に, sara ni mata さらにまた; (elsewhere) hoka no basho de 他の場所で; v (advance) saki ni susumeru 先に進める

fuse N hyūzu ヒューズ

fussy ADJ konomi ni urusai 好みにうるさい; kimuzukashi'i 気難しい

future N shōrai 将来, mirai 未来: *in the near future* chikai uchini 近いうちに

fuzzy ADJ aimai na あいまいな

G

gain N rieki 利益, toku 得, *(income)* shotoku 所得; VI toku o suru 得をする; VT eru 得る, moukeru もうける

gamble, gambling N kakegoto 賭け事, gyanburu ギャンブル

game N *(athletic)* shiai 試合, kyōgi 競技; gēmu ゲーム; asobi 遊び

gap N suki-ma すき間, suki 隙; wareme 割れ目, kireme 切れ目; zure ずれ, gyappu ギャップ

garage N *(for parking)* shako 車庫; *(for repairs)* jidōsha shūrikōjō 自動車修理工場

garbage N gomi ごみ, *(kitchen waste)* namagomi 生ごみ

garbage bin/can N gomibako ごみ箱

garden N *(yard)* niwa 庭; *(park)* kōen 公園

garlic N nin'niku にんにく

garment N irui 衣類

gas N *(natural)* gasu ガス; *(gasoline)* gasorin ガソリン

gasoline N gasorin ガソリン

gasoline station N gasorin sutando ガソリンスタンド;

kyūyujo 給油所

gate N mon 門, *(gateway)* deiriguchi 出入口; *(main/front)* seimon 正門

gather VI atsumaru 集まる, *(make a set)* sorou 揃う, *(congregate)* shūgō suru 集合する; VT *(collect up)* yose atsumeru 寄せ集める, atsumeru 集める; *(pluck, clip)* tsumu 摘む; N *(pleat)* hida ひだ, gyazā ギャザー

gear N gia ギア, giya ギヤ, haguruma 歯車

gem N hōseki 宝石

gender N seibetsu 性別

gene N idenshi 遺伝子

general ADJ *(all-purpose)* ippanteki na 一般的な, *(over all)* ippan no 一般の; *(common)* kyōtsū no 共通の

generation N sedai 世代, dōjidai 同時代, dōsedai 同世代: *for generations* daidai 代々

generator N hatsudenki 発電機

generous ADJ kandai na 寛大な, kimae ga ii 気前がいい

genius N tensai 天才

gentle ADJ yasashi'i やさしい, *(well-behaved)* otonashi'i お

となしい; *(docile)* sunao na 素直な; *(calm)* odayaka na 穏やかな

gentleman N dansei 男性, shinshi 紳士; *(middle-aged man)* oji-san おじさん, *(old man)* oji'i-san おじいさん

genuine ADJ hontō no 本当の

geography N chiri 地理; *(study/science)* chiri-gaku 地理学

German N *(language)* doitsu-go ドイツ語; *(people)* doitsu-jin ドイツ人; ADJ doitsu(-jin) no ドイツ(人)の

Germany N *(nation)* doitsu ドイツ;

gesture N miburi 身振り

get VI *(arrive)* tsuku 着く; VT *(arrive)* tōchaku suru 到着する; *(receive)* morau もらう, te ni ireru 手に入れる: *get down (get off)* oriru 降りる; *(crouch)* mi o fuseru 身を伏せる; *get in (enter)* hairu 入る; *get into (a vehicle)* (... ni) noru (〜に)乗る; *get old* toshi o toru 年を取る, fukeru 老ける; *get out (leave)* deru 出る; *(get it out)* dasu 出す; *get up (arise)* okiru 起きる

ghost N yūrei 幽霊; obake お化け

gift N okurimono 贈り物: *gift shop* miyagemono-ya みやげ物屋

gigabyte, GB N *(computer)* giga-baito ギガ・バイト

ginger N shōga 生姜

gingko N *(tree)* ichō イチョウ: *gingko nuts* gin'nan ギンナン

giraffe N kirin キリン

girl N on'na no ko 女の子; joshi 女子; *girlfriend* kanojo 彼女; gārufurendo ガールフレンド

give VT *(provide)* ataeru 与える, motaseru 持たせる, okuru 贈る, *(me)* kureru くれる, *(you/them)* ageru あげる, yaru やる; *(entrust temporarily)* azukeru 預ける; *(a party, etc.)* (pātī o) hiraku (パーティーを)開く, moyōsu 催す

glad ADJ ureshii 嬉しい

glamorous ADJ miryoku-teki na 魅力的な, miwaku-teki na 魅惑的な, hanayaka na 華やかな, iroppoi 色っぽい

glass N *(for drinking)* gurasu グラス, koppu コップ; *(material)* garasu ガラス

glasses N *(spectacles)* megane めがね

globe N *(shape)* tama/kyū 球, *(map)* chikyūgi 地球儀

gloomy ADJ inki na 陰気な

glorious ADJ hanayaka na 華やかな

glove N tebukuro 手袋, *(baseball, boxing)* gurabu グラブ, gurōbu グローブ

glow V hikaru 光る, N *(shine)* kagayaki 輝き, *(glow of sunset)* yūyake 夕焼け

glue N setchakuzai 接着剤, nori のり; V setchaku suru 接着する

glum ADJ inki na 陰気な

go V iku 行く; *go along (join)* sanka suru 参加する; *go around (visit)* tazuneru 訪ねる; *(curve)* magaru 曲がる; *(revolve)* mawaru 回る; *go back* modoru 戻る, kaeru 帰る; *go down* heru 減る; *go home* kitaku suru 帰宅する; *go out (of the house)* dekakeru 出掛ける, gaishutsu suru 外出する; *(fire, candle)* kieru 消える (火、ろうそく); *go over* yokogiru 横切る; *(exceed)* sugiru 過ぎる;

hamidasu はみ出す; *go up (climb)* noboru 登る

Go N *(board game)* go 碁, igo 囲碁

goal N gōru ゴール, mokuhyō 目標

goat N yagi 山羊

God N kami 神

god N gūzō 偶像, kami 神

goddess N megami 女神

gold N ōgon 黄金; kin 金

goldfish N kingyo 金魚

golf N gorufu ゴルフ

good ADJ ii いい, yoi 良い; *good at* umai うまい, jōzu na 上手な

Good afternoon. INTERJ kon'nichi wa. こんにちは.

Good evening. INTERJ konban wa. こんばんは.

good-looking ADJ hansamu na ハンサムな, kakkoii かっこいい, rukkusu no ii ルックスのいい

good luck N kōun o inoru 幸運を祈る

Good morning. INTERJ Ohayō (gozaimasu). おはようございます.

Good night. INTERJ O-yasumi nasai. おやすみなさい.

276

Goodbye GR sayōnara さようなら

goodness N aramā あらまあ

goods N shina(mono) 品(物); *(merchandise)* shōhin 商品

goodwill N kōi 好意, kokorozashi 志, shinsetsu 親切, zen'i 善意

Google N *(Internet search engine)* gūguru グーグル

goose N gachō ガチョウ

gorgeous ADJ gōka na 豪華な; rippa na 立派な; hanayaka na 華やかな; kakkōii 格好いい

gossip N uwasa うわさ; muda-/baka-banashi 無駄/ばか話, oshaberi おしゃべり

gourmet N gurume グルメ

government N seifu 政府

gown N gaun ガウン

graceful ADJ yūbi na 優美な

grade N hyōka 評価; tōkyū 等級; gakunen 学年

gradually ADV jojo ni 徐々に, dandan だんだん, sukoshizutsu 少しずつ

graduate N sotsugyōsei 卒業生: *graduate from* sotsugyō suru 卒業する; (daigaku o) deru (大学を) 出る

grain N tsubu 粒; *(cereal)* kokumotsu 穀物, kokurui 穀類; *(texture)* kime きめ

grammar N bunpō 文法

grand ADJ sōdai na 壮大な, subarashi'i すばらしい, erai 偉い

grandchild N mago 孫

grandparents N sofubo 祖父母

grant V ataeru 与える; N hojokin 補助金, joseikin 助成金

grapes N budō ぶどう

graph N grafu グラフ

graphic N zukei 図形, gurafikku グラフィック

grass N kusa 草; *(lawn)* shibafu 芝生

gratitude N kansha 感謝

grave N *(tomb)* (o-)haka (お)墓; ADJ *(serious)* omoi 重い, shinkoku na 深刻な

gravity N inryoku 引力

gravy N tare たれ; sōsu ソース; niku-jū/jiru 肉汁

gray ADJ hai'iro no 灰色の, nezumi-iro no ねずみ色の

gray hair N shiraga 白髪

greasy ADJ aburakkoi 油っこい・脂っこい

great ADJ *(grand)* sōdai na 壮大な; *(impressive)* migoto na 見事な

277

Great Britain N Eikoku 英国, igirisu イギリス

Greece N Girisha ギリシャ

greedy ADJ yokubari na 欲張りな, kuishinbō na 食いしん坊な

Greek N (langage) Girisha-go ギリシャ語, (people) Girisha-jin ギリシャ人; ADJ Girisha (-jin) no ギリシャ(人)の

green ADJ midori no 緑の

green light N (signal) aoshingō 青信号

green pepper N pīman ピーマン

green tea N (o-)cha (お)茶

greet V aisatsu o suru 挨拶をする; demukaeru 出迎える

greetings N aisatsu 挨拶

grill V yaku 焼く, aburu あぶる

grind V (into powder) suru する, suritubusu すりつぶす, hiku ひく; (polish) migaku 磨く

grip V nigiru 握る

grocer N (grocery store) shokuryōhin-ten 食品店

groceries N shokuryō-hin 食料品, shokuhin 食品

groom N hanamuko 花婿, shinrō 新郎

ground N jimen 地面, (on the ground) chijō 地上

group N gurūpu グループ, atsumari 集まり, dantai 団体, shūdan 集団

grow V seichō suru 成長する; (teeth, hair, mold, plant …) haeru 生える; (develops) hatten suru 発展する; (a crop) tsukuru 作る; (hair, beard, …) hayasu 生やす; (become) (… ni) naru (〜に) なる; (cultivate) yashinau 養う; *grow late* (yo ga) fukeru (夜が)更ける; *grow up* (child) sodatsu 育つ, seichō suru 成長する

growth N seichō 成長, hatsuiku 発育; (increase) zōka 増加, (development) hatten 発展

guarantee N hoshōsho 保証書; V hoshō suru 保証する

guard N ban 番, monban 門番, gādoman ガードマン; (vigilance) keikai 警戒; V mamoru 守る, keibi suru 警備する

guardian N hogosha 保護者

guess N (conjecture) suisoku 推測; V suisoku suru 推測する

guest N kyaku 客, (invitee) shōtaikyaku 招待客

H

guest room N kyakuma 客間

guide N gaido ガイド, an'nainin 案内人; *(book)* an'naisho 案内書; v an'nai suru 案内する; *(direct, counsel)* shidō suru 指導する

guidebook N ryokō an'naisho 旅行案内書, gaidobukku ガイドブック

guilt N tsumi 罪; *feeling/ sense of guilt* zaiakukan 罪悪感

guilty *(of a crime)* ADJ yūzai no 有罪の, ushirometai 後ろめたい: *feel guilty* zaiakukan o motsu 罪悪感を持つ, ki ga togameru 気がとがめる

guitar N gitā ギター

gum N *(chewing)* (chūin) gamu (チューイン)ガム; *(teethridge)* haguki 歯茎

gun N jū 銃, teppō 鉄砲

guts N harawata はらわた, chō 腸

gym, gymnasium N tai'ikukan 体育館, jimu ジム

gymnastics N taisō 体操

habit N shūkan 習慣; *(bad habit)* kuse くせ

hack, hacker N *(computer)* hakkingu ハッキング, hakkā ハッカー

hair N kami 髪, kami no ke 髪の毛, ke 毛

half N hanbun 半分; ADJ hanbun no 半分の; ADV hanbun hodo 半分ほど: *half a day/a half-day* han'nichi 半日; *half an hour* sanjuppun 30分, han-jikan 半時間; *half a year* han'toshi 半年

halfway ADV chūto de 中途で, tochū de 途中で

hall N hiroma 広間, *(entrance)* genkan 玄関; *(building)* kaikan 会館; *(lecture hall)* hōru ホール

ham N hamu ハム

hamburger N hanbāgā ハンバーガー; *(patty)* hanbāgu ハンバーグ

hammer N hanmā ハンマー, kanazuchi かなづち

hand N te 手; *(of clock)* hari 針: *hand out* teishutsu suru 提出する; *hand over* watasu 渡す

handbag N handobaggu ハンドバッグ, handobakku, ハンドバック

handbill N bira ビラ

handbook N hando-bukku ハンドブック, tebiki-sho 手引(き)書

handbrake N saido burēki サイドブレーキ

handicap N shōgai 障害, handikyappu ハンディキャップ, hande ハンデ

handicapped person N (shintai) shōgaisha (身体)障害者

handicraft N shukōgei 手工芸

handkerchief N hankachi ハンカチ

handle N totte 取っ手, handoru ハンドル, e 柄; V (a vehicle) (unten) dekiru (運転) できる; toriatsukau 取り扱う; (cope with it) shori suru 処理する; (use a tool) atsukau 扱う; (control, operate) sōjū suru 操縦する

handshake N akushu 握手

handsome ADJ hansamu ハンサム

handwriting N tegaki 手書き, nikuhitsu 肉筆

handy ADJ benri na 便利

な, yaku ni tatsu 役に立つ, atsukai yasui 扱いやすい

hang VI kakaru 掛かる, sagaru 下がる; VT kakeru 掛ける, (suspend) tsurusu 吊るす; (hang down) burasagaru ぶら下げる: *hang up* (phone) (denwa o) kiru (電話)を切る; *hang down* tareru 垂れる; sagaru 下がる; burasagaru ぶら下がる; sageru 下げる; burasageru ぶら下げる

hangover N futsuka-yoi 二日酔い

happen V okoru 起こる: *what happened?* dōshita (no) どうした(の)

happiness N kōfuku 幸福, shiawase 幸せ

happy ADJ ureshī'i うれしい; shiawase na 幸せな, kōfuku na 幸福な; (cheerful) yōki na 陽気な; yukai na 愉快な; (auspicious) medetai めでたい; (is delighted) yorokobashī'i 喜ばしい

Happy Birthday GR tanjōbi omedetō 誕生日おめでとう

Happy New Year GR akemashite omedetō 明けましておめでとう

harbor N minato 港

hard ADJ *(difficult)* kon'nan na 困難な, muzukashi'i 難しい; *(solid)* katai 固い; *(onerous)* kurushi'i 苦しい; *(hard to do)* shinikui しにくい, ADV *(cruelly, terribly)* hidoku ひどく; *(laboriously)* sesse to せっせと, *(intently)* shikiri ni しきりに

hard disk N hādodisuku ハードディスク

hardly ADV hotondo ... nai ほとんど～ない; *hardly before* ...suru to sugu ～するとすぐ

hardware N *(items)* kanamono 金物; *(machine)* kikai setsubi 機械設備; *(computer)* hādowea ハードウェア

hardworking ADJ kinben na 勤勉な

harmony N chōwa 調和

harvest N minori 実り, shūkaku 収穫

hasty ADJ isogi no 急ぎの

hat N bōshi 帽子 (tsuba no hiroi つばの広い)

hate V ken'o suru 嫌悪する, (... o) nikumu (～を)憎む

hatred N ken'okan 嫌悪感

have V shoyū suru 所有する, (...ga) aru (～が)ある, (...o) motteiru (～を)持っている; *(keep, retain)* kakaeru 抱える; ... o kau ～を飼う; *(time)* (jikan ga) aru (時間が)ある; *(eat, drink)* ... o taberu ～を食べる, ... o nomu ～を飲む; *(invite)* maneku 招く; *have already* ADV katsute かつて, sude ni すでに; *have been ...* ... ni ittakoto ga aru ～に行ったことがある; *have done ...* ... o shitakoto ga aru ～をしたことがある

hay N hoshikusa 干(し)草

hazard N hazādo ハザード, *(danger)* kiken 危険

he, him PRON kare wa/o 彼は/を

head N atama 頭, *(brains)* zunō 頭脳: *head for (toward)* ... ni mukau, ～に向かう; ... o mezasu, ～を目指す

headache N zutsū 頭痛

heading N *(caption)* midashi 見出し, *(title)* taitoru タイトル

headquarters N honbu 本部, honsha 本社

health N kenkō 健康, *(one's ~)* karada 体・身体, hoken 保健; *(state of one's ~)* kigen 機嫌; *(hygiene, sanitation)* eisei 衛生

healthcare N kenkōkanri 健康管理

health insurance N kenkōhoken 健康保険

healthy ADJ kenkōteki na 健康的な, genki na 元気な; *(sturdy)* jōbu na 丈夫な

hear V kiku 聞く

heart N shinzō 心臓; *(as seat of emotions)* kokoro 心; *(the very center)* chūshin 中心; *(core, spirit)* shin 芯; *(mind)* mune 胸, omoi 思い; *(spirit)* ki 気

heart attack N shinzō hossa 心臓発作

heat N netsu 熱; ondo 温度, atsusa 熱さ・暑さ

heating device N danbō sōchi 暖房装置, *(equipment)* danbō setsubi 暖房設備

heaven N ten 天; *(sky)* sora 空; *(paradise)* tengoku 天国

heavy ADJ omoi 重い; *(onerous)* kurushi'i 苦しい

hedge N ikegaki 生け垣

heel N kakato かかと

height N takasa 高さ

helicopter N herikoputā ヘリコプター

hell N jigoku 地獄

hello, hi GR *(on phone)* moshimoshi もしもし; *(greeting)* kon'nichiwa こんにちは, yā やあ; gokigenyō ごきげんよう

helmet N herumetto ヘルメット

help N *(assistance)* tetsudai 手伝い; *(good offices)* assen あっせん, sewa 世話; *(aid)* enjo 援助, hojo 補助; *(support)* ōen 応援; V *(assist)* tetsudau 手伝う; *(rescue)* tasukeru 助ける; *(save)* suku'u 救う; *(support)* ōen suru 応援する

helper N joshu 助手

her, hers ADJ/PRON kanojo o/no 彼女を/の

herb N kusa 草; yakusō 薬草, hābu ハーブ

here ADV koko ここ; kochira こちら, kotchi こっち

heredity N iden 遺伝

hide VT kakusu 隠す; VI kakureru 隠れる

high ADJ takai 高い

high-definition TV N haibijin-terebi ハイビジョンテレビ

highest N/ADJ saikō no 最高の, saijō no 最上の

highlight N midokoro 見所,

medama 目玉, hairaito ハイ
ライト

high school N kōtō-gakkō 高等
学校, kō-kō 高校

highway N kokudō 国道, kōdō
公道; (*expressway*) kōsokudōro 高速道路

hijack V (*airplane*) nottoru 乗
っ取る; N haijakku ハイジャック

hill N oka 丘

hike, hiking N haikingu ハイ
キング

hinder V samatageru 妨げる

hindrance N jama 邪魔,
bōgaibutsu 妨害物

hint N hinto ヒント; V honomekasu ほのめかす, anji
suru 暗示する

hip N (*buttock*) (o-)shiri (お)尻,
(*thigh*) momo もも; (*loins*)
koshi 腰

hire V yatou 雇う; N (*wages*)
chingin 賃金

his ADJ, PRON kare no 彼の

history N rekishi 歴史

hit N (*strike*) dageki 打撃,
hitto ヒット; atari 当たり; VI
butsukaru ぶつかる, utsu 打
つ; (*strike*) tataku 叩く; VT
ateru 当てる, butsukaru ぶつ
かる, ... ni tassuru 〜に達する

hobby N shumi 趣味

hold N (*handle*) totte 取っ手;
VI (*phone*) denwa o horyu
suru 電話を保留する, matsu
(待つ; motteiru 持っている;
VT (*grasp*) tsukamu つかむ;
(*te ni*) motsu (手に)持つ; (*in
arms*) daku 抱く; (*an open
umbrella*) sasu 差す; (*keep in
reserve*) totte oku 取って置く,
iji suru 維持する

hole N ana 穴

holiday N shukujitsu 祝日,
kyūjitsu 休日; (*vacation*)
kyūka 休暇

holy ADJ shinsei na 神聖な

home, house N ie 家; (*one's
residence*) jitaku 自宅;
(*household*) katei 家庭

homeland N bokoku 母国,
sokoku 祖国

homeless N furōsha 浮浪者,
hōmuresu ホームレス

homemade ADJ tesei no 手製
の, tezukuri no 手作りの

homestay N hōmusutei ホー
ムステイ

hometown N kokyō 故郷,
(*countryside*) inaka 田舎

homosexual N (ADJ) (*same sex*)
dōseiai (no) 同性愛(の)

283

honest ADJ shōjiki na 正直な; *(proper)* tadashi'i 正しい; *(earnest)* majime na 真面目な

honey N hachimitsu 蜂蜜

honor N meiyo 名誉

honorable ADJ *(respectable)* sonkeidekiru 尊敬できる, rippa na 立派な; *(famous)* chomei na 著名な

Hong Kong N Honkon 香港

hoodlum N furyō 不良

hoof N hizume 蹄

hook N kagi カギ; *(snap)* hokku ホック; V *(hook a fish)* (sakana o) tsuru (魚を)釣る; *(hang)* tsurusu 吊るす, hikkakeru 引っ掛ける

hope N nozomi 望み, kibō 希望, *(anticipation)* mikomi 見込み, *(ambition)* kokorozashi 志; V nozomu 望む, kibō suru 希望する

horizon N chiheisen 地平線, suiheisen 水平線

horrible ADJ osoroshi'i 恐ろしい

horse N uma 馬

hose N hōsu ホース

hospital N byōin 病院

hospitality N omotenashi おもてなし

host N shujin 主人

hot ADJ *(spicy)* karai 辛い; *(temperature)* atsui 熱い

hot dog N hotto doggu ホットドッグ

hot spring N onsen 温泉

hot water N o-yu お湯

hotel N hoteru ホテル

hour N jikan 時間

house N ie 家; *(one's residence)* jitaku 自宅; *(household)* katei 家庭

housewife N shufu 主婦

how? dono yō ni どのように, dō どう

how (about it)? ikaga いかが, dō どう

how are you? GR genki desu ka 元気ですか

How do you do? GR hajimemashite 初めまして

how far? dono-gurai/kurai *(distance)* どのくらい (距離)

how long? donokurai *(time)* どのくらい (時間); itsu made いつまで; itsu kara いつから

how many? donokurai *(number)* どのくらい, ikutsu いくつ (数)

how much? ikura *(price)* いくら (価格)

how old? ikutsu *(age)* いくつ (年齢)

however ADV shikashi nagara しかしながら, keredo (mo) けれど(も), shikashi しかし, demo でも, tokoro ga ところが, tadashi ただし, *(be sure)* mottomo もっとも

hug V dakishimeru 抱き締める

huge ADJ kyodai na 巨大な, bakudai na 莫大な

human N *(human being)* ningen 人間, jinrui 人類

human rights N jinken 人権

humanity N ningen-sei 人間性, hyūmanitī ヒューマニティー

humble ADJ *(modest)* kenkyo na 謙虚な

humid ADJ shimetta 湿った; shikke no aru 湿気のある; *(in summer)* mushiatsui 蒸し暑い

humorous ADJ omoshiroi おもしろい

hundred NUM hyaku 百

hundred thousand NUM jūman 十万

hungry ADJ kūfuku no 空腹の

hurdle N *(obstacle)* shōgai(-butsu) 障害物, *(sport)* hādoru ハードル

hurry V isogu 急ぐ; N isogi 急ぎ: *in a hurry* isoide 急いで; *hurry up* isogu 急ぐ; *(imperative)* isoide 急いで

hurt N kizu 傷; itami 痛み; VI *(pain)* itamu 痛む; VT itameru 痛める; *(cause pain)* kizutsuku 傷つく

husband N otto 夫, shujin 主人; *(one's husband)* go-shujin ご主人, dan'na-san/-sama 旦那さん/様

hut N *(shack)* koya 小屋

I

I, me PRON watashi wa/o 私は/を

ice N kōri 氷

ice cream N aisukurīmu アイスクリーム

icon N *(computer)* aikon アイコン

idea N kangae 考え; omoitsuki 思いつき, aidea アイデア; kokoroatari 心当たり; *(opinion)* iken 意見; *(intention, aim)* nerai 狙い; *(design)* an 案, *(proposal)* teian 提案

ideal ADJ risō-teki na 理想的な

285

identical ADJ dōitsu no 同一の, hitoshi'i 等しい

identity card N mibun-shōmei-sho 身分証明書, aidī-kādo IDカード

idiot N *(fool)* baka ばか, manuke 間抜け

idle ADJ *(is lazy)* namaketa 怠けた; *(useless)* muda na 無駄な

if CONJ moshi もし

ignorant ADJ muchi no 無知の

ignore V mushi suru 無視する

ill ADJ byōki no 病気の; fukō na 不幸な

illegal ADJ fuhō no 不法の, ihō no 違法の

illness N byōki 病気

illumination N iruminēshon イルミネーション, shōmei 照明

illustration N zukai 図解, irasuto (rēshon) イラスト(レーション)

ill-will N *(resentment)* urami 恨み, *(hostile feeling)* akui 悪意, teki-i 敵意

image N *(psychological/social)* imēji イメージ, gazō 画像, eizō 映像

imagination N sōzō 想像, *(imaginative power)* sōzō-ryoku 想像力

imagine V sōzō suru 想像する

imitation N *(fake)* mozōhin 模造品, nisemono 偽物

immediately ADV sassoku 早速, sugu (ni) すぐ(に), jiki (ni) じき(に), tadachi ni 直ちに, tachimachi (ni) たちまち(に)

immense ADJ bakudai na 莫大な

immigrant N ijūsha 移住者, imin 移民

immoral ADJ fudōtoku na 不道徳な

implant N *(tooth)* sashiba 差し歯, *(medical)* ishoku 移植

impolite ADJ shitsurei na 失礼な, burei na 無礼な

import N yunyū 輸入; *(goods)* yunyūhin 輸入品; V yunyū suru 輸入する

important ADJ jūyō na 重要な, taisetsu na 大切な, jūdai na 重大な, *(precious)* daiji na 大事な

impossible ADJ dekinai 出来ない, fukanō na 不可能な

impression N inshō 印象: *make an impression* inshōzukeru 印象付ける

impressive ADJ migoto na みごとな, inshōteki na 印象的な

improve vi naoru 直る, yoku naru 良くなる; vt naosu 直す, yoku suru 良くする

impudent ADJ atsukamashi'i 厚かましい, zūzūshi'i ずうずうしい

in PREP ... de ... で, *(located in)* ...ni ～に; *(inside)* ...no naka (de/ni) ～の中(で/に); *(time, years)* ... no aida ～の間, ... ni ～に: **in addition** ... ni kuwaete ～に加えて; **in order that** tame ni ために, yō ni ように

inappropriate ADJ futekisetsu na 不適切な

incense N okō お香; senkō 線香

incident N jiken 事件

include v fukumeru, 含める, tori'ireru 取り入れる, morikomu 盛り込む

income N shotoku 所得, shūnyū 収入

income tax N shotoku-zei 所得税

incomplete ADJ chūto hanpa na 中途半端な

inconsistent ADJ mujun shita 矛盾した

inconvenient ADJ fujiyū na 不自由な, fuben na 不便な

increase N zōka 増加, zōdai 増大, zōshin 増進; vi fueru 増える, ōkikunaru 大きくなる; vt ... o fuyasu ～を増やす

indecent ADJ gehin na 下品な; *(obscene)* waisetsu na わいせつな

indecisive ADJ ayafuya na あやふやな

indeed ADV tashika ni 確かに, hontō ni 本当に, jitsu ni 実に; *(of course)* mottomo 最も

independent ADJ dokuritsu shita 独立した

index N sakuin 索引, midashi 見出し, indekkusu インデックス

India N Indo インド

Indian N Indo-jin インド人; ADJ Indo(-jin) no インド(人)の

indicate v shimesu 示す; sasasu 指す; shiteki suru 指摘する, shiji suru 指示する

indigenous ADJ koyū no 固有の

indirect ADJ kansetsu-teki na 間接的な

individual ADJ kojin-teki na 個人的な; N *(person)* kojin 個人

Indonesia N Indoneshia インドネシア

Indonesian N *(language)*
Indonesia-go インドネシ
ア語; *(people)* Indonesia-
jin インドネシア人; ADJ
Indonesia(-jin) no インドネ
シア(人)の

industrious ADJ kinben na
勤勉な

industry N kōgyō 工業, sangyō
産業, gyōkai 業界

inexpensive ADJ yasui 安い,
anka na 安価な

inexpert ADJ heta na 下手な

infant N yōji 幼児, shōni 小児,
akanbō 赤ん坊, akachan
赤ちゃん

infection N kansen 感染;
(infectious disease)
densenbyō 伝染病

inflation N infure インフレ

influence N eikyō 影響;
(power) seiryoku 勢力; V
eikyō o ataeru 影響を与える

influenza N infuruenza インフ
ルエンザ

inform V shiraseru 知らせる;
kikaseru 聞かせる, tsugeru
告げる; *(instructs)* oshieru
教える

informal ADJ hi-kōshiki no
非公式の

information N jōhō 情報,
o-shirase お知らせ;
(guidance) an'nai 案内;
(reception) uketsuke 受付

information desk/booth N
an'nai-jo 案内所, furonto
フロント

ingredient N *(component)*
seibun 成分; *(raw material)*
zairyō 材料; *(cooking)*
shokuzai 食材

inhabitant N jūnin 住人

injection N chūsha 注射

injure V kega (o) saseru 怪我
(を)させる, itameru 痛める;
(damage it) sokonau 損なう;
kizutsukeru 傷つける

injury N fushō 負傷, kega 怪我

ink N sumi 墨, inku インク

inn N *(Japanese-style)* ryokan
旅館; yado 宿

inner ADJ *(inside)* naibu no
内部の, uchigawa no 内側の;
(secret) kakureta 隠れた;
(one's mind) naimen-teki na
内面的な

innocent ADJ adokenai あどけ
ない, mujitsu no 無実の,
junshin na 純真な, mujaki na
無邪気な, ubu na うぶな

inquiry N toiawase 問い合わせ,

(survey) chōsa 調査

insane ADJ kyōki no 狂気の

insect N konchū 昆虫, mushi 虫

insecure ADJ abunakkashi'i 危なっかしい

insert V hasamu 挟む, sashi-komu 差し込む

inside N naibu 内部, uchigawa 内側; *(inside of the house)* okunai 屋内; ADJ uchigawa no 内側の; naibu/naimen no 内部/内面の; PREP ... no naibu ni/de ～の内部に/で; ... no uchigawa de ～の内側で; ADV naka (de/ni) 中(で/に)

insipid ADJ ajike (no) nai 味気 (の)ない

inspect V tenken suru 点検する; kensa/kansatsu suru 検査/観察する

install V *(computer software)* instōru suru インストールする

installation N *(computer)* insutōru インストール

instance N *(example)* tatoe 例え, rei 例

instant N insutanto-shokuhin インスタント食品; ADJ insutanto no インスタントの, sokuseki no 即席の

instead of ADV ... no kawari ni ～の代わりに

institute N *(research)* kenkyū-jo 研究所

institution N *(facilities)* shise-tsu 施設; *(public)* kikan 機関, dantai 団体, kyōkai 協会

instruct V shiji suru 指示する, oshieru 教える, shidō suru 指導する; shiraseru 知らせる

instructor N shidōsha 指導者, kōshi 講師, insutorakutā インストラクター

instrument N *(implement)* dōgu 道具, kiki 機械; *(musical)* gakki 楽器

insufficiency N fusoku 不足

insult N bujoku 侮辱; V *(insult someone)* bujoku suru 侮辱する, baka ni suru ばかにする

insurance N hoken 保険

intellect, intelligence N chisei 知性, chinō 知能

intellectual N interi インテリ

intelligence quotient, IQ N chinō-shisū 知能指数

intend V ... suru tsumori de aru ～するつもりである

intention N ito 意図, ishi 意思, kokorozashi 志; *(aim)* nerai 狙い

intercom N intāhon インターホン

interest N *(pleasure)* kyōmi 興味, shumi 趣味; *(on money)* rishi 利子

interesting ADJ kyōmi bukai 興味深い, omoshiroi 面白い

interior N okunai 屋内, shitsunai 室内; uchigawa 内側; *(accessory)* interia インテリア

internal ADJ uchi no 内の, naibu no 内部の, naiteki 内的な

international ADJ kokusaiteki na 国際的な, *(worldwide)* sekaiteki na 世界的な

international exposition N bankoku-hakurankai 万国博覧会, banpaku 万博

Internet N intānetto インターネット

Internet bank N intānetto ginkō インターネット銀行, netto banku ネットバンク, onrain ginkō オンライン銀行

Internet café N intānetto kafe インターネットカフェ, netto kafe ネットカフェ

Internet shopping N īshoppingu イーショッピング,

intānetto shoppingu インターネットショッピング

interpreter N tsūyaku(sha) 通訳(者)

intersection N kōsaten 交差点

interval N aima 合間, ma 間; kankaku 間隔

interview N intabyū インタビュー, *(press interview)* kisha kaiken 記者会見

into PREP ... no naka ni 〜の中に

intrigue(s) N inbō 陰謀

introduction N shōkai 紹介

invalid ADJ *(not valid)* mukō na 無効な; N byōnin 病人;

invention N hatsumei 発明

inventory N mokuroku 目録, zaiko 在庫; *(inventory list)* zaikohyō 在庫表

investigate V shiraberu 調べる, chōsa suru 調査する; *(crime)* torishiraberu 取り調べる

invisible ADJ me ni mienai 目に見えない

invitation N sasoi 誘い, shōtai 招待; *(card)* shōtaijō 招待状

invite V *(ask along)* sasou 誘う, yobu 呼ぶ, maneku 招く; *(formally)* shōtai suru 招待する, mukaeru 迎える

invoice N seikyūsho 請求書;

okurijō 送り状; nōhinsho 納品書

involve v tomonau 伴う

Ireland n Airurando アイルランド

Irish n *(people)* Airurando-jin アイルランド; ADJ Airurando (-jin) no アイルランド(人)の

irregular ADJ fukisoku na 不規則な; fuzoroi na 不揃いな; futeiki no 不定期の

irrelevance ADJ futekisetsu na 不適切な

iron ADJ tetsu no 鉄の; v airon o kakeru アイロンをかける; n airon アイロン

Islam n Isuramu イスラム

island n shima 島

issue n hakkō(butsu) 発行(物); *(magazine issues)* -gō 号; v *(publishes)* hakkō suru 発行する

IT n *(information technology)* aitī アイティー

it PRON sore それ

Italian n *(language)* Itaria-go イタリア語; *(people)* Itaria-jin イタリア人; ADJ Itaria(-jin) no イタリア(人)の

italic n itarikku(-tai) イタリック(体); shatai 斜体

Italy n Itaria イタリア

itchy ADJ kayui かゆい; muzu-muzu suru むずむずする

It's all right. PHR daijōbu desu 大丈夫です

item n *(individual thing)* hinmoku 品目; kōmoku 項目

ivory n zōge 象牙

ivy n tsuta ツタ

J

jacket n jaketto ジャケット, uwagi 上着

jade n hisui ヒスイ

jail n keimusho 刑務所

jam n jamu ジャム

January n ichi-gatsu 一月, Shōgatsu 正月

Japan n Nihon/Nippon 日本

Japanese n *(language)* Nihon-go 日本語; *(people)* Nihon-jin 日本人; ADJ Nihon(-jin) no 日本(人)の; Nihonteki na 日本的な

Japanese cuisine n Nihon-ryōri 日本料理

Japanese food n washoku 和食

Japanese warrior n bushi 武士, samurai 侍

291

J

jar N *(with a large mouth)* kame かめ; *(with a small mouth)* tsubo つぼ; *(glass)* garasu-bin ガラスびん, bin びん

jaw N ago あご

jealous ADJ shittobukai 嫉妬深い; yakimochi o yaku 焼きもちを焼く, shitto suru 嫉妬する

jeans N jīnzu ジーンズ, jīpan ジーパン

jewel(ry) N hōseki 宝石

job N shigoto 仕事; ninmu 任務; gimu 義務 *(place)* tsutome-saki 勤め先: *getting a job* shūshoku 就職

job hopping N tenshoku 転職

job hunting N kyūshoku 求職

job transfer N tenkin 転勤, ten'nin 転任

join V awaseru 合わせる, *(graft, glue)* tsugu 接ぐ; *(enter)* …ni hairu ～に入る; *(in co-operation)* tsuku 付く: *join in* sanka suru 参加する

joint N *(in a statement)* fushi 節, ADJ gōdō no 合同の

joke N jōku ジョーク, jōdan 冗談

journal N jānaru ジャーナル; *(diary)* nikki 日記

journalist N kisha 記者, jānarisuto ジャーナリスト

journey N tabi 旅

joy N yorokobi 喜び

joyful ADJ ureshi'i うれしい, tanoshi'i 楽しい

judge V hihan suru 批判する

judgment N hanketsu 判決, hihan 批判

judo N jūdō 柔道

juice N jūsu ジュース, kajū 果汁

July N shichi-gatsu 七月

jumble ADJ gochagocha(shita) ごちゃごちゃ(した), gocha-maze no ごちゃ混ぜの

jump N tobu 跳ぶ; haneru 跳ねる

June N roku-gatsu 六月

jungle N janguru ジャングル, mitsurin 密林

junior ADJ *(younger)* toshi-shita no 年下の; *(colleague, fellow)* kōhai 後輩

junior college N tanki-daigaku 短期大学

junior high school N chūgakkō 中学校

junk e-mail/mail N janku mēru ジャンクメール, meiwaku mēru 迷惑メール

just ADJ *(fair)* kōhei na 公平
な; ADV *(only)* tatta no たった
の, ...dake 〜だけ; *(exactly)*
chōdo ちょうど; masa ni ま
さに; *(merely)* tada ただ:
just a moment chotto ちょ
っと; *just in case* ichiō 一
応; *just right* pittari ぴったり,
uttetsuke no うってつけの

justice N *(rightness)* seigi
正義, seitō-sei 正当性;
(judiciary) shihō 司法

juvenile N kodomo 子ども,
jidō-sho 児童書

K

keen ADJ nesshin na 熱心な

keep V tamotsu 保つ; *(retain)*
kakaeru 抱える; *(take in
trust)* azukaru 預かる; *(raise
animals)* kau 飼う: *keep cool
(calm down)* ochitsuku 落
ち着く

kelp N konbu 昆布

kennel N inugoya 犬小屋

kettle N yakan やかん,
yu-wakashi 湯沸かし

key N *(for computer)* kī キー
(コンピューター); *(for room)*
kagi 鍵

keyboard N *(for computer)*
kībōdo キーボード

keyhole N kagi-ana 鍵穴

kick V keru 蹴る: *kick out
(company)* kubi ni suru クビ
にする, *(school)* yame aseru
辞めさせる, taigaku-saseru 退
学させる

kid N kodomo 子供: *kid
around* fuzakeru ふざける

kidnap N yūkai 誘拐; V yūkai
suru 誘拐する

kidney N jinzō 腎臓

kill V korosu 殺す

killer N satsujinhan 殺人犯

kilogram N kiro(guramu) キ
ロ(グラム)

kilometer N kiro(mētā) キロ
(メーター)

kind ADJ *(of persons)* yasashi'i
やさしい(人); N *(type)* shurui
種類

kindergarten N yōchien 幼
稚園

kindness N on 恩, shinsetsu
親切

king N ō-sama 王様

kingdom N ō-koku 王国

kiosk N baiten 売店

kiss N kisu キス, seppun 接吻; V
kisu o suru キスをする

kit N *(of tools)* yōgu 用具, kitto キット

kitchen N daidokoro 台所, kitchin キッチン

kitchenware N *(kitchen utensils)* daidokoro yōhin 台所用品

kite N tako 凧; *kite-flying* tako-age 凧あげ; *fly a kite* tako o ager 凧をあげる

kitten N koneko 子猫

Kleenex N *(tissue)* tisshu(-pēpā) ティッシュ(ペーパー); chirigami ちり紙

kiln N kama 釜

knee N hiza 膝

kneel V hizamazuku ひざまずく

knife N kogatana 小刀, naifu ナイフ; *(big)* hōchō 包丁

knit V amu 編む

knitting, knitted goods N amimono 編み物

knob N *(in a statement)* fushi 節; *(bump)* kobu こぶ

knock N nokku suru ノックする; *knock down* taosu 倒す

knot N *(in a statement)* fushi 節; musubi(-me) 結び(目)

know V *(be acquainted with)* chishiki ga aru 知識がある; V shitteiru 知っている

knowledge N chishiki 知識

Korean N (ADJ) *(language)* Kankoku-go 韓国語; *(people)* Kankoku-jin (no) 韓国人(の)

Korean, North N (ADJ) Kita-chōsen (no) 北朝鮮 (の)

Korean, South ADJ Kankoku (no) 韓国(の)

L

label N *(tag)* fuda 札, rabel ラベル; V raberu o tsukeru/haru ラベルを付ける/貼る

labor N rōdō 労働; *labor union* rōdōkumiai 労働組合

laboratory N kenkyū-shitsu 研究室; jikken-shitsu 実験室, rabo ラボ

ladder N hashigo 梯子

ladle N shakushi 杓子; V kumu 汲む, sukū すくう

lady N fujin 婦人, go-fujin ご婦人; *(young)* ojō-san お嬢さん

lag N okure 遅れ; V okureru 遅れる; *time lag* jisa 時差

lake N mizu'umi 湖

lamb N kohitsuji 子羊, hitsujiniku 羊肉, ramu ラム

lamp N ranpu ランプ, shōmei 照明

land N tochi 土地; V *(plane)* chakuriku suru 着陸する (飛行機)

landmark N mejirushi 目印

landowner N ji-nushi 地主

landscape N fūkei 風景, keshiki 景色

lane N *(path)* komichi 小道; *(traffic, swim)* kōsu コース; *(highway)* shasen 車線

language N gengo 言語, kotoba 言葉, gengo 言語

lantern N chōchin ちょうちん

Laos N Raosu ラオス

Laotian N *(language)* Raosu-go ラオス語; *(people)* Raosu-jin ラオス人; ADJ Raosu(-jin) no ラオス (人)の

laptop N rapputoppu(-gata) konpyūtā ラップトップ(型)コンピューター, nōto(-gata) pasokon ノート(型)パソコン

large ADJ hiroi 広い, ōki'i 大きい

last ADJ saigo no 最後の; *(the last)* biri no ビリの: **at last** tōtō とうとう, yatto やっと, iyo-iyo いよいよ, tsuini ついに, yōyaku ようやく; **last month** sengetsu 先月; **last night** sakuya 昨夜; **last week** senshū 先週; **last year**

sakunen 昨年

late ADJ osoi 遅い; *(time)* okureru 遅れる; ADV osoku 遅く: **late at night** yoruosoku 夜遅く

later ADV sono go その後, ato de 後で

lately N, ADV kono aida この間; *(recently)* chikagoro 近頃, saikin 最近

laugh V warau 笑う: **laugh at ... o warau** ～を笑う

launch N hassha 発射, uchiage 打ち上げ

laundry N sentaku(-mono) 洗濯(物); *(cleaner)* kurīningu-ya クリーニング屋

lavatory N senmen-jo 洗面所, toire トイレ, otearai お手洗い

law N *(legislation)* hōritsu 法律, hō 法; *(rule)* hōsoku 法則; *(science/study of)* hōgaku(-bu) 法学(部)

lawyer N bengoshi 弁護士

lay V *(put)* oku 置く; *(lay the table)* tsukue o naraberu 机を並べる

lazy ADJ taiman na 怠慢な, namaketa 怠けた

lead V *(guide)* an'nai suru 案内する; *(as a leader)* michibiku

導く; *(coach them)* shidō suru 指導する; *(command them)* hiki'iru 率いる; N *(metal)* namari 鉛

leader N shidōsha 指導者, rīdā リーダー

leaf N ha 葉

leak VI moreru 漏れる, moru 漏る, moreru 漏れる; VT morasu 漏らす

leap year N urūdoshi うるう年

learn V narau 習う, manabu 学ぶ

learning N gakumon 学問; gakushū 学習

least N saishō 最小; ADJ *(smallest amount)* saishō no 最小の: *at least* sukunaku tomo 少なくとも

leather N kawa 皮

leave VI shuppatsu suru 出発する; saru 去る; VT *(for a far place)* tatsu 発つ; *(quit the company)* yameru 辞める; *(leave one's seat)* seki o hazusu 席を外す; wakareru 別れる; okiwasureru 置き忘れる; N wakare 別れ: *leave alone* hōtte oku 放っておく; *Leave me alone!* Hottoite! ほっといて!; *leave behind (by*

accident) okiwasureru 置き忘れる; *(for safekeeping)* hokan suru 保管する

lecture N kōgi 講義, *(talk)* kōen 講演

lecturer N *(at university)* kōshi (大学の) 講師

left N *(remaining)* nokori 残り; hidari(gawa) 左(側); ADJ hidari(gawa) no 左(側)の; ADV hidari e 左へ

left-handed ADJ hidarikiki no 左利きの

leftover N amari 余り, nokori 残り

leg N ashi 脚; *(shin)* sune すね

legal ADJ gōhō no 合法の, hōteki na 法的な, hōritsu-jō no 法律上の

legend N densetsu 伝説

leisure N *(spare time)* hima 暇, yoka 余暇; goraku 娯楽, rejā レジャー

lemon N remon レモン

lend V kasu 貸す

length N nagasa 長さ

lengthen V nobasu 伸ばす, enchō suru 延長する

leopard N *(animal)* hyō ヒョウ

less ADJ/ADV *(smaller amount)* yori sukunai/sukunaku より

少ない/少なく; **PREP** *(minus)* ... o hi'ita ～を引いた: *less than ...* ...ika ～以下

lessen **VI** sukunakunaru 少なくなる; heru 減る; **VT** sukunaku/chīsaku suru 少なく/小さくする; herasu 減らす

lesson **N** ressun レッスン, jugyō 授業

let **V** kyoka suru 許可する; *(as a favor)* (... ni sore o) saseru (～にそれを)させる, saseteyaru させてやる; yurusu 許す: *let alone* hotte/hōtte oku ほって/放っておく; *let loose/go* hanasu 放す; *let me know* o-shirase kudasai お知らせください; go-renraku kudasai ご連絡ください; *let someone know* **V** shiraseru 知らせる

let's *(suggestion)* ... shiyō ～しよう, (shi)mashō (し)ましょう: *Let's eat!* itadakimasu いただきます

letter **N** tegami 手紙; *(character)* moji 文字, ji 字

level **ADJ** *(even, flat)* taira na 平らな; *(height)* onajitakasa no 同じ高さの; **N** *(standard)* suijun 水準; *(extent)* teido 程度

library **N** toshokan 図書館; *(room)* toshoshitsu 図書室, *(home study)* shosai 書斎; *(collection)* zōsho 蔵書

license **N** menkyo 免許, raisensu ライセンス, menkyoshō 免許証; *(driver's license)* untenmenkyo 運転免許; *(permit)* kyoka 許可

lick **V** nameru 舐める

lid **N** futa ふた

lie **N** *(falsehood)* uso 嘘, itsuwari 偽り; **V** *(tell a lie)* uso o tsuku 嘘をつく

life **N** *(daily living)* seikatsu 生活, inochi 命, seimei 生命

lifetime **N** jinsei 人生, isshō 一生

lift **V** *(lift something)* (mono o) mochiageru (物を)持ち上げる; *(ride in car)* (kuruma ni) noseteageru (車に)乗せてあげる; *(raise)* takameru 高める; *(steal)* nusumu 盗む; **N** rifuto リフト

light **N** hikari 光, akari 明かり; *(lamp)* shōmei 照明; *(electric)* denki 電気, dentō 電灯; **ADJ** *(bright)* akarui 明るい; *(not heavy)* karui 軽い; *(pale)* usui 薄い

lighter N raitā ライター

lightning N inazuma 稲妻

like N konomi 好み; shumi 趣味; V (be fond of) …o tanoshimu ～を楽しむ; (be pleased by) konomu 好む, kini'iru 気に入る; (want) … o nozomu ～を望む; PREP (similar) …no yō na ～の様な; (be similar to) … ni niteiru ～に似ている

likely ADJ arisō na ありそうな; ADV (probably) tabun 多分

likewise ADV onaji yō ni 同じように

lime N (citrus) raimu ライム; (mineral) sekkai 石灰

limit N seigen 制限; gendo 限度; han'i 範囲; V seigen suru 制限する: time limit seigen (jikan) 制限(時間)

line N (mark) sen 線; (of letters) gyō 行; (queue) gyōretsu 行列; (phone) kaisen 回線; (thread) ito 糸; V sen o hiku 線を引く; naraberu 並べる: line up narabu 並ぶ

linen N asa 麻

link N wa 輪; (computer) rinku リンク; V tsunagaru つながる;

(computer) rinku suru リンクする

lion N raion ライオン

lips N kuchibiru 唇

liquid N ekitai 液体

liquor N sake 酒

list N hyō 表, risuto リスト; (of names) meibo 名簿; V hyō ni suru 表にする, (risuto ni) ireru (リストに)入れる

listen V kiku 聴く

listener N kiki-te 聞き手, risunā リスナー

literary ADJ bungaku no 文学の, bungaku-teki na 文学的な

literature N bungaku 文学

little N shōryō 少量; ADJ (not much) sukunai 少ない, (small) chīsai 小さい, chitchai ちっちゃい; (juvenile) osanai 幼い; (in quantity) sukoshi no 少しの: a little sukoshi 少し, wazuka わずか; little by little sukoshi zutsu 少しずつ; sorosoro そろそろ

live V (be alive) ikiteiru 生きている; (stay in a place) sumu 住む

lively ADJ (cheerful) yōki na 陽気な, (peppy) kappatsu na 活発な, genki na 元気な,

(flourishing) nigiyaka na に
ぎやかな

liver N kanzō 肝臓

living costs N seikatsu-hi
生活費

load N tsumini 積み荷, nimotsu
荷物: *load up* tsumikomu
積み込む

loathing ADJ daikirai na 大嫌
いな

lobby N robī ロビー

lobster N ise ebi 伊勢エビ,
robusutā ロブスター

local ADJ chihō no 地方の,
jimoto no 地元の

location N basho 場所, ichi
位置, haichi 配置

lock N jō 錠; VI kagi ga kakaru
鍵が掛かる, shimaru 閉まる;
VT jō/kagi o kakeru 錠/鍵を掛
ける; kotei suru 固定する

locker N rokkā ロッカー; *(coin-
operated)* koin-rokkā コイ
ンロッカー

lodge N rojji ロッジ, koya 小屋

lodgings N geshuku 下宿

log N maruta 丸太

logical ADJ ronri-teki na 論理
的な

login N *(computer)* roguin ログ
イン, setsuzoku 接続

log-out N roguauto ログアウト,
roguofu ログオフ, sainofu サ
インオフ, sainauto サインアウト

lonely ADJ sabishi'i 寂しい,
hitori no ひとりの,
kokorobosoi 心細い

long ADJ *(length)* nagai 長い
(距離); *(time)* nagai 長い (時
間): *for a long time* nagai
aida 長い間; *(in the past)*
mae kara 前から

long distance runner N chō-
kyori ran'na 長距離ランナー

long time ago ADV zutto
mukashi ni ずっと昔に; zutto
mae ni ずっと前に

long for V akogareru 憧れる

look N *(appearance)* yōsu
様子; *(personal appearance)*
kiryō 器量, mitame 見た目;
(a look in one's eyes)
metsuki 目付き; V nē ねえ,
chotto ちょっと: *look after*
sewa o suru 世話をする,
hikitoru 引き取る;
look at miru 見る, me o
mukeru 目を向ける; *look
back* furimuku 振り向く,
furikaeru 振り返る; *look for*
sagasu 探す; *look like* ... no
yō ni mieru 〜のように見え

る、... no yō ni omoeu ～のように思える); **look up** *(find in book)* kensaku suru (本を)検索する

loose ADJ yurui ゆるい、rūzu na ルーズな、*(lazy)* darashinai だらしない；*(wobbly)* guratsuita ぐらついた、*(not in packet)* tabanetenai 束ねてない

lose V *(be defeated)* makeru 負ける；nakusu なくす、ushinau 失う

loss N songai 損害、sonshitsu 損失；*(defeat)* make 負け；shippai 失敗

lost ADJ *(can't find way)* michi ni mayotta 道に迷った；*(missing)* ushinatta 失った、komatte 困って

lost property N funshitsubutsu 紛失物

lottery N takarakuji 宝くじ、chūsen 抽選

loud ADJ onryō no aru 音量のある、(oto ga) ōki'i (音が)大きい；urusai うるさい

love N ai 愛、koi 恋、ren'ai 恋愛；V aisuru 愛する、konomu 好む、kawaigaru 可愛がる

love affair N ren'ai-kankei 恋愛関係、romansu ロマンス

lovely ADJ suteki na 素敵な；airashi'i 愛らしい、kawaii かわいい

lover N koibito 恋人；aikōka 愛好家

low ADJ hikui 低い；*(cheap)* yasui 安い

low blood pressure N teiketsuatsu 低血圧

lowly ADJ iyashi'i いやしい

luck N un 運、unmei 運命；kōun 幸運、shiawase 幸せ

lucky ADJ *(a person)* kōun na 幸運な、un ga ii 運がいい；shiawase na 幸せな；*(strikes it lucky)* tsuiteiru ついている

luggage N tenimotsu 手荷物

lull V *(a child, baby)* ayasu あやす

lunar calendar N inreki 陰暦

lunch N chūshoku 昼食、hirugohan 昼ご飯、hirumeshi 昼飯、ranchi ランチ：*eat lunch* V chūshoku o toru 昼食をとる

lungs N hai 肺

lush ADJ *(midori no)* shigetta (緑の)茂った、aoao to shita 青々とした、mizumizushi'i みずみずしい

luxurious ADJ gōka na 豪華な；zeitaku na ぜいたくな

M

machine N kikai 機械

machinery N kikairui 機械類

mackerel N saba サバ

mad N ikari 怒り; ADJ ki ga kurutta 気が狂った; okotte 怒って: *get mad at* atama ni kuru 頭にくる

madam N *(term of address)* gofujin ご婦人; *(女性への敬称)* oku-san/-sama 奥さん/様

madness N kyōki 狂気

magazine N zasshi 雑誌

magic N tejina 手品; majikku マジック

magician N tejina-shi 手品師

magnet N jishaku 磁石

magnificent ADJ subarashi'i すばらしい

mahjong N mājan 麻雀

mail N *(post)* yūbinbutsu 郵便物; V yūsōuru 郵送する, tegami o dasu 手紙を出す

mail box N yūbinuke 郵便受け, posuto ポスト

mail order N tsūshin hanbai 通信販売

main ADJ *(most important)* omo na 主な, shuyō na 主要な: *main issue* hondai 本題

main store N honten 本店

main street N ōdōri 大通り; mein sutorīto メインストリート

maintenance N *(preservation)* hoshu 保守; *(support)* shiji 支持, *(upkeep)* iji 維持

major ADJ *(important)* jūyō na 重要な

majority N daibubun 大部分, daitasū 大多数, *(more than half)* kahansū 過半数

make V tsukuru 作る; *make up (invent)* decchiageru でっち上げる

maker N *(manufacturer)* mēkā メーカー, seizō-moto 製造元

makeshift ADJ maniawase no 間に合わせの

makeup N keshō 化粧; *(cosmetics)* keshō hin 化粧品; *(structure)* kumi-tate 組み立て, kōzō 構造

Malaysia N Marēshia マレーシア

Malaysian N *(people)* Marēshia-jin マレーシア人; ADJ Marēshia(-jin) no マレーシア(人)の

male N dansei 男性; ADJ otoko no 男の, dansei no 男性の

malice N akui 悪意

301

malignant ADJ akushitsu na 悪質な

mama N mama ママ, o-kāsan お母さん

mammal N honyū-rui 哺乳類, honyū dōbutsu 哺乳動物

man N otoko no hito 男の人, otoko 男

manage V *(run)* un'ei suru 運営する; *(cope with)* shori suru 処理する; *(run a business)* keiei suru 経営する; *(a team)* kantoku suru 監督する

management N keiei 経営; *(control)* shihai 支配; *(handling)* toriatsukai 取り扱い

manager N shihainin 支配人, kanrinin 管理人, manējā マネージャー; buchō 部長

Mandarin Chinese N Mandarin マンダリン, Chūgoku hyōjun-go 中国標準語, pekin-go 北京語

manga N *(comic)* manga マンガ

mankind N jinrui 人類

manner N yarikata やり方, shi-kata 仕方; furi ふり

manners N gyōgi 行儀, sahō 作法, manā マナー

manpower N rōdō-ryoku 労働力

manual N manyuaru マニュアル, tebikisho 手引き書

manufacture V seizō suru 製造する, seisan suru 生産する, tsukuru 作る

many ADJ takusan no たくさんの, ōku no 多くの

map N chizu 地図

maple N kaede カエデ, momiji モミジ

marathon N marason マラソン

March N san-gatsu 三月

march N kōshin 行進, māchi マーチ; *(music)* kōshin kyoku 行進曲; V kōshin suru 行進する

margin N *(white space)* yohaku 余白; yoyū 余裕; *(price difference)* mājin マージン

mark N *(sign)* shirushi 印, kigō 記号, māku マーク, ato 跡; *(score point)* ten 点, *(score)* tensū 点数; *(school grades)* seiseki 成績; V *(make a mark on)* (... ni) shirushi/kigō/ ten o tsukeru (...に)印/記号/点を付ける

market, marketplace N ichiba 市場

marriage N kekkon 結婚

marry V *(get married)* kekkon suru 結婚する

marsh N numa(chi) 沼(地)

martial arts N bujutsu 武術, budō 武道

marvelous ADJ suteki na すてきな, sugoi すごい

mask N masuku マスク; (o-)men (お)面

mass communications N masukomi マスコミ

mass media N masumedia マスメディア

massage N massāji マッサージ; V *(rubs with hands)* momu 揉む

master N *(of a shop, etc.)* dan'na 旦那, tenshu 店主; oyakata 親方; meijin 名人

masterpiece N kessaku 傑作, meisaku 名作

mat N matto マット

match N matchi マッチ; *(game)* shiai 試合; V *(equal)* taikō suru 対抗する; hitteki suru 匹敵する

matchbox N matchi-bako マッチ箱

mate N *(friend)* nakama 仲間, tomodachi 友達; *(spouse)* haigūsha 配偶者

material ADJ *(physical)* busshitsuteki na 物質的な

materials N *(ingredient)* zairyō 材料, genryō 原料, sozai 素材

mathematics N sūgaku 数学

matter N *(issue)* mondai 問題; busshitsu 物質: *it doesn't matter* dōdemoii どうでもいい, kamaimasen 構いません

maximum N saidai-gen 最大限

May N go-gatsu 五月

may MODAL V *(perhaps)*... ka mo shirenai ～かもしれない

maybe ADV tabun 多分, moshikashite もしかして; hyotto shita ra/shite/suru to ひょっとしたら/して/すると; aruiwa あるいは

mayor N shichō 市長

meal N shokuji 食事

mean V *(word)* imi suru 意味する *(intend)*... suru tsumori ～するつもり; ADJ *(cruel)* ijiwaru na 意地悪な; ototta 劣った

meaning N imi 意味, wake 訳

meanwhile ADV sono aida ni その間に

measles N hashika はしか

measure N *(ruler)* monosashi 物差し; V hakaru 計る

measurement(s) N sokutē 測定, sunpō 寸法

meat N shokuniku 食肉

mechanic N shūrikō 修理工, seibishi 整備士

medical ADJ igaku no 医学の

medical examination N shinsatsu 診察, kenkō shindan 健康診断

medicine N iyakuhin 医薬品; *(doctoring)* igaku 医学

meditation N meisō 瞑想; *(ascetic training)* shugyō 修行, gyō 行; *(Zen)* zazen 座禅

(the) Mediterranean N chichūkai 地中海

medium ADJ chūkan no 中間の; N chūkan 中間; baitai 媒体

meet V au 会う; *(happen to ...)* deau 出会う; *(encounter)* sessuru 接する; *(greet)* demukaeru 出迎える

meeting N ikaigō 会合, kai 会; *(by prior arrangement)* uchiawase 打ち合わせ

melody N merodī メロディー, senritsu 旋律

melon N meron メロン

melt VI tokeru 溶ける; VT tokasu 溶かす

member N kai'in 会員

memo(randum) N memo メモ

memorial N kinen hi 記念碑; ADJ kinen no 記念の

memorize V anki suru 暗記する

memory N kioku 記憶; *(computer)* memorī メモリー; *(capacity)* kioku-ryoku 記憶力; *(a recollection)* omoide 思い出

mend V naosu 直す

menstruate V gekkei ga aru 月経がある

mentality N chisei 知性知, chinō 知能

mention V noberu 述べる: ***Don't mention it.*** Dō itashimashite. どういたしまして。

menu N kondate 献立, menyū メニュー

merchandise N shōhin 商品

merely ADV tan ni 単に, tada ただ, tatta たった

merit N chōsho 長所

mess: in a mess N chirakari 散らかり

message N dengon 伝言, messēji メッセージ

messy ADJ gochagocha(shita) ごちゃごちゃ(した)

method N hōhō 方法、hō 法; shiyō 仕様

metropolitan ADJ tokai no 都会の、toshi no 都市の

microphone N maiku マイク

microscope N kenbi-kyō 顕微鏡

microwave N maikuro-ha マイクロ波、(kitchen microwave) denshi renji 電子レンジ

midday N shōgo 正午

midday meal N (lunch) ichūshoku 昼食

middle N (center) chūō 中央; man'naka 真ん中、chūshin 中心、naka ba 半ば; (medium size) chū 中間; (medium size) chū 中

(the) Middle East N Chūtō 中東

midnight, middle of the night N imayonaka 真夜中

midst N (… no) saichū (〜の) 最中

might MODAL V (shi)temo yoi (し)てもよい; (perhaps) moshi ka shitara … ka mo shirenai もしかしたら〜かもしれない

mild ADJ (not severe) odayaka na 穏やかな、yawarakai 柔らかい; (not spicy) amakuchi no 甘口の、(taste) maroyaka まろやか

military N, ADJ gunrai no 軍隊の、gunjin no 軍人の

milk N gyūnyū 牛乳

million NUM ihyakuman 百万

millionaire N hyakuman chōja 百万長者

mind N kokoro 心、omoi 思い、seishin 精神; kokorogamae 心構え; (brain) chiryoku 知力、chisei 知性; V (be displeased) ki ni naru 気になる; (take care) ki o tsukeru 気をつける; (manage) sewa o suru 〜の世話をする

mine PRON (my) wata(ku)shi no わた(く)しの; N (coal, etc.) kōzan 鉱山

minibus N maikurobasu マイクロバス、kogatabasu 小型バス

minimal ADJ (smallest, least) saishō no 最小の; (lowest) saitei no 最低の、saika no 最下の

minister N (Christian) bokushi 牧師

minor ADJ (not important) taishita koto nai 大したことない; sukunai 少ない

minus N mainasu マイナス; ADJ

305

... o (sashi)hi'ita 〜を(差し)引いた

minute N fun 分; ADJ (*fine, detailed*) seimitsu na 精密な, chimitsu na 緻密な

mirror N kagami 鏡; V (*reflect*) utsusu 映す

miscellaneous ADJ samazama na 様々な, zatta na 雑多な

miscellaneous goods N zakka 雑貨

misfortune N fukō 不幸

mismanagement N futegiwa 不手際

miss N (*mistake*) misu ミス; V (*bus, flight*) noriokureru (バス、飛行機に) 乗り遅れる; hazureru 外れる; (*loved one*) koishiku omou 恋しく思う, (*fail*) shippai suru 失敗する

Miss N (*for young woman*) ...-san 〜さん; ojō-san お嬢さん

mission N (*task*) ninmu 任務, (*operation*) sakusen 作戦, (*Christianity*) fukyō 布教 (katsudō) (活動)

mist N kiri 霧, moya 靄

mistake N machigai 間違い, ayamari 誤り, misu ミス; V machigau 間違う;

mistress N on'nashujin 女主人; aijin 愛人

misunderstanding N gokai 誤解

mix VI mazaru 混ざる; VT mazeru 混ぜる

mob N bōryoku-dan 暴力団

mobile phone N keitai denwa 携帯電話

model N mohan 模範, tehon 手本; (*mold*) mokei 模型; (*type*) kata 型; (*fashion model*) moderu モデル

modem N modemu モデム

modern ADJ gendai no 現代の

modest ADJ (*simple*) hikaeme na 控えめな, uchiki na 内気な

molester N (*sexual*) chikan 痴漢

moment N (*instant*) shunkan 瞬間; *in a moment* suguni すぐに; *just a moment* chotto matte kudasai ちょっと待って下さい, shōshō omachi kudasai 少々お待ちください

Monday N getsu-yōbi 月曜日

money N okane お金

money order N kawase 為替; (*postal*) yūbin kawase 郵便為替

monitor N *(of computer)* monitā (コンピューターの) モニター

monkey N saru 猿

monster N bakemono 化け物, obake お化け

month N tsuki 月: *month before last* sensen-getsu 先々月

monthly ADJ maitsuki no 毎月の

monument N kinenhi 記念碑

moon tsuki 月

moral N moraru モラル; ADJ dōtoku-teki na 道徳的な

more ADJ *(comparative)* ... yori ōku ～より多く, motto もっと, mō sukoshi もう少し: *a little more* mō sukoshi もう少し; *a lot more* motto takusan もっとたくさん; *more and more* masu-masu 益々, iyo-iyo いよいよ; *more or less* daitai だいたい

morning N asa 朝; go zen 午前

morning meal N chōshoku 朝食, asagohan 朝ご飯

mosque N mosuku モスク

mosquito N ka 蚊

moss N koke 苔

most ADJ mottomo ōku no 最

も多くの; mottomo ōki'i 最も大きい; ADV *(superlative)* mottomo 最も, ichiban 一番; *(the most of)* hotondo no ほとんどの; hijō ni 非常に; *(the most)* saidai no 最大の

moth N ga 蛾

mother N haha 母, hahaoya 母親, okā-san お母さん

mother country N bokoku 母国

mother-in-law N giri no haha 義理の母

motivation, motive N dōki 動機; yaruki やる気

motor N *(engine)* mōtā モーター, enjin エンジン

motorbike ōtobai オートバイ, baiku バイク

motor vehicle N jidōsha 自動車

mount N daishi 台紙

Mount Fuji N Fuji(-san) 富士(山)

mountain N yama 山

mountain-climbing N yama nobori 山登り, tozan 登山

mouse N *(animal)* nezumi ねずみ; *(computer)* mausu マウス (コンピューター)

mouth N kuchi 口

move N ugoki 動き; hikkoshi 引っ越し; V ugoku 動く; *(move residence)* utsuru 移る, *(change residence)* hikkosu 引っ越す; VT ugokasu 動かす: *move from ... to ...* ... kara ... ni idō suru ～から～に移動する

movie N eiga 映画

movie house/theater N eigakan 映画館

Mrs. … -fujin –夫人

much ADJ takusan no たくさんの, ōku no 多くの: *as much as* ... gurai ～位, ...no yōni ～のように[様]に; *much more ... (also)* issō いっそう

mud N doro 泥

murder N satsujin 殺人, hitogoroshi 人殺し; V *(kill a person)* korosu 殺す

muscle N kin'niku 筋肉

museum N hakubutsu-kan 博物館, *(art gallery)* bijutsu-kan 美術館

mushroom N kinoko きのこ

music N ongaku 音楽

musician N ongaku-ka 音楽家, myūjishan ミュージシャン

Muslim ADJ Isuramukyō(to) no イスラム教(徒)の

must MODAL V ...(shi)nakute wa ikenai ～なくてはいけない

mustache N kuchihige 口ひげ

mutton N maton マトン

my, mine ADJ, PRON watashi no ～の

Myanmar N Myanmā ミャンマー

my husband N otto 夫, shujin 主人

myself PRON jibun 自分, (jibun/watakushi) jishin (自分/私)自身; *by myself* jibun jishin de 自分自身で

mystery N nazo 謎, misuterī ミステリー, *(secret)* himitsu 秘密

myth N shinwa 神話

N

nail N *(finger, toe)* tsume 爪 (手、足); *(spike)* kugi 釘

nail clippers N tsumekiri 爪切り

naked ADJ hadaka no 裸の

name N namae 名前; meishō 名称; V nazukeru 名付ける

name card N meishi 名刺

name seal/stamp N *(chop)* hanko はんこ

nap N hiru-ne 昼寝; *take a nap* utatane suru うたた寝する

narcotic(s) N mayaku 麻薬

narrow ADJ semai 狭い; hosoi 細い

nasty ADJ iya na 嫌な

nation N *(country)* kuni 国, kokka 国家

nationalism N aikokushin 愛国心

nationality N kokuseki 国籍

nation-wide ADJ zenkokuteki na/ni 全国的な/に

native ADJ bokoku no 母国の; ten'nen no 天然の, shizen no 自然の

native language N bokoku-go 母国語

natural ADJ shizen no 自然の, ten'nen no 天然の

natural gas N ten'nen-gasu 天然ガス

nature N shizen 自然; seishitsu 性質, kishitsu 気質

naughty ADJ itazura na いたずらな, wanpaku na 腕白な

navigation N kōkai 航海; *(car navigation system)* kānabi カーナビ

near ADJ chikai 近い; ADV chikaku (ni) 近く(に)

nearby ADJ sugusoba no すぐそばの, chikaku 近く

nearly ADV hotondo ほとんど, hobo ほぼ; mazu まず

neat ADJ *(orderly)* kichin to shita きちんとした

necessary ADJ hitsuyō na 必要な

necessity N *(daily items)* hitsujuhin 必需品

neck N kubi 首

necktie N nekutai ネクタイ

need N hitsuyō 必要; MODAL V ... suru hitsuyō ga aru ～する必要がある

needle N hari 針

needy ADJ mazushi'i 貧しい, fu-jiyū na 不自由な, hinkon na 貧困な

negative ADJ shōkyoku-teki na 消極的な, hitei-teki na 否定的な, hikan-teki na 悲観的な, negatibu na ネガティブな; N *(film)* nega ネガ

neglect N hōchi 放置, hōki 放棄; *(child neglect)* ikujihōki 育児放棄; V *(disregard)* mushi suru 無視する; *(leave undone)* hōtteoku 放っておく; *(shirk)* okotaru 怠る

negotiate v hanashiau 話し合う; N kōshō 交渉

neighbor N rinjin 隣人

neighborhood N (go-)kinjo (ご)近所; *(neighbor)* rinjin 隣人

neither CONJ ... de nai ～でない: *neither ... nor* ADV ... mo... mo... nai ～も～も～ない; *neither one* ADV dochira (no ...) mo ...nai どちら(の～)もない

nephew N oi 甥

nervous ADJ shinkei-shitsu na 神経質な; *(chicken-hearted)* bikubiku suru びくびくする

nest N su 巣

net N ami 網

netizen N *(Internet)* netto-shimin ネット市民

network N hōsōmō 放送網, kairomō 回路網, jōhō-mō 情報網; *network address (computer)* nettowāku-adoresu ネットワークアドレス

never ADV kesshite ... nai 決して～ない

never mind ki ni shinai de 気にしないで

nevertheless ADV sore ni mo kakawarazu それにもかかわらず; sore ni shite mo それ

にしても, to wa itte mo とは言っても

new ADJ atarashi'i 新しい

newcomer N shinjin 新人

news N nyūsu ニュース; *(newspaper item)* kiji 記事

newsflash N nyūsu sokuhō ニュース速報

newspaper N shinbun 新聞

new year N shin'nen 新年: *Happy New Year.* Shin'nen/Akemashite o-medetō 新年/明けましておめでとう.

New Year's (Day) N ganjitsu 元日, gantan 元旦; O-shōgatsu お正月

New Year's eve N ō-misoka 大みそか

New York N Nyūyōku ニューヨーク

New Zealand N Nyūjīrando ニュージーランド

next ADJ *(in line, sequence)* tsugi no 次の: *next day* yokujitsu 翌日, tsugi no hi 次の日; *next month* raigetsu 来月; *next morning* yokuasa 翌朝, tsugi no hi no asa 次の日の朝; *next time* kondo 今度, jikai 次回, kono-tsugi 次の次; *next to* tonari ni 隣に

nice ADJ suteki na 素敵な; ii/yoi いい/良い; (weather) hare no 晴れの, ii (o-)tenki いい お天気; (delicious) oishi'i おいしい; (beautiful) kirei na きれいな, utsukushi'i 美しい; (kind) shinsetsu na 親切な, yasashi'i やさしい; bimyō na 微妙な

nickname N adana あだ名, aishō 愛称

niece N mei 姪

night N yoru 夜; ban 晩

nightmare N akumu 悪夢夜警; yakei-in 夜警員

nine NUM kyū 九

nineteen NUM jūkyū 十九

ninety NUM kyūjū 九十

no, not ADV (with nouns) ... de wa nai ~ではない (名詞につく); (with verbs and adjectives) ... nai ~ない, ... de wa nai ~ではない (動詞と形容詞につく); ADJ sukoshi mo ... nai 少しも~ない: no charge/fee muryō no 無料の, tada no ただの; No kidding! Masaka! まさか!, Jōdan deshō? 冗談でしょう!; no need to worry daijōbu 大丈夫; No parking chūsha

kinshi 駐車禁止; no problem daijōbu 大丈夫; No smoking kin'en 禁煙; No way! Tondemonai とんでもない; (Absolutely not.) Zettai ni dame desu. 絶対にだめです。

nobody PRON dare mo ... nai 誰も~ない

noise N oto 音; (buzz) sō'on 騒音, (static) zatsuon 雑音

noisy ADJ urusai うるさい, yakamashi'i やかましい, sōzōshi'i 騒々しい

nonsense N muimi na koto 無意味なこと, nansensu ナンセンス, bakageta koto 馬鹿げたこと; detarame でたらめ

no(n)-smoking N (sheet, booth) kin'en seki 禁煙席

noodles N menrui 麺類

noon N shōgo 正午, hiru 昼

nor CONJ ... de mo nai ~でもない

normal ADJ futsū no 普通の, hyōjun no 標準の

normally ADV futsū wa 普通は, itsumo wa いつもは, tsūjō wa 通常は

north N kita 北: north, the northern part hokubu 北部

North Pole N Hokkyoku 北極

North Star N hokkyoku-sei
北極星

Northern Europe N Hokuō
北欧

nose N hana 鼻

nostril N bikō 鼻腔

not ADV ... de wa nai ～では
ない; *not at all (you're
welcome)* dō itashimashite
どういたしまして; *not many/
(very) much* amari ...nai あ
まり～ない; *not only ... but
also* ... dake de naku... mo
mata ～だけでなく～もまた

note N (currency) shihei 紙幣;
(written) memo メモ

note pad N memo-chō メモ帳

notebook N nōto ノート,
(computer) nōto(gata)
pasokon ノート(型)パソコン

nothing PRON nani mo ... nai
何も～ない

notice N (notification) (o-)
shirase (お)知らせ, tsūchi 通
知; keikoku 警告; chūmoku
注目, chūi 注意; V kizuku 気づ
く; tsūchi suru 通知する

noun N meishi 名詞

novel N shōsetsu 小説

November N jūichi-gatsu
十一月

now N ima 今; *from now on*
kore kara これから, kongo
今後; *now and then* tama ni
たまに; *just now* tadaima
ただ今, tsui imashigata
つい今しがた; *until now* ima-
made 今まで

nowadays ADV kon'nichi de
wa 今日では, chikagoro 近ご
ろ; *now* imazai 今現在

nowhere ADV jitsuzaishinai
basho 実在しない場所; doko
ni mo ... nai どこにも～ない;
ADJ muda na 無駄な

nuclear ADJ kaku no 核の

nuclear weapon N kaku hēki
核兵器

nude N hadaka 裸, nūdo ヌー
ド; ADJ hadaka no 裸の, nūdo
no ヌードの

numb ADJ mahishita 麻痺した,
mukankaku na 無感覚な

number N kazu 数; ban 番;
(written numeral) sūji 数字;
(assigned) bangō 番号;
a number of ikutsu ka no
いくつかの

number one ADJ ichi-ban no
一番の

numeral N sūji 数字, sū 数

nurse N kangoshi 看護師; V

312

nursery N takuji-jo 託児所, *(nursery school)* hoikuen 保育園

nursing N *(a patient)* kango 看護, kanbyō 看病

nutrition N eiyō 栄養

nuts N nattsu ナッツ, ki-no-mi 木の実

nylon N nairon ナイロン

O

oar N kai 櫂, ōru オール

oath N chikai 誓い

obedient ADJ jūjun na 従順な, sunao na 素直な

obey V shitagau 従う, iu koto o kiku 言う事を聞く

object N taishō 対象; *(thing)* mono 物; *(objective, goal)* mokuteki 目的, ate 当て; *(aim)* nerai 狙い; V *(protest)* ... ni hantai suru 〜に反対する

objection N igi 異議, iron 異論, hantai 反対

oblique ADJ *(diagonal)* naname no 斜めの

obscure ADJ bakuzen 漠然

observatory N *(astronomical)* tenmon-dai 天文台; *(weather station)* kishō-dai 気象台; *(sightseeing)* tenbō-dai 展望台

observer N kansatsu-sha 観察者; tachiai-nin 立会人

obstruction N shōgai 障害, samatage 妨げ

obviously ADV *(clearly)* akiraka ni 明らかに, hakkiri to はっきりと

occasion N *(time)* toki 時, *(at that time)* koro 頃, *(opportunity)* kikai 機会; *(circumstance)* ba'ai 場合

occupation N shokugyō 職業; *(military)* senryō 占領

occur V okoru 起こる, hassei suru 発生する; shōjiru 生じる

ocean N umi 海

o'clock ADV ...-ji ...-時

October N jū-gatsu 十月

octopus N tako タコ

odor N *(bad smell)* akushū 悪臭

of PREP *(from)* ... no 〜の, ... kara 〜から

of course mochiron もちろん

off ADJ *(gone bad)* warukunatta 悪くなった; ADV *(turned off)* kiete 消えて, tomatte 止まって, *(leave)* hanarete 離れて;

313

PREP ... kara hanarete 〜から
離れて; *turn off (light, radio,
etc.)* kekesu 消す; *come
off (button, etc.)* toreru 取
れる, *(slip off)* nukeru 抜け
る; *take off (clothes, shoes)*
nugu 脱ぐ

offend v kanjō o gai suru 感情
を害する, ... o okoraseru 〜を
怒らせる; *(violate)* ... ni han
suru 〜に反する

offer N mōshikomi 申し込み;
v *(suggest)* teian suru 提案
する; *(provide)* teikyō suru
提供する; *(make an offer)*
mōshideru 申し出る

offering N teikyō 提供;
mōshide 申し出, mōshikomi
申し込み, mōshi'ire 申し入れ;
(the gods) o-sonae お供え

office N *(business)* jimusho 事
務所, ofisu オフィス; *(govern-
ment)* yakusho 役所; *(within
the company)* shanai 社内

official ADJ *(formal)* kōshiki no
公式の

officials N *(government)*
kōmuin 公務員; yakunin
役人 *(government)*

offline meeting N ofukai オフ
会, ofurain mītingu オフライ

ンミーティング

often ADV shibashiba しばしば,
yoku よく

oil N abura 油; *(petroleum,
machine oil)* sekiyu 石油

oily ADJ aburakkoi 油っこい・
脂っこい

ointment N nuri-gusuri 塗り薬,
nankō 軟膏

OK, okay ii いい, ōkē オーケー,
daijōbu 大丈夫

old ADJ *(of persons)* toshitotta
年取った(人); *(of things)* furui
古い(物); *(from way back)*
mukashi karano 昔からの:
in olden times mukashi
昔 mukashi

older ADJ toshiue no 年上の:
older brother N chōkei 長
兄; ani 兄, (o-)ni'i-san （お）
兄さん; *older sister* N chōshi
長姉; ane 姉, (o-)nē-san （お）
姉さん

omit v otosu 落とす, habuku
省く, nokeru 除ける, nuku
抜く, nozoku 除く; ryakusu
略す

on PREP *(of dates)* ... ni 〜に, ...
no toki ni 〜の時に; ADV
(turned on) haitta 入った; PREP
(at) ... no ue ni 〜の上に, ...

ni ~に: *on board* ... ni notte ~に乗って; *on fire* hi ga tsuita 火がついた; *on foot* toho de 徒歩で; *on the way* tochū de 途中で, chūto de 中途で; *on time* jikan dōri ni 時間通りに

once ADV ichido 一度, ikkai 一回; (*sometimes*) itsu ka いつか

one NUM ichi 一: *one by one* ichi'ichi いちいち; (*objects*) hitotsu-zutsu 一つずつ, (*people*) hitori-zutsu 一人ずつ; *one drink* hitokuchi 一口, ippai 一杯; *one minute* ippun 一分; *one night* hitoban 一晩; *one spoonful* hitosaji 一匙; *one year* ichi-nen 一年, ichinen-kan 一年間; *one year old* issai 一歳, hitotsu ひとつ

one day N aruhi ある日

one floor/story N ikkai 一階

one time ADJ ikkai no 一回の, ichi-do no 一度の

one-way N (*traffic, argument*) ippōtsūkō 一方通行; *one-way ticket* katamichi kippu 片道切符

oneself PRON jibunjishin 自分自身

onion N tamanegi 玉葱

online ADJ onrain no オンラインの: *online banking* onrain ginkō オンライン銀行; *online game* netto gēmu ネットゲーム, onrain gēmu オンラインゲーム; *online store* onrain sutoa オンラインストア, intānetto shoppu インターネットショップ

only CONJ tadashi ただし; ADJ tatta no たったの; yui'itsu no 唯一の; ADV tatta ... dake de っ~だけ; tatta たった; chōdo ちょうど

open ADJ hiraiteiru 開いている; hirakareta 開かれた; VI aku 開く; hajimaru 始まる; (*a shop*) kaiten suru 開店する; VT akeru 開ける; hiraku 開く; ...o kōkai suru ~を公開する; (*we're*) *open* eigyō-chū 営業中

opera N kageki 歌劇, opera オペラ

operating hours N eigyōjikan 営業時間

operating system N (*computer*) ōesu オーエス (OS)

operation N (*surgical*) shujutsu 手術; (*driving*)

315

unten 運転; *(handling)* sōjū 操縦; *(management)* keiei 経営; *(working)* sagyō 作業, shigoto 仕事

operator N sōjūshi 操縦士, operētā オペレーター; *(vehicle)* untenshu 運転手; *(business)* keieisha 経営者

opinion N iken 意見, kangae 考え, hyōka 評価

opponent N raibaru ライバル, *(sports)* aite 相手; *(rival)* teki 敵

opportunity N ii kikai いい機会; *(convenience)* tsugō no yoi toki 都合のよい時

oppose V ... ni hantai suru ～に反対する; *(reject)* ... o kobamu ～を拒む; *(resist)* ... ni hankō suru ～に反抗する, hanpatsu suru 反発する; *(conflict)* ... to tairitsu suru ～と対立する, ...ni taikō suru ～に対抗する

opposite N hantai 反対; ADJ *(contrary)* ... ni hanshite ～に反して; *(facing)* hantai gawa no 反対側の, mukō no 向こうの; *(contrary)* gyaku no 逆の; PREP *(opposite side)* ... no

hantai gawa ni ～の反対側に: *opposite sex (person of)* isei 異性

oppress V appaku suru 圧迫する

optional ADJ nin'i no 任意の; zui'i no 随意の

or CONJ ... ka ... ～か～; matawa または; *or else* soretomo それとも, matawa または, aruiwa あるいは

orange N *(color)* orenji'iro オレンジ色; *(citrus)* orenji オレンジ

order N *(command)* meirei 命令; *(placed for food, goods)* chūmon 注文; *(sequence)* junban 順番; V *(command)* meirei suru 命令する, ii'tsukeru 言い付ける, tsugeguchi suru 告げ口する; *(food, goods)* chūmon suru 注文する; *(arrange as a set)* soroeru 揃える

ordinary ADJ futsū no 普通の, tsūjō no 通常の, fudan no 普段の; tada no ただの; *(average)* heibon na 平凡な

organic ADJ ōganikku no オーガニックの, yūkisaibai no 有機栽培の

organization N soshiki 組織, *(group)* dantai 団体

organize V chōsei suru 調整する; *(set up)* kumitateru 組み立てる; hensei suru 編成する

Orient N Tōyō 東洋; Oriento オリエント

origin N kigen 起源, moto 元; gen'in 原因

original ADJ genkei no 原型の

originate V *(come from)* ... kara okoru 〜から起こる

ornament N sōshokuhin 装飾品, kazari 飾り

other ADJ hoka no 他の, betsu no 別の; *(the other one over there)* achira あちら

otherwise ADV samonakere ba さもなければ, sōshinai ni そうしないと

ought to MODAL V ... subeki de aru 〜すべきである, ...(shi)ta hō ga ii 〜(し)た方がいい

our ADJ wareware no 我々の, wata(ku)shitachi no わた(く)し達の

out N sotogawa 外側; ADV ... no soto e/ni 〜の外へ/に; *(away from home)* rusu no 留守の

outdoor(s) ADJ (ADV) soto no (de/ni/e) 外の(で/に/へ); yagai no (de) 野外の(で); autodoa no アウトドアの; okugai no (de/ni/e) 屋外の (で/に/へ): *outdoor bath* noten-buro 野天風呂

outer ADJ sotogawa no 外側の; *(appearance)* uwabe 上辺

outer lane/track N auto-kōsu アウトコース

outer space N uchū 宇宙

outing N ensoku 遠足

outline N *(synopsis)* gaiyō 概要, auto rain アウトライン

outrageous ADJ tondemonai とんでもない

outside N sotogawa 外側; ADJ okugai no 屋外の; gaibu no 外部の; PREP soto ni/de 外に/で; ADV sotogawa ni 外側に: *outside of* ... no soto ni 〜の外に

outsider N bugaisha 部外者, *(stranger)* yoso no hito よその人, yoso-mono よそ者

outstanding ADJ medatta 目立った, nukideta 抜きん出た

oval N *(shape)* daenkei 楕円形, ADJ daenkei no 楕円形の

oven N tenpi 天火, ōbun オーブン

over ADJ ue no 上の; ADV *(above)* ... no ue ni 〜の上に;

(finished) owatta 終った; **PREP** ...o koete ~を超えて, ijō 以上: *turn over* uragaesu 裏返す; *over there* achira gawa あちら側, asoko あそこ, mukō 向こう, mukai 向かい, sochira/sotchi そちら/そっち, atchi あっち

overall **ADJ** ippan no 一般の, *(composite)* sōgō-teki na 総合的な

overcast **ADJ** *(cloudy)* kumotta 曇った

overcoat **N** ōbā オーバー, kōto コート

overcome **V** uchikatsu 打ち勝つ

overestimate **N** kadai hyōka 過大評価; **V** kadai hyōka suru 過大評価する

overflow **V** afureru 溢れる, afureruderu 溢れ出る

overheat **V** kanetsu suru 過熱する, *(engine, etc.)* ōbā hīto suru オーバーヒートする

overlap **V** kasanaru 重なる

overseas **N** gaikoku 外国; **ADJ** kaigai no 海外の

owe **V** *(borrow money)* kari ga aru 借りがある

owl **N** fukurō フクロウ

own **V** shoji suru 所持する; **ADJ**

(personal) jibun no 自分の: *on one's own* hitori de 独りで

owner **N** mochinushi 持ち主, shoyūsha 所有者; *(master)* shujin 主人, ōnā オーナー; *(landowner)* jinushi 地主

ox **N** o-ushi 雄牛

oxygen **N** sanso 酸素

oyster **N** kaki 牡蠣

ozone layer **N** ozon sō オゾン層

P

Pacific Ocean **N** Taiheiyō 太平洋

pack **V** tsutsumu 包む; tsumeru 詰める, *(packing)* nizukuri o suru 荷造りをする

pack, package **N** kozutsumi 小包, nimotsu 荷物, tsutsumi 包み

packet **N** hōsōbutsu 包装物, kozutsumi 小包

page **N** pēji ページ

pain **N** itami 痛み; *(suffering)* kutsū 苦痛, kurushimi 苦しみ

painful **ADJ** itai 痛い; kurushi'i 苦しい, tsurai 辛い

paint **N** penki ペンキ, ganryō 顔料; **V** *(house, furniture)*

penki o nuru ペンキを塗る; *(picture)* e o kaku 絵を描く

painter N gaka 画家; *(house-painter)* penki-ya ペンキ屋

painting N *(picture)* e 絵, kaiga 絵画

pair N (it)tsui (一)対; (hito)kumi (一)組; V kumiawaseru 組み合わせる; *a pair of* ittsui no 一対の, hitokumi no 一組の

pajamas N nemaki 寝巻き, pajama パジャマ

palace N kyūden 宮殿

pale ADJ *(color)* (igo ga) usui (色が)薄い; usui iro no 薄い色の; *(face)* kaoiro ga warui 顔色が悪い

palm N *(tree)* yashi ヤシ; *(of hand)* te-no-hira 手のひら

pamper V amayakasu 甘やかす

pamphlet N bira ビラ

pan N nabe 鍋

pancake N hottokēki ホットケーキ, pankēki パンケーキ

panda N panda パンダ

panties N pantī パンティー

pantry N shokuryō-ko 食料庫

pants N zubon ズボン, *(slacks)* surakkusu スラックス, pantsu パンツ; *(underpants)*

zubonshita ズボン下

papa N papa パパ, o-tōsan お父さん

papaya N papaiya パパイヤ

paper N kami 紙; yōshi 用紙

paper bag N kami-bukuro 紙袋

paperfolding (art) N origami 折り紙

parade N parēdo パレード, gyōretsu 行列, *(march)* kōshin 行進; *(demonstration parade)* demo kōshin デモ行進

paradise N tengoku 天国, gokuraku 極楽, paradaisu パラダイス

paragraph N danraku 段落

parcel N kozutsumi 小包

pardon N yurushi 許し; INTERJ *pardon me?* shitsurei desu ga, ... 失礼ですが、...

parents N ryōshin 両親

park N kōen 公園; V *(car)* chūsha suru 駐車する

parking N *(parking lot)* chūsha-jō 駐車場; *No parking* chūsha kinshi 駐車禁止

parrot N ōmu オウム

part N *(not whole)* ichibu 一部, bubun 部分; *(portion)*

bun 分, *(section)* bu 部;
(of machine) buhin 部品;
vi wakareru 分かれる; vt
wakeru 分ける

partial ADJ ichibu no 一部の,
ichibubun 一部分: *(taking)*
partial charge N buntan 分担

participate v sanka suru 参
加する

particular ADJ *(especial)*
tokubetsu no 特別の;
(separate) betsu no 別の;
(peculiar, unique) tokushu
na 特殊な, tokuyū no 特有な

partition N shikiri 仕切り

partly ADV bubunteki ni 部
分的に

partner N *(in business)*
kyōdō keieisha 共同経営者に;
(spouse) tsureai つれあい

part-time ADJ arubaito no アル
バイトの, baito no バイトの;
pāto no パートの; hi-jōkin no
非常勤の

party N *(event)* enkai 宴会, pātī
パーティー (催し); *(political)*
tō 党 (政治的な): *birthday
party* tanjōbi-kai 誕生日会,
tanjō pātī 誕生パーティー;
drinking party nomikai 飲
み会, enkai 宴会; *opposition*

party yatō 野党; *ruling party* yotō 与党; *welcome party*
kangei kai 歓迎会

pass N *(commuter ticket)*
teikiken 定期券; *(mountain
pass)* yamamichi 山道; vi
(exam) gōkaku suru 合格
する, ukaru 受かる *(試験)*;
(time) tatsu 経つ, sugosu 過ご
す; *(exceed)* sugiru
過ぎる, vt *(go past)* tōrikosu
通り越す, oikosu 追い越す;
(hand over) te(watasu (手)
渡す: *pass away* iki o
hikitoru 息を引き取る

passenger N jōkyaku 乗客

passion N jōnetsu 情熱, gekijō
激情, netchū 熱中

passport N ryoken 旅券,
pasupōto パスポート

password N pasuwādo パスワ
ード, anshō-bangō 暗証番号

past ADJ *(former)* mukashi no
昔の, kako no 過去の:
go past tōrikosu 通り越す

paste N nori のり, *(pate)*
pēsuto ペースト, nerimono 練
り物; v norizuke suru のり
付けする

pastime N goraku 娯楽,
dōraku 道楽; shumi 趣味

320

pastry N (o-)kashi (お)菓子, kashipan 菓子パン

pat V (karuku) tataku (軽く) たたく

patent N tokkyo 特許, tokkyo-ken 特許権

path N komichi 小道, michi 道

patient N *(medical)* kanja 患者, *(ill person)* byōnin 病人; ADJ *(calm)* nintai no aru 忍耐の ある; *(put up with it)* gaman suru 我慢する

pattern N *(design)* patān パ ターン, moyō 模様, gara 柄; *(example)* tehon 手本, kata 型, gara 柄

pay N *(one's wage)* kyūryō 給料, chingin 賃金; V harau 払 う; *(taxes)* osameru 納める: *pay attention* chūi o harau 注意を払う; *pay one's share* buntan suru 分担する

payday N kyūryō-bi 給料日

payment N shiharai 支払い

peace N heiwa 平和

peaceful ADJ heiwa na 平和な; *(calm)* odayaka na 穏やかな, nodoka na のどかな

peach N momo 桃

peak N *(summit)* sanchō 山頂, tadaki 頂, chōjō 頂上; *(high point)* chōten 頂点

pear N nashi 梨

pearl N shinju 真珠

peculiar ADJ dokutoku no/na 独特の; okashina おかしな, kimyō na 奇妙な, hen na 変な

pedestrian N hokōsha 歩行者

pedestrian mall N hokōsha tengoku 歩行者天国

peel N *(rind)* kawa 皮; V (kawa o) muku (皮を)剥く

pen N pen ペン; *(fountain)* man'nenhitsu 万年筆

penalty N *(punishment)* bakkin 罰金

pencil N enpitsu 鉛筆

peninsula N hantō 半島

penis N penisu ペニス, dankon 男根; *(baby talk)* (o-)chinchin (お)ちんちん; *(medical)* inkei 陰茎

pension N nenkin 年金; *(bed & breakfast)* penshon ペン ション

people N hito 人; hitobito 人々, hitotachi 人達

peppermint N hakka ハッカ, pepāminto ペパーミント

percent, percentage N pāsento パーセント

perfectly ADV kanzen ni 完全に,

mattaku まったく、maru de まで、pittari ぴったり

perform v *(act)* enjiru 演じる; *(music, etc.)* ensō suru 演奏する

performance N kōen 公演; *(artistic)* engi 演技; *(musical instrument)* ensō 演奏; dekibae 出来映え

perfume N kōsui 香水

perhaps ADV *(maybe)* tabun 多分; *(probably)* osoraku おそらく; ...ka mo shirenai 〜かも知れない、moshikashitara もしかしたら、moshikasuru to も しかすると、

period N *(end of a sentence)* kutōten 句読点; *(menstrual)* seiri 生理; *(of time)* kikan 期間、*(limit)* kigen 期限; *(era)* jidai 時代

permanent ADJ eikyū no 永久の; eien no 永遠の; funen no 不変の; kawaranai 変わらない

permission N kyoka 許可、ninka 認可; menkyo 免許、raisensu ライセンス

permissive ADJ amai 甘い

permit N *(license)* menkyo 免許、kyoka(shō) 許可(証)、raisensu ライセンス; v *(allow)*

kyoka suru 許可する

perpetration N hankō 犯行

persimmon N *(fruit)* kaki 柿

person N hito 人

personal ADJ kojinteki na 個人的な; *(for one's own use)* jibunyō no 自分用の

personal business N shiyō 私用

personal computer, PC N pasokon パソコン

personal effects N temawarihin 手回り品

personal history N rireki 履歴; rirekisho 履歴書

personality N kosei 個性、seikaku 性格

perspire v ase o kaku 汗をかく

pessimistic ADJ hikanteki na 悲観的な

pet N *(animal)* aiganddubutsu 愛玩動物、petto ペット

petrol N gasorin ガソリン

petrol station N kyūyujo 給油所、gasorin sutando ガソリンスタンド

petroleum N sekiyu 石油

petty ADJ sasai na ささいな、sasayaka na ささやかな; *petty cash* koguchi-genkin 小口現金

pharmacy N yakkyoku 薬局

Philippines N Firipin フィリピン

phishing N *(Internet)* fisshingu フィッシング

phone N denwa 電話; *(cell/ mobile phone)* keitai denwa 携帯電話

photocopy N kopī コピー; V kopī suru コピーする

photographer N shashin-ka 写真家, kamera-man カメラマン

physical ADJ karada no 体の, shintai no 身体の: *physical exam* shintai-kensa 身体検査

physician N isha 医者, ishi 医師

physics N butsuri 物理, butsurigaku 物理学

piano N piano ピアノ: *plays the piano* piano o hiku ピアノを弾く

pick V *(choose)* erabu 選ぶ; *(pluck)* tsumu 摘む: *pick up* V *(someone)* kuruma ni noseru 車に乗せる (人を); *(something)* mochiageru 持ち上げる (物を)

pickpocket N suri すり; V suru する

picnic N ensoku 遠足, pikunikku ピクニック

picture N e 絵; *(photo)* shashin 写真; *(diagram, drawing)* zu 図

piece N *(item)* ikko 一個, hitotsu 一つ; *(portion, section)* hitokire ひと切れ: *a piece of* hitokire no 一切れの

pierce V tsukitōsu 突き通す

pig N buta 豚

pile VT tsumi-kasaneru 積み重ねる; VI tsumi-kasanaru 積み重なる

pillar N hashira 柱

pillow N makura 枕

pills N jōzai 錠剤

pilot N pairotto パイロット; *(plane captain)* kichō 機長

pimple N dekimono できもの, o-deki おでき

pin N *(for hair)* (hea)pin (ヘア)ピン, pindome ピンどめ; *(for sewing)* hari 針; mushipin 虫ピン

pinch N pinchi ピンチ, kiki 危機; V tsuneru つねる, tsumamu つまむ

pine N *(tree)* matsu 松

pink ADJ pinku no ピンクの

pipe N paipu パイプ; *(tube)* tsutsu 筒, kuda 管

pirate N kaizoku 海賊

piss N shōben 小便

pistol N pisutoru ピストル, kenjū 拳銃

pitcher N *(baseball)* tōshu 投手, pitchā ピッチャー; *(water)* mizusashi 水差し

pitiful, pitiable ADJ kawai-sō na かわいそうな, (o-)ki no doku na (お)気の毒な

pity N dōjō 同情; *what a pity* zan'nen da 残念だ

place N basho 場所, tokoro 所; V oku 置く

plain N *(flat land)* heiya 平野, heichi 平地; ADJ *(level ground)* taira na 平らな; *(not fancy)* heibon na 平凡な, jimi na 地味な, *(simple, frugal)* shisso na 質素な; assari (to) shita あっさり(と)した

plan N keikaku 計画, kikaku 企画, an 案; *(schedule)* yotei 予定; V keikaku suru 計画する, kikaku suru 企画する

plane N hikōki 飛行機

planet N wakusei 惑星

plant N shokubutsu 植物; *(factory)* kōjō 工場; V ueru 植える

plastic N purasuchikku プラスチック; *(vinyl)* binīru ビニール

plate N sara 皿

play V *(sports)* suru ～する; asobu 遊ぶ; *(a stringed instrument or piano)* hiku 弾く; *(musical instrument)* ensō suru 演奏する; N *(drama)* shibai 芝居, engeki 演劇; asobi 遊び

player N *(sports)* senshu 選手, *(instrument)* purēyā プレーヤー

plead V kongan suru 懇願する

pleasant ADJ kanji no ii 感じのいい; tanoshi'i 楽しい; omoshiroi 面白い; ureshi'i うれしい; kaiteki na 快適な

please V *(go ahead)* dōzo どうぞ; *(request)* onegai shimasu お願いします

pleasure N tanoshimi 楽しみ, yorokobi 喜び

pledge N chikai 誓い; V chikau 誓う

plug N *(bath)* sen 栓 (風呂); *(electric)* sashikomi 差込, puragu プラグ (電気)

plum N puramu プラム

plus ADJ tsukekuwawatta 付け加わった, purasu プラス

p.m. ADV gogo 午後, pī emu PM

pocket N poketto ポケット:

pocket money (o-)kozukai (お)小遣い

pocketbook N bunko(-bon) 文庫(本); handobaggu ハンドバッグ, handobakku ハンドバック

poet N shijin 詩人, kajin 歌人

point N (*in time*) jiten 時点 (時間); (*dot*) ten 点; (*points obtained*) tokuten 得点; (*gist*) yōten 要点; (*tip, end*) saki 先; v togaraseru 尖らせる; … o sasu 〜を指す: *point out* shiteki suru 指摘する; shiji suru 指示する

poisoning N chūdoku 中毒

polar bear N hokkyokuguma 北極グマ, shirokuma 白熊

pole N (*rod*) bō 棒, sao 竿, pōru ポール

police N keisatsu 警察

police officer N keisatsukan 警察官

policy N hōshin 方針, (*political*) seisaku 政策

polite ADJ reigitadashi'i 礼儀正しい; teinei na 丁寧な

politics N seiji 政治

pond N ike 池

pool N (*swimming pool*) pūru プール

poor ADJ (*needy*) mazushi'i 貧しい, binbō na 貧乏な; (*clumsy*) heta na 下手な; (*bad*) warui 悪い; (*pitiful*) kawaisō na かわいそうな: *poor at* futokui na/no 不得意な/の, heta na 下手な

pop v hajikeru はじける

popular ADJ ninki no aru 人気のある; hayari no 流行の; hyōban no 評判の; (*general*) ippan (muke) no 一般(向き)の

pop(ular) music N poppusu ポップス

population N jinkō 人口

pork N butaniku 豚肉

pornography N poruno ポルノ, ero-hon エロ本

porridge N o-kayu おかゆ

port N minato 港

portal website N pōtarusaito ポータルサイト (*MSN, Yahoo!, Google, etc.*)

portion N (*serve*) wakemae 分け前; toribun 取り分; (*part*) bubun 部分, bun 分, ichibu 一部

portrait N shōzō(-ga) 肖像(画)

position N chi'i 地位

positive ADJ sekkyoku-teki na

積極的な, maemuki na 前向きな, pojitibu ポジティブ

possess v *(own)* shoyū suru 所有する

possessions N shoyūbutsu 所有物

possibility N kanō-sei 可能性, jitsugen-sei 実現性

possible ADJ kanō na 可能な; *be possible* dekiru 出来る

post N *(column)* hashira 柱; *(mail)* yūbin 郵便

postage N yūbinryōkin 郵便料金, yūsōryō 郵送料

postcard N hagaki 葉書

post office N yūbinkyoku 郵便局

postpone v enki suru 延期する; ato ni mawasu 後に回す, atomawashi ni suru 後回しにする

pot N *(pan)* nabe 鍋; *(kettle)* potto ポット; *(jar)* tsubo つぼ; *(for plants)* hachi 鉢

potato N jagaimo ジャガイモ

pottery N yaki-mono 焼き物, tōki 陶器

poultry N toriniku 鶏肉

pour v sosogu 注ぐ

powder N kona 粉; funmatsu 粉末; paudā パウダー; *(face)* oshiroi おしろい

power N chikara 力; *(ability)* nōryoku 能力; *(influence)* seiryoku 勢力; *(electricity)* denryoku 電力

powerful ADJ chikarazuyoi 力強い; yūryoku na 有力な; kyōryoku na 強力な; hakuryoku ga aru 迫力がある

practical ADJ jitchi no 実地の, jissenteki na 実践的な; jitsuyōteki na 実用的な

practice N *(habit)* shūkan 習慣, *(drill)* renshū 練習; v renshū suru 練習する

praise N shōsan 賞賛; *(homage)* homekotoba 褒め言葉; v *(laud)* homeru 褒める; shōsan suru 賞賛する

prawn N ebi 海老

pray v inoru 祈る

prayer N inori 祈り; kigan 祈願

preacher N *(Christian)* bokushi 牧師

precious ADJ taisetsu na 大切な, daiji na 大事な, kichō na 貴重な; oshi'i 惜しい

preface N jobun 序文, maegaki 前書き

prefecture N ken 県

prefer v konomu 好む

pregnant ADJ ninshinshita 妊娠した

preparation(s) N yōi 用意, junbi 準備; shitaku 支度; *(anticipatory steps)* yobi 予備

prepare V *(make ready)* junbi suru 準備する; *(ready)* yōi ga dekiteiru 用意ができている; *(study ahead)* yoshū suru 予習する; *(be ready)* totonoeru 整える; *(make it)* tsukuru 作る

prescription N hōhōsen 処方箋

present N *(gift)* okurimono 贈り物, purezento プレゼント; ADJ *(at the moment)* genzai no 現在の; V okurimono o suru 贈り物をする, okuru 贈る; *(give)* ageru あげる, [POLITE] sashiageru 差し上げる; *be present (here)* koko ni iru ここにいる

president N *(of a nation)* daitōryō 大統領, *(of a society)* kaichō 会長, *(of a company/firm)* shachō 社長

press N *(journalism)* shinbun 新聞, masukomi マスコミ; V osu 押す, oshitsukeru 押し付ける; *(iron)* airon o kakeru アイロンをかける

pressure N atsuryoku 圧力; appaku 圧迫

pretend V ... o yosōu 〜を装う, ... no furi o suru ...のふりをする

pretty ADJ *(of places, things)* utsukushi'i 美しい, kogirei na こぎれいな (場所, 物); *(of women)* kawairashi'i かわいらしい (女性), chāmingu na

prevent V *(hinder)* samatageru 妨げる, (... no) jama o suru (〜の)邪魔をする; *(thwart)* habamu 阻む; *(block)* fusegu 防ぐ, *(ward off)* yobō suru 予防する

preview N shitami 下見; shisha 試写

previous ADJ mae no 前の

price N nedan 値段, kakaku 価格

pride N hokori 誇り, jisonshin 自尊心

priest N shisai 司祭; shinpu 神父

primary ADJ dai'ichi no 第一の; shokyū no 初級の

prime minister N shushō 首相

prince N ōji 王子, purinsu プリンス; *Crown Prince* kōtaishi 皇太子

princess N hime 姫, ohime-sama お姫様; ōjo 王女, purinsesu プリンセス; *Crown Princess* kōtaishi-hi 皇太子妃

principle N *(policy)* hōshin 方針, *(doctrine)* gensoku 原則, shugi 主義

print N insatsu(butsu) 印刷物, hanga 版画; v insatsu suru 印刷する, suru 刷る

printer N purintā プリンター

priority N yūsen(-ken) 優先(権); *order of priority* yūsen-jun'i 優先順位

prison N keimusho 刑務所

privacy N puraibashī プライバシー; shiseikatsu 私生活

private ADJ kojinteki na 個人的な, jibun-yō no 自分用の, shiyō no 私用の; *(secret)* himitsu no 秘密の, puraibēto プライベート; *(within the family)* uchiwa no 内輪の; *(privately established)* watakushi-ritsu/shiritsu no 私立の, shisetsu no 私設の

prize N shō賞, *(object)* shōhin 賞品, *(money)* shōkin 賞金; N *(reward)* go-hōbi ご褒美

pro, professional N puro プロ, senmon-ka 専門家

probably ADV osoraku おそらく, tabun たぶん

problem N mondai 問題

process N *(method)* yari-kata やり方, hōhō 方法; *(course, stage)* katei 過程, purosesu プロセス; *(development)* nariyuki 成り行き

produce v seisan suru 生産する, ... ga dekiru ～が出来る, ... o tsukuru ～を作る, ... o seizō/seisaku suru ～を製造/制作する; *(bring it about)* ... o shōjiru ～を生じる

product N seisanbutsu 生産物, seisanhin 生産品, seihin 製品

production N *(play, movie)* enshutsu 演出, seisaku 制作; *(manufacture)* seisan 生産, seizō 製造

profession N shokugyō 職業

professor N kyōju 教授

profile N purofīru プロフィール, ryakureki 略歴; *(face in profile)* yokogao 横顔

profit N rieki 利益; v mōkeru 儲ける

program N *(schedule)* yotei 予定, *(TV, etc.)* bangumi(hyō) 番組(表), puroguramu プログラム, enmoku 演目

programmer N *(computer program)* puroguramā プログラマー

progress N shinkō 進行, shinpo 進歩, shinchoku 進捗; keika 経過; V susumu 進む, shinpo suru 進歩する: *make good progress* hakadoru はかどる

project N keikaku 計画, kikaku 企画, purojekuto プロジェクト

prolong V enchō suru 延長する

prominent ADJ ichijirushi'i 著しい, medatta 目立った, *(famous)* chomei na 著名な

promise N yakusoku 約束; V yakusoku suru 約束する

promotion N *(salary rise)* shōkyū 昇給; *(incentive)* suishin 推進; *(betterment, increase)* hanbai sokushin 販売促進

prompt ADJ sassoku no 早速の, jinsoku na 迅速な, *(instant)* tossa no とっさの

pronunciation N hatsuon 発音

proof N shōko 証拠, shōmei 証明

proper ADJ *(appropriate)* tekitō na 適当な, tekisetsu na 適切な, kichintoshita き

ちんとした, chantoshita ちゃんとした

property N *(fortune)* shisan 資産, zaisan 財産; shoyū(ken) 所有(権)

proportion N ritsu 率; wariai 割合

proposal N an 案, kangae 考え, teian 提案 moushide 申し出; mōshi'ire 申し入れ; *(suggestion)* kikaku(an) 企画(案), kikaku-sho 企画書, teian-sho 提案書; *(of marriage)* endan 縁談; kyūkon 求婚

propose V teian suru 提案する; mōshikomu 申し込む, mōshideru 申し出る; *(publicly)* mōshi'-ireru 申し入れる; *(marriage)* kyūkon suru 求婚する

prosperity N hanei 繁栄, hanjō 繁盛, kō-keiki 好景気

protect V hogo suru 保護する, mamoru 守る, kabau かばう

protest V hantai suru 反対する

protrude V hamidasu はみだす

proud ADJ hokori ni omou 誇りに思う, hokorashi'i 誇らしい, tokuige na 得意気な; kōman na 高慢な: *be proud of* jiman suru 自慢する

prove v shōmei suru 証明する

provide v ataeru 与える, motaseru 持たせる: *provide a treat* gochisō suru ごちそうする

province N chihō 地方, chi'iki 地域

psychology N shinri 心理; *(science/study)* shinri-gaku 心理学

pub N *(Western-style)* pabu パブ; *(Japanese-style)* izakaya 居酒屋

public ADJ kōkyō no 公共の; kōshū no 公衆の; kōkai no 公開の; ōyake no 公の

public bath N sentō 銭湯, (o-)furo-ya (お)風呂屋

public holiday N shukujitsu 祝日, saijitsu 祭日

publication N shuppan 出版; shuppan-butsu 出版物; *(publishing)* hakkō 発行; *(books)* shoseki 書籍

publicity N senden 宣伝

pull v hiku 引く; hipparu 引っ張る; hikidasu 引き出す; *(refloats it)* hikiageru 引き上げる; *(stop)* tomeru 止める

pulse N myaku 脈, myakuhaku 脈拍

pump N ponpu ポンプ, asshukuki 圧縮機

pumpkin N kabocha カボチャ

punctual ADJ jikandōri no 時間どおりの

punish v bassuru 罰する

pupil N seito 生徒; *(apprentice)* deshi 弟子

puppy N koinu 小犬

pure ADJ junsui na 純粋な, jun na 純な; *(clean)* seiketsu na 清潔な

purple N murasaki 紫; ADJ murasaki(iro) no 紫(色)の

purpose N mokuteki 目的, ito 意図, kokorozashi 志

purse N *(for money)* saifu 財布

push v osu 押す, *(thrust)* tsuku 突く; oshitsukeru 押し付ける

put v *(place)* oku 置く: *put away* shimau しまう; *put between* hasamu 挟む; *put in* ireru 入れる; *put off (delay)* enki suru 延期する; *put on (clothes)* kiru 着る; *(performance)* kōen suru 公演する; *put out* dadasu 出す; *(extinguishes)* kesasu 消す; *put pressure on* appaku suru 圧迫する

puzzle N nazo 謎, pazuru パズ

Q

qualification N shikaku 資格

quality N shitsu 質, hin 品, hinshitsu 品質

quantity N ryō 量, bunryō 分量, sūryō 数量; *(large)* taryō 多量; tairyō 大量

guarantee V hikiukeru 引き受ける

quarrel V arasou 争う, kenka suru けんかする; N kenka けんか

quarter N yonbun no ichi 四分の一; *(of a year)* shihanki 四半期; *(time)* jūgo-fun 15分

queen N joō 女王

question N shitsumon 質問, *(problem)* mondai 問題, *(doubt, query)* gimon 疑問

questionable ADJ utagawashi'i 疑わしい, ikagawashi'i いかがわしい

questionnaire N ankēto アンケート

queue N *(line)* retsu 列; V *(line up)* retsu o tsukuru 列をつくる

juick ADJ kibin na 機敏な, hayai 速い

et ADJ shizuka na 静かな,

odayaka na 穏やかな, nodoka na のどかな

quit V yameru 辞める; *(computer)* shūryō suru 終了する

quite ADV *(fairly)* kanari かなり; *(very)* zuibun ずいぶん

quiz N kuizu クイズ

quotation N inyō 引用

R

rabbit N usagi うさぎ

race N kyōsō 競争, rēsu レース; *(of people)* jinshu 人種, minzoku 民族: *human race* jinrui 人類; V kyōsō suru 競争する

rack N tana 棚

radiation N *(nuclear)* hōshasen 放射線

radiator N danbō sōchi 暖房装置

radical ADJ kageki na 過激な

radio N rajio ラジオ

radioactivity N hōshanō 放射能

radish N daikon 大根

rage V abareru 暴れる, areru 荒れる, ikaru 怒る; N *(outrage)* gekido 激怒; *(passion)* jōnetsu 情熱

331

railroad, railway N senro 線路, tetsudō 鉄道

rain N ame 雨; V ame ga furu 雨が降る

rainbow N niji 虹

raise V (lift) ageru 上げる; (a flag) ageru 揚げる; (arouse) okosu 起こす; (price, wage, fee) hikiageru 引き上げる; (erect) tateru 立てる; (children) sodateru 育てる; (foster, nourish) yashinau 養う; (keep animals, etc.) kau 飼う; (collect money) tsunoru 募る

rake N kumade 熊手

ram N ramu ラム, o-hitsuji 雄羊

rampage V abareru 暴れる

ranch N bokujō 牧場

random ADJ ii'kagen na いい加減な; detarame na でたらめな; yatara na やたらな; (math, computer) musaku no 無作為の; **at random** musaku ni 無作為に, tekitō ni 適当に, teatarishidai ni 手当たり次第に, randamu ni ランダムに

range N han'i 範囲; (gas) gasu-renji ガスレンジ; (mountains) sanmyaku 山脈

rank N (station in life) kaikyū 階級, chi'i 地位

rape N (forcible intercourse) gōkan 強姦, reipu レイプ

rapid ADJ hayai 速い

rare ADJ (scarce) mezurashi'i 珍しい, (infrequent) mare na 稀な; (half-cooked) nama-yake no 生焼けの: **rare chance** N zekkō no chansu 絶好のチャンス

rat N nezumi ねずみ

rate N (tariff) ryōkin 料金; (ratio) ritsu 率, (percentage) wariai 割合: **rate of exchange** N (for foreign currency) kawase rēto 為替レート

rather ADV (fairly) kanari no かなりの; (partly) shōshō 少々; (preferably) mushiro むしろ: **rather than** ... yori mushiro ～よりむしろ

raw ADJ (uncooked) nama no 生の

raw material N zairyō 材料

raw silk N ki'ito 生糸

razor N kamisori 剃刀

reach VI (extend to) ... ni oyobu ～に及ぶ, nobiru 伸びる; VT (deliver) todoku 届く; (get to) tōchaku suru 到着する (arrive at) ...ni tsʊ

332

~に着く; *(achieve)* …ni
tassuru ~に達する
react v han'nō suru 反応する
read v yomu 読む
reader N *(person)* dokusha 読者
ready ADJ yōidekita 用意でき
た; ADV arakajime あらかじ
め, maemotte 前もって: *get
ready* junbi suru 準備する
real ADJ hontō no 本当の,
honmono no 本物の; *(actual)*
genjitsu no 現実の, *(present)*
jitsuzai no 実在の
real estate N fudōsan 不動産
realistic ADJ genjitsuteki na
現実的な
realize v *(comprehend)* satoru
悟る, … ga wakaru …が分
かる; *(carry out)* genjitsuka
suru 現実化する; nozomi ga
kanau 望みが叶う
really ADV *(in fact)* jissai ni 実
際に; *(truly, honestly)* hontō
ni 本当に: *Really?* Hontō
(desu ka) 本当 (ですか)
rear N (ADJ) *(tail)* ushiro (no) 後
ろ(の): *the rear* ADJ biri no
ビリの
reason N riyū 理由, wake 訳;
(logic) rikutsu 理屈, ronri 論
理; *(grounds)* konkyo 根拠

reasonable ADJ *(price)* tegoro
na 手ごろな (値段); *(sensible)*
bunbetsu no aru 分別のある;
(natural, proper) atarimae
no 当り前の; *(rational)*
gōriteki na 合理的な
rebel N hangyakusha 反逆者; v
(against) … ni somuku ~に
背く, hangyaku suru
反逆する
rebellion N hangyaku 反逆
recall N *(defective products)*
rikōru リコール; v *(remember)*
omoidasu 思い出す
receipt N ryōshūsho 領収書,
juryōsho 受領書
receive v uketoru 受け取る,
morau もらう, ukeru 受ける,
ukeireru 受け入れる; hikitoru
引き取る; sessuru 接する
receiver N *(telephone)* juwa-ki
受話器
recent ADJ saikin no 最近の,
kono-goro no この頃の,
chikagoro no 近頃の
reception N uketsuke 受付;
resepushon レセプション;
pātī パーティー
receptionist N *(person)*
uketsuke (no hito) 受付(の
人); uketsuke-gakari 受付係

recession N fukeiki 不景気, fukyō 不況

recipe N reshipi レシピ

reckon V kazoeru 数える

recognition N ninshiki 認識

recognize V mitomeru 認める

recommend V susumeru 勧める

recommendation N suisen 推薦, osusume おすすめ, (letter) suisen-jō 推薦状

reconfirm N saikakunin 再確認, (flight) rikonfāmu リコンファーム; (yoyaku o) saikakunin suru (予約を)再確認する

record N rekōdo レコード; (results, marks) seiseki 成績; (historic) kiroku 記録; V (sound) rokuon suru 録音する; (event) kiroku suru 記録する

recovery N kaifuku 回復

recreation N goraku 娯楽, rejā レジャー, rekurieshon レクリエーション

recruit N shin'nyū-shain 新入社員; V boshū suru 募集する; saiyō suru 採用する

rectangle N chōhōkei 長方形

recuperation N hoyō 保養

red N aka 赤; ADJ akai 赤い; aka

no 赤の: *red light* (signal) akashingo 赤信号

redo V yarinaosu やり直す

reduce V herasu 減らす; (curtail) habuki 省く; (summarize) chijimeru 縮める

refer to (reference) sanshō suru 参照する, ... ni fureru ... に触れる

reflect W hankyō suru 反響する; (ponder) ... o hansha suru 〜を反射する; hansei suru 反省する; (mirror) ... o utsusu 〜を映す

reflection N hanei 反映, hansha 反射; utsuri 写り; kage 影; (consideration) kōryo 考慮; hansei 反省

refrain V hikaeru 控える, enryo suru 遠慮する

refreshment N (drink) nomi-mono 飲み物

refrigerator N reizōko 冷蔵庫

refund N haraimodoshi 払い戻し, henkin 返金; V harai-modosu 払い戻す, henkin suru 返金する

refusal N kyozetsu 拒絶, kotowari 断り; kyohi 拒否

refuse V kotowaru 断る; jitai suru 辞退する; (reject)

334

kobamu 拒む, kyohi suru 拒否する; N *(waste)* kuzu くず

regarding PREP ... ni kanshite 〜に関して, ... ni tsuite no 〜 についての

region N chihō 地方, chi'iki 地域

register N *(of names)* meibo 名簿, *(enrollment)* kiroku 記録

registered post/mail N kakitome 書留

regret N kōkai 後悔; V kōkai suru 後悔する, kuyamu 悔やむ

regular ADJ *(normal)* tsūjō no 通常の; *(usual)* futsū no 普通の, *(ordinary)* nami no 並の; *(periodic/scheduled)* teiki no 定期の: *regular size* futsū saizu 普通サイズ

reject V kobamu 拒む, kyohi suru 拒否する

relationship N kankei 関係; aidagara 間柄; zokugara 続柄

relatives N shinseki 親戚

relax V kutsurogu くつろぐ; *(rest)* yasumu 休む

release N *(publication, etc.)* hatsubai 発売; *(movie, etc.)* kōkai 公開; *(free)* kaihō 解放; V hanasu 放す, hatsubai

suru 発売する, happyō suru 発表する

relics N ibutsu 遺物

religion N shūkyō 宗教

rely (on) V ... ni tayoru 〜に 頼る, *(request)* tanomu 頼む, irai suru 依頼する

remain V amaru 余る, *(get left behind)* nokoru 残る

remainder N *(leftover)* nokori 残り nokorimono 残り物, *(surplus)* amari 余り

remains N *(historical)* iseki 遺跡(歴史的); *(leftover)* nokori 残り; *(dead body)* itai 遺体

remarkable ADJ ichijirushi'i 著しい, ijō na 異常な

remember V oboeteiru 覚えている, *(recall)* omoidasu 思い出す

remind VI omoidasu 思い出す VT omoidasaseru 思い出させる; kizukaseru 気付かせる

reminder N hinto ヒント, saisoku 催促

remove V toru 取る, torinozoku 取り除く

renewal N kōshin 更新, rinyūaru リニューアル

renovate V *(repair)* shūri suru

修理する; *(rebuild)* rifōmu suru リフォームする, kaisō suru 改装する

repair N *(repairing)* naoshi 直し, shūri 修理; *(upkeep, care)* teire 手入れ; vт naosu 直す; *(mend, patch, sew)* tsukurou 繕う; shūri suru 修理する

repeat v kurikaesu 繰り返す

repel v *(water, etc.)* hajiku はじく

replace v sashikaeru 差し替える; torikaeru 取り換える; henkan suru 変換する

replica N fukusei(-hin) 複製品, mozō(-hin) 模造品, repurika レプリカ

reply N *(response)* henji 返事; *(answer)* kaitō 回答; v *(in speech)* hentō suru 返答する, *(in writing)* henji o kaku 返事を書く

report N *(announcement)* hōkoku 報告, hōkokusho 報告書, repōto レポート; *(notice)* (o-)shirase (お)知らせ, tsūchi 通知; v hōkoku suru 報告する

reporter N repōtā レポーター, kisha 記者

representative N daihyō 代表, daihyō-sha 代表者

reprint v saihan suru 再版する, zōsatsu suru 増刷する

reproduce v fukusei suru 複製する, saisei suru 再生する

reproduction N *(replication)* fukusei 複製, *(copy)* fukusha 複写; *(replay)* saisei 再生

reputation N hyōban 評判: *have a bad reputation* hyōban ga warui 評判が悪い

request N irai 依頼; yōkyū 要求, seikyū 請求; v *(formally)* irai suru 依頼する, *(informally)* tanomu 頼む

require v *(demand)* yōkyū suru 要求する

requirement N shikaku 資格, hitsuyōjōken 必要条件

rescue v tasukeru 助ける, suku'u 救う; kyūjo suru 救助する

research N *(investigation)* chōsa 調査, kenkyū 研究; v kenkyū suru 研究する

resemble v ... ni niteiru 〜に似ている, niru 似る; ... ni/ruiji suru 〜に/と類似する

reservation N yoyaku 予約

reserve N *(for animals)* hogoku 保護区 (動物); *(reticence)* enryo 遠慮; *(spare)* yobi 予備; ADJ yobi no 予備の; v *(ask for in advance)* yoyaku suru 予約する; *(put aside, hold)* totte oku 取って置く

resident N jūnin 住人, jūmin 住民

resign v *(job)* (shigoto o) yameru (仕事を)辞める

resist v hankō suru 反抗する, hanpatsu suru 反発する

resolve v *(problem)* kaiketsu suru 解決する (問題); *(prepare)* kakugo suru 覚悟する

resound v *(tune, noise, sound, voice)* hibiku 響く

respect N sonkei 尊敬; v sonkei suru 尊敬する, uyamau 敬う

respond v kotaeru 答える, ōjiru 応じる, hentō suru 返答する

responsibility N sekinin 責任; gimu 義務

responsible, be ADJ sekinin o motsu 責任を持つ

rest N *(a break/pause)* yasumi 休み, kyukei 休憩, hoyō 保養;

(remainder) nokori 残り

restaurant N resutoran レストラン, inshokuten 飲食店

restrain v osaeru 抑える

restricted ADJ fujiyū na 不自由な

restroom N keshōshitsu 化粧室, (o-)tearai (お)手洗い; *(bathroom)* toire トイレ

result N kekka 結果; *(outcome)* seika 成果; *(marks, grades)* seiseki 成績; *(effect)* eikyō 影響: *as a result* ... no kekkatoshite ...の結果として

retire v *(from job)* intai/taishoku suru 引退/退職する; *(withdraw)* shirizoku 退く; hikisagaru 引き下がる

return v *(give back)* kaesu 返す, modosu 戻す; *(go back)* modoru 戻る; *(turn back)* hikikaesu 引き返す *(go back/home)* kaeru 帰る, kitaku suru 帰宅する, *(one's home town)* kikyō suru 帰郷する; *(from abroad)* kikoku suru 帰国する

return ticket N ōfukukippu 往復キップ

reveal v *(make known)* akiraka ni suru 明らかにする; *(make visible)* arawasu 現す

revenge v fukushū o suru 復讐をする

reverse N hantai 反対; *(back, lining)* ura 裏; v *(go backwards)* gyakkō suru 逆行する; *(revert)* modosu 戻す; ADJ hantai no 反対の, gyaku no 逆の

review N hihyō 批評; v hihyō suru 批評する

revise v kaitei suru 改訂する

revival N *(regeneration)* fukkatsu 復活, saisei 再生, ribaibaru リバイバル

revolution N *(political)* kakumei 革命, reboryūshon レボリューション; *(revolving)* kaiten 回転

rewrite v kakinaosu 書き直す, kakikaeru 書き換える

rib N rokkotsu ろっ骨, abarabone あばら骨

rice N *(cooked)* gohan ご飯; *(uncooked)* kome 米; *(plant)* ine 稲

rice fields N tanbo 田んぼ

riceball N o-musubi おむすび, nigirimeshi にぎり飯, o-nigiri おにぎり

rich ADJ *(wealthy)* kanemochi no 金持ちの, yūfuku na 裕福

な; *(abundant)* yutaka na 豊かな, hōfu na 豊富な

rid: get rid of v *(remove)* torinozoku 取り除く; *(kick out)* oidasu 追い出す

ride N jōshajikan 乗車時間; doraibu ドライブ; v *(transport)* (norimono ni) noru (乗り物に) 乗る

right N migi 右; seigi 正義; ken'ri 権利; ADJ *(correct)* tadashi'i 正しい; *(not left)* migi no 右の; *(suitable)* ii (yoi) いい (良い); pittari ぴったり; *That's right* sō desu そうです

right away ADV *(at once)* sassoku 早速; sugu ni すぐに

right-handed ADJ migikiki no 右利きの

right-hand side migigawa 右側

right now ADV ima sugu ni 今すぐに; tatta ima たった今

rim N heri へり・縁, fuchi ふち・縁

ring N *(jewelry)* yubiwa 指輪; *(circle)* wa 輪, maru 円; vI *(a bell sounds)* naru 鳴る; vT narasu 鳴らす; *(on the phone)* denwa suru 電話する

ripe ADJ jukushita 熟した

rise N *(ascendancy)* jōshō 上昇; *(increase)* zōka 増加; *(in price, wage, fee)* hikiage 引き上げ, neage 値上げ; ... o okosu ...を起こす, shōjiru 生じる

risky ADJ atarihazure 当たり外れ risukī na リスキーな; kiken na 危険な

rival N kyōsōaite 競争相手, raibaru ライバル; teki 敵

river N kawa 川

revision N kaitei(-ban) 改訂(版), kōsei 校正

road N michi 道, dōro 道路

roast V *(grill)* aburu あぶる; yaku 焼く

rob V *(steal)* nusumu 盗む; *(plunder)* ubau 奪う

robber(y) N dorobō 泥棒, gōtō 強盗

rock N ishi 石, *(crag)* iwa 岩; *(music)* rokku ロック

rod N sao 竿; roddo ロッド

role N yakuwari 役割, yakume 役目; *(play)* yaku 役

roll VI korogaru 転がる; *(sway)* yureru 揺れる; VT korogasu 転がす; maku 巻く; N *(bread)* rōrupan ロールパン

ROM (read only memory) N

(computer) romu ロム

romance N romansu ロマンス, ren'ai 恋愛

romanization N rōma-ji ローマ字

roof N yane 屋根; V yane o fuku 屋根を葺く

room N *(in hotel/house)* heya 部屋; *(space)* kūkan 空間; *(room and board)* geshuku 下宿

root N *(plant)* ne 根 (植物); *(cause)* gen'in 原因

rope N rōpu ロープ, nawa 縄

rose N bara ばら

rot V itamu 傷む, kiusaru 腐る

rotation N kaiten 回転; kōtai 交代

rough ADJ *(coarse; wild)* arappoi 荒っぽい, zatsu na 雑な; arai 荒い; *(in texture)* zarazara (shita) ざらざら(した); *(bumpy)* dekoboko no でこぼこの; *(rowdy)* ranbō na 乱暴な; *(approximate)* ōyoso no おおよその: **get rough** V areru 荒れる

round N enkei 円形, wa 輪; shūi 周囲; ADV *(around)* ōyoso no おおよその; ADJ *(shape)* marui 丸い, enkei

no 円形の; v **marumeru** 丸める; PREP **mawatte** 回って; *final round* **kesshōsen** 決勝戦

round trip (ticket) N **ōfuku (-kippu)** 往復(切符)

route N *(bus, train)* **rosen** 路線

router N *(computer)* **rūtā** ルーター

routine N **nikka** 日課; *(computer program)* **rūtin** ルーティン

row N *(line)* **retsu** 列, **narabi** 並び; v *(a boat)* **kogu** 漕ぐ; *(quarrel)* **kōron suru** 口論する

royal family N **ōzoku** 王族, **ōshitsu** 王室; *(Japanese)* **kōshitsu** 皇室

royalties N **inzei** 印税

rub VT **kosuru** こする, **masatsu suru** 摩擦する; *(with both hands)* **momu** 揉む; VI **sureru** 擦れる

rubber N **gomu** ゴム

rubbish N **gomi** ごみ, **kuzu** くず, **garakuta** がらくた

rude ADJ **shitsurei na** 失礼な; **burei na** 無礼な, **busahō na** 不作法な

rug N **shiki-mono** 敷物, **jūtan** じゅうたん

ruin N **dainashi** 台無し

rule N **kisoku** 規則, **kitei** 規定, **rūru** ルール; *(law)* **hō** 法, **hōsoku** 法則

ruler N **jōgi** 定規, **monosashi** 物差し

rumor N **uwasa** うわさ

run V **hashiru** 走る: *run away* **nigeru** 逃げる, **iede suru** 家出する; *run into* ... **ni deau** に出会う

runaway N *(from home)* **iedenin** 家出人; *(escapee)* **tōbōsha** 逃亡者

rural ADJ **inaka no** 田舎の

rush V **isogu** 急ぐ: *with a rush (suddenly)* **ōisogi de** 大急ぎで

Russia N **Roshia** ロシア

Russian N *(people)* **Roshia-jin** ロシア人; *(language)* **Roshia-go** ロシア語; **Roshia no** ロシアの

rustic ADJ **inaka no** 田舎の, **shisso na** 質素な; **yabo na** 野暮な, **yabottai** 野暮ったい

rusty N **sabita** 錆びた

S

sack N (*bag*) fukuro 袋; (*dismissal from employment*) kaiko 解雇; (*bed*) beddo ベッド; (*pillage*) ryakudatsu 略奪; v kaiko suru 解雇する; kubi ni suru 首にする

sacred ADJ (*holy*) shinsei na 神聖な; (*religious*) shūkyō-teki na 宗教的な, shūkyō no 宗教の

sacrifice N gisei 犠牲; v gisei ni suru 犠牲にする

sad ADJ kanashi'i 悲しい; (*regrettable*) zan'nen na 残念な; (*miserable*) mijime na 惨めな

saddle N (*for horse*) kura 鞍; (*of bicycle*) sadoru サドル

safe ADJ anzen na 安全な; (*reliable*) daijōbu na 大丈夫な, jōbu na 丈夫な; (*steady*) tegatai 手堅い; (*certain*) tashika na 確かな

safeguard N (*protection*) hogo 保護; v hogo suru 保護する

safe(ly) ADV (*without incident*) chanto ちゃんと, tashika ni 確かに

sail N ho 帆; v (*make a voyage*)

kōkai suru 航海する, funatabi o suru 船旅をする

sailor N funanori 船乗り, suifu 水夫; (*crew*) sen'in 船員; (*navy*) suihei 水兵

salad N sarada サラダ

salary N kyūryō 給料; (*monthly*) gekkyū 月給

sale N hanbai 販売; (*special sale*) uridashi 売り出し, sēru セール; (*reduced prices*) yasu'uri 安売り, bāgen バーゲン: *not for sale* hibaihin 非売品

sales N uriage 売上; hanbai 販売; ADJ hanbai no 販売の: *sales assistant* ten'in 店員; *sales outlet* hanbaiten 販売店; *salesperson* hanbai'in 販売員; *sales promotion* hanbai sokushin 販売促進, hansoku 販促

salmon N sake 鮭, sāmon サーモン, shake シャケ: *salmon roe* ikura イクラ; sujiko 筋子

salt N shio 塩

salty ADJ shiokarai 塩辛い, shoppai しょっぱい

same PRON onaji 同じ; ADJ onaji yō na 同じ様な; ADV dōyō ni 同様に: *same time* (ni) dōji 同時(に)

sample N mihon 見本, sanpuru サンプル, shikyō-hin 試供品

sanctuary N *(asylum)* hinanjo 避難所; *(church)* kyōkai 教会

sand N suna 砂

sandals N sandaru サンダル

sandpaper N sandopēpā サンドペーパー, kami-yasuri 紙やすり

sandwich N sandoitchi サンドイッチ

sanitary ADJ eisei-teki na 衛生的な, eisei no 衛生の

sanitary napkin N *(seiri-yō)* napukin (生理用)ナプキン

sarcastic ADJ hiniku na 皮肉な, iyami na 嫌味な, iyamippoi 嫌味っぽい

sardine N iwashi イワシ

sash N *(girdle)* obi 帯; *(window-sash)* mado-waku 窓枠, sasshi サッシ

satan N akuma 悪魔

satellite N eisei 衛星: *artificial satellite* jinkō eisei 人工衛星

satisfy V manzoku saseru 満足させる; *(fulfill)* mitasu 満たす

Saturday N do-yōbi 土曜日

sauce N sōsu ソース; *(cooking)* tare たれ

saucer N kozara 小皿, sara 皿; *(for cup)* ukezara 受け皿

sausage N sōsēji ソーセージ

savage ADJ yaban na 野蛮な

save V *(rescue)* tasukeru 助ける; *(retain)* tamotsu 保つ; *(save up, hoard)* takuwaeru 蓄える; *(deposit money)* chokin suru 貯金する; *(accumulate)* tameru 溜める; *(economize on)* setsuyaku suru 節約する; *(computer)* (dēta o) hozon suru (データを)保存する

savings N takuwae 蓄え

savor V *(taste)* ajiwau 味わう

saw N *(tool)* nokogiri のこぎり; V nokogiri de hiku のこぎりで引く

say V iu 言う: *say goodbye* sayōnara to iu さようならと言う; *say hello* kon'nichiwa to iu こんにちはと言う, yoroshiku よろしく; *say sorry* ayamaru 謝る; *say thank you* arigatō to iu ありがとうと言う, orei o iu お礼を言う

scales N *(weighing)* hakari はかり; *(fish)* uroko うろこ

scallop(s) N hotategai 帆立貝

342

scandal N sukyandaru スキャンダル, fushōji 不祥事

scar N kizu-ato 傷跡

scarce ADJ sukunai 少ない, toboshi'i 乏しい

scarecrow N kakashi カカシ

scared ADJ obieta おびえた

scene N *(story, play)* bamen 場面; *scene of a crime* hankō genba 犯行現場

scenery N keshiki 景色, fūkei 風景, *(view)* nagame 眺め

schedule N kēkaku 計画, yotei(hyō) 予定(表); *(daily routine)* nittei 日程

scholarship N shōgaku-kin 奨学金

school N gakkō 学校: *school grounds/field* kōtei 校庭; *school uniform* gakusei-fuku 学生服, seifuku 制服

schoolchild N *(elementary school)* gakudō 学童, shōgakusei 小学生

schoolmaster N sensei 先生, kyōshi 教師

schoolroom N kyōshitsu 教室

science N kagaku 科学

scissors N hasami はさみ

scope N han'i 範囲

score N sukoa スコア, tokuten 得点, tensū 点数; *(musical score)* gakufu 楽譜; v ten o toru 点を取る

scotch tape N sero(han) tēpu セロ(ハン)テープ

Scotland N Sukottorando スコットランド

Scottish, Scot N (ADJ) Sukotto-rando-jin (no) スコットランド人(の)

scramble v *(mix)* kaki-mazeru かき混ぜる; *(climb)* hai-noboru はい登る; *(fight)* ubaiau 奪いあう

scrap N kuzu くず, danpen 断片, kuzu-mono くず物; *(refuse)* sukurappu スクラップ; v haiki suru 廃棄する, sukurappu ni suru スクラップにする

scratch v hikkaku ひっかく; N hikkaki-kizu ひっかき傷

scream N himei 悲鳴: *scream out* himei o ageru 悲鳴を上げる, akebu 叫ぶ

screen N *(folding)* byōbu 屏風; *(TV)* gamen 画面, *(movie)* sukurīn スクリーン; *(computer)* monitā モニター

screw N neji ねじ; v *(tighten)* (neji o) shimeru (ねじを)締める

script N daihon 台本, kyakuhon 脚本

scrub V ...goshigoshi arau ごしごし洗う, kosuru こする

sculpture N chōkoku 彫刻

scum N aku 灰汁

sea N umi 海

seafood N gyokairui 魚介類; kaisanbutsu 海産物

seagull N kamome カモメ

seal N inkan 印鑑, han 判, hanko 判子; *(label)* shīru シール; N *(animal)* azarashi あざらし, ashika あしか; V fū o suru 封をする, mippū suru 密封する, fusagu ふさぐ

sea mail N funabin 船便

search N *(investigation)* sōsa 捜査; *(retrieval)* kensaku 検索: *search for ...* o sagasu ～を探す

seashell N kaigara 貝がら

seasickness N funayoi 船酔い

seaside N umibe 海辺

season N kisetsu 季節; shīzun シーズン; V *(give flavor)* ajitsuke suru 味付する

seasoning N *(spice, flavoring)* chōmiryō 調味料; ajitsuke 味付け

seat N seki 席, zaseki 座席;

(chair) isu 椅子

seaweed N kaisō 海藻; nori のり; wakame わかめ; *(kelp)* konbu 昆布

second N byō 秒; ADJ daini no 第二の; nibanme no 二番目の

secondhand ADJ chūko/chūburu no 中古の, furui 古い; N *(goods)* chūko-hin 中古品; *secondhand shop/store* risaikuru shoppu リサイクルショップ

secret N himitsu 秘密; ADJ *(confidential)* himitsu no 秘密の, naisho no 内緒の: *keep a secret* himitsu o mamoru 秘密を守る

secretary N hisho 秘書

section N bumon 部門

section head N buchō 部長

sector N bumon 部門

secure ADJ anzen na 安全な, chanto shita ちゃんとした

security N *(stock, bond)* shōken 証券; *(secure feeling)* anshin 安心; *(computer)* sekyuritī セキュリティー

see V miru 見る; *(meet)* au 会う: *see you later* [FORMAL] sore dewa mata それではまた,

[INFORMAL] jā mata ne じゃあまたね、bai-bai バイバイ

seed N tane 種

seeing-eye dog N mōdōken 盲導犬

seek V motomeru 求める; sagasu 捜す

seem V ... to omowareru ～と思われる; (like) ... ni mieru ～に見える、... no yō desu ～の様です; ... rashi'i desu ～らしいです

seldom ADV hotondo (... nai) ほとんど(～ない)、metta ni (... nai) めったに(～ない); (infrequently) tama ni たまに

select V erabu 選ぶ

self N jishin 自身、jibun 自分

self-confidence N jishin 自信

selfish ADJ katte na 勝手な、jibunkatte na 自分勝手な、waga-mama na わがままな

self-service ADJ serufu sābisu no セルフサービスの

sell VI ureru 売れる; VT uru 売る、hanbai suru 販売する

sellout N uri-kire 売り切れ

semiconductor N handōtai 半導体

seminar N zemi ゼミ、zemināru ゼミナール、seminā

セミナー、kōshūkai 講習会

send V okuru 送る

sender N (mail, etc.) hassōnin 発送人、okurinushi 送り主; (mail, e-mail, etc.) sashidashi-nin 差出人、sōshin-sha 送信者

senior ADJ (older) toshi-ue no 年上の; N senpai 先輩

senior high school N kōtō-gakkō 高等学校、kō-kō 高校

sense N sensu センス、kankaku 感覚、chisei 知性: *sense of humor* yūmoa no sensu ユーモアのセンス

sensitive ADJ binkan na 敏感な; (delicate) kizutsukiyasui 傷つきやすい、sensai na 繊細な、derikēto na デリケートな

sentence N (written) bunshō 文章、bun 文

sentimental ADJ senchimen-taru na センチメンタルな; kanshōteki na 感傷的な

separate ADJ wakareta 分かれた; (different) betsu no 別の、betsubetsu na/no 別々な/の; VI wakareru 分かれる; (get distant) hanareru 離れる; VT wakeru 分ける; (separate something from) hanasu 離す

September N ku-gatsu 九月

sequence N *(order)* junjo 順序; zengo 前後

serial number N shiriaru nanbā シリアルナンバー; tōshi bangō 通し番号

serious ADJ *(not funny)* majime na まじめな; *(in earnest)* honki no 本気の; *(heavy, grave)* omoi 重い, jūdai na 重大な, shinkoku na 深刻な; *(severe)* hidoi ひどい; taihen na 大変な

servant N meshitsukai 召使; shiyōnin 使用人

serve V tsukaeru 仕える; *(a meal)* dasu 出す

server N *(computer)* sābā サーバー

service N hōshi 奉仕; *(in restaurant, etc.)* sābisu サービス; *(maintenance and repair)* afutāsābisu アフターサービス

sesame N goma ごま

set N *(collection)* kumi 組; ADJ shotei no 所定の; *(array)* soroi 揃い: *a set of* hitokumi no 一組の

set free V hanasu 放す

set meal N teishoku 定食, setto menyū セットメニュー

set up V setsuritsu suru 設立する, juritsu suru 樹立する; *(assemble)* kumitateru 組み立てる

setup N haichi 配置, junbi 準備, settei 設定

seven NUM nana, shichi 七

seventeen NUM jūnana, jūshichi 十七

seventy NUM nanajū 七十

several ADJ ikutsuka no いくつかの; nisan no 二三の, jakkan no 若干の

severally ADV sorezore それぞれ, ono'ono 各々

severe ADJ kibishi'i きびしい; kitsui きつい; *(terrible)* hidoi ひどい

sew V nu'u 縫う

sewage N gesui 下水, osui 汚水

sex N *(gender)* seibetsu 性別, seikō 性交, sekkusu セックス

sexual ADJ sei-teki na 性的な

shack N koya 小屋

shade N kage 陰; *(of trees)* kokage 木陰, hikage 日陰

shadow N kage 影, *(from sunlight)* hikage 日陰

shady ADJ ikagawashi'i いかがわしい

shake v furu 振る; furueru 震える, *(sway)* yureru 揺れる; **n** *(milkshake)* mirukusēki ミルクセーキ; sheiku シェイク

shall MODAL v ... deshō ～でしょう; *(have to)* ...shinakute wa ikenai ～しなくてはいけない; ... shimashō ka ～しましょうか

shallow ADJ asai 浅い

shame N *(disgrace)* chijoku 恥辱, haji 恥: *what a shame!* zan'nen 残念

shameful ADJ hazukashi'i 恥ずかしい

shameless ADJ zūzūshi'i ずうずうしい, atsukamashi'i 厚かましい

shampoo N shanpū シャンプー

shape N katachi 形, kata 型; *(figure)* sugata 姿, kakkō 格好; v *(form)* katachizukuru 形作る

share N *(portion)* toribun 取り分, wakemae 分け前; *(allotment)* buntan 分担, kyōyū suru 共有する: *one's share* wariate 割り当て; *share in, pay/do one's share* buntan suru 分担する, kyōyū 共有する

shark N same 鮫

sharp ADJ surudoi 鋭い; *(clever)* rikō na 利口な

shatter v konagona ni suru 粉々にする

shave v soru 剃る

shaver N kamisori かみそり

she, her PRON, ADJ kanojo wa/o 彼女は/を

sheep N hitsuji 羊

sheet N *(for bed)* shītsu シーツ; *(count flat things)* *a sheet of ...* ichimai no ... 一枚の～

shelf N tana 棚

shell N kara 殻; *(seashell)* ka-gara 貝がら; *(of tortoise etc.)* kōra 甲羅

shellfish N kai 貝

shield v hogo suru 保護する; N tate 盾

shift vi utsuru 移る; kawaru 変わる, *(alternate)* kōtai suru 交代する vt kaeru 変える, utsusu 移す; N idō 移動, shifuto シフト, kōtai 交代; henka 変化

shine N *(gloss)* tsuya つや; v hikaru 光る, *(gleam)* kagayaku 輝く; vt *(polish)* migaku 磨く

Shinto N shintō 神道

347

ship N fune 船: VI fune ni noru 船に乗る: VT (*load/carry*) (fune ni) noseru (船に)載せる, (fune de) hakobu (船で)運ぶ

shirt N shatsu シャツ

shit N daiben 大便, kuso くそ

shiver N furue 震え; V miburui suru 身震いする, zotto suru ぞっとする; furueru 震える

shock N dageki 打撃, shokku ショック, shōgeki 衝撃

shoe N kutsu 靴

shoelace N kutsuhimo 靴ひも

shoot V utsu 撃つ, (*bow*) iru 射る; (*film*) satsuei suru 撮影する: **shoot the breeze** abura o uru 油を売る

shop N mise 店; V (*shopping*) kaimono o suru 買い物をする

shoplift V manbiki suru 万引きする

shopping N kaimono 買い物, shoppingu ショッピング

short ADJ (*concise*) mijikai 短い; (*not tall*) hikui 低い; (*deficient*) tarinai 足りない: **short circuit** (*electric*) shōto suru ショートする; **short cut** chikamichi 近道; **short time** (*a moment*) tanjikan 短時間

shortage N fusoku 不足

shorten V mijikaku suru 短くする, chijimeru 縮める; herasu 減らす; (*abbreviate*) ryakusu 略す

shorts N tanpan 短パン; pantsu パンツ (下着)

shoulder N kata 肩

shout V sakebu 叫ぶ; (*yell*) donaru 怒鳴る

show N (*broadcast*) bangumi 番組; (*live performance*) shō ショー, moyōshi 催し, misemono 見せ物; V miseru 見せる; (*reveal*) arawasu 表す; (*indicate*) shimesu 示す; (*tell*) oshieru 教える: **show off** jiman suru 自慢する

shower N (*for washing*) shawā シャワー; (*rain*) kosame 小雨: **take a shower** shawā o abiru シャワーを浴びる

shrimp N ebi 海老

shrine N (*shinto*) jinja 神社, (*large*) jingū 神宮

shut VT tojiru 閉じる; shimeru 閉める; (*shut one's eyes*) me o tsuburu 目をつぶる; VI shimaru 閉まる

shut up! damare 黙れ, [POLITE] shizukani (shinasai) 静かに (しなさい)

shy ADJ uchiki na 内気な, hazukashigaru 恥ずかしがる

sibling N kyōdai きょうだい

sick ADJ byōki no 病気の; *(vomit)* hakike ga suru 吐き気がする

sickness N byōki 病気

side N yoko 横; *(beside, nearby)* soba 側; *(of body)* waki わき

sightseeing N kenbutsu 見物, kankō 観光: *sightseeing bus* kankō-basu 観光バス

sign N *(symptom)* shirushi しるし; *(omen)* zenchō 前兆; *(signboard)* kanban 看板; *(marker)* hyōshiki 標識; *(symbol)* kigō 記号; v shomei suru 署名する; aizu suru 合図する: *sign in* sain'in サインイン, roguin ログイン, roguon ログオン; *sign off* sainofu サインオフ, roguauto ログアウト, roguofu ログオフ

signal N shingō 信号; v aizu suru 合図する

signature N shomei 署名, sain サイン

silent ADJ mugon no 無言の: *be silent* damaru 黙る

silk N kinu 絹

silly ADJ bakabakashi'i ばかばかしい

silver N gin 銀; ADJ *(color)* giniro no 銀色の

similar ADJ ruiji shita/no 類似した/の, nita 似た, onaji yō na 同じ様な; *(even)* hitoshi'i 等しい

simple ADJ *(easy)* kantan na 簡単な, tanjun na 単純な, shinpuru na シンプルな; *(plain)* assarishita あっさりした; *(frugal)* shisso na 質素な; *(uncomplicated, modest)* jimi na 地味な

since ADV, PREP irai 以来, (sono) ato/go (その)後, shite kara …してから; CONJ … shite kara …してから

sing V utau 歌う

Singapore N Shingapōru シンガポール

singer N kashu 歌手

single ADJ *(not married)* dokushin no 独身の; *(only one)* yui'itsu no 唯一の; *(for one person)* hitori no ひとりの

sip N hitokuchi 一口

sir N *(term of address for male)* kika 貴下 (男性への敬称)

sister N shimai 姉妹; *(older)* ane 姉, (o-)nē-san (お)姉さん; *(younger)* imōto 妹

sister-in-law N *(older)* giri no ane 義理の姉, gishi 義姉; *(younger)* giri no imōto 義理の妹, gimai 義妹

sit V suwaru 座る; *(in chair)* (koshi) kakeru (腰)掛ける

situation N *(how things are)* jōkyō 状況, jōtai 状態, jitai 事態; *(circumstance)* ba'ai 場合

six NUM roku 六

sixteen NUM jūroku 十六

sixty NUM rokujū 六十

size N saizu サイズ

sketch N shasei 写生, suketchi スケッチ; shitae 下絵

ski, skiing N sukī スキー; V sukī o suru スキーをする

skill N udemae 腕前; ginō 技能; sukiru スキル

skillful ADJ jukurenshita 熟練した, jōzu na 上手な, umai うまい, takumi na 巧みな; *(proficient)* tassha na 達者な; *(nimble)* kiyō na 器用な

skim V *(graze)* kasumeru 掠める; kasumetoru 掠め取る

skin N hada 肌, hifu 皮膚

skip N sukippu スキップ; V sukippu suru スキップする; *(leave out)* nukasu 抜かす, tobasu 飛ばす

skirt N sukāto スカート

sky N sora 空: *the sky* tengoku 天国

skyscraper N kōsō-biru 高層ビル

slacks N surakkusu スラックス, zubon ズボン

slang N zokugo 俗語, surangu スラング

slash N surasshu スラッシュ; shasen 斜線, "/"

sleep N *(sleeping)* nemuri 眠り, suimin 睡眠; V nemuru 眠る; yasumu 休む; *(go to bed)* neru 寝る

sleeping pill N suimin-zai 睡眠剤, suimin-yaku 睡眠薬

sleepy ADJ nemui 眠い

sleeve N sode 袖

slender ADJ hosoi 細い, sumāto na スマートな

slide N suberidai すべり台; V suberu 滑る

slight ADJ wazuka na わずかな, chottoshita ちょっとした

slim ADJ surimu na スリムな, hosoi 細い

slip N *(woman's underwear)* surippu スリップ; *(slide)* surippu スリップ; v suberu 滑る; *(price)* sagaru 下がる

slippers N surippa スリッパ, uwabaki 上履き

slope N saka 坂; *(slant)* keisha 傾斜

slow ADJ osoi 遅い; *(sluggish)* noroi のろい, yurui 緩い; *(clock runs slow)* okureteiru 遅れている

small ADJ chīsai 小さい, chitchai ちっちゃい; *(fine)* komakai 細かい

small change N kozeni 小銭, o-tsuri おつり

smart ADJ *(intelligent)* kashikoi 賢い, atama ga ii 頭がいい, rikō na 利口な; *(stylish)* sumāto na スマートな, iki na 粋な

smartphone N *(multi-functional mobile phone)* sumātofon スマートフォン, sumaho スマホ

smell N *(bad odor)* akushū 悪臭; v niou 臭う

smile v warau 笑う; nikoniko suru にこにこする; hohoemu 微笑む; N *(smiling face)* egao 笑顔; hohoemi 微笑み

smoke N kemuri 煙; v *(tobacco)* tabako o su'u タバコをすう; ibusu いぶす

smooth ADJ *(of surfaces)* subesubeshita すべすべした, nameraka na なめらかな; *(slippery)* tsurutsurushita ツルツルした; *(flat)* taira na 平らな; v narasu ならす

smuggle v mitsuyunyū suru 密輸入する

snack N keishoku 軽食; *(mid-afternoon)* o-yatsu おやつ, sunakku スナック

snake N hebi 蛇

snap vi hajikeru はじける; vt *(water, etc…)* hajiku はじく

sneeze N kushami くしゃみ

snooze v inemuri 居眠り

snow N yuki 雪

SNS (Social Network Services) N esu-enu-esu エスエヌエス, sōsharu nettowāku sābisu ソーシャルネットワークサービス

so ADV *(therefore)* sorede それで, soreyue それゆえ; *(very)* totemo とても

so that CONJ dakara だから, … suru tame ni 〜するために

351

soak vi hitaru 浸る, tsukaru 漬かる; shimikomu しみ込む; vt tsukeru 漬ける

soccer n sakkā サッカー

society n shakai 社会; *(association)* kyōkai 協会; *(scholarly)* gakkai 学会

socket n *(electric)* soketto ソケット, ukeguchi 受け口 (電気の)

socks n kutsushita 靴下

sofa n sofā ソファー, nagaisu 長いす

soft adj yawarakai やわらかい

software n *(computer)* sofutowea ソフトウェア

soil n tsuchi 土; *(stain)* yogore 汚れ

soldier n heitai 兵隊

sole adj *(only)* tatta hitotsu no たったひとつの; n *(fish)* shita-birame 舌平目; *(foot)* ashi no ura 足の裏; *(shoe)* kutsuzoko 靴底

solid adj kotai no 固体の; *(firm)* katai かたい

solve v *(problem)* kaiketsu suru 解決する (問題を)

some adj *(certain number)* ikutsuka no いくつかの; *(certain amount)* ikura ka no いくらかの; *(certain)* nanraka no 何らかの; pron, adv tashō 多

少: *some other time* izure いずれ

somebody, someone pron dareka 誰か

someday adv izure いずれ, itsuka いつか

something pron nanika 何か: *something unusual/wrong* n *(the matter)* ijō 異状/異常

sometime adv itsuka いつか

sometimes adv tokidoki 時々; *(occasionally)* tama ni たまに

somewhere n dokoka どこか; adv dokoka ni/de/e どこかに/で/へ

son n musuko 息子

song n uta 歌

soon adv sugu ni すぐに, ima ni 今に: *as soon as ... suru to sugu* ～するとすぐに

sore adj *(painful)* itai 痛い

sorrow n kanashimi 悲しみ

sorry adj *(feel regretful)* kōkai suru 後悔する: *I'm sorry.* gomen'nasai ごめんなさい, sumimasen すみません

sort n *(type)* shurui 種類: *sort out* taisho suru 対処する

so-so adj mā-mā まあまあ

sound n oto 音, ne 音; vi naru

鳴る、*(make an animal sound)* naku 鳴く; **vt** narasu 鳴らす; **ADV** *(asleep)* gussuri (nemutteiru) ぐっすり(眠っている)

soup N sūpu スープ

sour ADJ suppai すっぱい

source N *(origin)* minamoto 源、kigen 起源、moto もと

south N minami 南

south-east N nantō 南東

south-west N nansei 南西

souvenir N miyagemono みやげ物、(o-)miyage (お)みやげ

soy sauce N shōyu しょう油

soybean N daizu 大豆

space N *(interspace)* kūkan 空間、*(available)* ma 間、*(between)* aida 間、sukima 隙間、*(outer space)* uchū 宇宙

Spain N Supein スペイン

spam N meiwaku mēru 迷惑メール、janku mēru ジャンクメール、supamu mēru スパムメール

Spanish N *(language)* Supein-go スペイン語、*(people)* Supein-jin スペイン人、Supein no スペインの

speak V hanasu 話す

special ADJ tokubetsu na/no 特別な(の)、betsu no 別の、*(peculiar)* tokushu no 特殊の、*(favorite)* tokui (na/no) 得意(な/の)、*(emergency)* rinji no 臨時の

specialist N senmon-ka 専門家、supesharisuto スペシャリスト、*(medical)* senmon-i 専門医

spectacles N *(glasses)* megane めがね

speech N supīchi スピーチ、hanashi 話、kotoba 言葉、*(public)* enzetsu 演説、kōen 講演; **make a speech** supīchi o suru スピーチをする

speed N hayasa 速さ、sokudo 速度、supīdo スピード

spell V (ji o) tsuzuru (字を) 綴る

spend V tsuiyasu 費やす、*(money)* tsukau 使う、*(pay)* dasu 出す、*(use time)* sugosu 過ごす

spices N kōshinryō 香辛料

spicy ADJ karai 辛い

spider N kumo クモ

spinach N hōrensō ほうれん草

spine N sebone 背骨

spiral ADJ rasenjō no らせん状の

spirit N seishin 精神、kokoro 心、tamashi'i 魂

spirits N *(hard liquor)* jōryshu 蒸留酒

spit N *(spittle)* tsuba/tsubaki 唾; V tsuba o haku つばを吐く

splash V haneru 跳ねる

split VT saku 裂く、waru 割る; wakeru 分ける; VI sakeru 裂ける、wareru 割れる; wakareru 別れる: *split up* bunkatsu suru 分割する

spoil VT waruku/dame ni suru 悪く/駄目にする; VI waruku naru 悪くなる、dainashi ni narau 台無しになる; *(sour)* kusaru 腐る、*(rot)* itamu 傷む

spoon N supūn スプーン

sport N supōtsu スポーツ、undō 運動

sports ADJ supōtsu no スポーツの、undōyō no 運動用の

spouse N haigūsha 配偶者

spray N supurē スプレー

spread VT hirogeru 広げる、*(diffuse)* hiromeru 広める; *(spread it out)* nobasu 伸ばす、noberu 伸べる; *(spread it on)* haru 張る; VI hirogaru 広がる; *(it gets diffused)* hiromaru 広まる、fukyū suru 普及する; *(spread out)* nobiru 伸びる; *(spread on)* (batā o)

nuru (バターを)塗る

spring N *(metal part)* supuringu スプリング、danryoku 弾力; *(of water)* wakimizu 湧き水、izumi 泉; *(season)* haru 春; *(of clock)* zenmai ぜんまい: *spring vacation* haruyasumi 春休み

square N shikaku 四角; *(plaza)* hiroba 広場、ADJ *(shape)* shikakui 四角い

squeeze V tsubusu 潰す; shiboru 絞る

squid N ika イカ

stadium N kyōgi-jō 競技場; *baseball stadium* yakyū-jō 野球場、kyūjō 球場

staff N sutaffu スタッフ、ichi'in 一員

stage N butai 舞台; *(process)* dankai 段階

stain N shimi しみ、yogore 汚れ; VT *(paint)* nuru 塗る; *(soil)* yogosu 汚す

stairs N kaidan 階段

stall N *(vendor)* baiten 売店、yatai 屋台; V *(car)* shissoku saseru 失速させる

stamp N inkan 印鑑、*(postage)* kitte 切手 *(郵便)*

stand N *(sales booth)* uriba

売り場, baiten 売店; *(stall)*
yatai 屋台; dai 台; vt tatsu 立
つ; vt tateru 立てる; *(tolerate)*
gaman suru 我慢する, shinbō
suru 辛抱する: *stand out*
(prominently) medatsu 目立
つ; *stand up* tachiagaru 立
ち上がる

standard N hyōjun 標準:
standard Japanese N
(language) hyōjungo 標準語

star N hoshi 星; *(symbol)*
hoshi-jirushi 星印; *(actor,*
actress) sutā スター

start N *(beginning)* hajimari
始まり, sutāto スタート, kaishi
開始; vi hajimaru 始まる;
shuppatsu suru 出発する; vt
hajimeru 始める, kaishi suru
開始する

state N *(of the U.S.)* shū 州; v
noberu 述べる

statement N hōkokusho 報告書

station N *(rail)* eki 駅

stationery N bunbōgu 文房具

statue N zō 像, *(bronze)* dōzō
銅像

status N chi'i 地位

stay N taizai 滞在; v taizai
suru 滞在する; iru いる;
(remain) nokoru 残る

steady ADJ chakujitsu na 着
実な

steal v nusumu 盗む

steam N jōki 蒸気, yuge 湯気; v
fukasu 蒸かす, musu 蒸す

steel N hagane はがね, tetsu 鉄

steer v kaji o toru かじをとる

stem N *(plant)* kuki 茎

step N *(stairs)* kaidan 階段,
ashidori 足取り, ippo 一歩

stepfather N mama-chichi
まま父

stepmother N mama-haha
まま母

steps, stairs N kaidan 階段

stew N shichū シチュー, nikomi
煮込み

stick N *(pole)* bō 棒; *(staff)* tsue
杖; vi ... ni kuttsuku 〜にくっ
つく; sasaru 刺さる; vt tsukeru
付ける; *(paste)* haru 貼る; ...
ni tsukisasu 〜に突き刺す:
stick to ... ni haru 〜に貼る

stiff ADJ katai 堅い; *(shoulder)*
(kata ga) koru 肩が凝る

still ADV *(even now)* mada まだ,
ima da ni 未だに; ADJ *(quiet)*
shizuka na 静かな: *still more*
... *(also)* issō いっそう

stink v akushū o hanatsu 悪臭
を放つ

stir v kakimawasu かき回す

stock N *(financial)* kabu 株; *(soup)* dashi だし; *(on hand)* zaiko(-hin) 在庫(品); vт shi'ireru 仕入れる; vı sutokku suru ストックする

stockings N kutsushita 靴下

stomach N *(strictly, belly)* o-naka おなか, hara 腹; i 胃

stone N ishi 石

stool N koshikake 腰掛, benki 便器

stop N *(bus, train)* teiryūjo 停留所, eki 駅 (バス、電車の); vı *(come to rest)* tomaru 止まる, todomaru とどまる; *(cease)* yamu 止む; *(in the midst)* chūshi suru 中止する; vт *(cease)* yameru やめる; *(halt)* tomeru 止める: ***stop it!*** yamete やめて

store N *(shop)* mise 店; *(saving)* takuwae 蓄え

storey / **story** N *(building)* kai 階 (建物)

storm N arashi 嵐; v *(rage)* abareru 暴れる

story N *(tale)* hanashi 話

stove N *(cooker)* konro コンロ

straight ADJ *(not crooked)* massugu na 真っ直ぐな:

straight ahead massugu mae ni 真っ直ぐ前に

strait N kaikyō 海峡

strange ADJ hen na 変な, fushigi na 不思議な; *(peculiar)* kimyō na 奇妙な, okashi'i おかしい

stranger N shiranai hito 知らない人; *(outsider)* yosono hito よその人, tanin 他人

strap N *(watch-band, etc.)* bando バンド; himo ひも, sutorappu ストラップ; *(hang on to)* tsurikawa 吊り革

strawberry N ichigo イチゴ

street N michi 道, tōri 通り

strength N *(power)* chikara 力; tsuyosa 強さ

strict ADJ *(severe)* kibishi'i 厳しい, katai 堅い, yakamashi'i やかましい; *(precise)* genmitsu na 厳密な; genjū na 厳重な

strife N arasoi 争い

strike N *(job action)* suto スト, sutoraiki ストライキ; *(baseball)* sutoraiku ストライク; v *(hit)* utsu 打つ; *(go on strike)* sutoraiki o suru ストライキをする

string N *(thread)* ito 糸; *(cord)* himo ひも; *(wire)* tsuru 弦: **string up** tsuru 吊る

stripe N shima (moyō) 縞模様

stroll V hōrō suru 放浪する

strong ADJ tsuyoi 強い; *(coffee, etc.)* koi 濃い; *(influential)* yūryoku na 有力な

stubborn ADJ *(determined)* ganko na 頑固な; danko to shita 断固とした

student N gakusei 学生

studio N atorie アトリエ, sutajio スタジオ

study N benkyō 勉強; gakushū 学習; *(observation)* kengaku 見学; *(room)* shosai 書斎; V benkyō suru 勉強する, gakushū suru 学習する, manabu 学ぶ

stuff N *(thing)* mono 物; V *(cram)* tsumeru 詰める

stuffy ADJ ikigurushi'i 息苦しい

struggle N arasoi 争い

stupid ADJ oroka na 愚かな, baka na 馬鹿な

style N *(shape)* katachi 形; yōshiki 様式, keishiki 形式; ... fū ～風

stylish ADJ sumāto na スマートな, iki na 粋な, ryūkō no

流行の, jōhin na 上品な, oshare na おしゃれな

subject N *(topic)* mondai 問題, *(conversation)* wadai 話題; tane 種; *(school)* kamoku 科目, gakka 学科; *(grammar)* shugo 主語

substance N busshitsu 物質

substitute, substitution N daiyaku 代役, kawari 代わり; daiyō 代用; daiyōhin 代用品; dairi 代理, dairinin 代理人

suburb N kōgai 郊外, shigai 市外, *(outskirts)* basue 場末; beddotaun ベッドタウン

succeed V seikō suru 成功する; *(take over for)* (uke)tsugu (受け)継ぐ; *(in a projection)* hikitsugu 引き継ぐ; *(in a test)* ukaru 受かる

success N seikō 成功, gōkaku 合格

such ADJ ... no yō na ～のような: **such as** tatoeba ... no yō na 例えば～のような

suck V su'u 吸う; shaburu しゃぶる

sudden ADJ totsuzen no 突然の, kyū na 急な

suddenly ADV kyūni 急に; fui ni 不意に, totsuzen 突然;

(unexpectedly) niwaka ni にわかに; *(urgently)* kyū ni 急に

suffer v kurushimu 苦しむ, nayamu 悩む, wazurau 煩う; *(incur)* kōmuru 被る, ukeru 受ける

sugar N satō 砂糖

suggest v teian suru 提案する

suggestion N teian 提案, an 案, kangae 考え

suicide N jisatsu 自殺

suit N *(business)* sūtsu スーツ, sebiro 背広; v *(match with)* …ni au 〜に合う

suitable ADJ fusawashi'i ふさわしい, oniai no お似合いの, tekitō na 適当な

sum N gaku 額, kingaku 金額; gōkei 合計

summary N yōyaku 要約, *(gist)* yōshi 要旨; gaiyō 概要

summer N natsu 夏

summit N *(peak)* sanchō 山頂, chōjō 頂上, itadaki 頂

summon v yobidasu 呼び出す

sun N taiyō 太陽

sunburn N hiyake 日焼け

Sunday N nichi-yōbi 日曜日

sunlight N hizashi 日差し

sunrise N hinode 日の出

sunset N hinoiri 日の入, higure 日暮れ

superb ADJ ichiryū no 一流の

superior ADJ yūshū na 優秀な; jōtō no 上等の; meue no 目上の; erai 偉い

supermarket N sūpāmāketto スーパーマーケット

supper N ban-gohan 晩ご飯, yūshoku 夕食, yūhan 夕飯

supplement N hosoku 補足, zōho 増補; *(pills)* sapurimento サプリメント, sapuri サプリ

supplies N *(necessities)* hitsuju-hin 必需品, *(expendables)* shōmō-hin 消耗品

supply N *(necessities)* hitsuju-hin 必需品, *(expendables)* shōmō-hin 消耗品

supply v hōkyū suru 供給する; hokyū suru 補給する; kyōkyū 供給; hokyū 補給

support N *(approval)* sansei 賛成, sandō 賛同; *(backing, help)* kōen 後援, bakkuappu バックアップ, ōen 応援; *(aid)* enjo 援助, sapōto サポート; v ōen suru応援する; *(prop)* sasaeru 支える; *(endorse)* shiji suru 支持する

suppose v dato omou 〜だと思う, sō omou そう思う

suppress v appaku suru 圧迫する

sure ADJ kakushinshita 確信した, tashika na 確かな: *make sure* tashikameru 確かめる, nen no tame 念のため

surface N hyōmen 表面; *(top)* uwabe うわべ

surgery N *(operation)* shujutsu 手術; *(specialty)* geka 外科

surname N myōji 苗字

surplus N amari 余り

surprising ADJ odorokubeki 驚くべき; omoigakenai 思いがけない

surroundings N kankyō 環境; shūi 周囲

survive VI ikinobiru 生き延びる; VT nagaiki suru 長生きする

sushi bar N sushi-ya すし屋

suspect N yōgisha 容疑者; V utagau 疑う

suspend V burasageru ぶら下げる; *(in the midst)* chūshi suru 中止する

suspicion N kengi 嫌疑, giwaku 疑惑

suspicious ADJ *(questionable)* fushin na 不審な; *(contrived)* ayashi'i 怪しい, ikagawashi'i いかがわしい

swallow N *(the bird)* tsubame つばめ; V nomikomu 飲み込む

swan N hakuchō 白鳥

swamp N numa 沼

swear V chikau 誓う

sweat N hakkan 発汗; ase 汗; V ase o kaku 汗をかく

sweater N sētā セーター

sweep V haku 掃く; *(cleaning)* sōji suru 掃除する

sweet ADJ amai 甘い; *(gentle)* yasashi'i やさしい; *(voice)* koe no ii 声のいい; *(lovely)* airashi'i 愛らしい

sweet potato N satsumaimo さつま芋

sweets N *(dessert)* dezāto デザート; okashi お菓子; amaimono 甘いもの; *(candy)* ame あめ

swelling N dekimono できもの, o-deki おでき

swim V oyogu 泳ぐ

swing VI yureugoku 揺れ動く; VT ugokasu 動かす, yurasu 揺らす; N buranko ブランコ

switch N suicchi スイッチ; V *(change)* kōkan suru 交換する; *(clothes)* kigaeru 着替える; *(turn on/off)* suicchi o ireru/kiru スイッチを入れる/切る

sword N katana 刀

symbol N shinboru シンボル, shōchō 象徴; *(mark)* kigō 記号

sympathy N dōjō 同情, kyōkan 共感

system N soshiki 組織, seido 制度, taikei 体系, chitsujo 秩序, shisutemu システム

systematic ADJ kichōmen na きちょうめんな, kisoku-tadashi'i 規則正しい

T

tab N tsumami つまみ; *(tag)* fuda 札

table N tsukue 机, tēburu テーブル

tablespoon N ō-saji 大さじ

table tennis N takkyū 卓球

tableware N shokki 食器

tablet (computer, PC) N taburetto タブレット

tablets, pills N jōzai 錠剤

tactics N *(strategy)* senjutsu 戦術, sakusen 作戦

tag N fuda 札; *(baggage tag)* ni-fuda 荷札, tagu タグ; *name tag* nafuda 名札

tail N o 尾, shippo しっぽ; *the*

tail end ADJ biri no ビリの

tailor N shitate-ya 仕立屋, yōfuku-ya 洋服屋

take V toru 取る; *(remove)* motteiku 持っていく; *(require)* yōsuru 要する; *(require time/money)* (jikan/ kane ga) kakaru (時間/金 が) かかる; *(incur)* ukeru 受 ける; *(accept; understand)* uketoru 受け取る; *(medicine)* (kusuri o) nomu (薬を)飲 む; *(picture)* shashin o toru/ utsusu 写真を撮る/写す; *take away (take out)* motte kaeru 持って帰る; *take back* hakushi ni modosu 白紙に戻 す; *take care of (look after)* sewa o suru 世話をする, … no mendō o miru ～の面倒 をみる; *(handle)* … o shori suru ～を処理する; *(care)* … no teire o suru ～の手入れを する; *take care (of yourself)* o-daiji ni お大事に; *take charge of* … o hikiukeru ～を引き受ける; *take it easy* goyukkuri ごゆっくり; jā (mata) ne じゃ(また)ね; *take off (clothes, shoes)* nugu (服を) 脱ぐ; *(remove)* hazusu 外す; *(plane)* ririku suru 離陸する; **take over** hikitsugu 引き継ぐ, hikitoru 引き取る; *(illegally seizes)* nottoru 乗っ取る

tale N hanashi 話, monogatari 物語; *folktale, ancient tale* mukashi-banashi 昔話

talented ADJ sainō no aru 才能のある

talk N hanashi 話; *(discussion)* hanashiai 話し合い; *(consultation)* sōdan 相談; V hanasu 話す: *talk about* ... ni tsuite hanasu ～について話す; *talk together* hanashiau 話し合う

tall ADJ takai 高い

tame ADJ jūjun na 従順な; V tenadukeru 手なづける

Taoism N dōkyō 道教

tap V *(karuku)* tataku (軽く)たたく; tōchō suru 盗聴する; N jaguchi 蛇口; *(tap-daicing)* タップダンス

tape N tēpu テープ, himo ひも: *adhesive tape* secchaku tēpu 接着テープ

target N mato 的, taishō 対象; *(goal)* mokuhyō 目標, tāgetto ターゲット

taste N aji 味; V *(try eating*

it) shishoku suru 試食する, tabete miru 食べてみる

tasty ADJ oishi'i おいしい, umai うまい

tattoo N irezumi 入れ墨・刺青, tatū タトゥー

tax N zei 税, zeikin 税金: *consumption tax* shōhi zei 消費税; *corporation tax* hōjin zei 法人税; *income tax* shotoku zei 所得税

tax-free ADJ menzei no 免税の

taxi N takushī タクシー: *taxi fare* takushī-dai タクシー代; *taxi stand* takushī noriba タクシー乗り場

tea N (o-)cha (お)茶; *(black)* kōcha 紅茶: *make tea* o-cha o ireru お茶を入れる

tea ceremony N o-cha お茶, chano-yu 茶の湯, sadō 茶道

teach V oshieru 教える

teacher N sensei 先生, kyōshi 教師

team N chīmu チーム

tear N namida 涙; VT *(rip)* yaburu 破る, saku 裂く; *(into pieces)* chigiru 千切る; VI sakeru 裂ける, yabureru 破れる; namida ga deru 涙が出る

tears N namida 涙

teaspoon N saji さじ, ko-saji 小さじ cha-saji 茶さじ

technical ADJ senmon-teki na 専門的な; tekunikaru na テクニカルな, gijutsu no 技術の

technique N gijutsu 技術, waza 技, tekunikku テクニック

teenager N shishunki no kodomo 思春期の子供 (13～19歳)

teeth N ha 歯

telephone V (a story) hanasu 話す: 言う; … ni kikaseru ～に聞かせる, … ni tsuguru ～に告げる; (let know) oshieru 教える: **tell on** ii'tsukeru 言い付ける, tsuguchi suru 告げ口する

telephone N denwa 電話

telephone number N denwabangō 電話番号

telescope N bōenkyō 望遠鏡

television N terebi テレビ

tell V (a story) hanasu 話す: 言う; … ni kikaseru ～に聞かせる, … ni tsuguru ～に告げる; (let know) oshieru 教える: **tell on** ii'tsukeru 言い付ける, tsuguchi suru 告げ口する

temperature N ondo 温度; (of body) taion 体温; (fever) netsu 熱; (air) kion 気温

temple N (ancient) koji 古寺; ji'in 寺院, (o-)tera (お)寺

temporary ADJ ichijiteki na 一時的な; rinji no 臨時の

ten NUM jū 十

ten percent N ichiwari 一割

ten thousand NUM ichiman 一万

tendon N ken 腱

tennis N tenisu テニス

tens of ADJ (multiples of ten) nanjūbaimono 何十倍もの

tense N kinchōshita 緊張した; (taut) hatte tsumeta 張り詰めた

tent N tento テント

tentative ADJ kari no 仮の

term N (period) kikan 期間, (time limit) kigen 期限; (school) gakki 学期; yōgo 用語; (stipulation) jōken 条件

terminal N (computer) tanmatsu 端末

terrible ADJ (severe) hidoi ひどい, taihen na 大変な; (frightening) osoroshi'i 恐ろしい; (shocking) tondemonai とんでもない

terribly ADV sugoku すごく, mono-sugoku ものすごく, to(t)temo と(っ)ても, taihen 大変; osoroshiku 恐ろしく

territory N ryōdo 領土, ryōchi 領地, teritorī テリトリー, nawabari 縄張り

test N shiken 試験, tesuto テスト; (check of blood, etc.) kensa 検査; V tamesu 試す

text N bun 文, tekisuto テキス
ト; v *(mobile phone)* mēru o
utsu メールを打つ(携帯電話)

text(book) N tekisuto テキスト,
kyōkasho 教科書

Thai N *(language)* Tai-go タイ
語; *(people)* Tai-jin タイ人;
ADJ Tai(-jin) no タイ(人)の

Thailand Tai タイ

than CONJ ... yori mo ～よりも

thank V kansha suru 感謝する,
o-rei o iu お礼を言う: *Thank
you* PHR arigatō ありがとう;
Dōmo. どうも; Sumimasen
すみません

thanksgiving N *(gratitude)*
kansha 感謝; *(thanksgiving
day)* kansha-sai 感謝祭

that PRON are あれ; sore それ;
(introducing a quotation) ...
to (iu) ～と（言う）: *that one
(of two) over there* PRON
achira あちら; *that person*
sono hito その人, aitsu あ
いつ; *that thing* sore それ;
that way achira あちら

theater N *(drama)* gekijo 劇場;
(drama, play) engeki 演劇,
shibai 芝居

their, theirs ADJ, PRON karera no
彼らの

them, they PRON *(people)*
anohito-tachi あの人達, karera
彼等; *(things)* sore-ra それら

theme N dai 題, daimoku 題目;
(topic) tēma テーマ, shudai
主題; *(composition)* sakubun
作文

then ADV sono go その後,
sorekara それから; *(at that
time)* sono toki その時

theory N riron 理論, rikutsu
理屈, seorī セオリー

there N *(ADV)* soko (ni/de) そこ
(に/で); *(over there)* asoko
(ni) あそこ(に): *there is/
are* ... ga aru ～がある, ... ga
iru ～がいる

therefore ADV *(consequently)*
sono kekka その結果,
yotte よって; *(accordingly)*
shitagatte 従って

thermometer N ondo-kei 温度
計; *(body)* taion-kei 体温計

these PRON korera no これらの

they, them PRON karera wa/o
彼らは/を

thick ADJ *(liquids)* koi 濃い
(液体); *(things)* atsui 厚い
(物); *(and round)* futoi 太い;
(dense, close) mitsu na 密
な, missetsu na 密接な

thief N dorobō 泥棒

thigh N momo もも

thin ADJ *(liquids)* usui 薄い (液体), *(person)* yaseta やせた (人); *(and round)* hosoi 細い

thing N mono 物; *(fact, matter)* koto 事

think V *(have an opinion)* omou 思う; *(ponder)* kangaeru 考える

third ADJ daisan no 第三の, sanbanme no 三番目の, mittsume no 三つ目の

thirsty ADJ nodo no kawaita のどの渇いた

thirteen NUM jūsan 十三

thirty NUM sanjū 三十

this PRON *(one)* kore これ, kono この: *this month* kongetsu 今月; *this time* ima 今; *this way* *(like this)* kō desu こうです; *(direction)* kochira/kotchi desu こちら/こっちです; *this year* kotoshi 今年

thorn N toge トゲ

those PRON sorera それら, arera あれら: *those days* tōji 当時

though CONJ ... ni mo kakawarazu ～にもかかわらず, demo でも, keredo(mo) けれど(も)

thoughts N shikō 思考, kangae 考え

thousand NUM sen 千

thread N ito 糸

threaten V odosu 脅す, kyōhaku suru 脅迫する

three NUM san 三

three hundred NUM sanbyaku 三百

three thousand NUM sanzen 三千

thrill N suriru スリル

thrilled ADJ waku-waku/zokuzoku suru わくわく/ぞくぞくします(する/して)

throat N nodo のど

through PREP *(past)* ... o tōrinukete ～を通り抜けて; *(coming ...)* ... o tōtte ～を通って; *(via)* ... keiyu (de/no) ～経由(で/の); *(throughout)* ...jū ～中; ... no aidajū ～の 間中

throw V nageru 投げる: *throw away/out* V suteru 捨てる

thumb N oya-yubi 親指

thunder N kaminari 雷

thunderstorm N raiu 雷雨

Thursday N moku-yōbi 木曜日

thus (so) ADV shitagatte 従って

ticket N *(for entertainment)*

ken 券, chiketto チケット (娯楽); *(for transport)* kippu 切符 *(乗り物)*

tickle v kusuguru くすぐる

tidy ADJ sētonsareta 整頓された, katazuita 片付いた; *tidy up* v seiton suru 整頓する; katazukeru 片付ける

tie N *(necktie)* nekutai ネクタイ; *(game)* hikiwake 引き分け; v musubu 結ぶ; *(fasten)* tsunagu つなぐ

tiger N tora トラ

tight ADJ pittarishita ぴったりした, kitsui きつい; *(hard)* katai 硬い; *(skimpy)* semai 狭い

tile N *(roof)* kawara 瓦; *(floor, wall)* tairu タイル

time N jikan 時間; *(specified)* jikoku 時刻; *(season)* kisetsu 季節; jiki 時期; *(opportunity)* jiki 時機: *next time* kondo 今度; *on time* jikandōri ni 時間通りに, teikoku ni 定刻に

time difference, time-lag N jisa 時差

times N *(period)* jidai 時代; *(season)* jiki 時期; SUFFIX *(multiplying)* ... bai 〜倍

timetable N jikokuhyō 時刻表

tin N buriki ブリキ

tiny ADJ totemo chīsana とても小さな

tip N *(end)* hashi 端; *(point)* saki 先; *(gratuity)* chippu チップ, kokorozuke 心付け

tips N kotsu コツ

tired ADJ *(sleepy)* nemui 眠い; *(worn out)* tsukareta 疲れた

tissue N tisshu-pēpā ティッシュペーパー; chirigami ちり紙

title N dai 題, *(of book, film)* daimei 題名 (本、映画), hyōdai 表題; *(of person)* katagaki 肩書き(人)

to PREP *(a person)* ... e 〜へ, ... ni 〜に, ... no hō ni 〜の方に (人); *(a place)* ... e 〜へ, ... no hōkō ni 〜の方向に (場所)

tobacco N tabako タバコ

today N kyō 今日

toe N tsumasaki つま先

tofu N tōfu 豆腐

together ADV tomo ni 共に, issho ni 一緒に

toilet N (o-)tearai (お)手洗い, toire トイレ; *(powder room)* keshōshitsu 化粧室

toll N tsūkō-ryō 通行料; *(telephone charge)* tsūwa-ryō 通話料

toll-free ADJ tsūwa-ryō muryō no 通話料無料の; furī daiyaru no フリーダイヤルの

tollgate N ryōkin-jo 料金所

tomato N tomato トマト

tomb N (o-)haka (お)墓

tomorrow N asu 明日, ashita 明日

tomorrow morning N ashita/ asu no asa 明日の朝

tomorrow night N ashita/asu no ban 明日の晩

tongue N shita 舌

tonight N konban 今晩

too ADV (also) ... mo mata ～も また; (excessive) amari ni... sugiru あまりに～過ぎる: *too much/many* ōsugiru 多過ぎる, anmari あんまり [+ NEGATIVE]: *be too much/ many* amaru 余る

tool N dōgu 道具, yōgu 用具

tooth N ha 歯

toothbrush N haburashi 歯ブラシ

toothpaste N hamigakiko 歯磨き粉

top N ue 上; (top side) hyōmen 表面; (highest part) teppen てっぺん, (summit) chōjō 頂上; (toy) koma こま; ADJ (topmost, best) saijō no 最上の, saikō no 最高の

topic N (of talk) wadai 話題; (hanashi no) tane/neta (話の) 種/ネタ; (problem) mondai 問題

torch N taimatsu たいまつ

total N (sum) gōkei 合計, (grand total) sōkei 総計

touch V ... ni sawaru ～に触る; ... ni fureru ～に触れる; ...ni (te o) tsukeru ～に(手を)付ける; (come in contact with) sessuru 接する, sesshoku suru 接触する: *keep in touch (with)* (...to) renraku o toru (～と) 連絡を取る; *touch upon* ... ni fureru ～に触れる

touch panel, touchscreen N tatchipaneru タッチパネル

tourist N kankōkyaku 観光客

tournament N taikai 大会; shiai 試合; senshuken 選手権

toward PREP ... no hō e ～の方へ; ... e mukau ～へ向かう; (confronting) ... ni kanshite ～に関して

towel N taoru タオル

tower N tō 塔, tawā タワー

town N machi 町; (urban) tokai 都会

toy N omocha おもちゃ

track N *(railtrack)* senro 線路; *(for running)* torakku トラック; V *(go back and investigate)* ato o tsukeru 跡を付ける

trade N *(business)* shōbai 商売; *(exchange)* bōeki 貿易; *(transaction)* torihiki 取り引き

trademark N shōhyō 商標, torēdo māku トレードマーク

trader N *(merchant)* shōnin 商人; *(international)* bōeki-shō 貿易商; *(stock)* tōki-ka 投機家

tradition N dentō 伝統; *(legend)* densetsu 伝説

traffic N kōtsū 交通; *traffic accident* kōtsū jiko 交通事故; *traffic jam* kōtsū-jūtai 交通渋滞

tragedy N higeki 悲劇

train N densha 電車, ressha 列車; V *(drill)* kunren suru 訓練する, *(practice)* renshū suru 練習する; *(brings up children, disciplines)* shitsukeru しつける

train station N eki 駅

training N kunren 訓練; *(practice)* renshū 練習

tram N romen densha 路面電車

transfer VI *(trains, etc.)* nori-kaeru 乗り換える; *(job)* ten'nin suru 転任する; VT utsusu 移す, furi-kaeru 振替える; N idō 移動, nori-kae 乗り換え

transform V henkan suru 変換する, henshin suru 変身する

translate V yakusu 訳す, hon'yaku suru 翻訳する

translation N hon'yaku 翻訳, yaku 訳

transport(ation) N unsō 運送, unpan 運搬, yusō 輸送; *(traffic)* kōtsū 交通

trash N *(scrap, junk)* kuzu くず, gomi ごみ

travel N ryokō 旅行; V ryokō suru 旅行する

travel agency N ryokō dairiten 旅行代理店

traveler N ryokōsha 旅行者

tray N (o-)bon (お)盆

treasure N takara 宝, takaramono 宝物, zaihō 財宝

treat N *(something special)* tanoshimi 楽しみ, gochisō ご馳走; V *(pay the bill)* ogoru おごる, gochisō suru ごちそうする; *(deal with)* atsukau 扱う; *(medically)* chiryō suru 治療する

treatment N teate 手当;
(*handling*) toritsukai 取り
扱い; (*reception*) taigū 待
遇; (*medical*) chiryō 治療,
ryōhō 療法

tree N ki 木

trend N (*tendency*) keikō 傾向,
(*inclination*) katamuki 傾き,
chōshi 調子; (*current*)
chōryū 潮流; (*movement*)
ugoki 動き; (*fashion*) ryūkō
流行; torendo トレンド

trial N (*legal*) saiban 裁判,
(*test*) shiken 試験, (*trying*)
tameshi 試し, kokoromi 試み,
toraiaru トライアル: **trial version** N taiken-ban 体験版

triangle N sankaku 三角,
sankakkei 三角形

tribe N buzoku 部族

tricky ADJ zurui ずるい, torikkī
トリッキー, bimyō na 微妙
な, (*difficult*) muzukashī'i
難しい

tricycle N sanrin-sha 三輪車

trigger N hikigane 引き金

trip N (*journey*) tabi 旅, ryokō
旅行; (*business*) shutchō 出張

triple N sanbai 三倍, ADJ sanbai
no 三倍の; toripuru トリプル

tropical ADJ nettai no 熱帯の;

toropikaru na トロピカルな

tropical rainforest N nettai
urin 熱帯雨林

troops N guntai 軍隊;
(*detachment*) butai 部隊

trouble N (*difficulty*) kon'nan
困難; (*inconvenience*)
tekazu/tesū 手数; (*time taken
up*) tema 手間; (*nuisance*)
meiwaku 迷惑, mendō 面倒,
(*bother*) yakkai 厄介

trousers N zubon ズボン

truck N torakku トラック

true ADJ hontō no 本当の; N
hon'ne 本音, honshin 本心

trunk N (*of tree*) miki 幹; (*of
elephant*) hana 鼻; (*baggage;
car trunk*) toranku トランク

trust N tanomi 頼み, irai 依
頼; shin'yō 信用, shinrai 信
頼; anshin 安心; V (*trust
them*) shin'yō suru 信用する,
shinjiru 信じる, shinrai suru
信頼する

truth N shinjitsu 真実, hontō
no koto 本当の事

try V (*strive*) doryoku suru
努力する; tamesu 試す,
kokoromiru 試みる, (*doing*)
(shi)te miru (し)てみる: **try
on** (*clothes*) shichaku suru

試着する
T-shirt N tī shatsu Tシャツ
tsunami N tsunami 津波
tube N kuda 管, kan 管;
(flexible, squeezable, inflatable) chūbu チューブ;
test tube shikenkan 試験管
Tuesday N ka-yōbi 火曜日
tuna N maguro マグロ; *(fatty)* toro トロ
tune N chōshi 調子, fushi 節
turkey N shichimen-chō 七面鳥
turn N *(order)* junban 順番; *(spin)* kaiten 回転; *(corner)* magarikado 曲がり角; VI *(go round)* mawaru 回る; VT mawasu 回す; *(direct one's face, etc.)* … ni mukeru 〜に向ける: *make a turn* v magaru 曲がる; *turn around* v furikaeru 振りかえる; *turn off* kesu 消す; *turn on* tsukeru 点ける; *turn over* uragaesu 裏返す
turtle N kame 亀; *(land)* riku-game 陸亀; *(sea)* umi-game 海ガメ
tusk N kiba 牙
tutor N kateikyōshi 家庭教師, chūtā チューター

tutoring school N juku 塾
TV N terebi テレビ
tweet V *(Internet)* (tsuittā de) tsubuyaku (ツイッターで)つぶやく; *(birds)* saezuru さえずる
tweezers N pinsetto ピンセット
twelve NUM jūni 十二
twenty NUM nijū 二十
twice ADV *(two times)* ni-do 二度, ni-kai 二回; *(double)* ni-bai 二倍
twilight N yūgata 夕方; tasogare 黄昏
twins N futago 双子
twist V nejiru ねじる, hineru ひねる
Twitter N tsuittā ツイッター
two NUM ni 二
type N *(sort)* shurui 種類; V *(typewrite)* taipu suru タイプする
typhoon N taihū 台風
typical ADJ tenkeiteki na 典型的な, daihyō-teki na 代表的な: *so typical* [IN NEGATIVE SENSE] arigachi na ありがちな, arikitari no ありきたりの

U

ugly ADJ minikui 醜い; migurushi'i 見苦しい

umbrella N kasa 傘

uncle N oji おじ

unclear ADJ aimai na あいまいな

unconscious ADJ ishiki fumei no 意識不明の

uncooked ADJ nama no 生の

under PREP ... no shita ni/de 〜の下に/で

undergo V keiken suru 経験する

underline V kasen o hiku 下線を引く

underpants N pantsu パンツ

undershirt N hadagi 肌着

understand V wakaru 分かる, rikai suru 理解する

undertake V hikiukeru 引き受ける

underwear N shitagi 下着, hadagi 肌着

undo V hazusu 外す; moto ni modosu 戻す; (untie) hodoku ほどく, toku 解く

undressed ADJ hadaka no 裸の: *get undressed* fuku o nugu 服を脱ぐ

unemployed ADJ shitsugyō-chū no 失業中の

uneven ADJ dekoboko no でこぼこの

unexpectedly ADV igai ni 意外に, omoigakenaku 思いがけなく; (suddenly) tōtotsu ni 唐突に, battari ばったり

unfavorable ADJ furi na 不利な

unfortunately ADV zan'nen nagara 残念ながら, ainiku あいにく

unhappy ADJ fukō na 不幸な, (moody) kigen ga warui 機嫌が悪い; (dissatisfied) fuman na 不満な

uniform N seifuku 制服, unifōmu ユニフォーム

unique ADJ dokutoku no/na 独特の/な, yui'itsu no 唯一の, yunīku na ユニークな

united ADJ gōdō no 合同の

United Kingdom N Eikoku 英国

United Nations N Kokusai-rengō 国際連合

United States (of America) N Amerika gasshūkoku アメリカ合衆国

university N daigaku 大学

unless CONJ ... de nai kagiri 〜でない限り; (shi)nakereba (し)なければ, (shi)nai to (し)ないと

370

unlucky ADJ fu'un na 不運な, un ga warui 運が悪い, tsuitenai ついてない

unnecessary ADJ fuhitsuyō na 不必要な, fuyō na 不要な; *(superfluous)* yokei na 余計な

unpleasant ADJ iya na 嫌な

unreasonable ADJ muri na 無理な, mucha na 無茶な; hidoi ひどい, rifujin na 理不尽な

unripe ADJ miseijuku no 未成熟の

unskillful ADJ heta na 下手な

untie V hodoku ほどく

until PREP ... made ～まで: *until now* ima made 今まで; *until when* itsu made いつまで

unusual ADJ ijō na 異常な

up, upward PREP ue no hōe 上のほうへ

update N appudēto アップデート, kōshin 更新; saishin(-ban) 最新(版); V kōshin suru 更新する, saishin(-ban) ni suru 最新(版)にする, appudēto suru アップデートする

upset VI hikkurikaeru ひっくり返る; *(be disturbed)* midareru 乱れる; VT

hikkurikaesu ひっくり返す; *(disturb)* midasu 乱す; *(get nervous)* dōyō suru 動揺する; ADJ dōyōshita 動揺した

upside down ADV sakasama ni 逆さまに, abekobe ni あべこべに

upstairs N nikai 二階; ADV nikai e 二階へ, jōkai e 上階へ

unsteady ADJ abunakkashi'i 危なっかしい

urban ADJ toshi no 都市の

urge N shōdō 衝動; V karitateru 駆り立てる; susumeru 勧める; unagasu 促す

urgent ADJ kyū no 急の, kinkyū no 緊急の, isogi no 急ぎの

urinate V shōben o suru 小便をする

use N shiyō 使用; V tsukau 使う

used ADJ *(secondhand)* chūko no 中古の: *used car* N chūkosha 中古車; *used to* ADV yoku ... shita mono da よく～したものだ; *be used to (accustomed)* nareteiru 慣れている

useful ADJ yakudatsu 役立つ, chōhō na 重宝な

useless ADJ mueki na 無益な,

muda na 無駄な; muyō no 無用の、fuyō no 不用の

user ID N *(computer)* yūzā-aidī ユーザーID

username N yūzāmei ユーザー名

usual ADJ itsumo no いつもの、futsū no 普通の、fudan no 普段の

usually ADV futsū wa 普通は、taitei たいてい、itsu mo いつも、fudan 普段

utensil N dōgu 道具

V

vacant ADJ *(open)* aiteiru 空いている

vacation N yasumi 休み、kyūka 休暇

vaccination N yobōsesshu 予防接種

vacuum cleaner N denki sōjiki 電気掃除機

vagina N chitsu 膣

vaguely ADV bakuzen to 漠然と

valid ADJ yūkō na 有効な、datō na 妥当な

valley N tani 谷

value N *(cost)* kachi 価値；*(good)* oneuchi お値打ち；

v nebumi o suru 値踏みをする

vanilla N banira バニラ

vase N *(for flowers)* kabin 花瓶

vast ADJ bakudai na 莫大な

vegetable N yasai 野菜

vehicle N norimono 乗り物

vending machine N hanbaiki 販売機

verb N dōshi 動詞

verify v tashikameru 確かめる；*(prove)* shōmei suru 証明する

versatility N ban'nō 万能

very ADV *(extremely)* hijō ni 非常に、zuibun ずいぶん、taihen 大変、totemo とても

vest N besuto ベスト、chokki チョッキ

via PREP ... o tōtte 〜を通って、... keiyu (de) 〜経由(で)；... o hete 〜を経て

vice- PREFIX fuku- 副-

vice-president N *(of a company)* fuku-shachō 副社長

vicious ADJ akushitsu na 悪質な、hidoi ひどい

vicious circle N akujunkan 悪循環

video recorder N bideo (rekōdā) ビデオ(レコーダー)

videotape N bideotēpu ビデオテープ; v rokuga suru 録画する

Vietnam N Betonamu ベトナム

Vietnamese N *(language)* Betonamu-go ベトナム語; *(people)* Betonamu-jin ベトナム人; ADJ Betonamu(-jin) no ベトナム(人)の

view N *(panorama)* keshiki 景色

viewpoint N mikata 見方, tachiba 立場

villa N bessō 別荘

village N mura 村

vinegar N su 酢

vinyl N binīru ビニール

violence N *(brute force)* bōryoku 暴力

violin N baiorin バイオリン

visa N biza ビザ, sashō 査証

visit N taizai 滞在; hōmon 訪問; *(of solicitude)* (o-)mimai (お)見舞い; *(interview)* menkai 面会; asobi 遊び; v *(pay a visit to)* hōmon suru 訪問する; tazuneru 訪ねる; asobu 遊ぶ

vitamin(s) N bitamin ビタミン; *(pills)* bitaminzai ビタミン剤

voice N koe 声

voicemail N rusubandenwa 留守番電話

volcano N kazan 火山

volume N boryūmu ボリューム

volunteer N borantia (katsudō) ボランティア(活動); v borantia (katsudō) o suru ボランティア(活動)をする

vomit N hedo へど, gero げろ; v hakidasu 吐き出す, haku 吐く

vote N hyō 票, tōhyō 投票; v tōhyō suru 投票する

vow N chikai 誓い; v chikau 誓う

vulgar ADJ gehin na 下品な, iyashi'i いやしい

W

wadding N tsumemono 詰め物

wafer N *(sweet)* uehāsu ウエハース

waffle N *(sweet)* waffuru ワッフル

wag v yureru 揺れる, yureugoku 揺れ動く, *(tail)* furu 振る

wages N chingin 賃金, *(salary)* kyūryō 給料

wagon N wagon ワゴン, daisha 台車; *(car)* wagon-sha ワゴン車

waist N (*loins*) koshi 腰, uesuto ウエスト; (*specifically*) koshi no kubire 腰のくびれ

wait for V ... o motsu ～を待つ

waiter, waitress N kyūji 給仕, bōi ボーイ, (*male*) uētā ウエーター; (*female*) uētoresu ウエートレス

waiting list N kyanseru machi risuto キャンセル待ちリスト, weitingu risuto ウェイティング・リスト

waiting room N machiai-shitsu 待合室

wake up V mezameru 目覚める, me ga sameru 目が覚める, (*rise*) okiru 起きる: *wake someone up* V okosu 起こす

wake-up call N mōningu kōru モーニングコール

walk V aruku 歩く; (*stroll*) sanpo suru 散歩する N (*way*) hodō 歩道; (*walking*) hokō 歩行

walking shoes N wōkingu shūzu ウォーキングシューズ

walking stick N (*cane*) sutekki ステッキ, tsue 杖

walkway N hodō 歩道

wall N kabe 壁; hei 塀

wallet N saifu 財布

wallpaper N kabegami 壁紙

walnut N kurumi クルミ

waltz N warutsu ワルツ

wander V (*walk around*) arukimawaru 歩き回る, (*hang round*) buratsuku ぶらつく, buraburasuru ぶらぶらする, samayou さまよう, hōrō suru 放浪する

want V ... ga hoshi'i ～が欲しい; ... shitai ～したい (*desire something*) hoshigaru 欲しがる: *wants to do (it)* (... ga) shitai (～が)したい, (... o) shitagaru (～を)したがる

war N sensō 戦争, arasoi 争い

ward N (*city district*) ku 区

wardrobe N yōfuku dansu 洋服だんす, ishō dansu 衣装だんす

warehouse N sōko 倉庫, kura 倉

warm ADJ (*not cool*) atatakai 暖かい, (*not cold*) atatakai 温かい; (*dedicated*) nesshin na 熱心な; V atatameru 温める: *warm up* atatamaru あたたまる

warmhearted ADJ kokoro ga atatakai 心が温かい, shinsetsu na 親切な

warmth N nukumori ぬくもり, atataka-sa あたたかさ, omoiyari 思いやり

warn V kēkoku suru 警告する, chūi suru 注意する

warning N kēkoku 警告; *(alert)* keihō 警報

warp N sori 反り; *(vertical threads)* tate-ito たて糸; VI soru 反る, *(get warped)* yugamu 歪む; VT sorasorasu 反らす, yugameru 歪める; *(crooked)* kuru'u 狂う

warranty N hoshō(-sho) 保証(書)

warrior N senshi 戦士; *(Japanese warrior)* samurai 侍, bushi 武士

wash V arau 洗う; *(launder)* sentaku suru 洗濯する; *the wash(ing)* sentaku 洗濯, sentaku-mono 洗濯物

washable ADJ sentaku no dekiru 洗濯のできる, araeru 洗える

washcloth N *(hand towel)* tenugui 手拭い, *(dishcloth)* fukin ふきん

washer, washing machine N sentaku-ki 洗濯機

washout N *(big mistake)* daishippai 大失敗; *(a failure)* shikkaku-sha 失格者

washroom N (o-)tearai (お)手洗い, senmen-jo 洗面所

wasp N hachi 蜂, suzume-bachi スズメバチ

waste N *(garbage)* haikibutsu 廃棄物, *(trash)* kuzu くず, kuzumono くず物; *(extravagance)* mudazukai 無駄遣い, rōhi 浪費; V muda ni suru 無駄にする; *(be extravagant with)* mudazukai suru 無駄使いする, rōhi suru 浪費する: *waste away* shōmō suru 消耗する; *waste of effort* mudabone 無駄骨, torō 徒労; *waste of money* mudazukai 無駄遣い, rōhi 浪費; *waste of time* jikan no muda 時間の無駄

wastebasket N kuzu-kago くずかご

wastewater N gesui 下水, osui 汚水, haisui 排水

watch N *(wristwatch)* ude-dokei 腕時計; V miru 見る; *(TV, movie)* miru 観る; *(observe)* kansatsu suru 観察する; *(guard)* … no ban o suru … の番をする: *watch* *for* nerau 狙う; *Watch your step!* Ashi-moto ni ki o tsukete! 足元に気を付けて!; *Watch out!* abunai! 危ない!

watchdog N banken 番犬

watchman N ban'nin 番人, keibi'in 警備員

water N mizu 水: *hot water* oyu お湯, yu 湯; *drinking water* nomimizu 飲み水

waterfall N taki 滝

waterfront N kashi 河岸

waterhole, watering hole N mizu tamari 水たまり

watermelon N suika スイカ

waterworks N suidō 水道

wave N *(in sea)* nami 波; *(permanent wave)* pama パーマ; V furu 振る

wax N wakkusu ワックス, rō ロウ

way N *(method)* hōhō 方法, shi-yō 仕様, yari-kata やり方; *(means)* shudan 手段; *(path)* michi 道: *the way of* ... suru hōhō 〜する方法; *by the way (incidentally)* tokorode ところで, chinami ni ちなみに; *get out of the way* doku 退く; *give way* yuzuru 譲る; *on the way* tochū (de) 途中(で);

way in iriguchi 入口; *way out* deguchi 出口

wayside N michibata 道端; gaitō 街頭

we, us PRON *(exclude the one addressed)* watashitachi wa 私たちは; *(include the one addressed)* watashitachi ni/o 私たちに/を

weak ADJ yowai 弱い; fujiyū na 不自由な: *weak at* futokui na/no 不得意な/の, heta na 下手な

wealth N tomi 富, zaisan 財産

wealthy ADJ yūfuku na 裕福な

weapon N heiki 兵器; buki 武器s; kyōki 凶器

wear N fuku 服, irui 衣類; V *(clothes)* kiru 着る; *(accessories)* tsukeru 着ける; *(footware, bottoms)* haku 履く, *(hat, headwear)* kaburu かぶる, *(necktie, belt)* shimeru 締める, *(on hands, fingers)* hameru はめる

weary ADJ tsukarekitta 疲れ切った

weather N tenki 天気

weather forecast N tenki-yohō 天気予報

weave V oru 織る

weaving N orimono 織り物

web browser n (*Internet*) webuburauza ウェブブラウザ

weblog N weburogu ウェブログ, burogu ブログ

website N webusaito ウェブサイト

wedding N kekkon 結婚; (*ceremony*) kekkonshiki 結婚式

wedding reception N kekkon hirōen 結婚披露宴

Wednesday N sui-yōbi 水曜日

weed N kusa 草, zassō 雑草

week N shū 週: *week after next* saraishū 再来週; *week before last* sensen-shū 先々週

weekend N shūmatsu 週末

weep v naku 泣く; (*lament*) nageku 嘆く

weigh v hakaru 量る

weight N omosa 重さ, jūryō 重量; (*body*) taijū 体重; (*object*) omoshi 重し: *gain/lose weight* taijū ga fueru/heru 体重が増える/減る

weight, weighing scales N hakari はかり

weird ADJ ayashi'i 怪しい, fushigi na 不思議な, sugoi す

ごい; (*feeling*) kimi ga warui 気味が悪い

welcome INTERJ yōkoso ようこそ, Irasshaimase. いらっしゃいませ; N (*a welcome*) kangei 歓迎; ADJ nozomashi'i 望ましい, arigatai ありがたい; v ... o mukaeru ...を迎える, demukaeru 出迎える: *You're welcome.* Dō itashimashite. どういたしまして.; *Welcome back/home.* O-kaeri nasai. お帰りなさい.; *welcome to ... e yōkoso* 〜へようこそ

welfare N fukushi 福祉

well N (*for water*) ido 井戸; ADJ (*good*) yoi 良い; (*healthy*) genki na 元気な; (*splendid*) rippa na/ni 立派な/に: *get well* naoru 治る; *very well* (*satisfactory*) yoroshi'i よろしい

well done yoku dekimashita よくできました

well now/then (*sore*) dewa (それでは, (*sore*) jā (それ)じゃあ, jā じゃあ, sate さて; ē-to ええと; *tokoro-de* ところで; (*let me think*) sōdesu ne そうですね; (*maybe*) mā まあ

well off ADJ (*wealthy*) yūfuku na 裕福な

well-behaved/mannered
ADJ gyōgi no ii 行儀のいい;
otonashi'i おとなしい

well-known **ADJ** yūmei na 有名
な, chomei na 著名な

well-liked **v** moteru もてる

west **N** nishi 西

western style **N** yō-fū 洋
風; (building) yōkan 洋館;
(room) yō-ma 洋間; (clothes)
yō-fuku 洋服

westerner **N** seiyōjin 西洋人

wet **ADJ** nureta 濡れた, (moist)
shimetta 湿った, shimeppoi
湿っぽい; **VI** nureru 濡れる;
VT (make it wet) nurasu 濡ら
す, (dampen it) shimerasu
湿らす

whale **N** kujira クジラ

what **PRON** nani 何: (in) what
(way) dō どう: what for nan
no tame ni 何のために; what
happened nani ga okita 何
が起きた; what kind/sort of
dono yō na どの様な, dōiu ど
ういう, don'na どんな; what
place doko どこ; dochira ど
ちら, dotchi どっち; what
time nanji 何時

whatever nan demo 何でも

wheat **N** komugi 小麦; mugi 麦

wheel **N** sharin 車輪, wa 輪,
hoīru ホイール; (steering
wheel) handoru ハンドル

wheelchair **N** kurumaisu 車
いす

when **PRON** itsu いつ; **ADV** (at the
time) ... suru toki ～する時;
about when itsugoro いつ頃;
since when itsu kara いつか
ら; until when itsu made い
つまで; by when itsu made ni
いつまでに

whenever **CONJ** itsudemo い
つでも

where **PRON** doko どこ, dochira
どちら: where to doko e ど
こへ

whereabouts **N** shozai 所在

whether **CONJ** ... ka dōka ...
かどうか

which **PRON** dore どれ, dono ど
の; (of two) dochira/dotchi
no どちら/どっちの

while **CONJ** (during) ... no aida
ni ～の間に; ... (shi)-nagara
～(し)ながら; ...-chu (ni) ～中(
に); (for) a while shibaraku
しばらく; a little while ago
sakihodo 先程, sakki さっき

whirlpool **N** uzu-maki 渦巻
き, uzu 渦

whisky N uisukī ウイスキー, wisukī ウィスキー; *whisky and water* mizuwari 水割り

whisper N kogoe 小声, sasayaki ささやき; v sasayaku 囁く; mimiuchi suru 耳打ちする

whistle N fue 笛, kuchibue 口笛, *(steam)* kiteki 汽笛

white N shiro 白; ADJ shiroi 白い

who PRON dare だれ, donata どなた, dochira(-sama) どちら(様)

whole ADJ *(all of)* subete no 全ての; *(be complete)* kanzen na 完全な; zentai no 全体の; *(the whole thing)* zenbu 全部

wholesale ADV oroshi(uri) de 卸(売)し(で)

whose PRON dare no 誰の

why ADV naze なぜ, dōshite どうして, dō どう: *that's why* dakara だから

wicked ADJ warui 悪い

wide ADJ hiroi 広い, habahiroi 幅広い

widen v hirogaru 広がる

widow N mibōjin 未亡人

width N haba 幅, yoko haba 横幅; hirosa 広さ

wife N fujin 夫人, *(someone's*

wife) oku-san/-sama 奥さん/様; *(my wife)* kanai 家内, tsuma 妻, nyōbo/nyōbō 女房; waifu ワイフ

Wi-Fi N *(wireless LAN)* musenran 無線LAN, waifai ワイファイ

wig N katsura かつら

wild ADJ wairudo na ワイルドな; *(disorderly)* ranbō na 乱暴な; *(rough)* arai 荒い; *(not cultivated)* yasei no 野性の; N *(roughneck)* abaremono 暴れ者; arechi 荒れ地, kōya 荒野

wildlife N yasei dōbutsu 野生動物, yasei seibutsu 野生生物

will MODAL V ... deshō ～でしょう; ... suru tsumori ～するつもり; N ishi 意志, omoi 思い; *(testament)* isho 遺書, yuigon 遺言

willow N yanagi 柳

win v *(game/war)* ... ni katsu ～に勝つ; *(prize)* jushō suru 受賞する

wind vi magaru 曲る; vт maku 巻く; *(reel)* makitoru 巻き取る; *(breeze)* kaze 風; *strong (heavy) wind* kyōfū 強風; *wind up (conclude*

window N mado 窓; *(wicket)* madoguchi 窓口

windowpane N mado-garasu 窓ガラス

windy ADJ kaze ga tsuyoi 風が強い

wine N wain ワイン, budōshu ぶどう酒

wing N *(of bird or plane)* tsubasa 翼; *(of insect)* hane 羽・羽根

wink N (V) mabataki (suru) まばたき (する), uinku (suru) ウインク (する)

winner N *(victor)* shōrisha 勝利者, yūshōsha 優勝者; *(awardee)* jushōsha 受賞者

winter N fuyu 冬

winter break/vacation N fuyuyasumi 冬休み

wipe V fuku 拭く: *wipe away* nugu'u 拭う

wire N harigane 針金; *(electric)* densen 電線, *(telephone line)* denwa-sen 電話線

wisdom N chie 知恵

wise ADJ kashikoi 賢い, kenmei na 賢明な

wish N (o-)negai (お)願い, kibō 希望, ganbō 願望; V nozomu 望む, ...ga hoshi'i ~が欲しい

wit N yūmoa ユーモア, kichi 機知, witto ウィット

with PREP ... to ～と, ... to issho ni ～と一緒に *(attached/included)* ...tsuki no ～付きの

withdraw V hakushi ni modosu 白紙に戻す, dattai suru 脱退する; *(leave)* hikiageru 引き上げる, hikitoru 引き取る; *(takes out money)* (yokin/okane o) orosu/hikidasu (預金/お金を) 下ろす/引き出す

withhold V hikaeru 控える; VT sashihiku 差し引く

within PREP ... no naka de/ni ～の中で/に; ... inai ni ～以内に; ADV naibu de 内部で

without PREP ... nashi ni ～なしに; *(omitting)* ... nuki de/no ～抜きで/の: *without notice/permission* mudan de 無断で

witness N mokugekisha 目撃者; *(in court)* shōnin 証人; shōko 証拠; V mokugeki suru 目撃する

wolf N ōkami オオカミ

woman N on'na 女, on'na no hito/kata 女の人/方; josei 女性, joshi 女子; *(lady)* fujin 婦人; go-fujin ご婦人

wonder v odoroku 驚く; N odoroki 驚き; fushigi 不思議

wonderful ADJ subarashi'i すばらしい, suteki na すてきな, sugoi すごい; *(delightful)* ureshi'i うれしい

wood N ki 木, *(lumber)* zaimoku 材木

woodblock print N mokuhanga 木版画, hanga 版画

wooden ADJ mokusei no 木製の

wool N yōmō 羊毛, ke 毛, ūru ウール

word N go 語, kotoba 言葉, tango 単語

work N *(occupation)* shigoto 仕事, gyōmu 業務; *(operations)* sagyō 作業; *(literature or art)* sakuhin 作品; v shigoto o suru 仕事をする, hataraku 働く, kinmu suru 勤務する

worker N *(laborer)* rodosha 労働者; *(employee, staff)* shain 社員, shokuin 職員

workstation N *(computer)* wākusuteshon ワークステーション

world N sekai 世界; *(at large)* yo-no-naka 世の中, *(people)* seken 世間

World Health Organization (WHO) N sekai-hokenkikō 世界保健機関

worldwide ADJ sekaiteki na 世界的な, sekai-jū 世界中

worm N mushi 虫

worn out ADJ *(clothes, machine)* tsukaifurushita 使い古した; *(tired)* tsukarekitta 疲れ切った

worry N shinpai 心配, kizukai 気遣い; v shinpai suru 心配する, kizukau 気遣う

worse ADJ yori warui より悪い; otoru 劣る

worship N sūhai 崇拝, raihai/reihai 礼拝; v shinkō suru 信仰する

worst ADJ saiaku no 最悪の; *(lowest)* saitei no 最低の

worth N kachi 価値

would like v ...ga hoshi'i ～が欲しい, ...shite moraitai ～してもらいたい, ... (shi)tai ～したい

wound N *(injury)* kizu 傷, kega

怪我; **w** kizutsuku 傷付く; **vt**
(injure) kizutsukeru 傷付ける

wrap v tsutsumu 包む, hōsō
suru 包装する; *(something
around it)* maku 巻く

wrapper, wrapping paper n
hōsōshi 包装紙

wreck n *(accident)* jiko 事故,
(collision) shōtotsu 衝突;
(ship) nanpa 難破, sōnan 遭
難; *(train)* ressha-jiko 列車事
故; *(wreckage)* zangai 残骸; **v**
(ruin) kowasu 壊す

wrinkle n shiwa しわ, **v** shiwa
ga dekiru しわができる

wrist n tekubi 手首

wristwatch n ude-dokei 腕時計

write v kaku 書く

writer n sakka 作家; *(author)*
chosha 著者, hissha 筆者

written explanation n
setsumeisho 説明書

wrong adj *(false)* ayamatta 誤
った, *(mistaken)* machigatta
間違った; *(morally)* warui 悪い

X

x-axis n ekkusu-jiku X軸

xenophobic adj *(hatred of
foreign country or people)*
gaikoku(-jin) girai no 外国
(人)嫌いの

Xmas n *(Christmas)*
Kurisumasu クリスマス

X-rating n seijin muki eiga
shitei 成人向き映画指定

X-ray n ekkūsusen エックス線,
rentogen (shashin) レントゲン
(写真)

Y

yacht n *(sailboat)* yotto ヨット;
(motor cruiser) kurūzā
クルーザー

Yahoo! n Yahū ヤフー

yak n *(animal)* yaku ヤク

yam n imo イモ, yamu imo
ヤムイモ

yap v hoeru 吠える

yard n niwa 庭

yard sale n *(garage sale)*
garējisēru ガレージセール

yarn n ito 糸; *(for knitting)*
ke-ito 毛糸

yawn v akubi o suru あくびをする

yeah! INTERJ ā ああ; un うん

year N toshi 年, nen 年: *year after next* sarainen 再来年; *year before last* ototoshi 一昨年, issaku-nen 一昨年; *year-end* kure no 暮れの, nenmatsu no 年末の; *year-end gift* (o-)seibo (お)歳暮; *year-end party* bōnenkai 忘年会

yearly ADJ nen ichido no 年1度の, nen ikkai no 年1回の, mainen no 毎年の; ADV nen (ni) ichido no 年(に)1度, maitoshi 毎年

yearn for V akogareru 憧れる

years old ... sai 〜歳

yeast N īsuto イースト

yell V sakebu 叫ぶ, wameku 喚く

yellow N ki'iro 黄色, ADJ ki'iroi 黄色い; *(coward)* okubyō na 臆病な

yen N en 円, ...-en ...円: *high value of the yen* en-daka 円高; *low value of the yen* en-yasu 円安

yes ADV hai はい, ee ええ; sōdesu そうです: *Yes, I see./Yes, I will (comply).* Wakarimashita. わかりました.

yesterday N kinō 昨日

yet ADV mada まだ: *not yet* mada... nai まだ〜ない

yield N *(product; income)* dekiagari 出来上がり; V *(gives in/up)* yuzuru 譲る

yoga N yoga ヨガ

yogurt N yōguruto ヨーグルト

yolk N *(egg)* kimi 黄身

yonder PRON achira あちら, atchi あっち

you PRON *(familiar)* anata あなた, *(intimate)* kimi 君, *(condescending)* omae お前

young ADJ wakai 若い: *very young* osanai 幼い; *young boy/girl* shōnen 少年/shōjo 少女; *young lady* ojō-san お嬢さん; musume(-san) 娘(さん); *young man* seinen 青年

young person, youth, youngster N waka-mono 若者

younger ADJ toshi-shita no 年下の; *younger brother* otōto 弟; *younger sister* imōto 妹, *(your)* imōto-san 妹さん

your(s) PRON anata-tachi/anata-gata no mono あなた達/あなた方の物

yourself, yourselves PRON
anata-jishin あなた自身

youth N *(state of being young)* wakasa 若さ;
(young person) wakamono 若者, seinen 青年; *(when young)* wakai toki/koro 若い時/頃

youth hostel N yūsu-hosuteru ユースホステル

Z

zapped ADJ *(dead tired)* tsukarehateta 疲れ果てた

zebra N shimauma シマウマ

Zen N *(Buddhism)* Zen 禅

zero N rei 零, zero ゼロ

zest N *(enthusiasm)* netsui 熱意; *(interest)* tsuyoi kyōmi 強い興味; *(enjoyment)*

yorokobi 喜び

zinc N aen 亜鉛

ZIP, zip code N yūbinbangō 郵便番号

zipper N chakku チャック, jippā ジッパー; fasunā ファスナー

Zodiac years N jūnishi 十二支

zone N *(area)* chitai 地帯, kuiki 区域; zōn ゾーン; ...-tai ...帯

zoo N dōbutsuen 動物園

zoological ADJ dōbutsu-gaku no 動物学の

zoology N dōbutsu-gaku 動物学

zoom N kakudai 拡大, *(camera)* zūmu ズーム

zoom lens N *(camera)* zūmu-renzu ズームレンズ

zucchini N zukkīni ズッキーニ